Android
Tips and Tricks

Guy Hart-Davis

que®

800 East 96th St
Indianapolis, Inc

ANDROID® TIPS AND TRICKS

COPYRIGHT © 2015 BY PEARSON EDUCATION, INC.

ISBN-13: 978-0-7897-5385-4

ISBN-10: 0-7897-5385-5

Library of Congress Control Number: 2014956782

Printed in the United States of America

First Printing December 2014

TRADEMARKS

WARNING AND DISCLAIMER

SPECIAL SALES

For information about buying this title in bulk quantities, or for special sales opportunities (which may include electronic versions; custom cover designs; and content particular to your business, training goals, marketing focus, or branding interests), please contact our corporate sales department at corpsales@pearsoned.com or (800) 382-3419.

For government sales inquiries, please contact governmentsales@pearsoned.com.

For questions about sales outside the U.S., please contact international@pearsoned.com.

EDITOR-IN-CHIEF
Greg Wiegand

ACQUISITIONS EDITOR
Michelle Newcomb

DEVELOPMENT EDITOR
William Abner

MANAGING EDITOR
Sandra Schroeder

PROJECT EDITOR
Seth Kerney

COPY EDITOR
Chuck Hutchinson

INDEXER
Rebecca Salerno

PROOFREADER
Jess DeGabriele

TECHNICAL EDITORS
Vince Averello
Christian Kenyeres

EDITORIAL ASSISTANT
Cindy Teeters

BOOK DESIGNER
Mark Shirar

COMPOSITOR
Mary Sudul

CONTENTS AT A GLANCE

TABLE OF CONTENTS

ABOUT THE AUTHOR

Guy Hart-Davis is coauthor of *My Samsung Galaxy Note 3* and *My HTC One*, and the author of nearly one hundred computer books.

DEDICATION

I dedicate this book to my son, Edward, who tests Android[†] hardware and software to destruction so that I don't have to.

ACKNOWLEDGMENTS

My thanks go to the people whose hard work helped create this book you're reading. In particular, I'd like to thank the following people:

- Michelle Newcomb, for asking me to write the book.
- William Abner, for developing the outline and content.
- Vince Averello and Christian Kenyeres, for reviewing the manuscript for technical accuracy and contributing suggestions for improving the book.
- Seth Kerney, for coordinating the book project.
- Chuck Hutchinson, for editing the manuscript with a light touch.
- Jess DeGabriele, for proofreading the book.
- Rebecca Salerno, for creating the index.

† and other!

WE WANT TO HEAR FROM YOU!

As the reader of this book, *you* are our most important critic and commentator. We value your opinion and want to know what we're doing right, what we could do better, what areas you'd like to see us publish in, and any other words of wisdom you're willing to pass our way.

We welcome your comments. You can email or write to let us know what you did or didn't like about this book—as well as what we can do to make our books better.

Please note that we cannot help you with technical problems related to the topic of this book.

When you write, please be sure to include this book's title and author as well as your name and email address. We will carefully review your comments and share them with the author and editors who worked on the book.

Email: feedback@quepublishing.com

Mail: Que Publishing
ATTN: Reader Feedback
800 East 96th Street
Indianapolis, IN 46240 USA

READER SERVICES

Visit our website and register this book at quepublishing.com/register for convenient access to any updates, downloads, or errata that might be available for this book.

Introduction

This short introduction is intended to make sure you know the essentials for navigating your Android device.

If you're already familiar with Android, feel free to skip the introduction and dive straight into Chapter 1, "Getting Up to Speed"—or into whichever chapter will be most helpful to you.

GRASPING THE ESSENTIALS OF ANDROID NAVIGATION

Google has made Android as easy to navigate as possible using straightforward taps and gestures on the touch screen.

This section covers navigating the lock screen, the Home screen, and the Apps screen; opening the Notifications panel and the Quick Settings panel; and opening the Settings app.

NAVIGATING THE LOCK, HOME, AND APPS SCREENS

As you work with your device, you will likely use three screens the most. These are the lock screen, which protects your security; the Home screen, which is your home base in Android; and the Apps screen, from which you launch the apps you want to use.

UNLOCKING THE LOCK SCREEN

When you start your Android device, it normally displays the lock screen. This security screen has two purposes: to prevent Android from responding to accidental touches on the screen and (optionally) to make the user authenticate himself by using the unlock method that the owner has set.

You can apply different unlock methods to the lock screen. The default unlock move is a simple swipe that provides no security at all, but you can apply strong security by requiring a PIN or passcode. Figure I-1 shows the lock screen secured with the PIN unlock method.

FIGURE I-1

To unlock a device secured with a PIN, type the PIN at the lock screen and tap the arrow below the 9 button.

> **!CAUTION** You can turn off the lock screen by tapping the None button on the Choose Screen Lock screen in the Settings app. This move is seldom wise except for devices you are using for demonstration purposes.

GETTING AROUND THE HOME SCREEN AND USING THE BUTTONS

After you've unlocked your device, the Home screen appears. The Home screen is your base for taking actions in Android and typically contains several types of items. Figure I-2 shows a Home screen with its essential parts labeled:

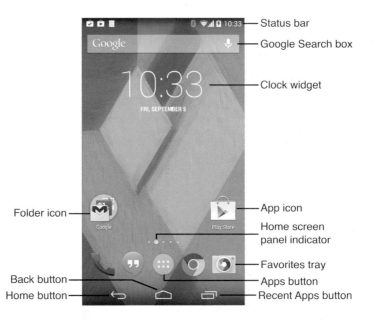

FIGURE I-2

The Home screen consists of a series of horizontal panels that give you access to many different Android features.

- **Status bar.** The status bar appears at the top of the Home screen and most other screens.
- **Google Search box.** This box enables you to search quickly straight from the Home screen. You can tap the microphone icon and speak your search terms.

- **Clock widget.** A *widget* is a small, single-purpose app, such as the Clock widget shown here. You can put any of a wide variety of widgets on the Home screen to display the information you find useful or entertaining.

- **App icon.** You can place icons for apps on the Home screen so that you can access them quickly.

- **Folder icon.** You can put your Home screen icons into folders to keep them organized.

- **Home screen panel indicator.** The Home screen consists of a series of panels that you can scroll among by swiping or dragging left or right. The larger dot shows the current panel in the series of panels.

- **Apps button.** Tap this button to display the Apps screen (discussed in the next section).

- **Favorites tray.** This tray contains a handful of icons for apps that you want to have available on every Home screen panel.

- **Back button.** Tap this button to return to the previous screen or to cancel out of a dialog box.

- **Home button.** Tap this button to display the Home screen. Android displays whichever Home screen panel you used last. Tap the Home button again to display your main Home screen panel.

> **TIP**   Tap and hold the Home button to access the Google Now information feature. You can also tap the Home button and swipe up to access Google Now.

- **Recent Apps button.** Tap this button to display the Recent Apps screen. You can then tap the app you want to display.

USING THE APPS SCREEN

From the Home screen, tap the Apps button to display the Apps screen. This screen (see Figure I-3) consists of one or more panels among which you can move by dragging or swiping left or right.

FIGURE I-3

On the Apps screen, drag or swipe left or right to find the app you want, and then tap its icon.

When you find the app you want to use, tap its icon. That app's screen then appears.

OPENING THE NOTIFICATIONS PANEL

The Notifications panel contains notifications raised by apps to alert you to events. For example, when you receive a message in Gmail, the Gmail app raises a notification in the Notifications panel. Similarly, when Android detects that a software update has become available, it displays a notification to let you know about the update.

To open the Notifications panel (shown in Figure I-4), drag or swipe down from the top of the screen with one finger. On a phone, you can drag or swipe down on the left, in the middle, or on the right; on a tablet, drag or swipe down in the left half of the top of the screen. You can then view your notifications, deal with any that need your attention, and close the Notifications panel again by dragging or swiping upward.

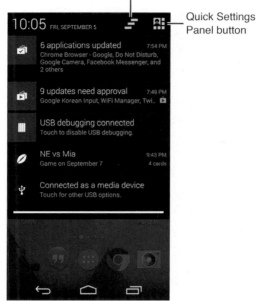

FIGURE I-4

Drag or swipe down from the top of the screen to open the Notifications panel.

OPENING THE QUICK SETTINGS PANEL

The Quick Settings panel is a screen that gives you swift access to frequently used settings. You can open the Quick Settings panel in any of these three ways:

- Pull down from the top of the screen with two fingers on a phone.
- Pull down in the right half of the top of the screen with one finger on a tablet.
- Open the Notifications panel and then tap the Quick Settings Panel icon in its upper-right corner.

Figure I-5 shows the Quick Settings panel on a phone.

Notifications
Panel button

FIGURE I-5

The Quick Settings panel gives you instant access to essential settings.

To close the Quick Settings panel, drag or swipe up.

>  **TIP**   On a phone, tap the Notifications Panel button to switch from the Quick Settings panel to the Notifications panel.

OPENING THE SETTINGS APP

Android has a vast number of settings that you can customize to configure your device the way you want it. You configure most of the settings through the Settings app. You can open the Settings app in three easy ways, as explained next. From here on, this book tells you to "Open the Settings app" rather than telling you which way to open it.

The quickest way to open the Settings app is to use the Quick Settings panel:

1. Open the Quick Settings panel by pulling down from the top of the screen with two fingers on a phone or with one finger on the right side of the top of the screen on a tablet.

2. Tap the Settings icon to open the Settings app.

Alternatively, you can open the Settings app from the Notifications panel:

1. Pull down from the top of the screen with one finger to open the Notifications panel.

2. Tap the Quick Settings icon to display the Quick Settings panel.

3. Tap the Settings icon to open the Settings app.

Or you can simply open the Settings app from the Apps screen like any other app:

1. Tap the Home button to display the Home screen.

2. Tap the Apps icon to display the Apps screen.

3. Tap the Settings icon to open the Settings app.

> **NOTE** Some Android skins make major changes to the Settings app, so if your device uses a skin, you may need to find your own way to the settings. See Chapter 14, "Using Samsung TouchWiz," and Chapter 15, "Using HTC Sense."

USING THE MENUS, CONTROLS, AND DIALOG BOXES

To enable you to give commands easily and clearly, Android uses menus, controls such as check boxes and radio buttons, and dialog boxes.

USING THE MENUS

Many apps include a Menu button that you can tap to display a menu of commands. For example, in Google's browser app, Chrome, you tap the Menu button (an icon with a vertical line of three dots) to display the menu (see Figure I-6), and then tap the command you want to use.

FIGURE I-6

Tap the Menu button (the three dots) to open the menu, and then tap the command.

WORKING WITH CONTROLS

Android uses check boxes to enable you to turn individual options on and off. For example, in Figure I-7, the Swipe to Archive box and the Sender Image box are checked, indicating that these options are turned on, while the Reply All box is unchecked, meaning that this option is turned off.

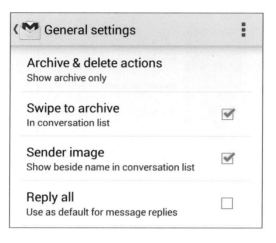

FIGURE I-7

Tap a box to check it (turning the option on) or uncheck it (turning the option off).

NOTE   This book uses the term *check* to mean tapping a box to put a check mark in it and the term *uncheck* to mean tapping a box to remove the check mark from it. If the box is already checked or unchecked (as appropriate), you don't need to change the setting.

Android uses groups of radio buttons to enable you to make a choice among two or more mutually exclusive options. For example, in the Archive & Delete Actions dialog box shown in Figure I-8, the Show Archive Only radio button is selected, showing the blue circle. Tapping the Show Delete Only radio button or the Show Archive & Delete radio button deselects the Show Archive Only radio button, because only one radio button in the group can be selected at any time.

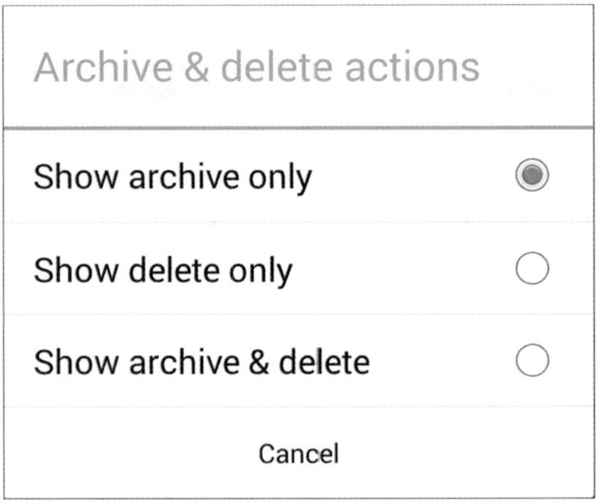

Archive & delete actions

Show archive only   ⊙

Show delete only   ○

Show archive & delete   ○

Cancel

FIGURE I-8

Tap a radio button to select that option, deselecting whichever other option in the group is currently selected.

MAKING CHOICES IN DIALOG BOXES

When you need to make a decision, Android displays a dialog box to present the choices clearly. You can't take other actions until you have dismissed the dialog box.

If a dialog box contains only radio buttons, as in Figure I-8, tapping a radio button closes the dialog box.

Otherwise, you normally tap a command button, such as the OK button or the Cancel button, to dismiss the dialog box. For example, in the Ringtones dialog box (see Figure I-9), you tap a radio button to select the ringtone you want to use, but the dialog box remains open. You then tap the OK button to close the dialog box, accepting the choice you have made, or tap the Cancel button to close the dialog box without making a choice.

Some dialog boxes appear only to confirm an action you have taken and so contain only an OK button.

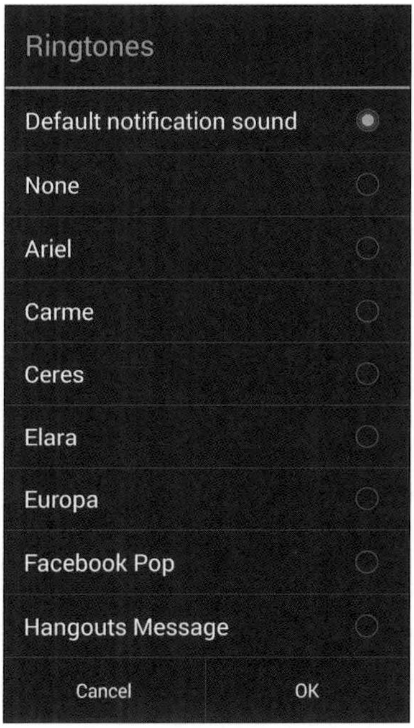

Ringtones	
Default notification sound	●
None	○
Ariel	○
Carme	○
Ceres	○
Elara	○
Europa	○
Facebook Pop	○
Hangouts Message	○
Cancel	OK

FIGURE I-9

Many dialog boxes contain command buttons, such as the OK button and Cancel button shown here.

USING THE TOUCHSCREEN

Android uses seven main gestures on the touchscreen:

- **Tap.** Tap the screen and then lift your finger.
- **Tap and hold.** Tap the screen and keep your finger on it, usually until a menu appears or another change occurs. This action is also called "long-press."
- **Double-tap.** Tap the screen twice in rapid succession.
- **Drag.** Tap an item on the screen, keep your finger on the screen, and then drag the item to its destination. In many cases, you need to tap and hold for a moment before the item becomes free for dragging.
- **Swipe.** Move your finger left, right, up, or down across the screen.
- **Pinch in.** Place your finger and thumb (or two fingers, if you prefer) apart on the screen and then pinch them together. This action is often used for zooming out (for example, on a map or a photo).

■ **Pinch out.** Place your finger and thumb (or two fingers) together on the screen and then spread them apart. This action is often used for zooming in.

Preventing the Screen from Rotating

Most Android devices include sensors (such as accelerometers) that detect the device's orientation. Android can automatically rotate the display to match the way the screen is pointing.

This automatic rotation is often handy, but you may want to turn it off at times, such as when you are holding your device nearly flat rather than upright. To turn off automatic rotation, open the Settings app, tap the Display button, and then uncheck the Auto-Rotate Screen box.

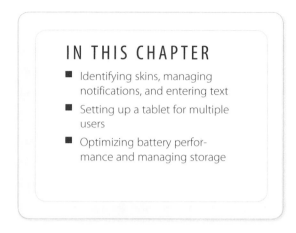

1

GETTING UP TO SPEED

This chapter will get you familiar with your Android device so that you can get the most benefit out of the rest of this book. You'll start by establishing which version of Android your device is running and whether it uses stock Android or a skin. You'll then move into setting volume levels for your various audio sources; managing your notifications; and entering text using the onscreen keyboard, hardware keyboards, and dictation. After that, it's time to examine how you set up a tablet for multiple users, get the best battery performance from your device, and manage files and storage on it.

IDENTIFYING YOUR DEVICE'S ANDROID VERSION AND ITS SKIN

At this writing, you can choose from a vast range of devices that run the Android operating system (OS). These devices not only have widely varying capabilities but also run different versions of Android. To make matters even more confusing, many devices also use what's called a *skin*, a layer

of software that runs on top of the Android OS, makes it look different, and gives it additional capabilities.

All this means that, to get the most out of this book, you need to know not only exactly what device you have but what version of Android it's running—and what skin, if any. Armed with this knowledge, you can identify which tips and tricks apply to your device, its version of Android, and its skin.

UNDERSTANDING ANDROID VERSION NUMBERS AND NAMES

Table 1.1 shows Android's versions as of fall 2014, starting with the latest version. Each version has a number and a name. For example, the latest version is Android 4.4, which is called KitKat; Android 5.0, Lollipop, is imminent.

Table 1.1   Android Version Numbers and Names

Version Numbers	Version Name
4.4	KitKat
4.1–4.3	Jelly Bean
4.0	Ice Cream Sandwich
3.0–3.2.6	Honeycomb
2.3	Gingerbread
2.2	Froyo
2.0–2.1	Éclair
1.6	Donut
1.5	Cupcake

At this writing, the current version of Android is KitKat (4.4). Jelly Bean (versions 4.1–4.3) is widely used, but so is Ice Cream Sandwich. Some Honeycomb (versions 3.0–3.2.6) are still in use.

FINDING OUT WHICH ANDROID VERSION YOUR DEVICE IS RUNNING

To find out which version of Android your device is running, follow these steps:

1. Open the Settings app.
2. Scroll down to the bottom of the list.

3. Tap the About Phone button or the About Tablet button to display the About Phone screen or the About Tablet screen. (On some devices, the button and screen may be called About Device.)

4. Look at the Android Version readout. You'll see a number such as 4.4.2 (which means your device is running KitKat) or 4.0.4 (which indicates Ice Cream Sandwich).

ESTABLISHING WHETHER YOUR DEVICE IS USING A SKIN

A skin is an extra layer of software that makes the Android user interface look different and work differently. Skins typically provide extra functionality that is not available in stock Android, so by adding a skin, a manufacturer can provide extra features to a device, make it more attractive, or make it easier to use.

These are all points in favor of skins. But because implementing a skin involves running extra software, a skin tends to make your Android device respond more slowly. If the device has a powerful processor and plenty of RAM, it may have enough punch to run Android and the skin without slowing down. But if the device is underpowered, a skin may make it slow and cumbersome to use.

Google periodically issues new versions of Android with new features, new looks, or other improvements. If you have one of Google's branded devices, such as the Nexus 5 phone or the Nexus 7 tablet, you can update to the newest version immediately. By contrast, manufacturers that provide custom versions of Android need to create new custom versions for their devices, which takes time and money. So if your device has a skin, you will likely have to wait months before a new version becomes available—and that's for one of the manufacturer's latest or biggest-selling devices. For older or lesser devices, manufacturers may not provide updated versions of Android.

The easiest way to tell whether your device has a skin is to see whether it's different from the stock Android screens shown in most of this book. For example, Figure 1.1 shows the Settings screen in stock Android on the left and the Settings screen in Samsung's TouchWiz skin on the right. You can clearly see the huge differences between the two.

FIGURE 1.1
Samsung's TouchWiz skin (right) makes huge visual changes from stock Android (left).

Tips for Choosing an Android Device

If you're looking for an Android device, take your time because there's a wide array of options. Here are four suggestions to help:

- **Android version.** If possible, get a device that has the latest version of Android. At this writing, that means KitKat (Android 4.4). You can get bargains on older devices, but be clear that you may not be able to update them to newer versions of Android.

- **Battery.** If you plan to use your device extensively, look for a model that enables you to easily change the battery.

- **Budget device.** When buying a budget Android device, choose a vanilla device—one without a skin—for better performance. A vanilla device is also more likely to receive Android OS updates quickly than a device with a skin.

- **SD card.** Look for one that accepts an SD card so that you can easily increase the storage, load your media files, and switch quickly between libraries of content.

SETTING DIFFERENT VOLUME LEVELS FOR DIFFERENT AUDIO SOURCES

Android enables you to set different volume levels for media playback, ringtones and notifications, and alarms. You can adjust the levels to make sure that notifications don't swamp the music you're enjoying and that alarms are loud enough to wake you or get your attention.

Here's how to set different audio levels for different audio sources:

1. Open the Settings app.

2. Tap the Sound button in the Device section to display the Sound screen.

3. Tap the Volumes button to display the Volumes dialog box (see Figure 1.2).

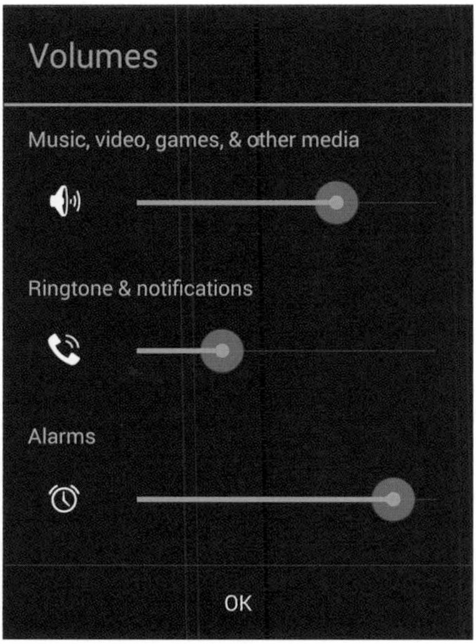

FIGURE 1.2

Drag the sliders in the Volumes dialog box to set the relative volumes for media playback, ringtones and notifications, and alarms.

> **NOTE** The Volumes dialog box on your device may display a different number of sliders than Figure 1.2 shows. For example, it may have a Ringtone slider and a Notifications slider instead of a Ringtone & Notifications slider.

4. Drag the sliders for Music, Video, Games, & Other Media; Ringtone & Notifications; and Alarms.

5. Tap the OK button.

MANAGING YOUR NOTIFICATIONS

Android displays notifications to help you keep up with your messages, appointments, and other events. You can choose which apps can give you notifications. If your device has a notification light, you can control whether Android pulses the light to make you aware of notifications you have not yet viewed.

RESPONDING TO A NOTIFICATION

When an app raises a notification, the notification appears briefly at the top of the screen and then disappears. Drag down from the top of the screen to display the Notifications pane (see Figure 1.3). You can then take the following actions:

■ Tap a button on the notification to take an action. For example, on a Missed Call notification, you can tap the Call Back button to return the call or tap the Message button to send a message to the caller.

■ Swipe a notification left or right to dismiss it.

■ Tap the Clear All button (the button that shows three horizontal bars staggered like a staircase) to clear all the notifications you can dismiss.

> **NOTE** You cannot dismiss system notifications such as the Connected as a Media Device notification shown in Figure 1.3.

■ If the notification is collapsed, tap it and drag down to expand it.

■ Tap and hold the notification until the App Info pop-up button appears, and then tap the button to display the App Info screen for the app.

■ Tap a notification to go to the app that raised it.

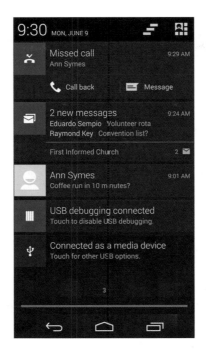

FIGURE 1.3

Tap a notification in the Notifications pane to go to the app that raised the notification.

Catching Up with Notifications You Missed

If you clear all notifications by mistake, or you clear them deliberately and realize that you didn't read something vital, don't worry—you can easily catch up with them by using a Settings Shortcut widget to display the Notifications screen.

Tap and hold empty space on the Home screen until the customization controls appear; then tap the Widgets icon to display the widgets list. Tap and hold the Settings Shortcut widget until it appears on the Home screen. When you lift your finger, the Settings Shortcut screen appears. Tap the Notifications button to make the Settings Shortcut widget take you to the Notifications screen.

You can now tap your Notifications widget to display the Notifications screen. This screen shows all your recent notifications, so you can easily catch up on what you missed. You can tap a notification to display the App Info screen for the app that raised the notification, not to go to the app itself.

Android clears the Notifications screen when you restart your device.

TURNING THE NOTIFICATION LIGHT ON OR OFF

If your device has a notification light, you can make the light blink to alert you to notifications you haven't yet seen. Here's how to control whether the light blinks:

1. Open the Settings app.
2. Tap the Display button to go to the Display screen.
3. Tap to check or uncheck the Pulse Notification Light check box.

TURNING OFF NOTIFICATIONS FOR AN APP

Here's how to turn off notifications for an app:

1. Open the Settings app.
2. Tap the Apps button in the Device section to display the Apps screen. The Apps screen displays the Downloaded tab at first.
3. If the app for which you want to turn off notifications does not appear on the downloaded tab, swipe left once to display the Running tab or twice to display the All tab.
4. Tap the app's button to display its App Info screen.
5. Tap to clear the Show Notifications check box.

> **TIP** Here are two ways to quickly display an app's App Info screen. If the app is currently running, tap the Recent Apps button, tap and hold the app's thumbnail in the Recent Apps list, and then tap the App Info button on the pop-up menu. If the app has raised a notification, tap and hold the notification on the Notifications panel, and then tap the App Info button on the pop-up menu.

CLEARING REPEAT NOTIFICATIONS

Sometimes Android may display the same notifications repeatedly. Usually, this happens with download notifications, but other apps can also raise notifications more than once.

If you find this happening, first restart your device. Restarting can solve any number of problems, and it takes only a minute or two.

If restarting doesn't suppress old download notifications, you may need to clear the cache and data for the Download Manager app. To do so, follow these steps:

1. Open the Settings app.
2. Tap the Apps button in the Device section to display the Apps screen.
3. Swipe left twice to display the All list.
4. Tap the Download Manager button to display the App Info screen for the Download Manager app.
5. Tap the Clear Cache button to clear the cached data.
6. Tap the Clear Data button. The Delete App Data? dialog box opens (see Figure 1.4).

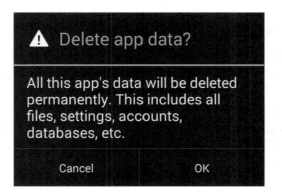

FIGURE 1.4

You may need to delete the app data for the Download Manager app to get rid of repeated download notifications.

7. Tap the OK button.
8. Tap the Force Stop button. The Force Stop? dialog box opens.
9. Tap the OK button.

Restart your phone after clearing Download Manager's cache and data.

> **TIP** Another way to clear old notifications is to install a notification-management app. You can find various notification-management apps on the Play Store, but watch out for two things. First, make sure the app doesn't require Internet access. Second, make sure that the app doesn't require your phone to be rooted. Rooting gives you access to the root account, which enables you to take full control of your device's software and hardware and install unapproved software on it.

ENTERING TEXT

To enter text on your Android device, you can use the onscreen keyboard, a hardware keyboard, or dictation. You can also enter emoticons to liven up your messages or documents.

USING THE KEYBOARD AND SPELLING CORRECTION

The most straightforward means of entering text in a document is the onscreen keyboard. Android automatically displays the onscreen keyboard when you touch a text field in a document or the user interface. The keyboard has a letters layout, a symbols and numbers layout, and an extended symbols layout.

Here's what you need to know about the keyboard:

- **Switch among layouts.** Tap the ?123 button to display the symbols and numbers layout. From there, tap the ABC button to return to the letters layout or tap the =\< button to display the extended symbols layout. From the extended symbols layout, tap the ABC button to display the letters layout or tap the ?123 button to return to the symbols and numbers layout.

> **NOTE** You can hide the keyboard by tapping the Back button (this button appears as a downward-caret icon when the keyboard is displayed). You may want to hide the keyboard so that you can read larger amounts of text or navigate to other text fields. To display the keyboard once more, tap in the text field again.

- **Type numbers from the letters keyboard.** The top row of letters on the letters layout has a number in the upper-right corner, from 1 on the Q key to 0 (zero) on the P key. To type the number, tap and hold the appropriate key until the pop-up panel appears, and then lift your finger. Some of the pop-up panels also contain alternate characters (discussed next), but the numbers are the default characters.

- **Type alternate characters.** The vowel keys, some letter keys (such as N, S, and C), and many of the symbol keys give access to pop-up panels containing alternate characters. For example, tapping and holding the A key opens a pop-up panel with alternate characters such as ã and æ (see Figure 1.5); and tapping and holding the asterisk key gives you access to star, dagger, and double-dagger symbols. So when you need to type a character that does not appear on any of the keyboard layouts, tap and hold the key for the base character, and then tap the character on the pop-up panel.

FIGURE 1.5

Tap and hold a character to display a pop-up panel of alternate characters, and then tap the character that you want to enter.

- **Type real fractions.** To type a real fraction, display the symbols and numbers layout, tap and hold the number key for the first part of the fraction, and then tap the fraction on the pop-up menu that appears. For example, tap and hold the 1 key to type ⅓, or tap and hold the 5 key to type ⅝.

- **Type quickly with Gesture Typing.** The Gesture Typing feature enables you to type words by sliding your finger from one letter to another over the keyboard without removing it. At the end of a word, you can either swipe over the spacebar to type a space and continue swiping the next word, or lift your finger off the screen and then put it back down to start the next word.

Turning On Gesture Typing and Configuring It

If Gesture Typing doesn't work on your device, you may need to turn it on. You may also need to configure it to work the way you prefer. Follow these steps:

1. Tap and hold the key to the left of the spacebar on the keyboard. Depending on your device and the keyboard, this may be the comma key or the Voice Input key (the microphone icon).

2. When the Settings icon appears, release the button to display the Input Options menu.

3. Tap the Google Keyboard Settings button to display the Google Keyboard Settings screen.

4. Select the Enable Gesture Typing check box to turn on Gesture Typing.

5. Select the Dynamic Floating Preview check box if you want to see a preview of the word as you slide.

6. Select the Phrase Gesture check box if you want to be able to type spaces by sliding your finger over the spacebar.

7. Tap the Back button to return to the document you were working in.

■ **Using suggestions.** By default, the Google Keyboard displays suggestions as you type in the area above the top row of the keyboard. The suggestion with three dots below it is the default one; you can enter this word by tapping the spacebar or a punctuation key (such as the period key). You can enter another suggestion by tapping it. To see the full list of suggestions, tap and hold any of the suggestions until the pop-up panel appears (see Figure 1.6).

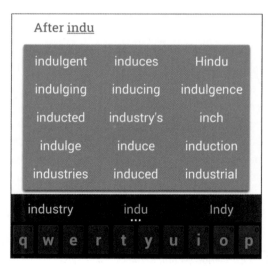

FIGURE 1.6

Tap and hold a suggestion to display the full list of suggestions. You can then tap a suggestion to insert it in the document.

CONFIGURING TEXT CORRECTION

Android's Text Correction feature automatically corrects words and phrases you type that appear to be wrong. You can control how aggressively Text Correction corrects text, so if you find Android changing too many words and phrases that you actually want to use, try turning down the degree of correction.

Here's how to configure Text Correction:

1. Open the Settings app.

2. Tap the Language & Input button in the Personal section to display the Language & Input screen.

3. Tap the Settings button (the sliders icon) to the right of the Google Keyboard button in the Keyboard & Input Methods section. The Google Keyboard Settings screen appears. Figure 1.7 shows the Text Correction section of this screen.

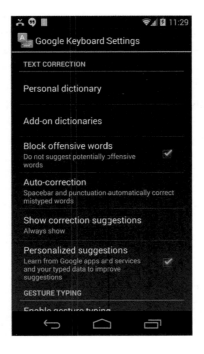

FIGURE 1.7

Use the controls in the Text Correction section of the Google Keyboard Settings screen to configure automatic corrections, correction suggestions, and add-on dictionaries.

4. Check the Auto-Capitalization check box in the General section if you want Android to automatically capitalize the first letter of each sentence or new paragraph.

> **TIP** If you want to load or remove add-on dictionaries, tap the Add-On Dictionaries button on the Google Keyboard Settings screen. On the Add-On Dictionaries screen that appears, tap the Refresh button to get the latest list of add-on dictionaries. You can then install an add-on dictionary by tapping its button and then tapping the Install button that appears, or delete a dictionary by tapping its button and then tapping the Delete button that appears.

5. Check the Block Offensive Words check box if you want Android to suppress words that some people may find offensive.

6. Tap the Auto-Correction button to display the Auto-Correction dialog box, and then tap the option button for the degree of correction you want: Off, Modest, Aggressive, or Very Aggressive. You'll probably want to experiment with the Modest and Aggressive settings to see which suits you best.

7. To control whether Android displays correction suggestions, tap the Show Correction Suggestions button, and then tap the appropriate button in the Show Correction Suggestions dialog box: Always Show, Show in Portrait Mode, or Always Hide.

> **TIP** The Show in Portrait Mode setting for Show Correction Suggestions is useful on phones and small tablets, on which the keyboard and correction suggestions together take up much of the screen in landscape mode.

8. Check the Personalized Suggestions check box if you want Google Keyboard to learn words and phrases from what you type. Personalized suggestions are usually helpful.

ADDING WORDS TO YOUR PERSONAL DICTIONARY

Android enables you to maintain a personal dictionary containing words that are correctly spelled but do not appear in Android's dictionary. By adding words to your personal dictionary, you can prevent Android from querying them. You can also create a shortcut for any word or phrase so that you can enter it by typing the shortcut.

1. Open the Settings app.

2. Tap the Language & Input button in the Personal section to display the Language & Input screen.

3. Tap the Personal Dictionary button to display the Personal Dictionary screen.

4. Tap the + button to display an input screen.

5. Type the word or phrase on the upper line.

6. Tap the Shortcut field and type any shortcut you want to use for the word or phrase.

7. Tap the Back button to finish adding the word.

> **TIP** You can also add a word to the personal dictionary when typing. Finish typing the word but don't type a space or punctuation. Tap the word in the suggestions bar, and then tap the Touch Again to Save prompt that appears. (On some devices, you may not see the Touch Again to Save prompt.)

> **NOTE** To edit or delete a word or shortcut, tap it on the Personal Dictionary screen. Android opens the word for editing. You can then change the word or shortcut or tap the Delete icon (the trash can) to delete it.

ENTERING TEXT USING A HARDWARE KEYBOARD

The stock Android onscreen keyboard is easy enough to use, but very few people are able to touch-type on it, especially on a phone rather than a tablet. So if you need to type large amounts of text on your Android device, you should think seriously about connecting a hardware keyboard to it.

You can connect a wide variety of keyboards via either Bluetooth or a cable. Bluetooth is handy, especially if you get a Bluetooth keyboard built into a case that fits your device. See Chapter 4, "Connecting to Networks and Devices," for instructions of connecting Bluetooth devices.

But if you simply need to enter a lot of text quickly, any regular USB keyboard will do the trick as long as your device supports the USB On-the-Go standard. Get a USB A female to micro USB B male adapter cable that also supports USB OTG, plug the keyboard into the USB female port, and plug the micro USB jack into your device.

> **NOTE** USB OTG is short for USB On-The-Go. USB OTG enables a device (such as an Android phone or tablet) to act as a USB host, so you can plug in USB hardware and use it.

After connecting a hardware keyboard, you can use the keyboard shortcuts explained in Table 1.2 to navigate through text.

Table 1.2   Keyboard Shortcuts for Hardware Keyboards

Keyboard Shortcut	What It Does
Left arrow	Moves the insertion point one character to the left.
Right arrow	Moves the insertion point one character to the right.
Up arrow	Moves the insertion point up one line.
Down arrow	Moves the insertion point down one line.
Ctrl+Left arrow	Moves the insertion point to the beginning of the current word (if the insertion point is within a word) or to the beginning of the previous word (if it is not).
Ctrl+Right arrow	Moves the insertion point to the beginning of the next word.
Alt+Left arrow	Moves the insertion point to the beginning of the line.
Alt+Right arrow	Moves the insertion point to the end of the line.
Alt+Up arrow	Moves the insertion point to the beginning of the document or text field.
Alt+Down arrow	Moves the insertion point to the end of the document or text field.
Alt+Delete	Deletes the current line.
Ctrl+A	Selects all the content of the document or the active field.
Ctrl+C	Copies the selection (if there is one) or the entire document (if not).

Keyboard Shortcut	What It Does
Ctrl+X	Cuts the selection (if there is one) or the entire document (if not).
Ctrl+V	Pastes the most recent Clipboard item.

> **TIP** You can select text using the keyboard by holding down Shift while you press the navigation keys or keyboard shortcuts. For example, press Shift+Right arrow to select the character to the right of the insertion point (or to extend the existing selection by one character to the right) or press Shift+Alt+Right arrow to select from the insertion point's current position to the end of the line.

Changing the Layout of a Hardware Keyboard

After connecting a hardware keyboard, you can change the layout if necessary. For example, you may prefer the Dvorak layout to QWERTY, or you may want the layout for a different language or region.

Open the Settings app, tap the Language & Input button, and then go to the Physical Keyboard section of the Language & Input screen.

Tap the keyboard's button (this shows the keyboard's description, such as Logitech USB Keyboard) to display the Choose Keyboard Layout dialog box. If the layout you want appears, tap it to apply it. If not, tap the Set Up Keyboard Layouts button to display the Keyboard Layouts screen, and then tap the check box for each keyboard layout you want to make available.

Tap the Back button, tap the appropriate keyboard in the Choose Keyboard Layout dialog box, and then start typing using that layout.

ENTERING TEXT USING DICTATION

Typing is the standard way of entering text, but you may be able to enter text more quickly—and accurately— by using the Google Voice Typing feature.

Google Voice Typing may already be set up on your phone or tablet. If so, you're good to go, but you may want to set up your input languages or install offline speech recognition.

Follow these steps to set up and configure Google Voice Typing:

1. Open the Settings app.
2. Tap the Language & Input button in the Personal section to display the Language & Input screen.
3. Check the Google Voice Typing check box.
4. Tap the Settings button on the right of the Google Voice Typing button to display the Google Voice Typing Settings screen.
5. If you want to select input languages, tap the Choose Input Languages button and work on the Choose Input Languages screen.
6. Check the Block Offensive Words check box if you want Google Voice Typing to censor your input.
7. Tap the Offline Speech Recognition button to display the Download Languages screen. This screen has three tabs: Installed, All, and Auto-Update. The Installed tab appears first.
8. Review your current languages on the Installed tab.
9. If you need to install another language for offline speech recognition, tap the All tab, and then tap the language you want to download and install.
10. Tap the Auto-Update tab to reveal its controls, and then tap the option button for the way you want to update. Your choices are Do Not Auto-Update Languages; Auto-Update Languages At Any Time; Data Charges May Apply; and Auto-Update Languages over Wi-Fi Only.

> **TIP** The Auto-Update Languages over Wi-Fi Only setting is the best choice for keeping your Google Voice Typing languages up to date without incurring data charges from downloading over the cellular network.

After you've turned on Google Voice Typing, tap the microphone button to the left of the spacebar on the onscreen keyboard to start dictation.

> **TIP** If you plan to dictate a lot, use a high-quality headset microphone. Google Voice Typing delivers impressive results with just the open microphone built into your device, but you can get much clearer input by using a headset microphone.

ENTERING EMOJI

The Google Keyboard provides a large selection of emoticons that you can enter in your messages and documents. To access the emoticons, tap and hold the Enter key at the lower-right corner of the onscreen keyboard, and then tap the smiley-face icon on the pop-up panel.

> **NOTE** Depending on your device and keyboard configuration, you may be able to access emoticons by tapping an emoticon key that appears on the keyboard or by tapping and holding the key to the left of the keyboard and then tapping the Emoticons button on the pop-up panel.

With the emoticons displayed (see Figure 1.8), tap the Tab button for the category you want to view, and then scroll right to see further characters. Tap the Recents tab button (the leftmost button, with the clock icon) to see the characters you've used recently. Tap the ABC button to return to the letters keyboard.

FIGURE 1.8
You can easily enter emoticons in your messages and documents by using the Google Keyboard.

USING ALTERNATIVE KEYBOARDS

If you find the Google Keyboard difficult to use, you can install another keyboard that suits you better. You'll find a wide variety of alternative keyboards in the Play Store. Here are three alternative keyboards to consider:

- Hacker's Keyboard (free) is a highly customizable keyboard that includes keys you normally find on hardware keyboards, such as Ctrl and Tab, but not on Android keyboards. This keyboard is great for remote access to computers.

- SwiftKey is a trace keyboard (like the Gesture Typing feature on the Google Keyboard) with strong predictive text features. Download the SwiftKey Trial app to give the keyboard a spin and see if you want to pay for the full version.

- Smart Keyboard Pro ($2.75) is a customizable keyboard that includes skins for different looks and optional transparency. You can customize the key height separately for portrait and landscape orientations; hide the period and comma keys; and switch among Normal mode, T9 mode, and Compact mode. Smart Keyboard Pro includes a calibration tool that you can run to improve accuracy if you find you tend to tap the wrong keys. Download the free Smart Keyboard Trial to test; you can then pay for the upgrade to Pro if you like it.

SETTING UP A TABLET FOR MULTIPLE USERS

Android includes multiuser features for tablets, so if you have a tablet, you can set it up with a separate account for each user. By creating user accounts, you give each user his own home screen, settings, and storage for documents. Each user can send and receive email and browse the Web without sharing his messages and history with other users. Each user can choose a different unlock method to keep his data safe.

Instead of creating a user account for another person, you can create a *restricted profile*, a kind of limited account that enables the user to access only some apps and content on your account. Like a user account, a restricted profile has a separate space and data on the tablet. You might want to create a restricted profile for a child that you allow to occasionally use your tablet.

CREATING A USER ACCOUNT

When you create a new user account, it is best to have the person who will use the account with you so that she can set up the account immediately. In this way, you can ensure that the right person sets up the user account; you can also insist that the person sets an unlock method on the account to help protect the tablet.

If you must set up the new user account when the person is not available, the account appears on the lock screen without a security method. Anyone with access to the tablet can set up the user account, and there is no obligation to set an unlock method.

Here's how to create a user account:

1. Open the Settings app.
2. Tap the Users button in the Device section to display the Users screen.
3. Tap the Add User or Profile button to display the Add dialog box (see Figure 1.9).

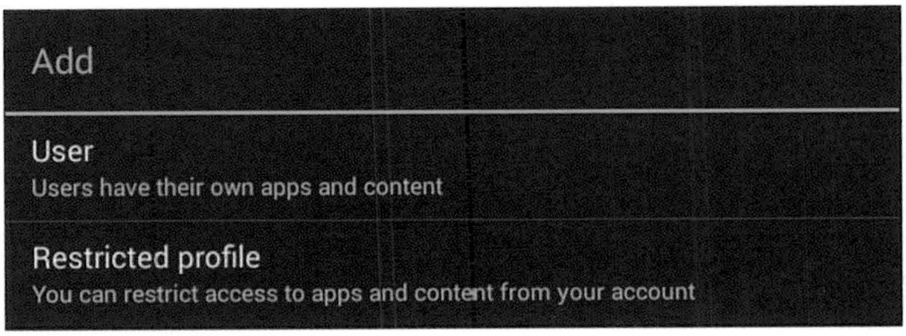

Add

User
Users have their own apps and content

Restricted profile
You can restrict access to apps and content from your account

FIGURE 1.9

In the Add dialog box, tap the User button to start creating a new user account on your tablet.

4. Tap the User button to display the Add New User dialog box (see Figure 1.10).

Add new user

After you create a new user, that person needs to go through a setup process.

Any user can accept updated app permissions on behalf of all other users.

Cancel   OK

FIGURE 1.10

Tap the OK button in the Add New User dialog box.

5. Tap the OK button. Android displays the Set Up User Now? dialog box (see Figure 1.11).

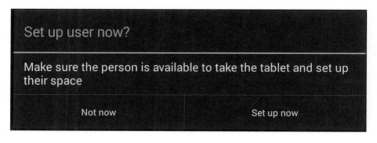

FIGURE 1.11

In the Set Up User Now? dialog box, tap the Set Up Now button if the user is available to set up her user account. Otherwise, tap the Not Now button.

6. If the user is with you and can set up the account now, tap the Set Up Now button and hand over the tablet to the user. Otherwise, tap the Not Now button.

7. Assuming you tap the Set Up Now button, the lock screen appears, showing an account button called New User. This account button is selected automatically. The user can swipe to unlock the screen, tap the Next button on the Welcome screen that appears, and then follow through the steps to set up the account.

If you tap the Not Now button in the Set Up User Now? dialog box, the user account appears in the Users & Profiles list on the Users screen as New User, Not Set Up. When the user is present and can set up the account, lock the tablet by opening the Quick Settings panel and tapping your account picture. The user can then tap the New User icon, swipe to unlock the screen, and follow through the screens to set up the account.

Understanding Owner and Nonowner Accounts

To create a new user account on your tablet, you must log in using the owner account. This is the account you used when you first set up the tablet. As long as that account is the only account that your tablet contains, there's no confusion; but if your tablet already contains multiple user accounts, and you find that the Add User or Profile button does not appear on the Users screen, the reason is most likely that you are using a nonowner account.

CREATING A RESTRICTED PROFILE

Here's how to create a restricted profile for a user:

1. Open the Settings app.

2. Tap the Users button in the Device section to display the Users screen.

3. Tap the Add User or Profile button to display the Add dialog box.

4. Tap the Restricted Profile button to display the Application and Content Restrictions screen (see Figure 1.12).

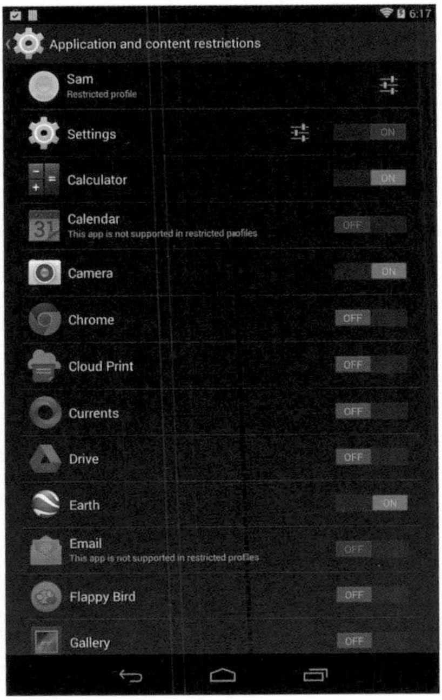

FIGURE 1.12

On the Application and Content Restrictions screen, choose which apps to make available in the restricted profile.

Setting a Screen Lock to Protect Your Apps and Data

For the restricted profile feature to work, you must use a screen lock to protect your apps and data. So if you haven't yet set a screen lock, Android prompts you to set a lock when you tap the Restricted Profile button in the Add dialog box. Tap the Set Lock button to display the Unlock Selection screen, tap the lock type you want (Pattern, PIN, or Password), and then follow through the steps for setting the lock. Android then displays the Application and Content Restrictions screen, and you can continue with step 5 in the main text.

5. Tap the New Profile button at the top to display the Profile Info dialog box.

6. To add a custom icon to the profile, tap the default icon on the left side of the dialog box, tap the Take Photo button or the Choose Photo from Gallery button on the pop-up menu, and then take the photo or select the existing photo to use. You can then crop the photo as needed.

7. Type the name for the profile, replacing the default name, New Profile.

8. Tap the OK button to close the Profile Info dialog box and apply the name.

9. Touch the Settings icon to the left of the On/Off switch on the Settings button to display the list of settings. You can then tap a check box to control whether the user can use the feature. For example, select the Location check box to enable the user to use the Location feature.

10. Specify which apps you want the user to be able to use by setting its switch to the On position. Make sure the switch for each app you don't want the user to use is set to the Off position.

11. Tap the Back button to return to the Users screen.

SWITCHING AMONG USER ACCOUNTS AND PROFILES

After you set up an account for each full user and a restricted profile for each person who needs less freedom, you can easily switch among the accounts and profiles. Follow these steps:

1. Pull down from the upper-right corner of the screen to display the Quick Settings panel.

2. Touch your user account icon to lock the tablet. The lock screen appears, showing the list of users as circular buttons at the bottom. The larger circle indicates the last user. The lock screen shows that user's lock screen wallpaper and unlock method (for example, swipe or password).

> **✓ TIP** You can also lock your tablet by pressing the Power button briefly. The tablet turns off, and the screen goes dark. Press the Power button again to wake the tablet. The lock screen appears, and you can choose which account or profile to use.

3. Tap the button for the user account or restricted profile to which you want to switch. The circle for that account or profile grows larger, and the lock screen changes to show the wallpaper and unlock method set for that account or profile.

4. Unlock the screen by using that unlock method. For example, type the password and press the Enter key.

DELETING A USER ACCOUNT OR RESTRICTED PROFILE

If you no longer need a particular user account or restricted profile, you can delete it from your tablet. Follow these steps:

1. Open the Settings app.

2. Tap the Users button in the Device section to display the Users screen.

3. Tap the Delete icon (the trash can) on the button for the account. The Remove User? dialog box or the Remove Profile? dialog box opens, warning you that the user's or profile's space and data will disappear from the tablet.

4. Tap the Delete button to finish removing the user account or profile.

UNDERSTANDING AND AVOIDING PROBLEMS

Sharing a tablet with others can be a great way to get more computing out of your hardware budget, but it may bring some problems with security, storage space, and performance.

Apart from actually having to share the physical device, you need to ensure security for your data and that of each user. Make sure you lock the tablet consistently so that nobody can access it without entering a PIN or passcode.

Be aware that each user can accept updated app permissions for the tablet as a whole. This means you should create full user accounts only for people you can trust to deal sensibly with app updates.

With several users storing data and files (especially media files) on the tablet, space may run low. You will need to manage the device's storage using the techniques discussed later in this chapter.

If several users have sessions open at the same time, the tablet may start running more slowly because it is low on memory. You can try closing apps, or getting other users to close their apps so yours will run better, but you will normally be better off restarting the tablet.

GETTING THE BEST BATTERY PERFORMANCE

To get the most use out of your Android phone or tablet, you will need to manage its battery life. You can do this using either the tools that come with the device or with extra tools that you add. You can identify features and apps that consume large amounts of power so that you can either disable them or simply not use them. You can reduce the amount of power your device needs by choosing settings to spare power. And you can give yourself the means to recharge your device at every opportunity.

IDENTIFYING POWER HOGS

To identify power-hogging features and apps, follow these steps:

1. Open the Quick Settings panel. For example, pull down from the top of the screen with two fingers.

2. Tap the Power icon to display the Battery screen (see Figure 1.13). This screen shows currently running features and apps listed in descending order by power consumption—in other words, greediest first.

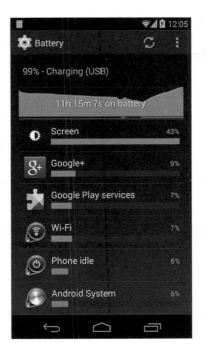

FIGURE 1.13

Look at the Battery screen to see which features and apps have been consuming the most battery power.

3. Tap the Battery graph at the top to display the History Details screen (see Figure 1.14). This screen shows a larger battery chart, enabling you to see the relative rates of power consumption more clearly, and bar charts showing when each feature was consuming power.

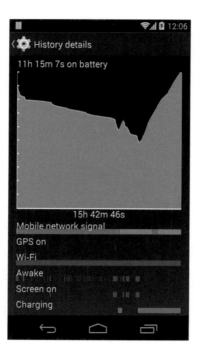

FIGURE 1.14

The History Details screen shows you exactly when each feature was consuming power.

4. Tap the Back button to return to the Battery screen.

5. Tap the button for a feature or app whose usage details you want to view. The Use Details screen appears. Figure 1.15 shows the Use Details screen for Google Play services.

> **NOTE** The Use Details screen for some apps and features includes controls for adjusting the battery usage.

FIGURE 1.15

The Use Details screen gives you specifics on what an app has been doing.

EKING OUT BATTERY LIFE

To get the most runtime out of your device, you need to reduce power consumption to an acceptable minimum. What that means depends on what the device is and what you're doing with it.

Here are 10 ways you can easily reduce the amount of power your device consumes:

- **Turn down the display brightness.** Open the Quick Settings panel, tap the Brightness icon, and then drag the slider as far to the left as you can bear. The display gets through a huge amount of power, especially on a tablet with a large screen.

- **Set a short sleep interval.** Open the Settings app, tap the Display button, and then tap the Sleep button to display the Sleep dialog box. Tap a short time, such as 15 Seconds or 1 Minute, to save power by turning off the screen quickly when you're not using it.

- **Use Airplane mode when you can go offline.** Open the Quick Settings panel and tap the Airplane Mode icon to quickly shut down all communications services. Repeat the move when you need to go back online.

> **☑ TIP** Turn on Airplane mode when you don't absolutely need connectivity and you're in a place with no signal or poor signal, such as rural wastelands or convention centers. Otherwise, your device will happily squander valuable battery power on chasing will-o'-the-wisp signals.

■ **Turn off communications services you don't need.** Open the Quick Settings panel and tap the icon for any communications service that is currently turned on but which you can afford to turn off: Cellular (on a phone or cellular-capable tablet), Wi-Fi, or Bluetooth. If your device has Near Field Communication (NFC), turn that off as well.

■ **Set the Location mode to Battery Saving.** Open the Settings app and tap the Location button in the Personal section to display the Location screen. Tap the Mode button at the top to display the Location Mode screen, and then tap the Battery Saving button. Alternatively, set the Location switch on the Location screen to the Off position to turn off location tracking entirely.

■ **Check for email less frequently.** Unless it's vital that you receive all your messages as soon as possible, reduce the frequency of checking for new messages to a minimum. See Chapter 6, "Taking Gmail to the Pro Level," for instructions on configuring the Gmail app and Chapter 7, "Becoming Expert with the Email App," for instructions on configuring the Email app.

■ **Store copies of cloud files on your device.** Services such as Dropbox are great because they enable you to access your documents from anywhere you have an Internet connection. But to save power, you can store copies of files on your phone or tablet so that you don't need to download them. For example, in Dropbox, you can mark a file as a favorite to make Android store a copy of it locally.

■ **Avoid playing videos and music.** Playing videos eats through battery power quickly because it uses the screen, but even playing back music takes a fair amount of power. If you find your Android device runs out of power regularly, consider getting a minute music player (such as an iPod shuffle or one of its competitors) so that you can listen to your essential music without running down the battery on your phone or tablet.

■ **Turn off live wallpapers.** Live wallpapers look pretty, but they make your device's processor work harder and consume power. To turn off live wallpapers, open the Settings app, tap the Display button to go to the Display screen, and then tap the Wallpaper button to display the Choose Wallpaper From screen. You can then tap the Wallpapers button to set a static wallpaper, tap the Gallery button to choose a picture from the Gallery app, or touch the Photos button to use a photo from the Camera app.

- **Streamline your Home screens.** Widgets that require updating, such as those for email or social networking, consume power both through updating and network connections, so run as few widgets as possible if you're trying to squeeze more time out of your battery.

> **TIP**   Some skins and devices offer extra power-management features. For example, the Samsung Galaxy S 5's Ultra Power Saving mode enables you to shut off all nonessential features and even uses black-and-white output to reduce the power draw. Look into any extra features that your device provides for getting you through power shortages.

RECHARGING SECRETS

As you saw in the previous sections, you can take various actions to reduce your device's power consumption. But given that most of these actions make your device not only less useful but also harder to use, you may prefer to take a damn-the-torpedoes approach and confront the power problem head on by running your device at full bore but also recharging it whenever you get the chance.

Here are suggestions for recharging your Android device:

- **Carry a spare battery.** If your phone or tablet enables you to easily change batteries, carry one or two spare—and fully charged—batteries with you wherever you go and swap them out as needed. Being able to easily change batteries is one of the great advantages of some Samsung phones, such as the Galaxy Note 4 and the Galaxy S 5.

- **Get a battery case.** If your phone or tablet is a high-profile device, you may be able to find a case with a built-in battery. If you consistently need more battery power than the built-in battery delivers, a battery case can be a great solution.

- **Get an external battery or portable charger.** No matter which device you have, you can choose from a wide range of external batteries, also called *portable chargers*, to which you connect your device via USB to recharge it. If you live in a sunny climate, consider getting one with a solar charger.

- **Upgrade the battery.** If your device's battery is user-replaceable, you may be able to replace it with a higher-capacity version. First, if your device is still under warranty, check whether replacing the battery will invalidate the warranty; if so, decide whether this is a sacrifice you're prepared to make in your pursuit of power or whether to wait until the warranty expired. Next, look up the specs for your device's battery, and then search on the Internet for a higher-capacity version.

! CAUTION When buying a third-party charger or battery for your Android device, read professional and user reviews to make sure you choose a quality unit. A poorly made charger can not only overload your device, damaging the battery, but can also be a fire hazard to the place where you use it. A poorly made battery can damage your Android device directly. Also check the battery's date of manufacture before buying. A lithium-ion battery gradually loses capacity over two to three years because of oxidization, so make sure the battery you buy is fresh.

- **Get a car charger.** If you drive a car, get a car charger so that you can plug your device in to charge for the duration of each journey. That should more than offset the power taken by using your device for navigation in the car.
- **Get a spare charger.** Carrying a charger to and from work is a headache, especially when you leave the charger at your workplace for the weekend. Get a spare charger to keep at work.
- **Carry a USB cable.** When no external battery or dedicated charger is available, plug your device into the USB port on whichever computer is handy. The battery may charge more slowly, but you'll pick up at least some power.

Understanding How Device Batteries Charge

These days, most devices use lithium-ion batteries, which deliver a good amount of power relative to their size, are usually very stable, and prefer frequent charging to full discharging and recharging.

To get the most out of your device's battery, you need to understand the essentials of how it works so that you can charge it in the ways that work best for the battery and for yourself.

Some manufacturers recommend charging the battery fully at the first charge. Most experts agree that this isn't necessary, suggesting that the manufacturers have carried the recommendation over from the days of nickel batteries, which *did* require a full charge at first. But if you want to go ahead and give your device's battery a full charge at first, it will do no harm.

A battery's life is measured in charge cycles; a typical lithium-ion battery gives around 500 charge cycles. A *charge cycle* involves charging and discharging the battery fully. Normally, you'll use partial charge cycles rather than full charge cycles for your device's battery, using the device for a while and then plugging it into a power source to recharge. Partial charge cycles add up to full charge cycles as you'd expect, so if you discharge your battery 50% on Monday, 25% on Tuesday, and 25% on Wednesday, charging it up again each evening, you've consumed a full charge cycle.

Using partial charge cycles like this is in general the best way to treat a lithium-ion battery. This is in contrast to some older battery technologies, in which partially discharging and recharging the battery could cause a "memory effect" that reduced the battery's charge capability to the amount you had used.

If you want to keep your device's battery working well, it's a good idea to give it a full discharge and recharge every 30 or so charge cycles—say, once a month if you use your device heavily, or once every couple of months for moderate use. This full discharge and recharge helps to sync the battery's fuel gauge with the actual state of the battery's charge. Without this discharge and recharge, the fuel gauge gradually becomes less accurate, so the power status Android reports to you may not be correct.

Most recent lithium-ion batteries charge relatively quickly up to the 80% level and then charge more slowly for the last 20%. So charging your device for 20 minutes can bump up the level substantially if the battery is depleted, but if the battery is above the 80% level, it may add only a few percent.

Some third-party chargers claim to be able to charge a lithium-ion battery fully in just a few minutes. Experts agree that such instant charging is not possible and that attempting to charge in this way is likely to damage the battery.

Never charge a lithium-ion battery in freezing conditions, because doing so can damage the battery. If the battery gets really cold (for example, because you leave your phone in the car in winter), allow it to warm up before you try to charge it.

MANAGING FILES AND STORAGE

You might be familiar with Parkinson's Law, which states that "work expands so as to fill the time available for its completion"—but do you know the Law's corollary that states "Storage requirements will increase to meet storage capacity"?

Sadly, this corollary seems to be all too true: However much storage space you have, on your Android device in this case, you'll find you want to carry around that quantity of files—or usually more. Between the songs and movies you bring for entertainment, the books and documents you need for work or study, and the files you create directly on your device, the built-in storage can quickly become full. This is especially true if you record video, which can chew through several gigabytes of storage space in next to no time.

Most devices come with only a modest amount of storage space. At this writing, manufacturers pretend that 16GB is a generous size and charge a savage premium for higher-capacity devices. So chances are that you'll need to manage the files and storage on your device.

> **NOTE**   Whether you can use SD cards with your device or not, back it up frequently in case it suffers an accident or you delete a priceless file by accident.

ADDING AN SD CARD

If your device accepts an SD card, add the highest-capacity SD card that works. If your device's SD card is awkward to insert and remove, you will probably want to leave a single card in place, but if you can swap SD cards easily, you can use several of them. This gives you an easy way to quickly load files onto your device from your computer: Copy them to the SD card, and then insert it in your Android device.

> **TIP**   Before adding an SD card, read your device's documentation to find out the largest size of SD card it supports. Then search online to see if other people who have the device have gotten a larger SD card to work—and if so, which make and model of card. The manufacturers' recommendations are often conservative or out of date, so be prepared to research your device and SD cards if you need the maximum storage possible.

Understanding KitKat's Limitations on SD Card Storage

Android devices have a strange relationship with SD cards. On the one hand, few manufacturers sell high-capacity devices, so you pretty much need to add an SD card in order to give yourself plenty of storage. On the other hand, Google's own devices don't have SD card slots, and Google keeps making changes to the ways in which Android apps can use SD cards. Most of the recent changes have been restrictive, limiting the ways in which apps can use SD cards.

The latest changes, introduced in KitKat, largely prevent third-party apps from writing data to the SD card. Before this, if you gave a third-party app permission to access the SD card, it could read and write to any folder on the SD card. But now, even with permission to access the SD card, a third-party app can write only to folders it creates or folders of which it takes ownership. And if you uninstall the third-party app, you also delete the app's folders and their contents.

Google made these changes for good reason: The SD card uses the old file allocation table (FAT) file system, which doesn't support file and folder permissions of the type that most modern operating systems co. So whereas in the Windows NT File System (NTFS for short), the Mac HFS Plus file system (also called Mac OS Extended file system), and most Linux file systems, you or the OS can set separate permissions on each file or folder, in FAT you cannot: Any app that has access to a FAT volume can access all that volume's folders and files. This lack of security enables any malicious or ill-programmed app to compromise sensitive data on the SD card.

Locking down the SD card like this increases your security, but it makes the SD card that much less useful to you. For example, a third-party camera app may no longer be able to store photos and videos on the SD card, or a video-editing app may no longer be able to edit videos. The problem is most acute for file-management apps, which can no longer create folders, move files, or perform other essential actions in areas of the SD card they don't themselves own.

If you need to run apps that worked using the SD card on older versions of Android but don't work under KitKat, you may need to root your device. This book doesn't cover rooting, but you can find instructions by searching online for *root* and your device's name. Proceed with great care because rooting can "brick" a device, rendering it useless (even as a brick).

If you root your device, you can install a fix such as the KitKat External SD Card Patch (free from the Play Store), which enables apps to write to the SD card again. You can also connect a physically external storage device, such as a USB memory stick or a USB drive, to your device. The result is physically awkward but enables you to add massive amounts of storage to the device.

Android expects SD cards to use the FAT file system. Almost all SD cards come formatted with FAT, so if you've got a new card, you're good to go. If the SD card is formatted with another file system, you need to reformat it before your device can use it.

You can reformat the SD card on your device itself or by using a computer. The following sections explain how to reformat an SD card on Android, on Windows, and on OS X.

> **! CAUTION**   Reformatting an SD card removes any files and folders it currently contains. You may also want to reformat an SD card to remove all its contents.

FORMATTING AN SD CARD ON ANDROID

Here's how to format an SD card on Android:

1. Insert the SD card into the slot.
2. Open the Settings app.
3. Tap the Storage button in the Device section.
4. Tap the Unmount SD Card button to unmount the SD card from the file system.
5. Tap the Format SD Card button.
6. Tap the OK button in the confirmation dialog box that opens.

FORMATTING AN SD CARD ON WINDOWS

Here's how to format an SD card on Windows:

1. Insert the SD card into a card reader built into or connected to your computer.
2. Open a File Explorer window showing This PC (on Windows 8) or a Windows Explorer window showing Computer or My Computer (on earlier versions).
3. Right-click the SD card and then click Format on the shortcut menu to open the Format dialog box.
4. Click the File System drop-down list and then click FAT32.
5. Clear the Quick Format check box to make Windows check the SD card for errors while formatting it.

6. Click the Start button.

7. Click the OK button in the confirmation dialog box that opens.

8. When the Format Complete dialog box opens, click the OK button.

9. Right-click the SD card and then click Eject to eject the card.

10. Remove the card from the card reader.

FORMATTING AN SD CARD ON OS X

Here's how to format an SD card on OS X:

1. Insert the SD card into a card reader built into or connected to your Mac.

2. Click the Launchpad icon on the Dock, type **dis**, and then click the Disk Utility icon to launch Disk Utility.

3. In the left pane, click the SD card. The right pane displays controls for managing the card.

4. Click the Erase tab to display its controls.

5. Click the Format pop-up menu and then click ExFat.

6. Click the Name field and type the name you want to give the card.

7. Click the Erase button.

8. Click the Erase button in the confirmation dialog that opens.

9. After the format operation finishes, click the Eject button on the toolbar.

10. Remove the card from the card reader.

CHOOSING A FILE MANAGER

You can manage files and folders on your device by running a file manager on the device itself. Some devices include file managers, whereas others don't. If your device doesn't have a file manager, download and install one from the Play Store.

Both ES File Explorer (see Figure 1.16) and ASTRO File Manager are powerful file managers that are easy to use. Both are free from the Play Store; ASTRO File Manager also offers a paid version, ASTRO File Manager Pro, which removes the ads.

FIGURE 1.16

If your device doesn't come with a file manager, you can install one from the Play Store, such as ES File Manager.

> **NOTE** Because of the KitKat limitations discussed in the previous section, file managers can manage only the apps on the internal storage, not on the SD card.

CHECKING FREE SPACE AND SEEING WHAT'S TAKING UP SPACE

To see how much space you have left on your device, open the Settings app and touch the Storage button. The Storage screen appears (see Figure 1.17), showing the Internal Storage section at the top and the SD Card (if your device has an SD card) further down the screen.

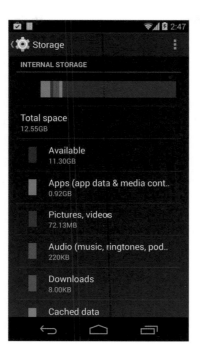

FIGURE 1.17

Use the Storage screen to identify which types of files are taking up your device's storage space.

The Storage screen is easy to read:

- The bar chart at the top of the Internal Storage section shows what proportion of your device's storage is in use and how much is free. The color bars show you the file types.

- The Total Space readout gives your device's total capacity.

> **NOTE** The Total Space readout on the Storage screen shows a capacity lower than your device's nominal capacity for two reasons. First, manufacturers give the nominal capacity in gigabytes calculated using billions of bytes (1000^3 bytes) rather than the gigabytes that computers actually use (1024^3 bytes), which are 7.4% bigger; so a device with 16GB nominal capacity has a true capacity of 14.9GB. Second, the operating system takes up several gigabytes of space.

- The Available readout shows how much space is available.
- The Apps readout shows how much space the apps are taking up. You can tap the Apps button to display the Apps screen, from which you can uninstall apps to recover space.
- The Pictures, Videos readout shows how much space your pictures and videos are occupying. You can tap this button to view your photos in the Gallery app or the Photos app. You can delete photos using these apps if necessary.
- The Audio readout shows how much space your audio files—such as songs, ringtones, and podcasts—are taking. You can tap this button to display the Open From panel, which gives you several ways to browse the files. But usually it is easier to manage your music from your computer if you sync your device with it.
- The Downloads readout shows the amount of space occupied by files you have downloaded. You can tap the Downloads button to display the Downloads screen, from which you can delete files to free up space.
- The Cached Data readout shows how much space is devoted to cached data. *Cached data* is data saved by apps to enable them to display it more quickly; for example, web browsers cache recent web pages in case you visit them again.
- This Misc. readout shows how much space miscellaneous files are occupying.

RECOVERING SPACE

After reading the previous section about the Storage screen, you can likely see several straightforward ways of recovering space on your device: You can delete apps you no longer need; remove pictures, videos, and audio items; delete any downloaded files; and clear your cached data.

DELETING APPS

If you've installed a lot of apps, deleting any that you don't use is a good way to start recovering space on your device.

Open the Settings app and tap the Apps button in the Device section to display the Apps screen. This screen can display the apps sorted either by name in alphabetical order or by size in descending order. If the apps appear in alphabetical order, tap the Menu button and then tap Sort by Size to get a list with the biggest apps at the top.

If you want to see what's taking up space, tap the Menu button and then tap Sort by Size (see Figure 1.18) to get a list of apps in descending order of size.

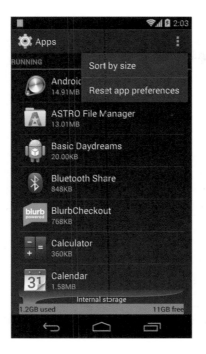

FIGURE 1.18

On the Apps screen, tap the Menu button and then tap Sort by Size to see which apps are taking up the most room.

To remove an app, tap its button on the Apps screen. The App Info screen for the app appears, and you can tap the Uninstall button to uninstall the app.

REMOVING PICTURES AND VIDEOS

Pictures can take up a large amount of space on your device, and videos can eat up all your remaining storage in just a few minutes of shooting.

You can access your photos and videos by tapping the Pictures, Videos button on the Storage screen. If the Complete Action Using dialog box opens, tap the app you want to use (such as Gallery) and then tap the Always button or the Just Once button, as appropriate. You can then use the app to select individual photos or videos and delete them as necessary.

> **✓ TIP** Managing your photos and videos using the Gallery app or the Photos app on your device works fine up to a point. But if you need to remove whole swaths of photos or reels of videos, it's easier to connect your device to your computer and manage them from there.

REMOVING AUDIO ITEMS

If you need to remove audio items from your device, tap the Audio button on the Storage screen. Android displays the Open From pane, in which you can touch the app in which you want to view the files.

> **✓ TIP** As with photos and videos, removing large numbers of audio items from your Android device using the device itself tends to be awkward. If you use your device with a computer, use the computer to remove to remove the files.

DELETING DOWNLOADED FILES

If you no longer need files you have downloaded to your device, delete them to recover space on it. Tap the Downloads button on the Storage screen to display the Downloads folder. You can then tap and hold a file to select it, select other files as needed, and then tap the Delete icon (the trash can).

CLEARING YOUR CACHED DATA AND MISCELLANEOUS FILES

If you've deleted all other content you can spare from your device, but you're still short of space, you may want to clear your cached data and delete your miscellaneous files.

You can clear your cached data by tapping the Cached Data button and then tapping the OK button in the Clear Cached Data? dialog box (see Figure 1.19).

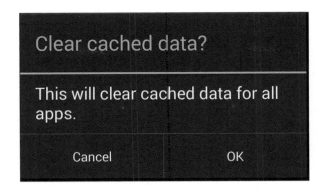

FIGURE 1.19

You can clear cached data to free up space on your Android device.

You can tap this button to display the Misc Files screen, which provides controls for selecting the files and deleting them. Normally, the miscellaneous files take up only a small amount of space.

IN THIS CHAPTER

- Choosing the best sync app for your device
- Syncing your device and loading files
- Updating, backing up, and using remote lock and wiping

2

SYNCING YOUR DEVICE

To get the most use and enjoyment out of your Android device, you'll probably need to put some of your existing files on it: songs, photos, videos, documents, and so on. Likewise, you'll probably want to copy or move files from your device to your computer or other storage. For example, if you take photos and videos on your device, you will likely want to copy or move them to a computer so that you can enjoy them on a bigger screen—and so that the videos you shoot don't take up all the space on your device.

In this chapter, you'll look at your options for copying and moving files back and forth between your device and your computer. You can either control the copying and moving manually or sync the files between the device and your computer.

> ✎ **NOTE** There's no need to sync your Android device with a computer. You can use your phone or tablet as a standalone device if you prefer, loading it with files using whatever means you find convenient and backing it up online.

Later in this chapter, you'll dig into how to keep your device updated, how to back it up to keep your data safe, and how to restore the device from backup when problems occur. Finally, you'll learn how to set up Remote Lock and Wiping for your device in case you lose it.

UNDERSTANDING YOUR OPTIONS FOR SYNCING YOUR DEVICE

If you want to copy, move, or sync files between your Android device and your computer, your first decision is which sync app to use. Your choices depend on your computer's operating system and the Android device you're using.

> ✎ **NOTE** Google has designed Android to use the Internet as extensively as possible for setting up, syncing, and managing devices. Because of this approach, Google doesn't provide a desktop companion app for Android except for Android File Transfer for Mac, which you'll meet later in this chapter. By contrast, Apple offers iTunes as a one-stop means of syncing media files with your PC or Mac as well as providing the iCloud service as an online sync, backup, and restore option.

CHOOSING THE RIGHT SYNC APP

Google doesn't provide an app for syncing Android devices with Windows. You can either access your device directly through Windows File Explorer or Windows Explorer (depending on which version of Windows you have) or use a third-party app.

Unlike Windows, OS X doesn't let you access an Android device's storage directly through the file system. Whereas Android devices show up in Windows File Explorer like other drives, they don't appear in the Finder in OS X.

To enable you to access the file systems of Android devices on OS X, Google provides the free app called Android File Transfer. If you're using OS X with your Android device, Android File Transfer is a good place to start unless your device's manufacturer provides a desktop app.

Major Android manufacturers provide sync and management software for Windows and for OS X. Here are three examples:

- **Samsung.** Samsung provides the Kies app for managing a wide range of its devices.

> [✎ **NOTE**] Kies for Windows comes in two main versions as of this writing: Kies3 for the latest Samsung devices, such as the Galaxy S 5 and Galaxy Note 4, and Kies (no number) for older devices. Before downloading a version of Kies, make sure that it supports your device.

- **Motorola.** Motorola provides the Motorola Device Manager app for managing Motorola devices.
- **HTC.** HTC provides the HTC Manager app for managing HTC devices.

If your device's manufacturer provides a desktop app for managing your device, you'll probably want to start with that app, because it will normally provide features tailored to that manufacturer's hardware and software. For example, Samsung Kies includes features for backing up and restoring Samsung devices.

Using a Third-Party Sync App for Windows or OS X

If your device's manufacturer doesn't provide a desktop app, or if you don't find that app useful, you can go for an app from an independent developer instead. Of these, the most promising is doubleTwist, which you can download from the doubleTwist website, www.doubletwist.com. doubleTwist syncs your iTunes library, so it's great if you use iTunes to manage your music.

doubleTwist consists of a free desktop app that runs on Windows and Mac and a free Android app that offers in-app purchases for extra features. The most compelling extra feature is AirSync, which enables you to sync music and videos with your iTunes library on your computer via Wi-Fi and to play music from your Android device to AirPlay devices such as Apple's AirPort Express wireless access point.

GETTING AND INSTALLING YOUR SYNC APP

After deciding which sync app you want to use, you need to get its distribution file and install it. In this section, you look at the general installation procedure on Windows, using one app as an example, and then go through how to download and install Android File Transfer on OS X.

INSTALLING A SYNC APP ON WINDOWS

After deciding which sync app to use, go to the manufacturer's website and download the latest version. In most cases, your browser gives you the choice of running the app or saving it; usually, it's best to save the app in case the installation fails and you need to launch it again. After the download completes, click the Run button to launch the installer.

TIP Even if your device's manufacturer includes a CD containing an installation file of its management app, you're better off downloading the app from the manufacturer's website because it is highly likely to be a newer version. Most of these apps check for updates and heavily encourage you to update them, so if you install a version from CD, you'll probably have to download and install the new version anyway almost immediately. Just make sure you're on the manufacturer's official website. Don't download a file from a third-party website, because you run the risk that someone may have tampered with it.

NOTE HTC devices usually have a distribution file of the HTC Manager app on an extra partition that appears when you connect the device to your computer. You can open this file to launch the installer, but in this case too, you'll usually be better off downloading the latest version of HTC Manager from the HTC website.

When you launch the installer, Windows usually displays the User Account Control dialog box (see Figure 2.1) to make sure it's you who's running the software rather than a malicious process having launched it. Look at the Program Name readout and the Verified Publisher readout to make sure the software is genuine, and then click the Yes button.

FIGURE 2.1

In the User Account Control dialog box, look at the Program Name readout and the Verified Publisher readout before clicking the Yes button.

After you've got the installer running, the installation procedure is usually straightforward, but watch out for the installer offering to create desktop shortcuts, change settings, or install extra software. For example, the InstallShield Wizard for Samsung Kies 3 includes the Create Shortcut on Desktop check box (see Figure 2.2), which you'll need to uncheck if you don't want a Kies 3 shortcut cluttering up your desktop.

FIGURE 2.2

You may need to deselect options in the installer—for example, uncheck the Create Shortcut on Desktop box here unless you want a desktop shortcut for Kies 3.

Some of the installers have an option for running the app on the final setup screen, which is handy. Otherwise, run the app as usual from the Start screen or the Start menu.

CHOOSING WHAT HAPPENS WHEN YOU CONNECT YOUR DEVICE TO WINDOWS

When you connect your device to Windows, the OS finds and loads any driver needed to communicate with the device. Windows then displays a pop-up window asking what you want to do with the device (see Figure 2.3).

FIGURE 2.3

In this pop-up window, choose which action (if any) you want Windows to take when you connect your device.

These are the choices you typically have:

- **Sync Digital Media Files to This Device.** Click this button to use Windows Media Player (or the other player identified) to sync music and video to the device.

- **Open Device to View Files.** Click this button to open a Windows File Explorer window showing the contents of the device. You can then copy files back and forth manually.

- **Import Photos and Videos.** Click this button to import photos and videos from your device to your PC using the Photos app (or the other app identified).

- **Take No Action.** Click this button to have Windows take no action with the device. You can then decide what to do.

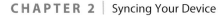

INSTALLING ANDROID FILE TRANSFER ON OS X

Here's how to download and install Android File Transfer on OS X:

1. Open your web browser and go to www.android.com/filetransfer/.

> 📝 **NOTE** Android File Transfer isn't available on the Mac App Store.

2. Click the Download Now button to download the disk image file containing the app.

3. If Safari (or whichever browser you're using) doesn't automatically mount the disk image on your Mac's file system and open a Finder window displaying the disk image's contents, click the Downloads icon on the Dock and then click the Android File Transfer disk image. The Android File Transfer disk image's icon appears on your desktop unless you have unchecked the External Disks box on the General tab in Finder Preferences.

> 📝 **NOTE** The name of the Android File Transfer disk image file varies, but it should be easy to identify. If it's the last file you downloaded, it'll be the file at the top or in the upper-left corner of the Downloads stack.

4. Drag the Android File Transfer icon to the Applications icon in the folder. OS X copies the app file.

5. Drag the Android File Transfer disk image's icon to the Trash to eject the disk image.

> ✅ **TIP** Ejecting the Android File Transfer disk image unmounts the disk image from your Mac's file system. The disk image file remains in your Downloads folder, and you can delete it later if you don't want to keep it.

You can now launch Android File Transfer by clicking the Launchpad icon on the Dock and then clicking the Android File Transfer icon.

There's one complication you may run into at this point: OS X's Gatekeeper feature may block you from running Android File Transfer because it is not from the Mac

App Store. If this happens, follow these steps to permit the installation of apps from identified developers as well as from the Mac App Store:

1. Click the System Preferences icon on the Dock. If the icon doesn't appear there, click the Apple menu and then click System Preferences. The System Preferences window opens.

2. Click the Security & Privacy icon to display the Security & Privacy pane.

3. Click the lock icon in the lower-left corner, type your password (and an Administrator account name if necessary), and then click the Unlock button to unlock Security & Privacy preferences.

4. Click the Mac App Store and Identified Developers radio button (see Figure 2.4).

5. Run Android File Transfer by clicking the Launchpad icon on the Dock and then clicking the Android File Transfer icon.

6. Go back to the Security & Privacy pane and click the Mac App Store radio button again.

7. Click the Close button (the red button at the left end of the title bar) to close System Preferences.

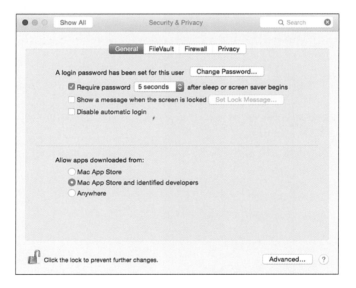

FIGURE 2.4

You may need to unlock Security & Privacy preferences and select the Mac App Store and Identified Developers radio button to launch Android File Transfer.

USING YOUR SYNC APP

After installing your sync app, you can use it to sync files between your device and your computer. Most sync apps also enable you to back up your device to your computer and restore it from the computer when things go wrong.

USING SYNC APPS ON WINDOWS

After you've installed your sync app on Windows, the app should launch automatically when you connect your device to your PC. If not, you can launch the app manually as usual—for example, by clicking its icon on the Start screen or the Start menu.

> **NOTE** For security, most sync apps require you to unlock your device before the app can control it.

Once the app is open, it connects your device automatically, and the controls appear for working with the device. Figure 2.5 shows Samsung Kies 3 on Windows with a Galaxy Note phone connected. Kies 3 has a fairly typical user interface, but other apps have different looks and capabilities, as you'd expect.

> **NOTE** If you connect multiple devices of types that the app can manage, click the device you want to work with.

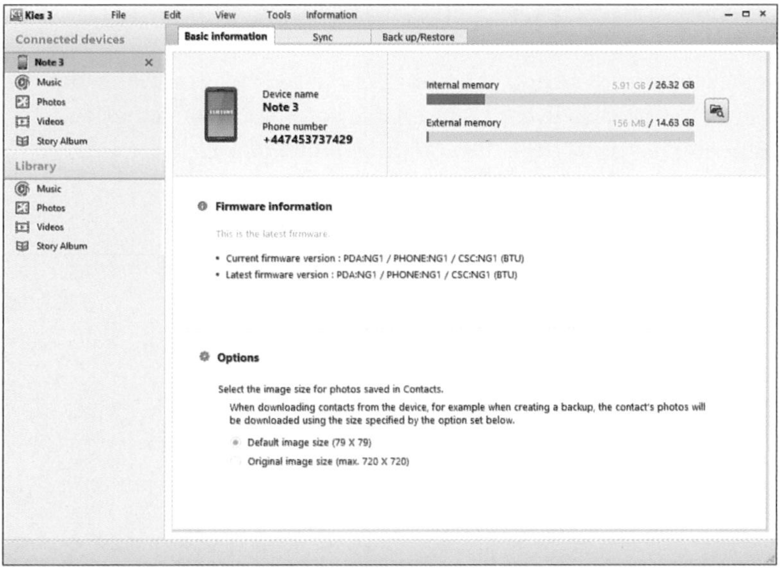

FIGURE 2.5
Samsung Kies 3 has a fairly typical user interface for management apps.

Most sync apps include a setting for automatically checking for updates. If you will find this feature helpful, locate this setting in the Options or Preferences and turn it on.

LOADING MUSIC, VIDEOS, OR PHOTOS

To load items onto your device, you switch to the list that contains the items, choose the items to load, and then specify where to put them. For example, here's how to load music from the Music section of the Library in Kies 3:

1. With your device connected, click the Music item in the Library section to display the songs you have added to Kies.
2. Check the box for each song you want (see Figure 2.6).
3. Click the Send to Device button on the toolbar, and then click the Internal Memory item or the External Memory item on the pop-up menu, as needed. Internal Memory is the device's built-in memory; External Memory is the SD card.

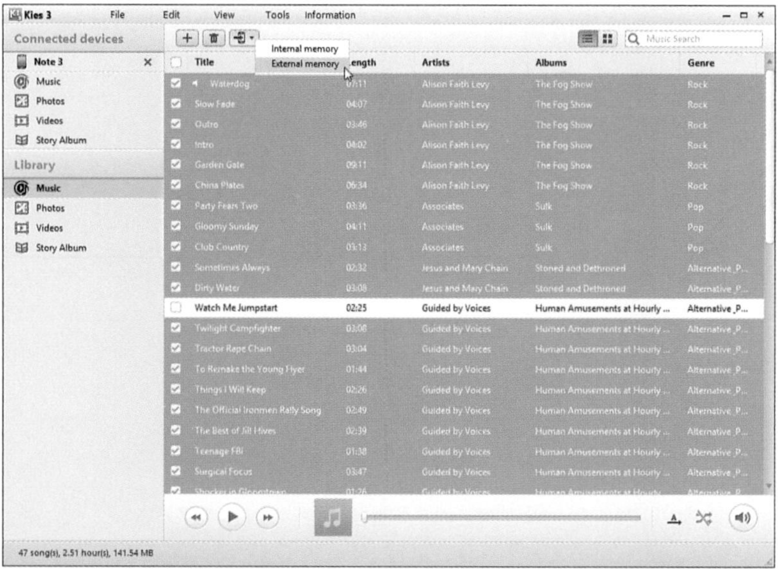

FIGURE 2.6

Select the songs you want to sync, click the Send to Device button, and then click Internal Memory or External Memory, as needed.

SYNCING INFORMATION BETWEEN YOUR COMPUTER AND YOUR DEVICE

To sync information between your computer and your device, use the sync controls to specify which information to sync, and then set the sync running. For example, here's how to sync data using Kies 3:

1. Click the Sync tab to display its contents (see Figure 2.7).

2. Check the boxes for the information you want to sync. You may want to check the Select All Items box at the top of the tab to check all the other boxes.

3. In each radio button group, select the appropriate radio button for your needs.

4. Click the Sync button.

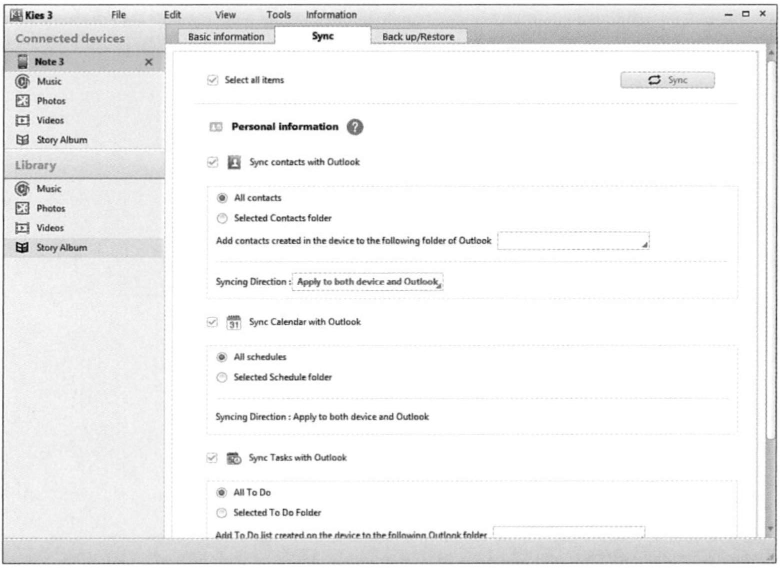

FIGURE 2.7

Use the sync controls in your sync manager to choose which information to sync between your computer and your device.

USING ANDROID FILE TRANSFER ON OS X

Unlock your Android device before you connect it to your Mac. Otherwise, Android File Transfer cannot access the device, and you must restart Android File Transfer after unlocking the device.

Android File Transfer on OS X provides a straightforward window (see Figure 2.8) for browsing your device's file system and managing files on it. These are the actions you'll need most often:

- **Copy files from your Mac to your device.** Drag the files from a Finder window to the appropriate folder in the Android File Transfer window.
- **Copy files from your device to your Mac.** Drag the files from their folder in the Android File Transfer window to a Finder window showing the destination folder.
- **Create a folder on your device.** Click the New Folder button in the upper-right corner, type the name for the folder, and then press Return.
- **Delete a file or folder from your device.** Ctrl+click the file or folder in the Android File Transfer window, click Delete on the contextual menu, and then click the Delete button in the confirmation dialog box that opens.

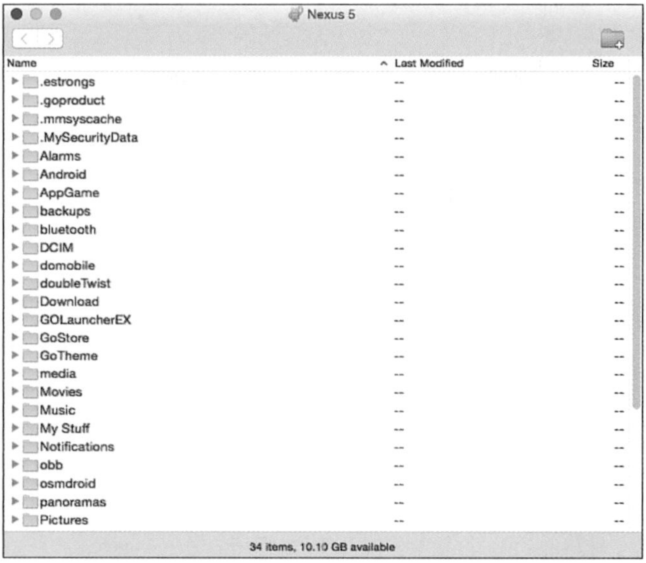

Name	Last Modified	Size
▶ .estrongs	--	--
▶ .goproduct	--	--
▶ .mmsyscache	--	--
▶ .MySecurityData	--	--
▶ Alarms	--	--
▶ Android	--	--
▶ AppGame	--	--
▶ backups	--	--
▶ bluetooth	--	--
▶ DCIM	--	--
▶ domobile	--	--
▶ doubleTwist	--	--
▶ Download	--	--
▶ GOLauncherEX	--	--
▶ GoStore	--	--
▶ GoTheme	--	--
▶ media	--	--
▶ Movies	--	--
▶ Music	--	--
▶ My Stuff	--	--
▶ Notifications	--	--
▶ obb	--	--
▶ osmdroid	--	--
▶ panoramas	--	--
▶ Pictures	--	--

34 items, 10.10 GB available

FIGURE 2.8

Android File Transfer enables you to browse the files on an Android device and copy files to it.

> **! CAUTION** Android File Transfer has a 4GB size limit on files. This is seldom a problem unless you're heaving huge video files around, but it's worth knowing about.

LOADING FILES ON YOUR DEVICE

As you saw in the previous section, you can load files onto your device by using a sync app. This is great for those types of files that the app supports, such as songs, photos, and videos. But to load other file types, you may need to use other means, such as these:

■ **Load files using the SD card.** If your device has an SD card slot, you can use SD cards to load files onto your device or transfer files off it. Simply connect the SD card to a card reader attached to your computer (or another device that contains the files), copy the files to the SD card, and then reinsert it in your device.

> **⌇ NOTE** How convenient it is to load files via SD card depends on how easy your device—and any case you keep it in—make inserting and removing the SD card. If getting to the SD card involves surgery, you won't want to go switching SD cards unless you have to. But if you change SD cards in seconds (as you can do with the Samsung phone models whose backs pull straight off), this is a great way of moving files to and from your device.

> **⌇ TIP** Using multiple SD cards is a great way to switch among having different sets of files on your device. For example, by carrying an SD card full of songs and another full of videos, you can switch between the two without having to skimp on either your music library or your movie library.

- **Load files using wireless connections.** You can use Wi-Fi, Bluetooth, or Near Field Communication (NFC) to transfer files between your Android device and your computer or other device.

- **Load files using Google Drive.** Google Drive enables you to store your files securely on the Internet. You can upload files to your Google Drive account from your computer and download them to your device by using the Google Drive app—or vice versa.

- **Load files using Dropbox.** Like Google Drive, Dropbox enables you to store your files online and then download them to your device. If your device doesn't have the Dropbox app, you can install it for free from the Play Store.

- **Transfer files using email.** When you need to transfer files individually and other means of sharing aren't convenient, email can be a great solution: Simply attach the file or files to an email message and send it to an account that you can access from your device. The main constraint is that most email servers limit messages to between 5MB and 10MB total. But if you keep any message to less than 5MB, including the overhead needed to encode the file attachments for transmission via email, the messages should transfer fine.

UPDATING, BACKING UP, AND RESTORING YOUR DEVICE

To keep your Android device running well, you should keep its software up to date with the latest versions that the manufacturer provides. To protect yourself against disaster, you should back up your device regularly so that you can restore from backup if necessary.

> ## NOTE   Many manufacturers of Android devices customize each new release of Android for their devices. This development work takes time, so new versions of Android become available for different devices at different times. As you'd expect, the newest, most popular, and most expensive devices tend to get new versions of Android sooner than older devices do.

KEEPING YOUR DEVICE UPDATED

Android devices automatically check for software updates and download them when they are available.

Android then displays a notification such as "System Update Downloaded" on the Notifications panel to let you know that the update is ready for installation.

Tap this notification to launch the installer for the update. The installer's screen (see Figure 2.9) summarizes the changes that the update brings.

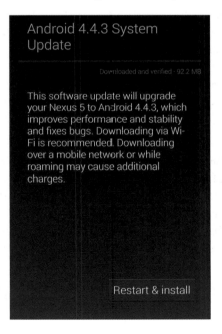

FIGURE 2.9

Tap the Restart & Install button on the System Update screen to restart your device and install the update.

Controlling Automatic Checking for Software Updates

Stock Android doesn't let you turn off automatic checking for software updates, but Samsung's TouchWiz does, while HTC Sense enables you to turn off automatic downloading of updates. (The only way to turn off automatic checking in stock Android is to root your device, which this book doesn't cover.)

In TouchWiz on a Samsung device, open the Settings app, tap the About Device button, and then tap the Software Update button on the About Device screen. On the Software Update screen, uncheck the Auto Update box. From the Software Update screen, you can tap the Update Now button to check for updates manually whether Auto Update is turned on or off.

In HTC Sense, open the Settings app, tap the About button to display the About screen, and then tap Software Updates. On the Software Updates screen, uncheck the Auto-Download System Updates box if you want to turn off automatic downloading. You can also uncheck the Auto-Update Apps box if you want to turn off automatic downloading and installation of apps. Note the "and installation" bit there: If you check the Auto-Update Apps box, HTC Sense not only downloads but also installs updates to system apps.

KEEPING YOUR APPS UPDATED

To keep your apps updated, you use the Play Store app like this:

1. Tap the Play Store icon on the Home screen or on the Apps screen. The Play Store app opens.

2. Tap the Play Store icon or text in the upper-left corner to display the menu pane, and then tap My Apps to display the My Apps screen (see Figure 2.10).

3. Tap the Update All button to download and install all available updates.

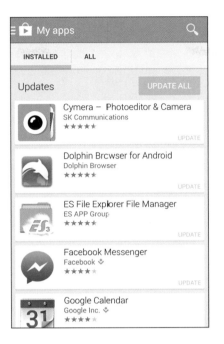

FIGURE 2.10

From the My Apps screen in the Play Store app, you can tap the Update All button to apply all available updates at once, or tap an app's button to update that app individually.

📝 **TIP** Updating all your apps at once is usually the most convenient approach. But sometimes, such as when your device has a slow Internet connection or is using the cellular network (or both), you may prefer to update apps individually. In this case, tap the app's button in the Updates list to display the app's screen in the App Store, and then tap the Update button to download and apply the update.

Recovering from Update or Restore Problems

If a system update or a restore operation goes wrong, you may find your device doesn't start properly. For example, it may start to boot but then restart partway through the boot process.

If you run into this problem, you can perform a hard reset to recover from the problem. See the section "Performing a Hard Reset" in Chapter 3, "Customizing Your Device," for details on this procedure.

BACKING UP YOUR DEVICE

Most likely your Android device contains a treasure trove of valuable information, so it's vital that you keep it backed up in order to be able to recover your data if something goes wrong.

ASSESSING YOUR CHOICES OF BACKUP METHODS

Depending on your device and its manufacturer, and maybe on your computer setup, you have a choice of ways to back up your Android device. These are the options that you may have:

- **Back up to your Google account.** This is the easiest way to back up your essential data, including your app data, your Wi-Fi passwords, and your settings.
- **Back up to another online destination.** You can back up some or all the data on your device to a cloud backup service such as G Cloud (www. gcloudbackup.com). These services typically charge a subscription fee that varies depending on how much space you need.

!CAUTION Backing up to an online destination can be a great way to keep your data safe—with two main caveats. First, choose a service that will be around for the long haul; this may mean paying higher subscription fees than bargain-basement services charge. Second, backing up a device's worth of data (say 32GB or 64GB) over a normal broadband connection will take a long time. This is a concern only on the first backup, because after you have made a complete backup, the following backups are incremental, with each containing only the files that have changed since the previous backup.

- **Back up to your computer.** If you use an app such as Samsung Kies or HTC Manager to manage your device from your computer, you can back up specific items to your computer. This method works well but presupposes you have a computer and that you'll keep it safe enough, and in good enough condition, to be able to restore your device from it.
- **Back up to a USB On-the-Go drive.** If you want a compact solution that you can take with you anywhere, invest in a USB On-the-Go drive and use an app such as ES File Explorer to copy files to it for backup.

BACKING UP YOUR DEVICE TO YOUR GOOGLE ACCOUNT

If you have a stock Android device, the easiest solution is to back up your essential data to your Google account. This backup is set-and-forget and takes only moments to turn on.

> **TIP** Even if you use another form of backup, such as a sync app, you may want to back up essential data to your Google account for belt-and-braces security.

Here's how to set your device to back up to your Google account:

1. Open the Settings app.
2. Tap the Backup & Reset button to display the Backup & Reset screen (see Figure 2.11).

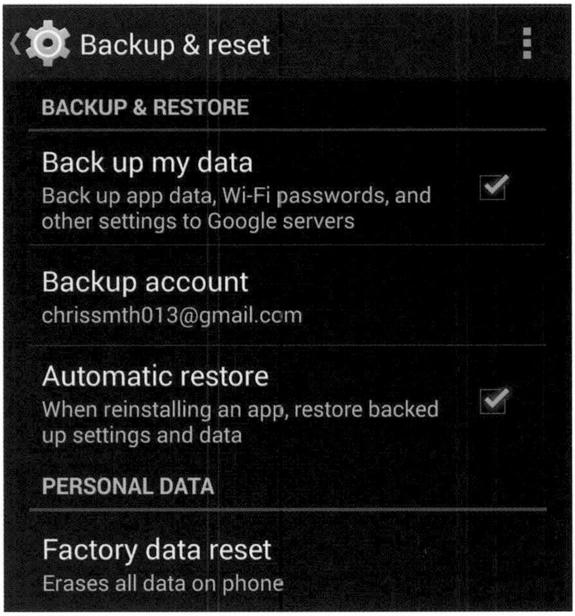

FIGURE 2.11

On the Backup & Reset screen in the Settings app, specify your backup account and check the Back Up My Data box.

3. Check the Back Up My Data box.
4. If the Backup Account button shows the wrong Google account, tap the button, and then tap the right account in the Set Backup Account dialog box.

> **✎ NOTE** In the Set Backup Account dialog box, you can tap the Add Account button to use another account for backup that is not currently set up on your device.

5. Check the Automatic Restore box if you want Android to automatically restore backed-up settings and data when you restore an app to your device. This setting is usually helpful.

> **✎ NOTE** Backing up your device to your Google account doesn't back up your apps, but it does back up details about them. When you restore your data, you can download all your apps again from the Play Store by using the My Apps list in the Play Store app.

BACKING UP YOUR DEVICE USING A SYNC APP

Most sync apps include features for backing up your device to your computer and restoring it afterward. Here is what you do with Samsung Kies 3:

1. Connect your device to your computer.

2. Launch Kies if it doesn't launch automatically.

3. When your device appears in the Connected Devices list, click it to display the control screens.

4. Click the Back Up/Restore tab to display its controls.

5. Click the Data Backup button on the vertical tab bar to display the backup controls (see Figure 2.12).

6. Check the box for each item you want to include. You can check the Select All Items box at the top of the list to quickly check all the other boxes.

7. Click the Backup button.

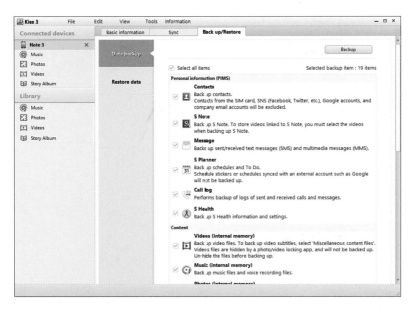

FIGURE 2.12

On the Back Up/Restore tab, choose which data to back up, and then click the Backup button.

RESTORING YOUR DEVICE

After things go wrong, you can restore your device from your last backup to get it back to its previous state (or as near as possible).

RESTORING YOUR DEVICE FROM A GOOGLE BACKUP

To restore your device from a Google backup, reset the device as explained in the section "Performing a Hard Reset" in Chapter 3.

> **TIP** You can also use your backup from one device to restore your data to another device. So if you drop your phone onto an unforgiving surface or into too much water, you can set up your new phone (in its bulletproof and waterproof case) by restoring your data onto it from the latest backup.

When your device restarts, tap the Yes button on the Got Google? screen, and then type your email address and password on the Sign In screen. When the Google Services screen appears, check the box called Back Up Your Data to a

Google Account. Restore Previous Backups to This Device. Tap the Continue button (the arrow), and Android downloads the latest backup and installs it on your device.

> **NOTE** After restoring the backup, Android downloads the apps from the Play Store that were previously installed on your device. This may take awhile, so be prepared to be patient.

RESTORING DEVICES WITH A SYNC MANAGER

If you've backed up your device using a sync manager, you can restore it by using the Restore functionality. You'll normally find the controls for restore near those for backup.

For example, here's how to restore a Samsung device that you've backed up with Kies:

1. Connect your device to your computer.

2. Launch Kies if it doesn't launch automatically.

3. When your device appears in the Connected Devices list, click it to display the control screens.

4. Click the Back Up/Restore tab to display its controls.

5. Click the Restore Data button on the vertical tab bar to display the restore controls (see Figure 2.13).

6. Click the Select the Backup File to Restore pop-up menu and select the backup file you want to use.

7. Check the box for each item you want to include. You can check the Select All Items box at the top of the list to quickly check all the other boxes.

8. Click the Restore button.

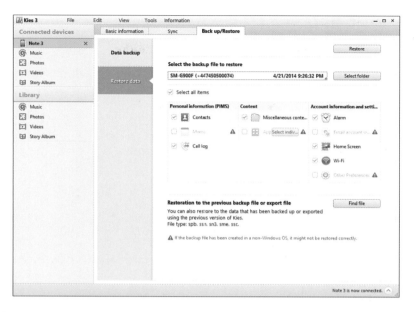

FIGURE 2.13
On the Restore Data tab, select the backup to restore, choose which items to include, and then click the Restore button.

SETTING UP AND USING REMOTE LOCK AND WIPING

Being portable, valuable, and highly covetable, your Android device makes a tempting target for those with light fingers and loose morals. And even if you manage to keep your device safe from others, you may manage to lose it yourself.

Before this happens, you should configure Android Device Manager to enable you to find or lock your device if you mislay it, or wipe it if someone else takes it.

> **!CAUTION** Remotely erasing your device may not be able to wipe the content of the SD card. In any case, someone who has grabbed your device can remove the SD card. So it's best to put any valuable or sensitive data on the device's main storage rather than on the SD card.

SETTING UP REMOTE FIND AND WIPING

Here's how to set up Remote Find and Wiping:

1. From the Home screen, tap the Apps button to display the Apps screen.

2. Tap the Google Settings icon to open the Google Settings app.

3. Tap the Android Device Manager button to display the Android Device Manager screen (see Figure 2.14).

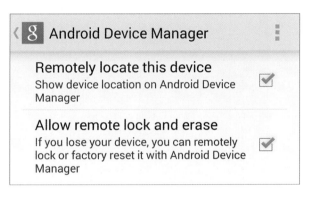

FIGURE 2.14

On the Android Device Manager screen in the Google Settings app, check the Remotely Locate This Device box and the Allow Remote Lock and Erase box.

4. Check the Remotely Locate This Device box.

5. Check the Allow Remote Lock and Erase box. The Activate Device Administrator? screen appears (see Figure 2.15), making sure you understand that allowing Android Device Manager to lock the screen, change the password, and erase all data without warning will perform exactly those actions.

6. Tap the Activate button. Android activates Remote Lock and Erase and displays the Android Device Manager screen again.

Now you're all set for your device to go missing. I hope it doesn't, but the next section tells you what to do if it does.

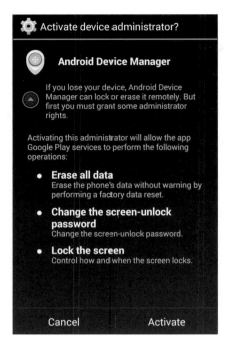

FIGURE 2.15

Tap the Activate button on the Activate Device Administrator? screen to enable remote locking and wiping of your device.

REMOTELY LOCKING AND WIPING YOUR DEVICE

Here's how to remotely lock and wipe your device if it goes missing:

1. Open a web browser on your computer or on another device that you have. These instructions are for a computer, but you can follow them easily enough on a device.

2. Go to the Android Device Manager website, www.google.com/android/devicemanager.

3. Log in using the Google account you use on your device.

4. On the Welcome to Android Device Manager screen, click the Accept button. Android Device Manager displays a map showing the location of your device (see Figure 2.16).

> **NOTE** If you have multiple devices registered to this account, click the pop-up menu showing the first device's name, and then click the device you want to locate.

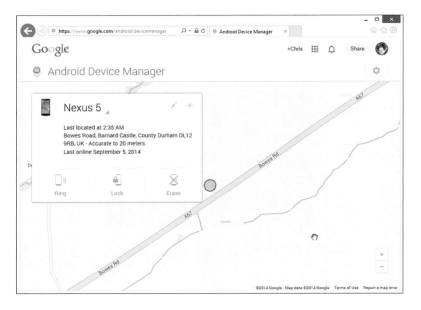

FIGURE 2.16

Android Device Manager locates your device and displays the location on a map.

5. If you want to make your device ring, click the Ring button, and then click the Ring button again in the Ring Device? dialog box that opens.

> **TIP** Ringing a device is good both for finding the device yourself if the map shows that you've misplaced it at home or for causing someone else to pick it up if you've left it somewhere else. If the device is somewhere else, it's best to lock the device before ringing it.

> **NOTE** Using the Ring feature makes the device ring at full volume for five minutes or until someone presses the Power button to stop the ringing.

6. To lock the device, click the Lock button, and then enter a new password, a recovery message, and a phone number in the New Lock Screen dialog box that opens (see Figure 2.17). The new password is compulsory. The recovery message and phone number are optional but are important if you want whoever finds your phone to contact you about returning it.

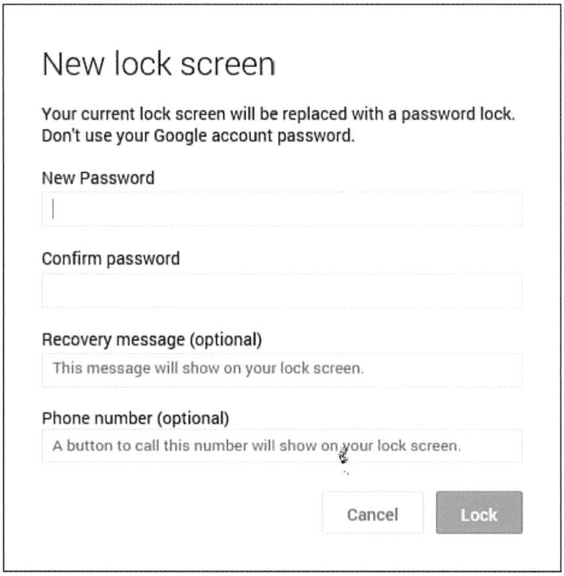

New lock screen

Your current lock screen will be replaced with a password lock. Don't use your Google account password.

New Password

Confirm password

Recovery message (optional)

This message will show on your lock screen.

Phone number (optional)

A button to call this number will show on your lock screen.

Cancel   Lock

FIGURE 2.17

When locking your device remotely, you must specify a new password in the New Lock Screen dialog box. You can also enter a recovery message and a contact phone number.

7. If you've lost hope of recovering your device, click the Erase button to display the Erase All Data? dialog box (see Figure 2.18), and then click the Erase button.

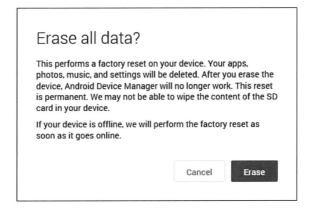

FIGURE 2.18

Click the Erase button if there's no hope of getting your device back and you want to erase its data.

NOTE   The Erase feature performs a factory reset on the device to erase the data. If the device is online when you give the command, the reset happens almost immediately. If the device is offline, the factory reset happens as soon as it goes back online.

IN THIS CHAPTER

- Setting up your home screens
- Using a different launcher
- Securing your device with locking, location settings, and encryption

3

CUSTOMIZING YOUR DEVICE

In this chapter, you'll learn to customize your device. You'll start with the Home screens, because setting these up the way you prefer can make a huge difference in how you use your phone or tablet.

Android gives you access to a wide range of settings, enabling you to configure your device to work the way you prefer. You can access most of these settings through the Settings app.

SETTING UP YOUR HOME SCREENS

Your Home screens are your base camp for getting things done in Android, so you will want to make them as useful as possible. This means adding the icons and widgets you use the most and arranging them into your preferred order. You may also want to add Home screens (or remove existing ones) and change the wallpaper.

> ☑ **TIP**   This section explains how to customize the Home screens using stock Android. If your device has a skin, you may need to use different techniques. See Chapter 14, "Using Samsung TouchWiz," for instructions on customizing the Home screens on the Samsung TouchWiz skin and Chapter 15, "Using HTC Sense," for instructions on the HTC Sense skin.

How you customize Home screens depends on the version of Android and the launcher it is running. For example, Google Now Launcher, the default launcher on the Nexus 5 on KitKat, uses different methods than the launcher (simply called Launcher) that is the default on the Nexus 7 on KitKat.

ADDING AND REMOVING HOME SCREENS

To give yourself space for your icons and widgets, you can create extra Home screens. If you no longer need a Home screen, you can remove it.

> ✐ **NOTE**   Some versions of Android with certain launchers provide a set number of Home screens and don't let you add or delete Home screens. In this case, you can install a third-party launcher to enable yourself to add and delete Home screens.

Google Now Launcher makes it easy to add Home screens. Follow these steps:

1. Swipe left one or more times to display the last Home screen (the one on the right).
2. Tap and hold an icon to make it mobile, and then drag it to the right edge of the screen. Android automatically creates another Home screen.
3. Release the icon.

> ☑ **TIP**   You can create further Home screens in the same way. Before you do, though, you must put at least one more icon on the new Home screen you've just created so that there will be at least one icon left on that Home screen when you drag an icon to create another Home screen.

To remove a Home screen with Google Now Launcher, you remove all the icons from it. Android then gets rid of the surplus Home screen automatically.

ADDING APPS TO YOUR HOME SCREENS

You can run any app from the Apps screen, but you'll probably want to put the apps you use most on your first Home screen for quick access.

Here's how to add an app's icon to a Home screen:

1. On the Home screen, tap the Apps icon to display the Apps screen.

2. Tap and hold the icon for the app you want to add to the Home screen. Thumbnails of the Home screens appear.

3. Drag the icon to the destination Home screen, position it where you want it, and then drop it.

> **NOTE** If you need to move the app's icon again on the Home screen, tap the icon and hold down until it becomes mobile, drag it to the new location, and then drop it.

ADDING WIDGETS TO YOUR HOME SCREENS

You can also add widgets, tiny apps that display specific information, to your Home screens. Android comes with an extensive selection of widgets built in. If you need widgets beyond these, you can find many more on the Play Store and other online sites.

ADDING WIDGETS TO YOUR HOME SCREENS WITH LAUNCHER

Here's how to add a widget to a Home screen with Launcher:

1. On the Home screen, tap the Apps icon to display the Apps screen.

2. Tap the Widgets tab in the upper-left corner of the screen to display the Widgets screen.

3. Swipe left or right until you find the widget you need (see Figure 3.1).

> **✎ NOTE** Each widget has its size to the right of its name, such as 1 × 1 for the Email Folder widget, 3 × 3 for the Gmail widget, or 3 × 1 for the Google Keep widget. You can use these sizes to judge where the widgets will fit on your Home screens.

FIGURE 3.1

Locate the widget you want to add, and then tap and hold it.

4. Tap and hold the widget to pick it up. The Home screen then appears as a thumbnail.

5. Drag the widget to where you want it to appear, and then drop it.

> **✎ NOTE** If the current Home screen doesn't have room for the widget, drag it to the left or right to display another Home screen.

6. If the widget displays any configuration options, choose suitable settings. For example, when you add the Gmail widget to a Home screen, you get to choose which folder to display in the widget.

ADDING WIDGETS TO YOUR HOME SCREEN WITH GOOGLE NOW LAUNCHER

Here's how to add a widget to a Home screen with Google Now Launcher:

1. Tap and hold open space on the Home screen to display the customization controls.

2. Tap the Widgets button to display the Widgets screen.

3. Swipe left until you find the widget you want to add.

4. Tap and hold the widget to pick it up. The Home screen then appears as a thumbnail.

5. Drag the widget to where you want it to appear, and then drop it.

6. If the widget displays any configuration options, choose suitable settings. For example, when you add the Gmail widget to a Home screen, you get to choose which folder to display in the widget.

ADDING WEB ADDRESSES TO YOUR HOME SCREENS

If you need to be able to quickly access particular websites, you can add their addresses to your Home screens. Follow these steps:

1. Open the Chrome browser and go to the web page or website.

2. Tap the Menu button to open the menu.

3. Tap the Add to Homescreen button to display the Add to Homescreen dialog box (see Figure 3.2).

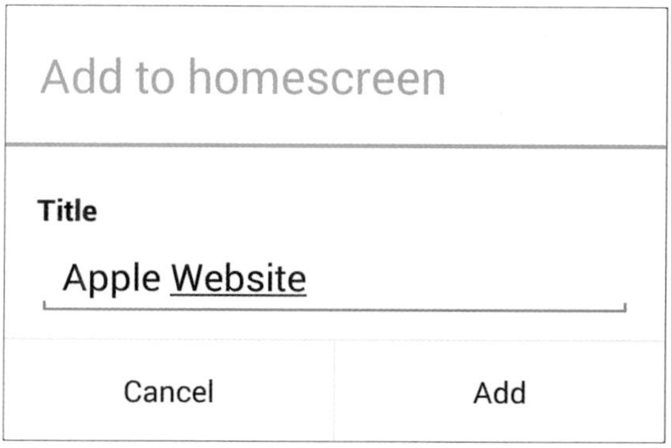

Add to homescreen

Title

Apple Website

Cancel   Add

FIGURE 3.2

In the Add to Homescreen dialog box, type the name you want to see for the icon on the Home screen, and then tap the Add button.

4. Either accept the default name for the icon or type a descriptive name that will enable you to identify it.

5. Tap the Add button. Android adds the icon to your Home screen. You can then tap and hold it and move it to another location if you want.

ORGANIZING HOME SCREEN ITEMS INTO FOLDERS

Your device's Home screens provide enough space for an almost infinite number of icons, but you'll probably need to keep them organized in a human-friendly way. To organize your icons, you can create folders either on the Home screens themselves or in the Favorites tray.

Here's how to create a folder:

1. Navigate to the Home screen that contains the icons. You can drag icons from screen to screen, but it's easier to start with them on the same screen.

2. Tap and hold an icon until it becomes mobile.

3. Drag the icon on top of another icon you want to put in the same folder. Android puts the two icons in a folder and assigns it the default name *Unnamed Folder*.

NOTE   When you drag one icon on top of another icon, a highlighted circle appears behind the second icon to show that the icon is in the right place. If you miss the target icon, it moves out of the way on the assumption that you are rearranging the icons rather than creating a folder.

4. Tap the folder to open it.

5. Tap the folder's default name (*Unnamed Folder*) as shown in Figure 3.3 and then type the name you want to give it.

FIGURE 3.3

To rename a folder you've created, open it, tap the default name, and then type the name you want to use.

6. Tap the Done button or tap outside the folder's name to apply the name.

> **TIP** To take an icon out of a folder, tap the folder to open it. Tap and hold the icon until it becomes mobile, and then drag it out of the folder to where you want it on the Home screen. To delete a folder, remove all its icons; when only one icon is left, the folder disappears, and that icon moves to the Home screen.

ADDING DROPBOX FOLDERS TO YOUR HOME SCREENS

If you've installed the Dropbox app on your device, you may want to give yourself an easy way to access key folders. To do so, add one or more instances of the Dropbox widget to your Home screen using the technique explained earlier in this chapter. When you add the widget, Android prompts you to choose the folder that the widget will open. Android gives the widget the name of the folder.

REPOSITIONING ITEMS ON YOUR HOME SCREENS

To reposition an item on a Home screen, tap and hold it until it becomes mobile, and then drag it to where you want to place it.

REMOVING ITEMS FROM YOUR HOME SCREENS

To remove an item from a Home screen, tap and hold the item's icon until the Remove button appears at the top of the screen. Drag the icon to the Remove button so that both the icon and the Remove button turn red, and then drop the item.

REARRANGING YOUR HOME SCREENS

On some devices and versions of Android, you can rearrange your Home screens by dragging them into the order you prefer. Other devices and Android versions don't provide this functionality, but you can add it by installing a launcher as discussed later in this chapter.

To rearrange your Home screens with Google Now Launcher, open the Home screens for customization, and then tap and hold the thumbnail for the Home screen you want to move. When it becomes mobile, drag it to its destination and drop it there.

TIP If you want to reset your Home screens to their defaults, open the Settings app, tap the Apps button, and then swipe left twice to display the All screen. Tap the Google Search button to display the App Info screen, and then tap the Clear Data button. In the Delete App Data? dialog box that opens, tap the OK button. Tap the Home button to return to the Home screen.

SETTING THE WALLPAPER

To change the overall look of your Home screens, you can change the wallpaper. Android comes with a set of colorful wallpapers, and you can download other wallpapers to add variety. You can also use a photo of your own.

NOTE Each Home screen uses the same wallpaper on stock Android. Some skins enable you to use different wallpapers on different Home screens.

SETTING THE WALLPAPER WITH LAUNCHER

Here's how to set the wallpaper with Launcher:

1. Tap and hold open space on a Home screen. The Choose Wallpaper From dialog box opens (see Figure 3.4).

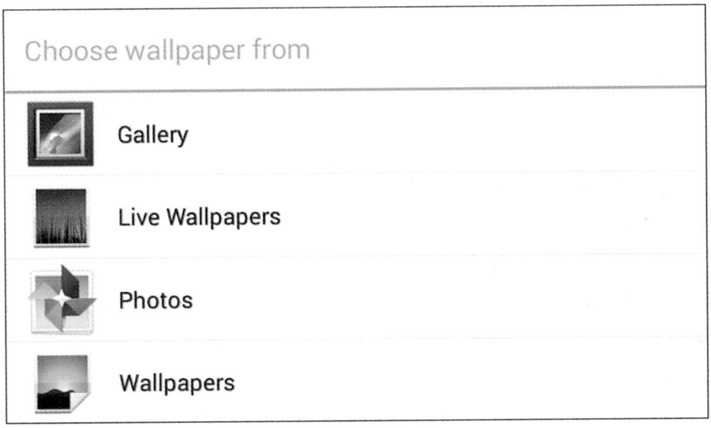

FIGURE 3.4

In the Choose Wallpaper From dialog box, tap the source of wallpapers you want to use.

2. Tap the source of wallpapers to use: Gallery, Live Wallpapers, Photos, or Wallpapers. Gallery and Photos enable you to use your own images.

> **TIP** The live wallpapers include motion, which can make the Home screens look more entertaining when you're not working in an app. However, because they take up more processing power, you should avoid them if you want maximum performance or maximum runtime on the battery.

3. Scroll the list of wallpapers and tap the one you want to preview.
4. After you've chosen your wallpaper, tap the Set Wallpaper button.

SETTING THE WALLPAPER WITH GOOGLE NOW LAUNCHER

Google Now Launcher streamlines the process of setting the wallpaper. Follow these steps:

1. Tap and hold open space to open the Home screen for customization.
2. Tap the Wallpapers button to display the Wallpapers screen.

3. Tap the Pick Image button if you want to use one of your own images for the wallpaper; when you find the image, tap it to preview it. Otherwise, scroll the list of wallpapers and tap the one you want to preview.

4. When you've selected the wallpaper you want, tap the Set Wallpaper button to apply it.

TIP You can find vast numbers of wallpapers on both the Play Store and on the Web. For best results, make sure you get wallpapers of the right resolution for your device—for example, 1080×1920 for a device such as the Nexus 5. If you're not sure of your device's resolution, look it up online.

CAUTION Before downloading a wallpapers app from the Play Store, read user reviews to determine its quality. If you decide to install it, carefully review the permissions it requires. If it requires permissions it shouldn't need, such as accessing your contacts, cancel the installation.

USING A DIFFERENT LAUNCHER

A *launcher* is an app that enables you to launch other apps. The launcher controls how your device's Home screen and other main screens appear, including any live widgets you place on them.

Android includes a default launcher that runs by default and which you summon each time you press the Home button. But you can install different launchers to change how Android looks and acts on your device.

NOTE Different versions of Android include different launchers, making the Home screens, the Apps screen, widgets, and so on look different and work differently. For example, the Nexus 5 has a launcher called Google Now Launcher rather than the launcher (called Launcher) that the Nexus 7 has.

CHOOSING A LAUNCHER

If you want to change your launcher, you have plenty of choices because developers have built many different launchers. You can find various launchers by opening the Play Store app, tapping the Apps button, and then searching for *launcher*.

Here are three of the top launchers at this writing:

■ **Google Now Launcher.** Google Now Launcher is a launcher developed by Google that enables you to upgrade the launcher functionality on devices running new versions of Android. Google Now Launcher runs best on stock Android, but you also can try running it on skinned versions of Android. Google Now Launcher is free.

■ **Nova Launcher.** Nova Launcher is a slick launcher that makes substantial changes to the Android user interface. The basic version of Nova Launcher is free and provides a slew of customization features, but the Prime version (which costs $4) has even more, including the use of gestures on the Home screens. With Nova Launcher, you can even put small horizontal widgets in the app drawer if you find that helpful. Figure 3.5 shows the Nova Launcher's Add to Home Screen dialog box.

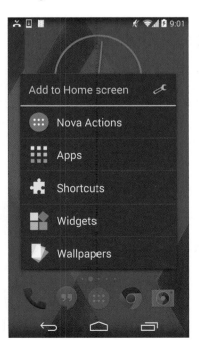

FIGURE 3.5

The Nova Launcher includes a long list of actions for configuring your Home screens.

- **GO Launcher EX.** Go Launcher EX offers a wide range of customizations including themes that dramatically change the look of Android. Some themes are free; others you must pay for. Go Launcher EX includes shortcuts to many recommended apps, some of which are free. Figure 3.6 shows the Home screen in Go Launcher EX.

FIGURE 3.6

Go Launcher EX comes with shortcuts to many recommended apps.

! CAUTION   A launcher typically needs many permissions to run successfully. For safety, it is best to avoid launchers from sources other than the Play Store unless you are certain of their provenance, integrity, and coding.

INSTALLING A LAUNCHER

To install a launcher, you download it from the Play Store like any other app. When the download completes, open the launcher by tapping the Open button on the app's screen in the Play Store app or by tapping the launcher's icon on the Apps screen.

Some launchers walk you through a setup routine on first run. For example, Nova Launcher prompts you to import items from your existing launcher, saving you the trouble of rebuilding your existing Home screens for the new launcher. If the launcher cannot import widgets, you will need to add them manually.

After you finish any setup routine, the launcher displays your Home screen in all its transformed glory (or otherwise), and you can start exploring the launcher.

SETTING YOUR DEFAULT LAUNCHER

After installing a launcher, you can set it as your default app if you want to use it all the time. The default launcher is the one that Android activates when you tap the Home button.

NOTE Some launchers may set themselves to be the default automatically. You'll know this has happened if pressing the Home button displays the new launcher instead of a dialog box for choosing which launcher to use.

Here's how to set your default launcher:

1. Tap the Home button to display the Select a Home App dialog box (see Figure 3.7).

NOTE You may see the Complete Action Using dialog box instead of the Select a Home App dialog box. Tap the right launcher, and then tap the Always button.

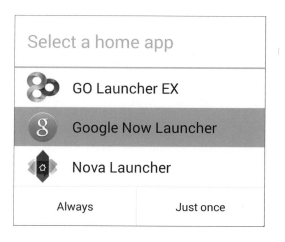

FIGURE 3.7

In the Select a Home App dialog box, tap the button for the launcher you want to make the default, and then tap the Always button.

2. Tap the launcher you want to make the default launcher.

3. Tap the Always button.

> **TIP** Tap the Just Once button in the Select a Home App dialog box if you want to switch quickly from launcher to launcher, comparing them.

SWITCHING AMONG LAUNCHERS

After you've set your default launcher, that launcher comes up each time you tap the Home button, but you can switch to another launcher temporarily by tapping its icon on the Apps screen.

The launcher opens, and you can use it as usual. But when you tap the Home button, the Home screen shows your default launcher once more.

CHANGING YOUR DEFAULT LAUNCHER

Here's how to change your default launcher:

1. Open the Settings app.

2. Tap the Home button in the Device section to display the Home screen (see Figure 3.8).

FIGURE 3.8

Use the Home screen in the Settings app to choose your default launcher. You can also delete
any launcher you no longer want.

3. Tap the launcher you want to make the new default, selecting its radio
   button.
4. Tap the Home button.

> **TIP** To delete a launcher, tap the Delete button (the trash can) on the
> right of its button on the Home screen in the Settings app.

MAKING NO LAUNCHER THE DEFAULT

When you're experimenting with launchers, you may want to try making no
launcher the default so that you can easily switch among the launchers. By
removing your default launcher, you can make Android display the Select a Home
App dialog box each time you tap the Home button.

> **TIP** If your device is running an Android version below 4.3, you need
> to use this technique to switch from your current default launcher to another
> launcher.

Here's how to remove your default launcher:

1. Open the Settings app.

2. Tap the Apps button in the Device section to display the Apps screen.

3. Swipe left twice to display the All screen.

4. Scroll down and find the launcher that's currently running.

5. Tap the launcher to display its App Info screen.

6. Tap the Clear Defaults button. A confirmation dialog box normally opens.

7. Tap the OK button.

8. Press the Home button. Because you've cleared the defaults, the Select a Home App dialog box opens.

9. Tap the button for the launcher you want to use. For example, tap the Launcher button to return to the standard launcher for older versions of Android.

10. Tap the Always button.

> **NOTE** The rest of this book assumes that you are using a standard launcher, such as Google Now Launcher or plain Launcher.

> **NOTE** On Samsung TouchWiz, go to the App Info screen for your current launcher and tap the Set Default Home button, and then tap the OK button in the Clear Defaults dialog box that opens. You can then clear your default launcher by opening the Settings app, tapping Default Applications, going to the entry for the launcher, and tapping the Clear button to its right.

CONFIGURING INPUT OPTIONS

Android supports various different input options to enable you to get text into your device using your preferred language and a keyboard that suits your needs. You can also input text using your voice with the Google Voice Typing feature.

To set up your input options, you work on the Language & Input screen in the Settings app (see Figure 3.9). To display this screen, open the Settings app and tap the Language & Input button in the Personal section.

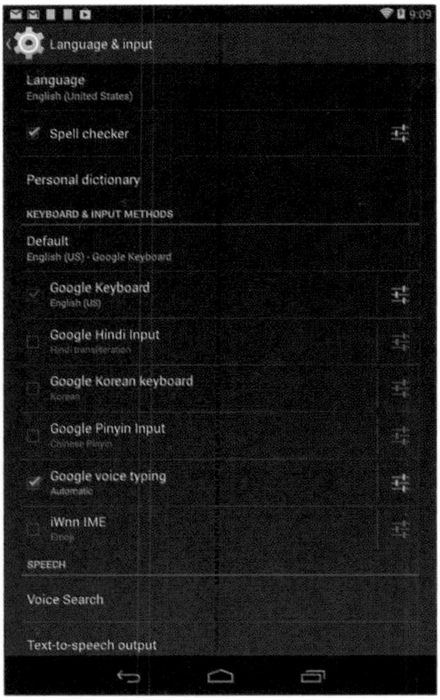

FIGURE 3.9

Use the Language & Input screen to set your input language and configure input options.

First, make sure the Language button at the top shows the language you want to use, such as English (United States). If not, tap this button to display the Language screen and then tap the correct language.

Next, in the Keyboard & Input Methods section, set up the keyboards and other input methods you want to use on your device. Tap to check the check box for each of the keyboards you want to have available:

- The Google Keyboard is normally the default keyboard, so its check box will be checked until you uncheck it.

- Google Voice Typing enables you to enter text by tapping the microphone button to the left of the spacebar and then speaking into your device's microphone (or an attached microphone). Make sure this check box is checked if you want to be able to use this feature.

- Check the box for any other keyboard that you have installed and that you want to have available.

> ✏️ **NOTE** Chapter 1, "Getting Up to Speed," discusses some alternative keyboards you may want to try on your device.

After checking the check box for a keyboard, you can tap the Settings icon on the right side of the keyboard's button to display the settings screen for the keyboard.

For example, Figure 3.10 shows the Google Keyboard Settings screen, where you can set your input language (such as U.S. English), turn auto-capitalization and keypress sounds on or off, set up text correction, enable gesture typing, and choose other options. Chapter 1 explains your choices on the Google Keyboard Settings screen.

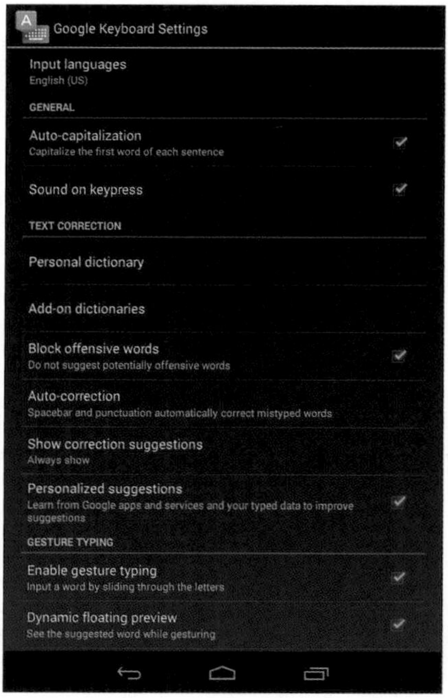

FIGURE 3.10

Choose options for a keyboard on its settings screen.

After choosing which keyboards to make available, set your default keyboard by tapping the Default button at the top of the Keyboard & Input Methods list and then tapping the appropriate keyboard in the Choose Input Method dialog box.

Making the Most of the Input Options Dialog Box

Android's Input Options dialog box gives you quick access to keyboard settings and enables you to switch among input methods. You can display the Input Options dialog box quickly by tapping and holding the key to the left of the spacebar on the keyboard until the pop-up panel appears, and then either tapping the Settings button on the pop-up panel or simply lifting your finger. (The Settings button is the default button on the pop-up panel, so lifting your finger has the same effect as tapping the button.)

After you've opened the Input Options dialog box, you can tap the Google Keyboard Settings button to go straight to the Google Keyboard Settings screen.

If the Select Input Method button appears in the Input Options dialog box, you can tap it to display the Select Input Method dialog box. This dialog box enables you to switch to a different keyboard or input method, such as Google Voice Typing.

CONFIGURING THE LOCK SCREEN

The lock screen is the screen that appears when you start your device or when you wake your device after sleep. You can choose different lock strengths or even turn off locking altogether. You can add widgets to the lock screen, and you can display your owner information on it.

CHOOSING THE BEST LOCKING METHOD

To keep your data safe, lock your device. Android offers five ways to unlock the screen, but only two are worth using if your device contains any personal or sensitive information, as almost all devices do.

These are the five unlock methods:

- **Slide.** You tap the lock icon on the lock screen and slide your finger across the screen to unlock your device. Slide provides no security at all, but it does prevent your device from becoming unlocked by accident in your pocket or bag.

- **Face Unlock.** You register your face as the means of unlocking your device, adding either a pattern or a PIN for those times when Face Unlock doesn't work. You can then unlock your device by aiming the screen-side camera at your face.

> **!CAUTION** Face Unlock is more a fun feature than a serious locking method. Someone who looks like you to the camera and its algorithms may be able to unlock your device. If you use Face Unlock, be sure to use the Improve Face Matching feature to scan your face from different angles and to turn on Liveness Check, which requires you to blink to prove you're not a picture, a mannequin, or a corpse.

- **Pattern.** You draw a pattern on a nine-dot grid on the screen to unlock your device. A pattern is useful only for light security. You can draw a complex pattern to make this harder for a determined attacker to break, but the result may be more difficult for you to use than a PIN or password.

- **PIN.** You type in a numeric personal identification number (PIN) and tap the Enter button to unlock your device. PIN is a good choice for medium security. The PIN must be at least four digits long (giving 1,000 possible combinations), but it is sensible to use eight digits (10,000,000 combinations) or more.

> **NOTE** If you enter the wrong PIN or password five times in succession, Android makes you wait 30 seconds before trying again. This delay is to make it awkward for someone to guess your PIN or password—for example, by entering the names of your family, friends, or pets. It also helps delay an attacker breaking your PIN by "brute force," simply entering every possible PIN value in turn until stumbling on the correct PIN.

- **Password.** You type in a password using any characters—letters, numbers, or symbols—but containing at least one letter. Password is the only choice for serious security on your device. Android requires the password to be at least four characters long, but you should consider eight characters a minimum to secure your device effectively. The longer the password, the harder it is for an attacker to break by brute force.

SETTING UP LOCKING ON YOUR DEVICE

Here's how to set up locking on your device:

1. Open the Settings app.
2. Tap the Security button in the Personal section to display the Security screen.

> **NOTE** The screen locking settings may be in a different location on your device, such as a screen called Lock Screen or Security & Screen Lock.

3. Tap the Screen Lock button in the Screen Security section to display the Choose Screen Lock screen. If you have already applied a lock, you will need to use the unlocking method to proceed. For example, type your PIN and tap the Continue button.

4. Tap the unlock method you want to use, and then follow through any screens that appear. For example, if you tap the Password button, you must type a password and then confirm it.

> **NOTE** If you choose Face Unlock, select the check box called Liveness Check on the Security screen. To pass Liveness Check, you must blink your eyes while unlocking the screen. It's also a good idea to tap the Improve Face Matching button and rescan your face several times.

5. Back on the Security screen, tap the Automatically Lock button to display the Automatically Lock dialog box, and then tap the button for the delay between the device going to sleep and the screen locking. The best choice is Immediately, but you may want to have a short delay, such as 5 Seconds or 15 Seconds, if you find yourself needing to wake your device soon after you put it to sleep.

6. Also on the Security screen, tap the Power Button Instantly Locks button, selecting its check box so that you can lock your device quickly by pressing the Power button.

Locking is now set up. To try it, press the Power button once to lock your device, press the Power button again to wake it, and then use the unlock method to unlock the device.

PUTTING WIDGETS ON THE LOCK SCREEN

In its default state, the lock screen enables you to take two actions:

■ **Open Google Now.** Swipe up from the bottom of the screen. If you have set an unlock method other than Swipe, you will need to unlock your device.

■ **Open the Camera app on a phone.** The Camera icon appears in the lower-right corner of the lock screen. You can swipe left to access the Camera app quickly without unlocking your device. Tap the Home button to return from the Camera app to the lock screen so that you can unlock your device.

Android enables you to put widgets on the lock screen so that you can see essential information without unlocking your device. For example, you can add the Gmail widget to the lock screen so that you can see the new messages in your inbox, or add the Calendar widget to help you keep track of your upcoming appointments.

!**CAUTION** Any information you display on the lock screen is accessible to anybody who can pick up your device and press the Power button. So you'll need to balance your desire for instant access to information against your need to keep that information private.

Here's how to add widgets to the lock screen:

1. Select the Enable Widgets check box on the Security screen in the Settings app.
2. Lock your device by pressing the Power button once.
3. Wake your device by pressing the Power button again. The lock screen appears.
4. Swipe to the right so that a + icon appears.
5. Tap the + icon to display the list of widgets.
6. Tap the widget you want to add to the lock screen. If the widget has options, such as choosing which mailbox to display, make your choices.

PUTTING YOUR OWNER INFORMATION ON THE LOCK SCREEN

You can also add your owner information—or any text you care to display—on the lock screen. To do so, follow these steps:

1. Open the Settings app.
2. Tap the Security button to display the Security screen.
3. Tap the Owner Info button to display the Owner Info screen.
4. Select the Show Owner Info on Lock Screen check box.
5. Type the text you want to display.

CHOOSING LOCATION SETTINGS TO PROTECT YOUR PRIVACY

Carrying a cell phone is like carrying a beacon that constantly tracks your location, and even a Wi-Fi–only tablet keeps track of your whereabouts so that it can provide map information and other location-dependent data. Besides, electronics devices are exposed to snooping, so it's essential to choose privacy settings that suit your needs.

Here's how to choose location settings:

1. Open the Settings app.
2. In the Personal section, tap the Location button to display the Location screen (see Figure 3.11).

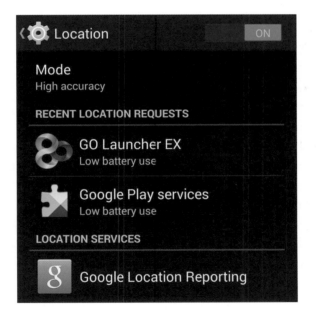

FIGURE 3.11

On the Location screen, you can turn location tracking off altogether, choose which mode to use, and configure Location Services.

3. Set the Location switch to the On position to use location tracking.
4. Tap the Mode button to display the Location Mode screen (see Figure 3.12).

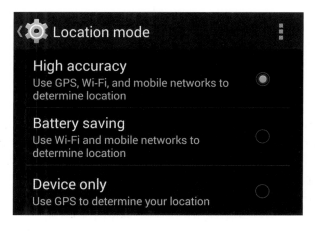

FIGURE 3.12

On the Location Mode screen, choose how you want Android to track your device's location.

5. Tap the button for the location mode you want to use: High Accuracy, Battery Saving, or Device Only.

6. Tap the Back button to return to the Location screen.

7. Review the apps and services in the Recent Location Requests list to make sure that all are apps you want to use location services.

8. In the Location Services list, tap Google Location Reporting to display the Google Location Settings screen (see Figure 3.13).

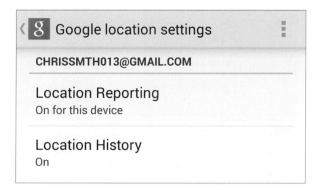

FIGURE 3.13

From the Google Location Settings screen, you can turn off location reporting, location history, or both.

> **TIP** If you have set up multiple Google accounts on your device, make sure the Google Location Settings screen is showing the account you want to configure.

9. Review the Location Reporting readout to see whether location reporting is on or off. If you need to change the setting, tap the Location Reporting button to display the Location Reporting screen, and then set the Location Reporting switch to the On position or to the Off position, as appropriate. Tap the Back button to return to the Google Location Settings screen.

10. Review the Location History readout to see whether location history is on or off. If you need to change the setting, tap the Location History button to display the Location History screen, and then set the Location History switch to the On position or to the Off position, as needed.

11. If you want to delete all the location history entries for this Google account, tap the Delete Location History button at the bottom of the Location History screen. In the Permanently Delete? dialog box that appears (see Figure 3.14), tap to check the I Understand and Want to Delete check box, and then tap the Delete button.

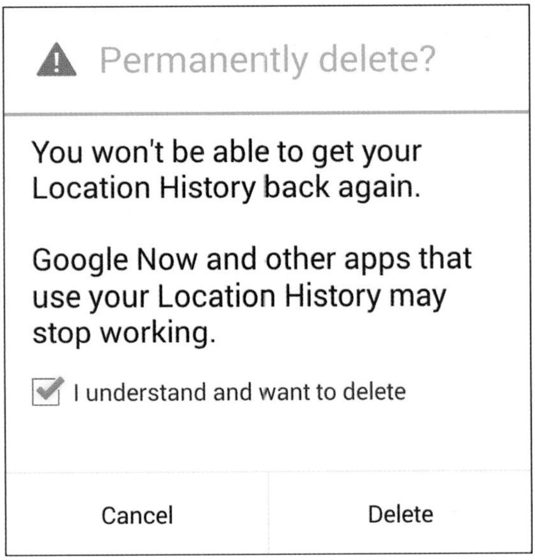

⚠ Permanently delete?

You won't be able to get your Location History back again.

Google Now and other apps that use your Location History may stop working.

☑ I understand and want to delete

Cancel   Delete

FIGURE 3.14

Tap the Delete button in the Permanently Delete? dialog box to confirm you want to delete your location history entries.

!CAUTION Deleting your location history entries may stop apps that use your location history from working. Google Now is the app most likely to be affected, but other apps also can be affected.

Opening the KitKat Easter Egg

Android version 4.4, KitKat, includes an *Easter egg*, a hidden feature for your entertainment. To open the Easter egg, follow these steps:

1. Open the Settings app.

2. Tap the About Phone button or About Tablet button at the bottom of the screen.

3. Triple-tap the Android version readout.

4. Tap and hold the symbol that appears.

5. Tap and hold the graphic that appears.

6. Watch the animation, or drag objects about.

7. Swipe up from the bottom of the screen to display the control buttons, and then tap the Home button to display the Home screen.

ENCRYPTING YOUR DEVICE

To protect your device against unauthorized access if you lose it, you can encrypt its contents. Encryption deliberately scrambles the content using an encryption key, leaving the content unreadable without the key to decrypt it.

NOTE Encryption can take an hour or more, depending on the amount of data your device contains and its processor speed; and if encryption fails to complete, your data may get corrupted. So Android ensures enough power is available by making the encryption controls unavailable unless the device's battery is fully charged *and* the device is connected to a power supply.

For the encryption to work, you must set a lock screen PIN or password to prevent others from unlocking your device. If you've already set a PIN or password, you're good to go; if not, go back to the section "Setting Up Locking on Your Device," earlier in this chapter, and set one or the other.

Understanding the Disadvantages of Encryption

Encryption has three disadvantages you must understand before you encrypt your device.

First, your device must decrypt data to present it to you, so it may run more slowly. Depending on the device's hardware, the difference may not be noticeable, but it may be enough to be annoying.

Second, you must enter your PIN or passcode to decrypt the storage each time you restart the device. This is easy enough, but if you forget your PIN or passcode, you won't be able to access your data.

Third, the only way to remove encryption is by restoring your device to factory settings. Doing this removes all your data and apps from the device, so you have to set it up again from scratch.

For a tablet that has multiple user accounts set up, there's a fourth disadvantage: Even if you encrypt the tablet from your owner account, the other accounts remain unencrypted and aren't required to set a PIN or passcode. This raises the possibility that an attacker can use the other accounts to attack your data.

! CAUTION Android's encryption is strong enough to prevent civilian attackers from unencrypting it. However, you should assume that law-enforcement agencies and government security agencies have tools strong enough to break the encryption without breaking a serious sweat.

ENCRYPTING THE DATA ON YOUR DEVICE

Here's how to encrypt your device:

1. Fully charge the battery, and leave the device connected to power.
2. Open the Settings app.

3. Tap the Security button in the Personal section to display the Security screen.

> **📝 NOTE** Depending on your device, the encryption settings may be in a different location. If necessary, search for "encrypt."

4. Tap the Encrypt Phone button or the Encrypt Tablet button (whichever one appears). The Encrypt Phone screen or the Encrypt Tablet screen appears. (Some devices have the Encrypt Device button and Encrypt Device screen instead.)

5. Read the information and then tap the Encrypt Phone button or the Encrypt Tablet button. The Confirm Your PIN screen or Confirm Your Password screen appears.

> **📝 NOTE** If your device doesn't have a PIN or password set, the No Lock Screen PIN or Password dialog box opens, telling you that you need to set a PIN or password. Turn back to the section "Setting Up Locking on Your Device," earlier in this chapter, and return when you have set a PIN or password.

6. Type your PIN or password.

7. Tap the Continue button. The Encrypt? screen appears, warning you that encryption is irreversible and that your device will restart several times during the encryption process.

8. Tap the Encrypt Phone button or the Encrypt Tablet button. Android starts the encryption process. You'll see the Encrypting screen with a progress readout as it works.

9. When the Type Password to Decrypt Storage prompt appears, type your PIN or password and tap the Done button on the keyboard. Android then decrypts your data, the lock screen appears, and you can type your PIN or password (again) to unlock the device as usual.

> **📝 NOTE** If you have a PIN rather than a password, don't worry that the Type Password to Decrypt Storage prompt asks for a password. Type in your PIN, and all will be well.

TIP If encryption fails on a tablet that has multiple user accounts set up, try updating to the latest version of Android before encrypting the tablet.

DECRYPTING THE DATA ON YOUR DEVICE

The only way to decrypt the data on your device is to perform a factory data reset. This move wipes all your apps and data off your device and restores it to its original settings.

!CAUTION Back up your device's data to your computer or to an online account—or, better, to both—before performing a factory data reset.

TIP You may want to perform a factory data reset before selling your phone or tablet or giving it to someone else.

Here's how to perform a factory data reset:

1. Open the Settings app.
2. Tap the Backup & Reset button in the Personal section to display the Backup & Reset screen.
3. Tap the Factory Data Reset button. The Factory Data Reset screen appears (see Figure 3.15).

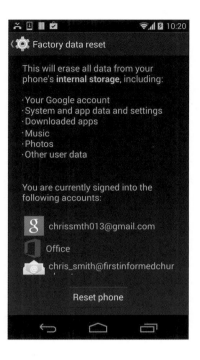

FIGURE 3.15

On the Factory Data Reset screen, read the warnings, and then tap the Reset Phone button or Reset Tablet button.

4. The Confirm Your PIN screen or Confirm Your Password screen appears.

5. Type your PIN or password.

6. Tap the Continue button. The Reset? screen appears, displaying a final, excited warning (see Figure 3.16).

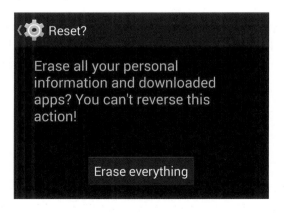

FIGURE 3.16

On the Reset? screen, take a deep breath, and then tap the Erase Everything button.

7. Tap the Erase Everything button. The Power Off dialog box opens for a few seconds. The device then shuts down and restarts. The Erasing screen appears while Android erases the data.

Android then resets the operating system to factory defaults and displays the Welcome screen. You can then set up your device again as you did when you first got it.

> **TIP**   The quickest and easiest way to get your device up and running again is to restore data from your Google account to it. Tap the Yes button on the Got Google? screen, and then type your email address and password on the Sign In screen. When the Google Services screen appears, check the check box called Back Up Your Data to a Google Account. Restore Previous Backups to This Device.

PERFORMING A HARD RESET

As well as the factory data reset explained a moment ago, there's another type of reset called a *hard reset*. A hard reset is a move you typically perform when your device won't start correctly; for example, it crashes while loading Android.

> **!CAUTION**   Exactly how you perform a hard reset depends on the device you're using and the version of Android it's running. The following list gives you the general steps needed, but you may need to search online to find the different key presses or commands your device and version of Android need.

Here's how to perform a hard reset:

1. Power down your phone or tablet. Press and hold the Power button until the Power dialog box opens, tap the Power Off button, and then tap the OK button in the Power Off dialog box that opens to confirm the move.

> **NOTE**   If the Power dialog box doesn't appear because your device is frozen, keep holding down the Power button until the device turns off.

2. Hold down the Volume Up button, the Volume Down button, and the Power button for several seconds. Your device turns on and displays a picture of an

Android lying on its back with its cover open for maintenance. Release the buttons.

> **☑ TIP** Different devices use different combinations of hardware buttons to perform a hard reset. If the combination given here doesn't work for your device, search online for the device's name and *recovery buttons*.

3. Press the Volume Up button or the Volume Down button one or more times until the Recovery Mode button appears at the top of the screen.

4. Press the Power button to give the Recovery Mode command. Your device restarts and displays another screen showing an Android lying on its back, cover open for maintenance, a red triangle with an exclamation point, and the message No Command.

5. Press and hold the Volume Up button and the Power button at the same time until your device restarts again.

6. Press the Volume Up button or the Volume Down button to select the Wipe Data/Factory Reset command on the menu.

7. Press the Power button to give the command. A confirmation screen appears because this is a drastic move.

8. Press the Volume Up button or the Volume Down button to select the Yes – Erase All User Data command.

9. Press the Power button to give the command. Android erases the data, restarts, and displays the Welcome screen. You can then set up the device from scratch.

4

CONNECTING TO NETWORKS AND DEVICES

To get the most out of your Android device, you'll want to connect it to wireless networks as often as possible, and to cellular networks if it is a phone or has cellular capability. You'll likely also want to connect it to Bluetooth devices, such as keyboards or headphones, to make full use of its features. You may also want to connect your device to a virtual private network, or VPN, to establish a secure connection to a server across the Internet.

USING AIRPLANE MODE

Android's Airplane mode feature turns off all of your device's wireless communications. Airplane mode is primarily designed for those times when you're in an airplane and FAA regulation or crew intransigence forbids you from using wireless communications. But you can also use Airplane mode at any time to save power.

To turn on Airplane mode, open the Quick Settings panel and tap the Airplane Mode icon, changing the icon from an outline to solid white. A white airplane icon appears at the right end of the status bar, just to the left of the battery icon, to remind you that Airplane mode is on.

To turn off Airplane mode, open the Quick Settings panel and tap the Airplane Mode icon again.

> **TIP** You can also turn Airplane mode on or off by opening the Settings app, tapping the More button in the Wireless & Networks section, and then checking or unchecking the Airplane Mode check box on the Wireless & Networks screen. Usually, though, it's easier to use the icon on the Quick Settings panel. On some devices, you may find an Airplane Mode switch directly on the Settings screen, which is handy.

While Airplane mode is on, you can turn on Wi-Fi and establish connections to wireless networks if necessary. You can also turn on Bluetooth so that you can use Bluetooth devices.

> **TIP** Turning on Airplane mode generally enables your device to charge faster.

TAKING CONTROL OF CELLULAR CONNECTIONS

If your Android device is a phone or a cellular-capable tablet, you'll want to manage its cellular connections. This means using data roaming deliberately rather than by accident to avoid extra charges, making sure you keep within your data plan (likewise), and switching between 3G and 4G networks as needed to maintain connectivity.

DISPLAYING THE MOBILE NETWORKS SCREEN

Most of the settings you'll need for controlling your cellular connection are on the Mobile Network Settings screen (see Figure 4.1). To reach this screen, open the Settings app, tap the More button in the Wireless & Networks area, and then tap the Mobile Networks button.

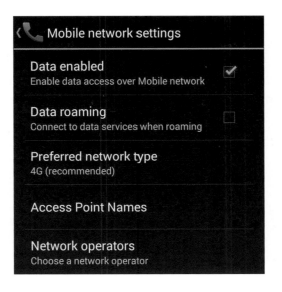

FIGURE 4.1

From the Mobile Network Settings screen, you can control data roaming and select your preferred network type.

ENABLING AND DISABLING DATA AND ROAMING

The Mobile Network Settings screen has two check boxes: the Data Enabled check box and the Data Roaming check box. It's essential you understand the difference between the two.

The Data Enabled check box controls whether your device can transfer data across the cellular connection—for example, getting your email. This uses the data allowance on your cellular plan. Normally, you'll want to keep the Data Enabled box checked so that you can receive data. You'll turn it off only if you run through the data on your data plan and need to avoid racking up extra charges.

> **NOTE** Your device may show a different name for the data roaming control, such as the Global Data Roaming Access check box.

The Data Roaming check box controls whether your device can transfer data *when it's connected to other carriers' cellular networks*. Normally, when you're on your home turf, you'll want to use your regular carrier. (That's why you chose it, I hope.) But when you go outside your carrier's area, especially if you go outside the country, you may need to connect to another carrier to get your device working.

! CAUTION Connecting to another carrier's network can be expensive for calls, so check the cost first. Double-check the costs for data roaming because they can be exorbitant. Some carriers have the grace to warn you (usually by sending a text message) when you cross country borders and start roaming; some even point out what roaming will cost you. But don't rely on such warnings.

TIP When using data roaming, transfer as little data as possible. Downloading movies or TV shows is obviously unwise, but you should also watch out for other data hogs such as streaming audio and email attachments. Instead of streaming audio, put your music on your device for when you travel. For email, reduce the sync frequency or set it to never sync, checking manually for messages when necessary—and preferably when you have a Wi-Fi connection rather than a cellular connection.

When you check the Data Roaming box, the Attention dialog box (see Figure 4.2) opens to warn you that you may incur significant charges. Tap the OK button if you're sure you want to use roaming.

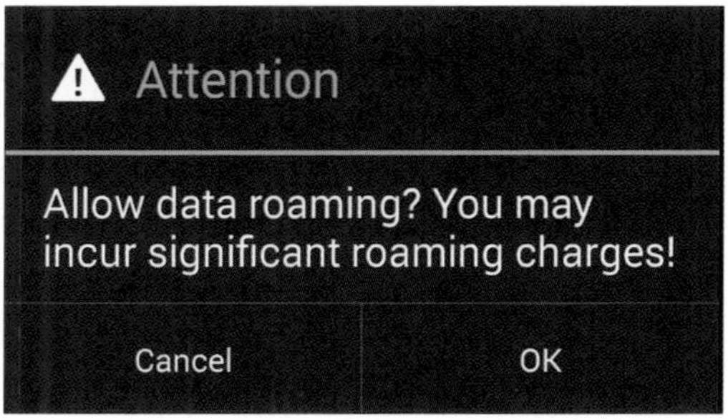

FIGURE 4.2

The Attention dialog box warns you that data roaming may hit you in the pocketbook.

CHOOSING BETWEEN 3G AND 4G NETWORKS

If you have both 3G and 4G networks available, you should tell your device which you want to use. Tap the Preferred Network Type button on the Mobile Network Settings screen to display the Preferred Network Type dialog box (see Figure 4.3), and then tap the appropriate radio button. These vary depending on your device and carrier, but you'll see options such as 4G, 3G, or 2G; or Global, LTE/CDMA, or GSM/UMTS.

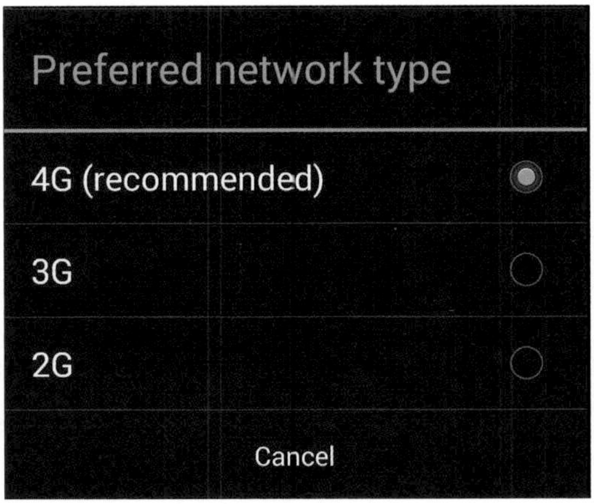

Preferred network type

4G (recommended)   ⦿

3G   ○

2G   ○

Cancel

FIGURE 4.3

In the Preferred Network Type dialog box, tap the radio button for the network type you want to use.

CONFIGURING A NEW ACCESS POINT

Cellular devices connect to a carrier's network through access points. The Access Point Name (APN) setting on your device controls which access point your device uses.

Normally, your device's SIM card causes the device to connect to the right APN, so you don't need to change the setting. But in special circumstances you may need to specify the APN for your device. To do so, tap the Access Point Names button on the Mobile Network Settings screen, and then work on the APNs screen. Here you can tap an existing APN to edit its settings or tap the Add (+) button to set up a new APN from scratch.

> **TIP** If you mess up your APN settings, tap the Menu button on the APNs screen, and then tap Reset to Default on the menu.

CONNECTING TO A DIFFERENT CARRIER

To connect to a different carrier, tap the Network Operators button on the Mobile Network Settings. The Available Networks screen appears, and Android automatically searches for carriers. You can then tap the carrier to which you want to connect.

> ✎ **NOTE** Some carriers prevent you from connecting to other carriers' networks.

To return to your normal carrier, tap the Choose Automatically button on the Available Networks screen.

KEEPING WITHIN YOUR DATA PLAN

Android includes a Data Usage tool to help you keep within your data plan and not overrun your mobile data limit. On most devices, you can set a limit for your data usage and set a warning level to let yourself know you're approaching the cutoff point.

Open the Settings app and tap the Data Usage button in the Wireless & Network section to display the Data Usage screen (see Figure 4.4).

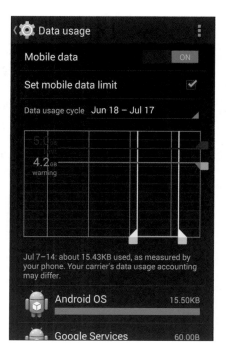

FIGURE 4.4

Visit the Data Usage screen to keep informed of your data usage.

Here you can set the Mobile Data switch to On or Off to control mobile data as a whole. Normally, you'll want to leave it On unless you've run out of data plan.

SETTING A WARNING LEVEL AND A LIMIT

To set a limit for data usage, tap the Set Mobile Data Limit check box, tap the OK button in the Limiting Data Usage dialog box that opens, and then drag the red bar up or down the diagram to set the limit. Drag the orange bar up or down to set the warning level.

Tap the Data Usage Cycle pop-up menu and choose the dates to use for the billing cycle. You can either tap one of the suggested date ranges on the pop-up menu or tap Change Cycle and set the appropriate date in the Usage Cycle Reset Date dialog box.

To see how much data you've used in a specific time frame, tap the white handles and drag the left start bar and the right end bar to the appropriate points on the timeline.

IDENTIFYING DATA HOGS

Look at the list at the bottom of the Data Usage screen to identify data hogs. The list items are shown in descending order of appetite, so you can easily see which apps have been greediest.

Tap an app to display the Data Usage screen for that app alone. Figure 4.5 shows an example for Chrome. Use the Data Usage cycle pop-up menu and the histogram at the top to specify the time period you want to see. You can then look at the Foreground readout and Background readout to see how the app has been using data.

FIGURE 4.5

On the Data Usage screen for an app, you can check the Restrict Background Data box to prevent the app from using mobile data when it is in the background.

If you don't want the app to use mobile data when it's in the background, check the Restrict Background Data box.

WORKING ON THE DATA USAGE SCREEN'S MENU

The menu on the main Data Usage screen (see Figure 4.6) contains essential commands for managing your data usage:

FIGURE 4.6

Use the menu on the Data Usage screen to manage your data usage.

- **Data Roaming.** Check this box to turn on roaming. Because roaming may rack up charges, the Allow Data Roaming? dialog box opens to confirm the action. Tap the OK button if you want to go ahead.

- **Restrict Background Data.** Check this box to prevent all apps and services from using mobile data when they're in the background. Android displays the Restrict Background Data? dialog box to warn you that restricting background data prevents some apps and services from working unless they have a Wi-Fi connection. Tap the OK button if you want to proceed.

- **Auto-Sync Data.** Check this box to enable Android to sync data automatically.

- **Show Wi-Fi Usage.** Check this box to display Wi-Fi data usage on a separate tab. Being able to check Wi-Fi usage is useful if you're on a metered Wi-Fi connection (such as at a hotel) or if you suspect an app of hogging Wi-Fi bandwidth. Otherwise, if you're on an all-you-can-eat Wi-Fi connection, you probably don't care how much data you're shifting over it.

- **Mobile Hotspots.** Tap this button to display the Mobile Hotspots screen (see Figure 4.7), and then check the box for each Wi-Fi network that is a hotspot rather than a regular wireless network. You can then restrict apps in the background from using the hotspots.

> ✅ **TIP** The other difference that marking hotspots makes is that when your device is connected to a known hotspot, apps may also warn you before downloading large files.

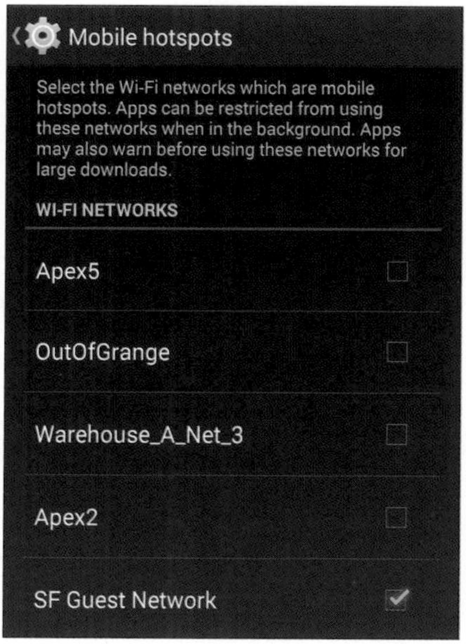

FIGURE 4.7

On the Mobile Hotspots screen, check the box for each available Wi-Fi network that is a hotspot.

MANAGING YOUR WI-FI CONNECTIONS

Even if you've got a cellular device with a generous data plan, Wi-Fi tends to be essential to getting the most out of your device. In this section, you'll learn how to find and identify networks; connect to them using passwords, WPS, and Wi-Fi Direct; install digital certificates; whitelist your device; configure IP settings; connect through a proxy server; and more.

TURNING WI-FI ON AND OFF

You can quickly turn Wi-Fi on or off by opening the Quick Settings panel and tapping and holding the Wi-Fi icon. When Wi-Fi is off, this icon shows the text "Wi-Fi"; when Wi-Fi is on and your device has connected to a wireless network, the icon shows three pieces of information (see Figure 4.8):

- The network's name under the icon (abbreviated if necessary).
- The connection's strength—one to four of the gray bars turn white.

> **NOTE** The bars on the Wi-Fi icon appear orange when your device is establishing a connection.

- Whether the connection is transferring data. An up arrow indicates data going to the server, while a down arrow indicates data coming to your device.

FIGURE 4.8

The Wi-Fi icon on the Quick Settings panel shows the current Wi-Fi network's name, strength, and whether it is transferring data upstream and downstream.

> **TIP** Instead of using the icon on the Quick Settings panel to turn Wi-Fi on or off, you can set the switch on the main Settings screen or the switch on the Wi-Fi screen.

When you turn Wi-Fi on, Android checks to see if any of the Wi-Fi networks to which you've previously connected your device are available. If a network is available, Android connects to it.

> **TIP** For instant access to the Wi-Fi screen, create a Settings shortcut to it on the Home screen.

CONNECTING TO WI-FI NETWORKS

To choose which Wi-Fi network your Android device connects to, open the Wi-Fi screen in one of these ways:

- Tap the Wi-Fi icon on the Quick Settings panel.
- Open the Settings app and tap the Wi-Fi button (not the Wi-Fi switch) on the Settings screen.

If the Wi-Fi switch on the Wi-Fi screen is set to Off, set it to On. Android then searches for available networks and displays a list of them. If a network to which you've previously connected is available, Android connects to it.

If no such network is available, or if you want to connect to a different network, tap it on the Wi-Fi screen. If the network requires a password, Android displays a dialog box (whose title bar bears the network's name) to prompt you for it (see Figure 4.9). Type the password—check the Show Password box if you need to see what you're typing—and then tap Connect to connect.

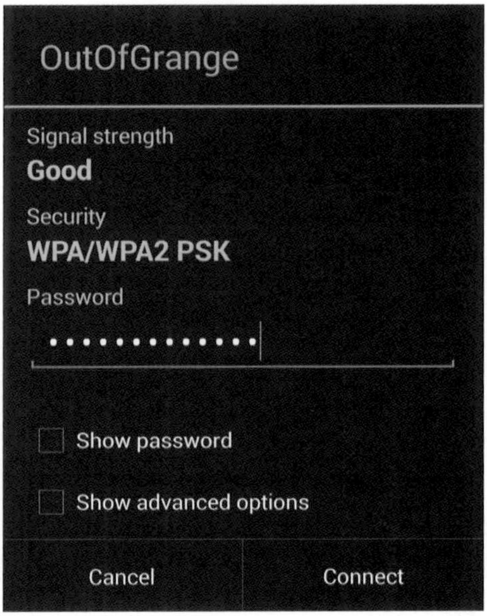

FIGURE 4.9

Android prompts you to enter the password for the wireless network you're trying to join.

TIP If the Wi-Fi network you're expecting to see doesn't appear on the Wi-Fi screen, tap the Menu button and then tap Scan on the menu to force another scan. If the network still doesn't appear, you may need to provide the network name; see the next section for details.

Each Wi-Fi network has a network name to identify it. The administrator assigns the name when setting up the network. The name contains alphanumeric characters—letters and numbers—and has a maximum length of 32 characters.

NOTE The technical term for a wireless network's name is service set identifier, or SSID.

When setting up a Wi-Fi network, the administrator can decide whether to have the router broadcast the network's name—as networks normally do—or whether to create a *closed* network, one that doesn't broadcast its name.

NOTE Creating a closed network is one of the security measures an administrator can take for a wireless network. It is only moderately effective: Casual intruders may miss the network, but anyone with a Wi-Fi scanner will still be able to detect the network.

CONNECTING TO A CLOSED NETWORK

To connect to a closed network, you need to provide the network name as well as the password or other security measure. Tap the + button, which appears at the bottom of the Wi-Fi screen on a phone and at the top of the Wi-Fi screen on a tablet, to display the Add Network dialog box (see Figure 4.10). Then enter the details and tap the Save button.

NOTE SSIDs are case sensitive, so use the exact case.

FIGURE 4.10

Use the Add Network dialog box to connect to a closed network.

📝 **TIP** You can also use the Add Network dialog box to add an open network that is not currently in range.

After adding the closed network to the list on the Wi-Fi screen, you can tap the network to connect to it.

SETTING UP A NETWORK USING WPS

Some Wi-Fi routers include a feature called Wi-Fi Protected Setup (WPS) to help you set up networks securely. If your router includes WPS, and you have direct access to the router, you can set up the wireless network easily on your Android device. Android supports two types of WPS:

- **WPS.** You press a hardware button on your Wi-Fi router to permit the connection.

- **WPS PIN Entry.** You enter a PIN in your Wi-Fi router's configuration interface to permit the connection.

> **NOTE** WPS is mostly used by Wi-Fi routers designed for the home market. It is a moderately secure way of establishing a connection to a Wi-Fi network.

To connect via WPS, tap the WPS button (the icon with curling arrows going up and down). The WPS Setup dialog box opens (see Figure 4.11).

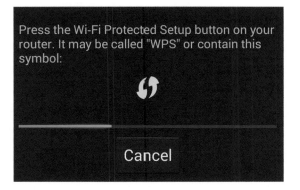

FIGURE 4.11

To set up a Wi-Fi network using WPS, tap the WPS button on the Wi-Fi screen, and then press the WPS button on your Wi-Fi router.

To connect via WPS PIN Entry, tap the Menu button on the Wi-Fi screen, and then tap WPS PIN Entry on the menu. The WPS PIN Entry dialog box opens, showing the PIN you need to enter on your Wi-Fi router (usually through a browser-based configuration utility). After you enter the PIN correctly, your device can connect to the network.

USING WI-FI DIRECT

Wi-Fi Direct is a Wi-Fi standard for connecting two devices to each other without using an access point, enabling you to share files between the devices or share one device's Internet connection with the other. Wi-Fi Direct uses WPS to negotiate the link between the devices.

> **!CAUTION** Only some Android devices support Wi-Fi Direct. If the Wi-Fi Direct item doesn't appear on the menu on the Wi-Fi screen in Settings, your device doesn't support Wi-Fi Direct.

Here's how to establish a connection using Wi-Fi Direct:

1. On the Wi-Fi screen on each device, tap the Menu button and then tap Wi-Fi Direct on the menu. The Wi-Fi Direct screen appears, displaying a list of peer devices and a list of remembered groups (see Figure 4.12).

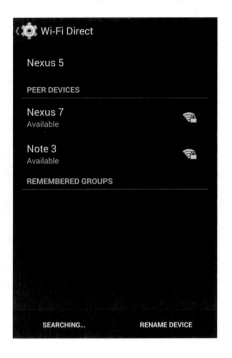

FIGURE 4.12

On the Wi-Fi Direct screen, tap the device to which you want to connect.

> **TIP** If the Wi-Fi Direct screen shows a generic name (such as Android_54d8) for your device, tap the Rename Device button, type a descriptive name (such as Nexus 5), and then tap the OK button. If the Rename Device button doesn't appear on your device, tap the Menu button and then tap Configure Device to reach a screen that enables you to rename the device.

2. Tap the device to which you want to connect. The word *Invited* appears under the device's name while Wi-Fi Direct waits for the user of the other device to accept the invitation to connect.

3. After Wi-Fi Direct establishes the connection, the word *Connected* appears under the device's name in the Peer Devices list. You can now transfer files as needed between the devices.

4. When you are ready to stop using Wi-Fi Direct, tap the connection. The Disconnect? dialog box opens.

5. Tap the OK button.

Troubleshooting Wi-Fi Direct Connections

Wi-Fi Direct is great when it works, but often it doesn't. You may find that other devices don't appear on the Wi-Fi Direct screen, even when they're physically right next to your device. Or you may find that the device is listed, but Wi-Fi Direct fails to establish a connection to the device you tap. Or Wi-Fi Direct may connect, but your device doesn't enable you to transfer the file type you want to.

If you're having trouble with Wi-Fi Direct, tap the Back button to return from the Wi-Fi Direct screen to the Wi-Fi screen. Turn Wi-Fi off, wait a few seconds, turn it back on, and then tap the Menu button and tap Wi-Fi Direct to display the Wi-Fi Direct screen again. If Wi-Fi Direct still isn't working, try turning off your device and then restarting it.

At this point, you'll probably want to turn to a different means of connection. NFC and Bluetooth are both options, but if you need to transfer large files, you'll do better with an app such as SuperBeam or HitcherNet. Each offers a limited free version to persuade you to pay for an upgrade. For example, SuperBeam plays ads at you until you pay the premium for the Pro version, which offers extra features and no ads.

INSTALLING DIGITAL CERTIFICATES

For some connections, you may need to use a digital certificate to authenticate your device to a server. A digital certificate is a unit of encrypted code that you install on your device and tell it to use for specific tasks.

You can install a digital certificate either from an email message or from a folder on your device. You start the installation process in different ways, but the rest of the process is the same.

To start installing a digital certificate from an email message, tap the attachment button for the digital certificate in the message. The Extract Certificate dialog box opens.

> **✓ TIP** If you receive a digital certificate in an email message but you don't want to install it now, tap the Menu button on the attachment and tap Save on the menu to save the file to your Downloads folder.

To start installing a digital certificate from a folder, follow these steps:

1. Open the Settings app.
2. Tap the Security button in the Personal section.

> **✎ NOTE** You may need to tap a different button on your device, such as Security & Screen Lock. The button for installing digital certificates from the SD card may also have a different name (such as Install from SD Card), but you should have no trouble finding it.

3. Tap the Install from Storage button in the Credential Storage section. The Open From panel appears.
4. Navigate to the folder that contains the certificate.
5. Tap the certificate. The Extract Certificate dialog box opens.

In the Extract Certificate dialog box, type the password for the certificate. Normally, you'll need to find this out from the person who sent you the certificate.

Tap the OK button, and the Name the Certificate dialog box opens (see Figure 4.13). Type a descriptive name in the Certificate Name box so that you can easily distinguish this certificate from any others on your device. Then tap the Credential Use pop-up menu and tap the appropriate button:

- **VPN and Apps.** Tap this button to make this digital certificate available for connecting to VPN servers or for use in apps (such as for connecting to an Exchange Server system).
- **Wi-Fi.** Tap this button to make this digital certificate available for connecting to Wi-Fi networks.

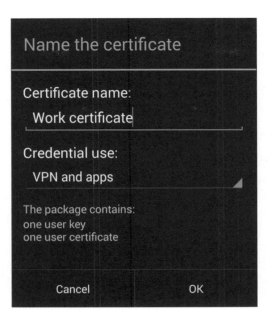

FIGURE 4.13

In the Name the Certificate dialog box, type a descriptive name for the certificate and specify what you will use it for.

Tap the OK button to close the Name the Certificate dialog box. Android installs the certificate and briefly displays a readout saying that it has been installed.

CHOOSING ADVANCED WI-FI SETTINGS

The Wi-Fi screen gives you access to the essential settings for configuring Wi-Fi networks, but to take full control of Wi-Fi, you'll need to configure advanced settings. Tap the Menu button on the Wi-Fi screen to open the menu, and then tap Advanced to display the Advanced Wi-Fi screen (see Figure 4.14).

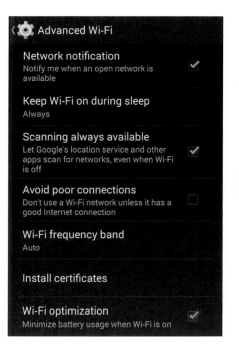

FIGURE 4.14

From the Advanced Wi-Fi screen, you can set your device to keep Wi-Fi on during sleep, avoid poor connections, and use specific frequency bands.

> **NOTE** Your device may not have all the options shown on the Advanced Wi-Fi screen here. For example, it may lack the Wi-Fi Optimization button or the Avoid Poor Connections button. Conversely, it may have extra features such as a Sort By button, which enables you to sort available wireless networks by signal strength or alphabetically.

These are the settings you can choose:

- **Network Notification.** Check this box to have Android notify you when an open network is available. Some devices call this Wi-Fi Notifications rather than Network Notification.

- **Keep Wi-Fi On During Sleep.** Tap this button to display the Keep Wi-Fi On During Sleep dialog box, and then tap the Always radio button, the Only When Plugged In radio button, or the Never radio button.

> **!CAUTION** Selecting the Never radio button in the Keep Wi-Fi On During Sleep dialog box on a phone or cellular-capable tablet will increase your data usage because apps will use the cellular connection to check for data. Normally, it's best to choose Only When Plugged In if you need to conserve battery power. Choose Always if having the latest data available is more important than battery power.

- **Scanning Always Available.** Check this box to allow the Google Location Service and other apps to scan for Wi-Fi networks even when Wi-Fi is turned off. Uncheck this box if you want "off" to mean "off."

- **Avoid Poor Connections.** Check this box if you want to let Android reject a Wi-Fi network that has a poor Internet connection. This setting can save you the frustration of struggling to use a poor connection, but if you're stuck somewhere with only poor connections available, you may need to uncheck this box to get online at all.

- **Wi-Fi Frequency Band.** To control which frequency band your device uses, tap this button, and then tap the appropriate radio button in the Wi-Fi Frequency Band dialog box: Auto, 5 GHz Only, or 2.4 GHz only.

- **Install Certificates.** Tap this button to start installing digital certificates. This is an alternative way of beginning the installation process explained in "Installing Digital Certificates," earlier in this chapter.

- **Wi-Fi Optimization.** Check this box to minimize battery usage while Wi-Fi is turned on. This is normally a good idea.

> **NOTE** You can also make Android forget a wireless network. See the section "Forgetting a Network," later in this chapter.

WHITELISTING YOUR DEVICE ON A WI-FI NETWORK

Some Wi-Fi networks use whitelists to determine which devices are allowed to connect to them. A whitelist is a list of approved MAC addresses on devices.

> **NOTE** MAC is the abbreviation for Media Access Control. A MAC address is a unique hexadecimal identifier (such as f8:a9:d0:73;c4:dd) burned into the network hardware of a device.

You can find your device's MAC address in two places:

- **The MAC Address readout on the Advanced Wi-Fi screen.** Open the Settings app, tap the Wi-Fi button, tap the Menu button, and then tap Advanced on the menu.

- **The Wi-Fi MAC Address readout on the Status screen or in the Status dialog box.** Open the Settings app, tap the About Phone button or the About Tablet button (or the About Device button on some devices), and then tap the Status button.

> **CAUTION** If you're administering a wireless network, a whitelist of MAC addresses is a useful security measure for preventing unauthorized devices from connecting. But it's not foolproof, because software can *spoof* (fake) an authorized MAC address that an attacker has grabbed using a network sniffer tool.

There's no way to copy the MAC address, so you'll need to write it down. You can then give it to your network's administrator to add to the MAC whitelist—or, if the network is your own, add the address yourself.

CONFIGURING IP SETTINGS MANUALLY

To connect to a wireless network, your device must have suitable Internet Protocol (IP) settings: the IP address, the gateway address, the network prefix length, and the DNS server addresses. Typically, the device receives these settings automatically from the network, but you can also set them manually if necessary.

Most Wi-Fi networks use Dynamic Host Configuration Protocol (DHCP), a protocol in which a DHCP server or DHCP allocator automatically provides IP addresses and network configuration information to devices that connect. DHCP is an efficient way of sharing available IP addresses among devices, so it's widely used. But some networks use static IP addresses instead, assigning a particular address to each device. For such networks, you must configure your device's IP settings manually.

You can configure IP settings either when setting up the network in the first place (tap the network on the Wi-Fi screen) or afterward by tapping and holding the network's button on the Wi-Fi screen and then tapping Modify Network on the pop-up menu. Either way, you work in the dialog box for the network. This dialog box's title bar shows the network's name.

Tap to check the Show Advanced Options box, and the dialog box expands to show the Proxy controls and the IP Settings controls.

You'll look at the Proxy controls in the next section. For now, tap the IP Settings pop-up menu and then tap Static instead of DHCP. The dialog box expands again (see Figure 4.15) to reveal the following fields for you to fill in:

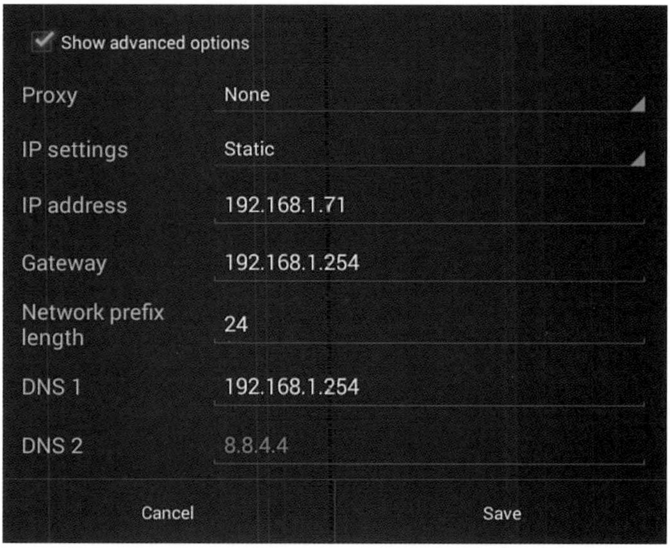

FIGURE 4.15

Choose Static in the IP Settings pop-up menu if you need to enter a static IP address and other network information.

- **IP address.** Type the static IP address for your device.

> **NOTE** Normally, you'll be using an IPv4 address, which consists of four groups of numbers in the 0–255 range, separated by periods—for example, 192.168.1.44 or 10.0.0.250. If you're connecting to an IPv6 network, the address consists of six hexadecimal groups separated by colons—for example, fe80:0000:faa9:d0fe:fe72:c4dd. If a group consists of zeros, you can collapse it to nothing, simply putting a pair of colons to indicate where it would be. For example, the previous address can also be written fe80::faa9:d0fe:fe72:c4dd, with the group of zeros removed.

- **Gateway.** Type the IP address of the network gateway or router.
- **Network Prefix Length.** Leave the default setting, 24, unchanged for IPv4 networks. For IPv6 networks, type the length the administrator has specified, such as 64.

> **TIP** The Network Prefix Length setting replaces the subnet mask setting (such as 255.255.255.0) that was previously used for IPv4 networks.

- **DNS 1.** Type the IP address of the first DNS server your administrator or ISP has given you, or use Google's primary DNS server, 8.8.8.8.
- **DNS 2.** Type the IP address of the second DNS server your administrator or ISP has given you, or use Google's secondary DNS server, 8.8.4.4.

Tap the Save button after you make your choices.

CONNECTING THROUGH A PROXY SERVER

Instead of directly connecting to websites, your device can connect through a proxy server. This server fulfills network requests for your device, either by providing data that the server has previously cached or by relaying the requests to a suitable server. For example, instead of requesting a web page directly from the web server, your device requests it from the proxy server. The proxy server either delivers the web page from its cache, quickly providing the data and reducing Internet use, or requests the web page from the web server and passes it along to your device.

> **TIP** Normally, you'd connect through a proxy server in a corporate or organizational setting, where the proxy server not only caches data but also prevents access to blocked sites. You can also connect through a proxy server with the aim of disguising the location where the network requests are coming from.

To set up a Wi-Fi connection to use a proxy server, follow these steps:

1. On the Wi-Fi screen, tap and hold the Wi-Fi connection, and then tap Modify Network on the pop-up menu to open the configuration dialog box for the network.

> **NOTE**   You can also set up a proxy connection when first connecting to a Wi-Fi network.

2. Tap to check the Show Advanced Options box. The dialog box expands to show the Proxy controls and the IP Settings controls.

3. Tap the Proxy pop-up menu and then tap Manual instead of None on the menu. The proxy settings appear (see Figure 4.16).

4. Type the proxy server's hostname (such as eproxy.surrealmacs.com) or IP address (such as 208.42.68.13) in the Proxy Hostname box.

5. Type the port number in the Proxy Port box. The default port is 8080.

6. In the Bypass Proxy For box, type any domains or hosts that you want your device to access without the requests going through the proxy server.

7. Tap the Save button to close the dialog box and save the changes.

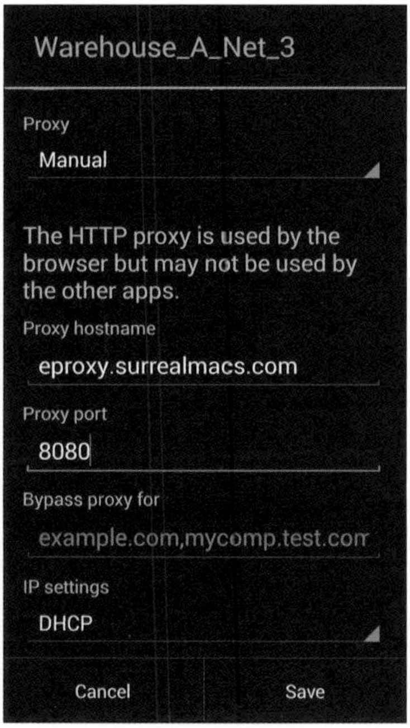

FIGURE 4.16

Choose Manual in the Proxy pop-up menu to display the fields for configuring a Wi-Fi connection to use a proxy server.

IMPROVING YOUR WI-FI CONNECTIONS

By this point, your Android device should be establishing connections to the Wi-Fi networks you want to use. But what if the connections aren't working as well as you need them to?

First, if your device keeps dropping the connection and then having to reestablish it, try turning Wi-Fi off and back on again. If that doesn't help, try powering down your device and restarting it. Restarting is tedious if you're in a hurry, but it can clear up any number of niggling problems.

If the connection is still problematic, and it's a network that you administer, restart the wireless router.

Second, look at the connection's status to see if anything is obviously wrong. Open the Wi-Fi screen in the Settings app and tap the button for the network to which your device has connected. In the dialog box that opens (see Figure 4.17), look at the Signal Strength readout. This readout uses plain English terms—Excellent, Good, Fair, Poor, and Out of Range—to indicate the connection's strength or lack thereof. If the Signal Strength is Poor, you may want to try another wireless network instead if one is available.

OutOfGrange

Status
Connected

Signal strength
Good

Link speed
72Mbps

Security
WPA/WPA2 PSK

IP address
192.168.1.121

Cancel   Forget

FIGURE 4.17

Look at the Signal Strength readout and Link Speed readout to identify anything obviously wrong with a Wi-Fi connection.

Look also at the Link Speed readout. If the speed is lower than usual, try dropping the connection and then reconnecting. The easiest way to drop the connection is to set the Wi-Fi switch to Off for a moment, and then set it back to On.

> **NOTE** Android usually connects at the highest link speed possible. But if you establish the connection when your device is relatively far from the wireless access point and the signal is correspondingly weak, you may get a low link speed that persists even when you move your device closer to the wireless access point. If this happens, drop the connection and reconnect to try to get a higher link speed.

Third, you may need to change channels to get a decent connection. A wireless network can use any of a variety of channels, which the administrator can choose using whatever configuration utility the wireless access point provides. If many of the wireless networks in your immediate vicinity use the same channels, you may get lower throughput.

To see which network is using which channels, you can install a Wi-Fi analyzer app or Wi-Fi stumbler app from the Play Store. Many are available with different features, but most show you the available networks, their relative signal strength, and the channels they are using. Armed with this information, you can set your wireless network to avoid the channels your neighbors are using.

> **TIP** A Wi-Fi analyzer app or Wi-Fi stumbler app is also useful for locating available wireless networks when you need to get online.

FORGETTING A NETWORK

When you no longer want to use a particular network, you can tell your device to forget it. Tap the network's button on the Wi-Fi screen to display the dialog box for the network, and then tap the Forget button.

> **NOTE** You can also tap and hold the network on the Wi-Fi screen, and then tap Forget Network on the pop-up menu.

> ☑ **TIP**   If your device cannot connect to a network to which it has successfully connected before, forget the network and then rejoin it, entering the password again.

SHARING YOUR DEVICE'S INTERNET CONNECTION

If you have a phone or a cellular-capable tablet, you can share your cellular Internet connection with your computer or other devices. You have three options for sharing:

- **USB Tethering.** Connect your device to your computer via USB and enable the computer to use the device's Internet connection across the USB cable.
- **Portable Wi-Fi Hotspot.** Share your device's Internet connection via Wi-Fi with multiple devices.
- **Bluetooth Tethering.** Share your device's Internet connection via Bluetooth with other devices. You'll look at this in the section "Sharing an Internet Connection via Bluetooth Tethering," later in this chapter.

> ☑ **NOTE**   Some cellular providers disable the Portable Wi-Fi Hotspot feature unless you pay an extra fee for it.

To control sharing, you use the Tethering & Portable Hotspot screen (see Figure 4.18). To display this screen, open the Settings app, tap the More button in the Wireless & Networks section, and then tap the Tethering & Portable Hotspot button.

FIGURE 4.18

From the Tethering & Portable Hotspot screen, you can set up USB tethering, portable Wi-Fi hotspot, or Bluetooth tethering.

> **! CAUTION** Sharing your device's cellular connection puts more stress on the device and may cause it to wear out sooner. For this reason, you may decide to use Internet sharing only when absolutely necessary rather than everyday.

SHARING THE INTERNET CONNECTION VIA USB TETHERING

To share your device's Internet connection via USB sharing, connect your device to your computer via USB and then check the USB Tethering box.

> **TIP** Windows normally picks up the tethered connection immediately without your intervention. On Mac, you may need to select the tethered network interface manually: Click the Apple menu and then click System Preferences, and then click Network in the System Preferences window. In the Network pane, click your device's name in the list of network interfaces, and then click the Apply button.

SHARING THE INTERNET CONNECTION VIA PORTABLE WI-FI HOTSPOT

To share your device's Internet connection via Portable Wi-Fi Hotspot, first set up the hotspot. Tap the Set Up Wi-Fi Hotspot button on the Tethering & Portable Hotspot screen and choose suitable settings in the Set Up Wi-Fi Hotspot dialog box (see Figure 4.19):

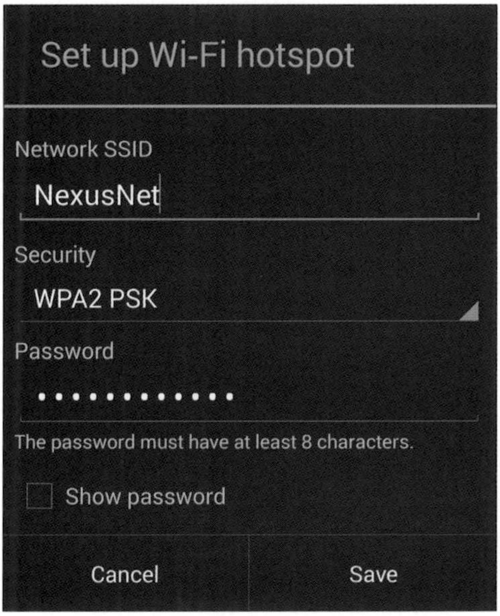

FIGURE 4.19

In the Set Up Wi-Fi Hotspot dialog box, name your hotspot and choose the security type.

- **Network SSID.** Type a name that you can easily identify from other nearby Wi-Fi hotspots. Many people leave the default name, AndroidAP, so it's a good idea to change the name.
- **Security.** Tap this pop-up menu and choose WPA2 PSK.

> **NOTE** The other choices on the Security pop-up menu are None and WPA PSK. Don't use None, because any device within Wi-Fi range will be able to use your hotspot. Use WPA PSK if you find that older devices can't connect to the hotspot because they don't support WPA2 PSK.

- **Password.** Type the password for the connection. Use at least 8 characters for the password, and preferably 12–20 characters. (If you choose None in the Security pop-up menu, the Password field disappears.)

!CAUTION Sharing your Internet connection via Portable Wi-Fi Hotspot can eat through your data plan at high speed. Use the Data Usage screen in the Settings app to monitor how much data your device has used and how much remains.

Tap the Save button to close the Set Up Wi-Fi Hotspot dialog box, and your hotspot is ready for use. Check the Portable Wi-Fi Hotspot box on the Tethering & Portable Hotspot screen to turn on the hotspot. Computers and devices can then connect to the hotspot using the same techniques as for any other wireless network.

NOTE The maximum number of simultaneous connections for the hotspot depends on the device but is usually between three and eight. Android doesn't give you any indication of how many clients have connected to the hotspot, so it can be hard to tell how much use it's getting.

While the hotspot is active, the hotspot icon appears at the left end of the status bar (see Figure 4.20), and the notifications panel displays a notification that you can touch to go straight to the Tethering & Portable Hotspot screen. To turn off the hotspot, uncheck the Portable Wi-Fi Hotspot box on the Tethering & Portable Hotspot screen.

Hotspot icon

FIGURE 4.20

The hotspot icon indicates that the hotspot is active.

CONNECTING BLUETOOTH DEVICES

Most Android devices include Bluetooth capabilities, enabling you to wirelessly connect a wide variety of devices through the Bluetooth protocol. For example, you can connect Bluetooth headphones to listen to music comfortably or connect a Bluetooth keyboard so that you can enter text at full speed in documents. If your device is a phone or a cellular-capable tablet, you can also use Bluetooth to share its Internet connection with other devices.

The first time you connect a Bluetooth device, you must pair it with your Android device. After pairing the devices, you can subsequently connect them quickly and easily.

PAIRING A BLUETOOTH DEVICE WITH YOUR ANDROID DEVICE

Here's how to pair a Bluetooth device with your Android device:

1. Open the Settings app.

2. Tap the Bluetooth button to display the Bluetooth screen.

3. Set the switch to On.

4. Turn on the Bluetooth device and make it visible via Bluetooth.

> **NOTE** To make a device visible, you may need to press a dedicated button or press its other control buttons in combination. Typically, the device gives an indication that it is visible—for example, flashing lights of different colors or emitting beeps—so you'll know when you've got it right.

5. If the Bluetooth device doesn't appear in the Available Devices list on your Android device (see Figure 4.21), tap the Search for Devices button.

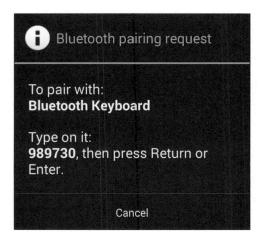

FIGURE 4.21
Tap the Bluetooth device's button in the Available Devices list to start pairing it with your Android device.

6. If the Bluetooth Pairing Request dialog box opens (see Figure 4.22), type the code shown and press Enter or Return.

FIGURE 4.22
Devices such as a Bluetooth keyboard require you to enter a pairing code.

7. When the pairing is complete, the Bluetooth device appears in the Paired Devices list. Tap the Settings button (the icon with three horizontal sliders) to display the Paired Bluetooth Device screen (see Figure 4.23).

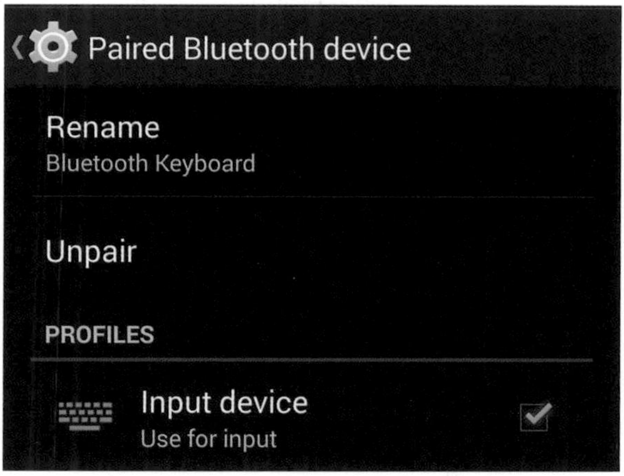

FIGURE 4.23

Use the Paired Bluetooth Device screen to rename a Bluetooth device, unpair it, or turn off its profile.

8. If you want, tap the Rename button, type a descriptive name in the Rename dialog box, and then tap the OK button.

NOTE On the Paired Bluetooth Device screen, you can uncheck the device's box in the Profiles list to stop using a device for the purpose shown. For example, Android lists a keyboard as an input device. You can uncheck the box to stop using the keyboard for input temporarily.

TIP When you're not using Bluetooth, turn it off to save battery power and to prevent other devices from trying to connect to your device via Bluetooth. The quickest way to turn Bluetooth on and off is by opening the Quick Settings panel and then tapping and holding the Bluetooth icon.

TRANSFERRING FILES TO ANOTHER DEVICE VIA BLUETOOTH

You can transfer files to another device via Bluetooth by using the Share feature.

1. Open the app that owns the files.

2. Select the files. How you do this depends on the app, but in many apps, you can turn on Selection mode by tapping and holding a file.

3. Give the Share command. This also depends on the app, but in many apps you can either tap the Share button on the toolbar or tap the Bluetooth button on the toolbar.

4. In the Share Via dialog box, tap Bluetooth to display the Bluetooth Device Chooser screen.

5. Tap the device to which you want to send the files.

The target device then receives a prompt about the files. If the user accepts the file, Android transfers it.

When another device tries to transfer a file to your device via Bluetooth, your device displays a Bluetooth Share notification. Tap the notification to display the File Transfer dialog box (see Figure 4.24), and then tap the Accept button or the Decline button, as appropriate. You can then go to the file by tapping the Bluetooth Share: Received File notification in the notifications panel or by tapping the Menu button on the Bluetooth screen and then tapping Show Received Files on the menu.

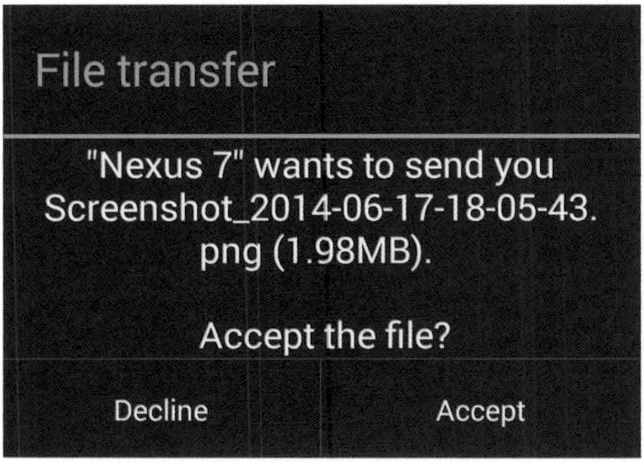

File transfer

"Nexus 7" wants to send you Screenshot_2014-06-17-18-05-43. png (1.98MB).

Accept the file?

| Decline | Accept |

FIGURE 4.24

Android prompts you to accept each Bluetooth file transfer.

SHARING AN INTERNET CONNECTION VIA BLUETOOTH TETHERING

To share your device's Internet connection via Bluetooth, check the Bluetooth Tethering box on the Tethering & Portable Hotspot screen. Other devices can then connect to your device via Bluetooth and use its Internet connection to access the Internet.

The general theory is plain enough, but as usual, the devil is in the details. If you're looking to use an Android device to share the Internet connection via Bluetooth, you're in the right place. The following subsections explain how to pair Android devices via Bluetooth and share an Internet connection.

PAIRING TWO ANDROID DEVICES

To pair another Android device with your device, first make your device visible by tapping the button at the top of the Bluetooth screen. This button shows the device's Bluetooth name and the readout "Only visible to paired devices." When you tap the button, the readout changes to "Visible to all nearby Bluetooth devices" and a countdown of the remaining visibility time (see Figure 4.25).

> **TIP** You can change your device's Bluetooth name by tapping the Menu button, tapping Rename Phone or Rename Tablet on the menu, typing the new name in the Rename Phone dialog box or the Rename Tablet dialog box, and then tapping the Rename button.

FIGURE 4.25

Tap your device's name on the Bluetooth screen to make it temporarily visible via Bluetooth.

On the other device, tap the button for your device in the Available Devices list on the Bluetooth screen. If your device doesn't appear there, tap the Search for Devices button.

> ☑ **TIP** You can change how long your device remains visible for Bluetooth devices. On the Bluetooth screen, tap the Menu button and then tap Visibility Timeout on the menu to open the Visibility Timeout dialog box. You can then tap the appropriate radio button—2 Minutes, 5 Minutes, 1 Hour, or Never Time Out.

Each device then displays the Bluetooth Pairing Request dialog box. Verify that each instance of the dialog box shows the same number, and then tap the Pair button on each device. Android establishes the connection, and each device appears in the Paired Devices list on the other device.

SHARING THE INTERNET CONNECTION VIA BLUETOOTH ON AN ANDROID DEVICE

Now that you've paired the devices, you need to turn on the Internet Access profile for the device that will use the shared Internet connection.

On this device, tap the Settings button to the right of the device's name in the Paired Devices list on the Bluetooth screen. On the Paired Bluetooth Device screen that appears, check the Internet Access box in the Profiles list. You can then use the Internet connection, but Android turns off the Internet Access profile when the device locks.

USING VPNS

Virtual private networking (VPN) enables you to create a secure connection to a server across an insecure network. You'd typically use a virtual private network (also abbreviated VPN) for connecting across the Internet to a work network.

> ☑ **TIP** Here are two more uses for VPN. First, when you connect to a Wi-Fi hotspot, you can use a VPN to secure your Internet traffic against snooping. Second, when you need to make your device appear to be in a different location than it actually is. For example, if you subscribe to a U.S.-based media service, you may not be able to access it when you travel abroad. But by connecting to a VPN server within the United States, you can make your computer appear to be in the country, enabling you to use the service. Leading VPN services include IPVanish (www.ipvanish.com), StrongVPN (www.strongvpn.com), and CyberGhost VPN (www.cyberghostvpn.com).

SETTING UP A VPN CONNECTION

To set up a VPN connection on your Android device, you'll need to know the following:

- **VPN type.** This can be PPTP, L2TP/IPSec PSK, L2TP IPSec RSA, IPSec Xauth PSK, IPSec Xauth RSA, or IPSec Hybrid RSA.

- **Server address.** This can be a server name (such as vpnserv.notionalpress.com) or an IP address (such as 209.14.241.1).

- **L2TP secret.** This is a text string used for securing some L2TP connections.

- **IPSec identifier.** This is a text string used for some IPSec connections.

- **IPSec preshared key.** This is a text string used for some IPSec connections.

> **NOTE** For some types of VPN, you may also need to provide a digital certificate. See the section "Installing Digital Certificates," earlier in this chapter, for instructions on installing a digital certificate.

Ask the VPN's administrator for this information. Ask also for your username and password for the VPN connection. You don't need these for setting up the connection, but you'll need them when you connect.

Armed with the right information, follow these steps to set up the VPN on your device:

1. Open the Settings app.

2. Tap the More button in the Wireless & Networks section to display the Wireless & Networks screen.

3. Tap the VPN button to display the VPN screen.

4. Tap the + button to open the Edit VPN Profile dialog box (see Figure 4.26).

5. Type a descriptive name in the Name box.

6. Tap the Type pop-up menu and select the type, such as L2TP/IPSec PSK. The Edit VPN Profile dialog box changes to display fields for the information required.

7. Fill in the other information required for the VPN using the data the administrator has given you.

> **NOTE** If you need to fill in DNS search domains, DNS servers, or forwarding routes, check the Show Advanced Options box to reveal the fields in which you can enter this information.

8. Tap the Save button. The VPN appears on the VPN screen.

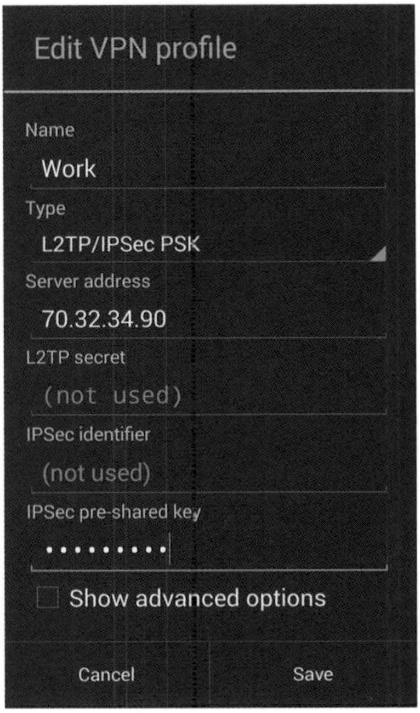

FIGURE 4.26

In the Edit VPN Profile dialog box, select the VPN type and enter its details.

CONNECTING VIA THE VPN

After you've set up a VPN connection, you can connect via the VPN using the following steps:

1. Tap the VPN's button on the VPN screen. The Connect To dialog box opens (see Figure 4.27), showing the VPN's name (for example, Connect to Work for a VPN called "Work").

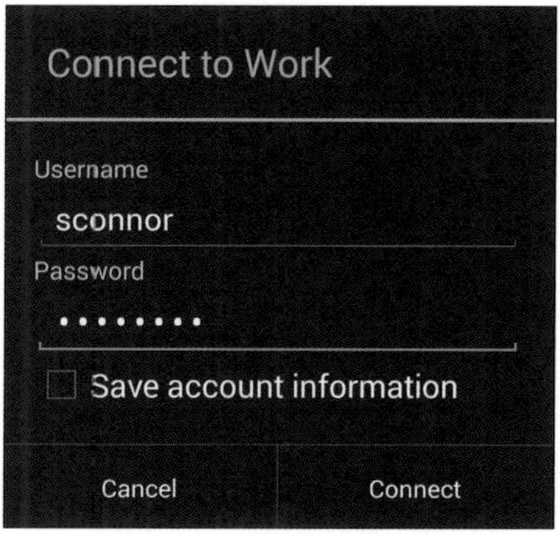

Connect to Work

Username

sconnor

Password

••••••••

☐ Save account information

Cancel   Connect

FIGURE 4.27

In the Connect To dialog box for the VPN, check the Save Account Information box if you want to save your credentials for future use.

> **TIP**   Early versions of KitKat (Android 4.4) had some bugs in the VPN software, which Google had recoded for KitKat. If your device has trouble establishing VPN connections, can establish connections but cannot transfer data over them, or unexpectedly disconnects from the VPN, make sure you have updated it to the latest version of Android.

2. Type your username and password.

3. Check the Save Account Information box if you want to save your username and password so you don't have to type them next time.

4. Tap the Connect button. Android connects to the server and displays the readout "Connected" under the connection's name. The VPN symbol appears in the status bar (see Figure 4.28).

VPN icon

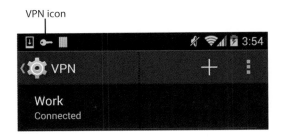

FIGURE 4.28

The VPN screen with a VPN connection connected.

After connecting, you can work across the VPN connection in much the same way as a local network connection. Normally, the speeds will be much slower across the VPN, so you may need to be patient while transferring data.

When you're ready to stop using the VPN, tap its button on the VPN screen or on the Notifications panel. The VPN Is Connected dialog box opens (see Figure 4.29), and you can tap the Disconnect button to disconnect the connection.

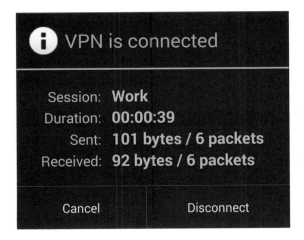

FIGURE 4.29

Tap the Disconnect button in the VPN Is Connected dialog box when you're ready to disconnect the VPN.

> **NOTE** If your device changes its Internet connection from Wi-Fi to cellular or vice versa while you are using a VPN connection, Android disconnects the VPN automatically as a safety measure. If you cannot reconnect the VPN over the new means of connection, restart your device.

IN THIS CHAPTER

- Installing or sideloading the apps you need
- Running apps and switching among apps
- Troubleshooting apps and rebooting into Safe mode

5

INSTALLING, RUNNING, AND MANAGING APPS

In this chapter, you learn how to install, run, and manage apps on your Android device. Along the way, you learn how to install apps from the Play Store, how to sideload apps from other sources, and how to force apps to stop when they misbehave.

EVALUATING PERMISSIONS WHEN INSTALLING APPS

As I'm sure you know, the main source for apps for Android devices is Google's Play Store. By launching the Play Store app from its icon on your device's Home screen or Apps screen, you can visit the Play Store and browse or search through the hundreds of thousands of apps approved by Google for Android devices.

After you've found the app you want to install, you can install it by tapping the Install button (if the app is free) or the price button (if it is not).

> **✓ TIP** If you have a Samsung device, one of the perks of signing up for a Samsung account is a $10 credit on the Play Store.

The key question during installation is which permissions the app needs. Don't just "click through" this step by tapping the Accept button; instead, read the list of permissions, and make sure they fit the app and what you understand it to do.

There are no hard-and-fast rules for what you should allow and what you should refuse, because everything depends on the app and what it does. For example, a social-media app such as Facebook Messenger (see Figure 5.1) will need access to your contacts and calendar, location, photos, camera and microphone, and so on if it is going to revolutionize your social life, so you would accept the permissions if you wanted to install the app. By contrast, if a spreadsheet app requested the same permissions, you should run for the hills.

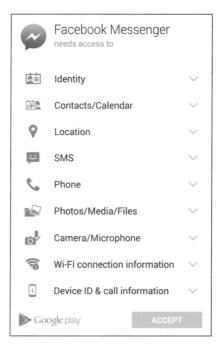

FIGURE 5.1

Verify that the list of permissions requested is appropriate to the app.

After you've tapped the Accept button, the installation proceeds. After the app is installed, you can run it easily by tapping the On button on its screen in Google Play. If you've displayed other screens elsewhere in the meantime, you can also launch the app from its Successfully Installed notification, or simply launch the app from the Apps screen as usual.

GETTING A REFUND ON AN APP

If you buy an app and decide you don't want to keep it—or you realize that you bought the wrong app—you can get a refund for it. Within two hours of making the purchase, return to the app's screen in the Play Store app and tap the Refund button (see Figure 5.2).

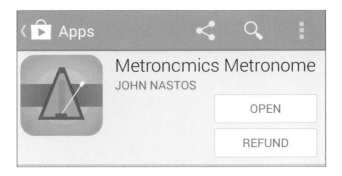

FIGURE 5.2

You can request a refund within two hours by tapping the Refund button on the app's screen in the Play Store app.

> **TIP** After two hours, you may still be able to get a refund. Open your web browser, go to the Play Store (play.google.com), and then sign in. Click the Store button in the left column; then tap or click the Menu button (the three vertical dots) in the row for the purchased item and select Report a Problem. In the Report a Problem dialog box, open the pop-up menu and select I'd Like to Request a Refund. Type an explanation in the text box and click or tap the Submit button.

CONFIGURING YOUR PLAY STORE ACCOUNT

To make the Play Store app work the way you prefer, and to avoid getting unwanted notifications about updates to apps and games, spend a few minutes configuring your Play Store account. Open the Play Store app by tapping its icon on the Home screen or on the Apps screen; then tap the Play Store button in the upper-left corner and tap Settings on the menu panel to display the Settings screen (see Figure 5.3).

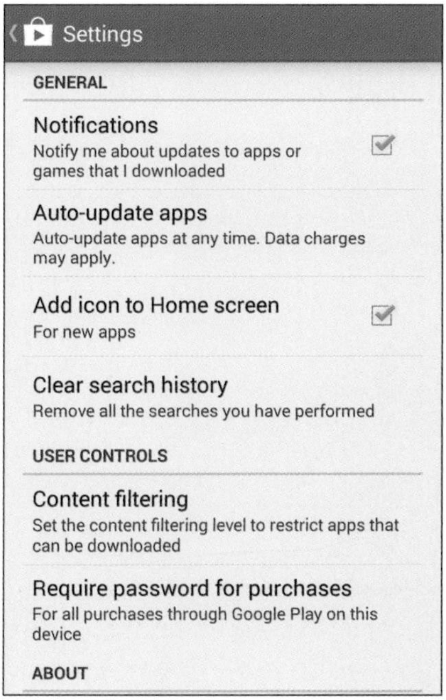

FIGURE 5.3
Use the Settings screen to configure the Play Store app to work your way.

These are the settings you can choose:

- **Notifications.** Uncheck this box (it's checked by default) if you don't want to receive notifications about updates to apps or games you've bought or downloaded.

- **Auto-Update Apps.** Tap this button to display the Auto-Update Apps dialog box (see Figure 5.4), and then tap the appropriate radio button: Do Not Auto-Update Apps; Auto-Update Apps at Any Time. Data Charges May Apply; or Auto-Update Apps over Wi-Fi Only.

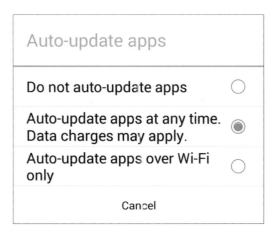

FIGURE 5.4

In the Auto-Update Apps dialog box, choose whether to update apps automatically over cellular or Wi-Fi, over Wi-Fi only, or not at all.

> **TIP** Auto-Update Apps over Wi-Fi Only is usually the best choice in the Auto-Update Apps dialog box. Unless you have an unlimited data plan, it's a mistake to update apps over the cellular connection.

■ **Add Icon to Home Screen.** Check this box if you want each new app to add an icon to the Home screen. Usually, it's best to uncheck this box, run most apps from the Apps screen, and add to the Home screen only icons for those apps you use the most.

■ **Clear Search History.** Tap this button to clear the history of the searches you've performed on the App Store. When you tap this button, no dialog box opens and no confirmation readout appears.

■ **Content Filtering.** Tap this button to display the Allow Apps Rated For dialog box (see Figure 5.5). You can then tap the appropriate radio button: Everyone, Low Maturity, Medium Maturity, High Maturity, or Show All Apps.

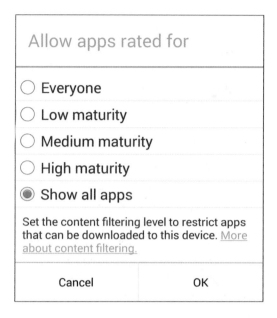

FIGURE 5.5

In the Allow Apps Rated For dialog box, choose the level of content filtering you want to apply for the App Store.

■ **Require Password for Purchases.** Tap this button to display the Require Password dialog box, and then tap the appropriate radio button: For All Purchases Through Google Play on This Device, Every 30 Minutes, or Never.

SIDELOADING APPS

When you want to install an app that isn't available on the Play Store, you can *sideload* it. Sideloading is a manual installation technique in which you get the app in a distribution file called a package file (which uses the .apk file format), copy the package file to your device, and then install the app. You may need to change a security setting in order to enable sideloading.

INSTALLING A FILE MANAGER

To sideload apps, you need to use a file-management app such as ES File Explorer or Astro File Manager. If you already have such an app installed, you're ready to begin. If not, open the Play Store app and install a file-management app. This section shows screens from ES File Explorer, which is free and works well.

GETTING THE PACKAGE FILE FOR THE APP

Next, you need the package file containing the app you want to load. These are the three main ways of getting the package file:

■ **Download the package file from the Internet.** You can find many Android package files in online repositories. Some of the files are shared illegally, and some may contain malware as well as the apps, so you need to be careful.

■ **Get the package file from a company or organization.** If your company or organization provides an Android app, the website may provide it for download, or an administrator may provide it on a physical device such as a USB On-the-Go drive.

■ **Get the package file from another device.** If you already have the app on another device, you can create a package file containing the app.

How you create a package file depends on the file-management app you're using, but here's an example using ES File Explorer:

1. Open ES File Explorer.

2. Navigate to the App Manager folder.

3. Tap and hold the icon for the first app you want to package. ES File Explorer turns on selection mode and checks the check box on the icon.

4. Tap to check the box for any other app you want to package (see Figure 5.6).

FIGURE 5.6

In ES File Explorer, check the box for each app you want to package, and then tap the Backup button.

    5. Tap the Backup button at the bottom of the screen. The message "Backup application successfully" appears briefly.

You can now navigate to the /sdcard/backups/apps/ folder to locate the package file and copy it to the device on which you want to install it. You can copy the package file in any convenient way, such as these:

- **Bluetooth.** Transfer the file using Bluetooth, as discussed in Chapter 4, "Connecting to Networks and Devices."

- **USB On-the-Go.** Connect a USB On-the-Go memory stick to the source device and copy the file to the memory stick. Then connect the memory stick to the destination device and copy the file across.

- **Dropbox or a similar service.** Upload the file to your Dropbox account from the source device and then download it to the destination device.

- **Email.** If the file is small enough to go through email servers, you can simply send the file to an account that's set up on the destination device.

> **TIP**   If you need an easier way to transfer a file from one Android
> device to another, install the app called File Beam (Touch to Send) written by
> Mohammad Abu-Garbeyyeh. This app enables you to transfer pretty much any
> file type, including .apk files, through Near Field Communication (NFC). You select
> the file in an app such as ES File Explorer, give the Share command, and then tap
> Beam File in the Share Via dialog box. Your device then prompts you to bring the
> devices back to back so that the NFC chips identify each other. You then tap the
> Touch to Beam prompt, and your device sends the file.

SETTING ANDROID TO ALLOW APPS FROM UNKNOWN SOURCES

Android has a security mechanism that prevents you from installing apps from
what it calls "unknown sources"—in other words, from anywhere other than the
Play Store. Follow these steps to allow yourself to sideload apps:

1. Open the Settings app.

2. Tap the Security button to display the Security screen. On some devices,
   you'll need to use a different screen, such as Security & Screen Lock.

3. In the Device Administration section, check the Unknown Sources box. A
   warning dialog box opens (see Figure 5.7).

4. Tap the OK button.

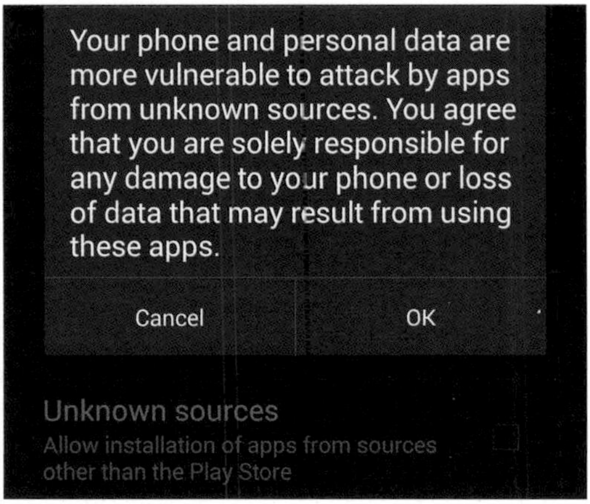

FIGURE 5.7

When you check the Unknown Sources check box, Android warns you that apps may attack your device and data.

SIDELOADING THE APP

You can now sideload the app on your device. To start the installation, tap the package file to open it. For example, if you have copied the file to a folder, open your file-management app to that folder and tap the file. If you have received the app attached to an email message, tap the attachment file in the email app.

Android displays a screen showing the app's name at the top. The Device Access list shows the permissions that the app requires (see Figure 5.8).

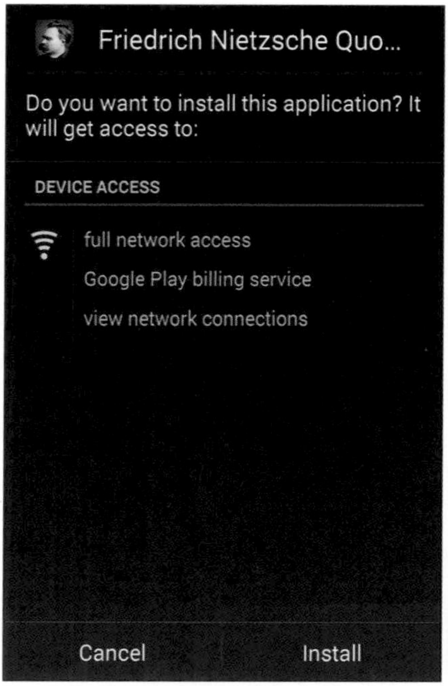

FIGURE 5.8

When sideloading an app, be sure to review the permissions in the Device Access list before tapping the Install button.

Review the permissions and tap the Install button if you want to proceed. When the installation is complete, you can run the app from the Apps screen.

RUNNING APPS

After installing an app, you can run it from the Apps screen like any other app. If you will need to run the app frequently, create a shortcut for it on the Home screen.

If you have a keyboard attached, you can run apps by using the keyboard shortcuts shown in Table 5.1.

Table 5.1   Keyboard Shortcuts for Running Apps

Keyboard Shortcut	Opens This App
Search+B	Default browser (for example, Chrome)
Search+C	Contacts
Search+E	Email app
Search+G	Gmail
Search+I	Calendar
Search+M	Maps
Search+P	Music
Search+S	Messages
Search+Y	YouTube

> **TIP**   If you need to prevent other people who use your device from running particular apps or using certain features on it, try the AppLock app. This app enables you to choose which items to lock, so if you share your device with other people, you can prevent them from using apps and features without entering the AppLock password.

WORKING WITH THE RECENT APPS SCREEN

Android displays each app full screen, so you can work with only one app at a time. However, you can quickly switch from one app to another by using the Recent Apps screen. This screen also enables you to close an app or display its App Info screen.

> **NOTE** Some skins include the ability to display multiple windows at the same time. For example, Samsung's TouchWiz skin includes the Multi-Window feature, which works on both phones and tablets. Because of the amount of screen real estate involved, multiple windows tend to be more useful on tablets than on phones.

SWITCHING APPS WITH THE RECENT APPS SCREEN

To switch apps, tap the Recent Apps button. The Recent Apps screen appears (see Figure 5.9), showing a list of the apps that are running. The most recent apps are the ones at the bottom of the list, which is the part of the list that appears on the screen at first. Swipe or drag down to scroll the list so that you see other apps.

When you find the app you want to display, tap its button.

FIGURE 5.9

From the Recent Apps screen, you can tap the app you want to view, remove an app from the list, or display the App Info screen for an app.

CLOSING AN APP FROM THE RECENT APPS SCREEN

You can close an app from the Recent Apps screen by swiping it off the list to the left or to the right, whichever you find more convenient.

Alternatively, tap and hold the app's button to display the pop-up menu, and then tap Remove from List on the menu.

OPENING THE APP INFO SCREEN FOR AN APP

When you need to force an app to stop, or you need to uninstall an app, you use the App Info screen for that app. You can display the App Info screen in two easy ways:

- **Running app.** If the app is running, tap the Recent Apps button to display the Recent Apps screen. Tap and hold the app's button to display the pop-up menu, and then tap App Info.

- **Any app.** Open the Settings app, tap the Apps button to display the Apps screen, and then tap the button for the app.

FORCING AN APP TO STOP

If an app stops responding to the touchscreen, you can force it to stop. To do so, display the App Info screen for the app and then tap the Force Stop button. In the Force Stop? dialog box that opens (see Figure 5.10), tap the OK button.

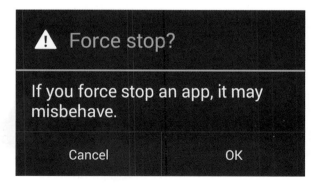

FIGURE 5.10

Tap the OK button in the Force Stop? dialog box to stop an app.

CLEARING AN APP'S CACHE, DATA, OR DEFAULTS

If an app starts acting oddly, you may need to clear its cache or its data. If you have set it to be the default app for a particular action or file type, you can clear its defaults when you need to use another app for those purposes.

You can take all these actions from the App Info screen for an app:

- **Clear Data.** Tap this button, and then tap the OK button in the Delete App Data? dialog box that opens to delete all the app's data, including any accounts you have set up in the app.

- **Clear Cache.** Tap this button to delete all the data that the app has cached. You'd normally want to do this if the cached data appears to have become corrupted and is making the app unstable or if you suspect the cache of containing sensitive data that you want to get rid of.

- **Clear Defaults.** Tap this button to clear any default settings associated with the app. For example, if you've installed a Home screen launcher and made it the default, tapping the Clear Defaults button stops the launcher from running when you press the Home button. Instead, you can choose the launcher you want, and you can decide whether to make it the new default.

> **TIP** If you need to clear the cached data from all your apps, you don't need to go through them one by one. Instead, open the Settings app, tap the Storage button, and then tap the Cached Data button. In the Clear Cached Data? dialog box, tap the OK button, and Android wipes out all the data that apps have cached.

UNINSTALLING APPS

When you no longer need an app, you can uninstall it. Here's how:

1. Open the App Info screen for the app.
2. Tap the Uninstall button. A confirmation dialog box opens, with its title bar showing the app's name (see Figure 5.11).

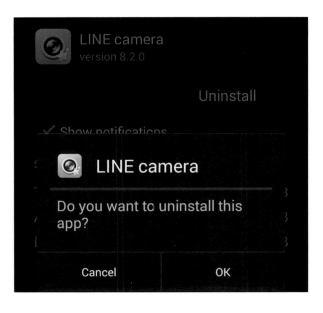

FIGURE 5.11
To uninstall an app, tap the Uninstall button on the App Info screen, and then tap the OK button in the confirmation dialog box.

3. Tap the OK button.

> **TIP** After uninstalling an app, you can reinstall it easily from the My Apps list in the Play Store app.

> **NOTE** You can't uninstall the apps built into Android. Instead, you can tap the Disable button on the App Info screen for the app. In the Disable Built-In App? dialog box that opens, tap the OK button. If you need to enable the app again, tap the Enable button that then appears on the App Info screen.

REBOOTING INTO SAFE MODE

If your device becomes unstable and crashes when you restart it, you can boot into Safe mode to prevent third-party apps from loading.

Here's how to reboot into Safe mode:

1. Press and hold the Power button until the Power Off dialog box opens.

2. Tap and hold the Power Off button until the Reboot to Safe Mode dialog box opens (see Figure 5.13).

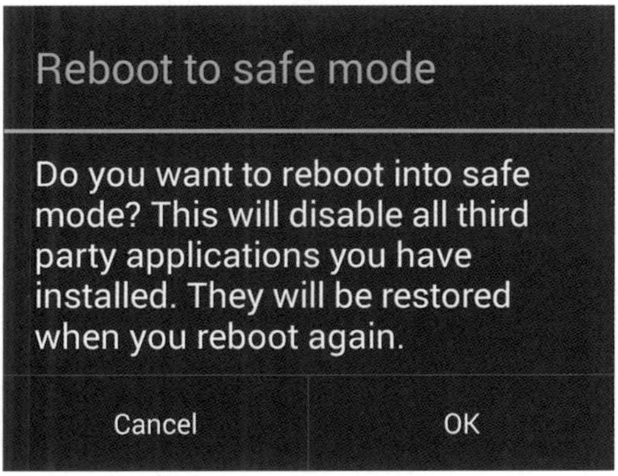

Reboot to safe mode

Do you want to reboot into safe mode? This will disable all third party applications you have installed. They will be restored when you reboot again.

Cancel   OK

FIGURE 5.12

You can reboot into Safe mode to disable third-party apps that may be making your device unstable.

3. Tap the OK button.

> ✓ **TIP** If the method for rebooting into Safe mode doesn't work for your device, turn it off and then hold down the Volume Up button while you restart it.

After your device restarts, the words "Safe mode" appear in the lower-left corner of the screen so you can't forget Safe mode is on. You can then uninstall apps as needed.

To leave Safe mode, power your device off as normal, and then power it back on.

RESETTING APP PREFERENCES

When you need to return the settings on all your apps to their default state, you can reset your device's app preferences. Normally, you'd do this either if configuration changes you've made have rendered your device unstable and you can't work out which change caused the problem or if you want to be able to choose your default apps for particular tasks again.

Here's how to reset app preferences:

1. Open the Settings app.

2. Tap the Apps button to display the Apps screen.

3. Tap the Menu button and then tap Reset App Preferences on the menu. The Reset App Preferences? dialog box opens (see Figure 5.13).

4. Tap the Reset Apps button.

Reset app preferences?

This will reset all preferences for:

· Disabled apps
· Disabled app notifications
· Default applications for actions
· Background data restrictions for apps
· Any permission restrictions

You will not lose any app data.

Cancel   Reset apps

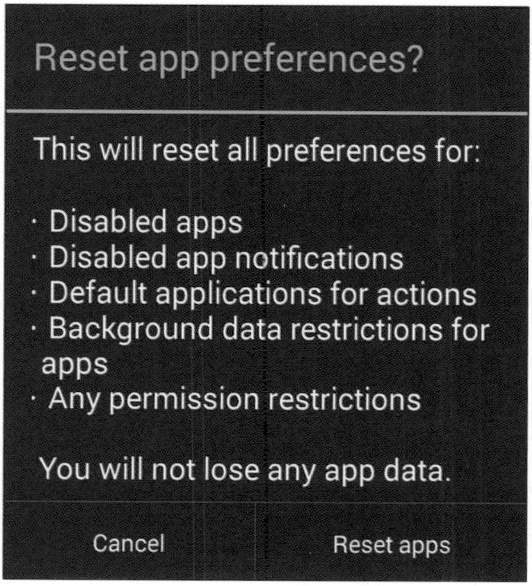

FIGURE 5.13

Tap the Reset Apps button in the Reset App Preferences? dialog box to reset the preferences for all the apps on your device.

Should You Use a Task-Killer App?

As you know, your device uses random access memory (RAM) to store the apps you're running. Your device has a fixed amount of RAM, typically ranging from 1GB for a low-end device to 3GB for a powerhouse. The more RAM, the more apps you can run at once.

You can find task-killer apps for Android—apps that enable you to kill (in other words, close) apps that are running in the background. The idea is to reclaim memory by removing apps from it, making more memory available to the apps you're actually using.

Killing apps like this makes sense on the face of it, but it's seldom if ever necessary. Android is pretty smart about managing memory and is designed to keep apps running in the background. When you display the Home screen or jump to another app, Android pauses the app you've just left unless it's doing something that needs to continue, such as playing music or downloading the Library of Congress. Android keeps the app in memory, so your device can display the app almost instantly when you go back to it.

If you use a task killer to close the app, you do free up some memory. But if the app interprets its killing as an error having occurred, the app may restart automatically, taking up memory again and also consuming processor cycles to load.

The other point to bear in mind is that Android is designed to use memory efficiently. This means using as much of the memory as possible as much of the time, not trying to keep memory free for use in the future. So if you look at a breakdown of the memory your apps are using, you'll probably see that the memory is full. That's not a problem; it's how it should be.

A task-killer app can be useful if an app keeps crashing, but normally you can close such an app using Android's regular tools, as discussed earlier in this chapter. You should then remove the problem app from your device.

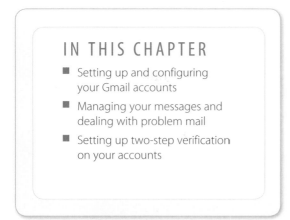

IN THIS CHAPTER

- Setting up and configuring your Gmail accounts
- Managing your messages and dealing with problem mail
- Setting up two-step verification on your accounts

TAKING GMAIL TO THE PRO LEVEL

Your Android device gives you access to Gmail everywhere you go, so chances are you'll want to maximize your usage of Gmail. Your first move in this chapter is to get all your Gmail accounts set up on your device. Your second move is to configure all those accounts to work the way you prefer and to fully exploit the features that Gmail offers.

After that, you'll put those features into use triaging and reading your messages, writing messages and managing your mail, and dealing with problem mail and problem senders. You'll also learn how to search for messages using advanced search operators and how to set up 2-Step Verification to protect your Gmail account.

SETTING UP YOUR OTHER GMAIL ACCOUNTS

Normally, you'll have set up your primary Gmail account while setting up your device for the first time. Now is the time to set up any other Gmail accounts you have.

Here's how to add a Gmail account to your device:

1. Open the Settings app from the Quick Settings panel or the Apps screen.

TIP You can also get to the Settings app from within the Gmail app, but doing so takes longer and is barely worthwhile. Open the menu panel and tap Settings to display the Settings screen. Then tap the Menu button there, tap Manage Google Accounts, and then tap the Continue button in the dialog box that opens.

2. Tap the Add Account button to display the Add an Account screen.
3. Tap the Google button to display the Add a Google Account screen.
4. Tap the Existing button to display the Sign In screen.
5. Type your email address and password, tap the Next button, and then tap the OK button in the confirmation dialog box.

TIP When you type your email address, you can omit the "@gmail.com" part of the address. Settings fills that in for you automatically.

6. On the Google Services screen, uncheck the Keep Me Up to Date with News and Offers from Google Play box unless you really want to receive these messages.
7. On the Set Up Payment Info screen, tap the Add Credit or Debit Card radio button or the Redeem radio button and tap the Continue button if you want to set up a means of payment now. Otherwise, tap the Skip button.
8. On the Account Sign-In Successful screen (see Figure 6.1), tap to uncheck the box for any item you don't want to sync.
9. Tap the Next button to make Settings finish setting up the account. The main Settings screen then appears.

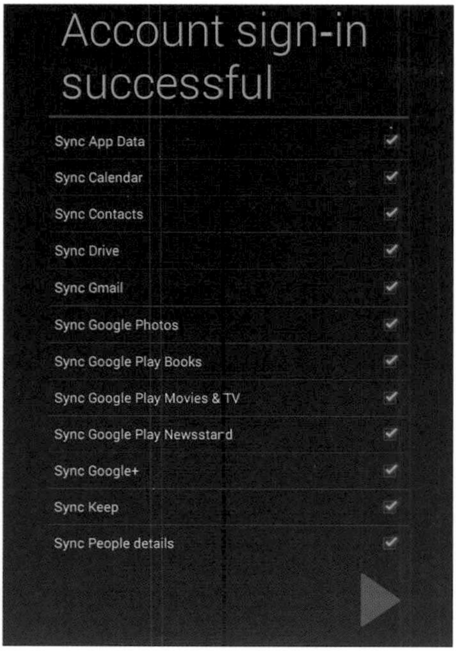

FIGURE 6.1

When setting up a Gmail account, choose which items to sync to your device.

CONFIGURING YOUR GMAIL ACCOUNTS TO WORK YOUR WAY

The Gmail app provides a wide variety of settings that you can configure to make your Gmail accounts work the way you prefer. To get started with configuration, open the menu panel and tap the Settings button to display the Settings screen. As you can see in Figure 6.2, this screen contains a General Settings button and a button for each of your Gmail accounts, enabling you to configure each of them separately.

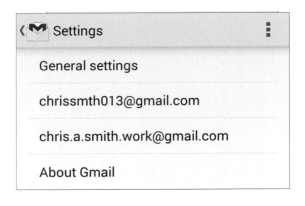

FIGURE 6.2

The Settings screen gives you access to general settings and to each of your Gmail accounts.

CHOOSING GENERAL SETTINGS

Normally, you'll want to start by tapping the General Settings button to display the General Settings screen (see Figure 6.3) so that you can choose options for how the Gmail app works overall.

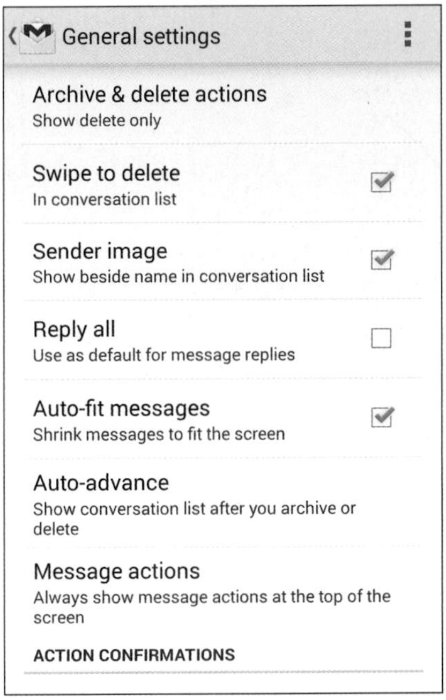

FIGURE 6.3

The General Settings screen enables you to choose Gmail-wide settings such as Archive & Delete, Auto-Advance, and Action Confirmations.

CONTROLLING ARCHIVING AND DELETION

Gmail gives you all the space you need to keep all your messages indefinitely and encourages you to archive your old messages instead of deleting them. Some people think keeping all their old messages is a good idea, while others prefer to keep only important messages. Depending on which you prefer, you can set the Gmail app to show only the archive action, only the delete action, or both the archive and delete actions.

To choose which actions appear, tap Archive & Delete Actions, and then tap the appropriate radio button in the Archive & Delete Actions dialog box: Show Archive Only, Show Delete Only, or Show Archive & Delete.

The second setting on the General Settings screen changes depending on your choice for the Archive & Delete Actions setting: If you select the Show Archive Only radio button or the Show Archive & Delete radio button, the Swipe to Archive check box appears. If you select the Show Delete Only radio button, the Swipe to Delete check box appears.

Check this box if you want to be able to archive messages—or delete messages, if you chose Show Delete Only—by swiping them off the conversation list. This action is usually helpful unless you find yourself performing it by accident—for example, when being jostled on public transit.

CHOOSING SENDER IMAGE, REPLY ALL, AND AUTO-FIT MESSAGES SETTINGS

Check the Sender Image box if you want the sender image to appear to the left of the sender's name in the conversation list. The sender image shows the sender's photo if it's available in your contacts; otherwise, it displays the first letter of the sender's name. You can tap the sender image to select a message quickly.

Check the Reply All box if you want to use Reply All as the default action for replying to messages that have multiple recipients.

> **! CAUTION** Check the Reply All box only if you're required to include all recipients in your replies. Some companies and organizations require this. Otherwise, use Reply All manually and sparingly to help keep down unnecessary emails.

Check the Auto-Fit Messages box if you want the Gmail app to automatically shrink messages to fit on your device's screen. This setting is usually helpful unless you find it makes the messages too small to read.

CONFIGURING AUTO-ADVANCE

The Auto-Advance feature enables you to control what the Gmail app displays next when you deal with a message by archiving or deleting it. Your choices are to display the next newer item, display the next older item, or return to the conversation list so that you can pick the next item you want to deal with. What to choose here depends on the messages you receive and the way you prefer to work with them.

Tap the Auto-Advance button to display the Advance To dialog box, and then tap the Newer radio button, the Older radio button, or the Conversation List radio button, depending on which you want.

CHOOSING WHETHER TO SHOW MESSAGE ACTIONS

On a phone, your next choice is whether to make the message action buttons appear at the top of the screen even when you scroll down the message. The message action buttons are the star button, Reply button, and message Menu button that appear at the top of the message. These buttons always appear at first, but you can choose to keep displaying them always, only when your device is in portrait orientation, or not display them once you scroll down.

To control when the message action buttons appear, tap the Message Actions button, and then tap the Always Show radio button, the Only Show in Portrait radio button, or the Don't Show radio button.

CHOOSING ACTION CONFIRMATIONS

In the Action Confirmations section of the General Settings screen, you can check or uncheck the Confirm Before Deleting box, the Confirm Before Archiving box, or the Confirm Before Sending box to control which actions the Gmail app confirms and which it doesn't.

> **TIP** Action confirmations can be useful if you use your device in a moving or busy environment, such as on public transit. If you're stationary and have a sure touch, you may prefer to turn confirmations off.

After you finish on the General Settings screen, tap the Back button to return to the Settings screen.

CONFIGURING ACCOUNT-SPECIFIC SETTINGS

Apart from the General settings, Gmail's remaining settings are account-specific, so you can set them differently for your various accounts if you need to.

To start configuring account-specific settings, tap the button for one of your accounts on the Settings screen. Figure 6.4 shows an account settings screen on a phone.

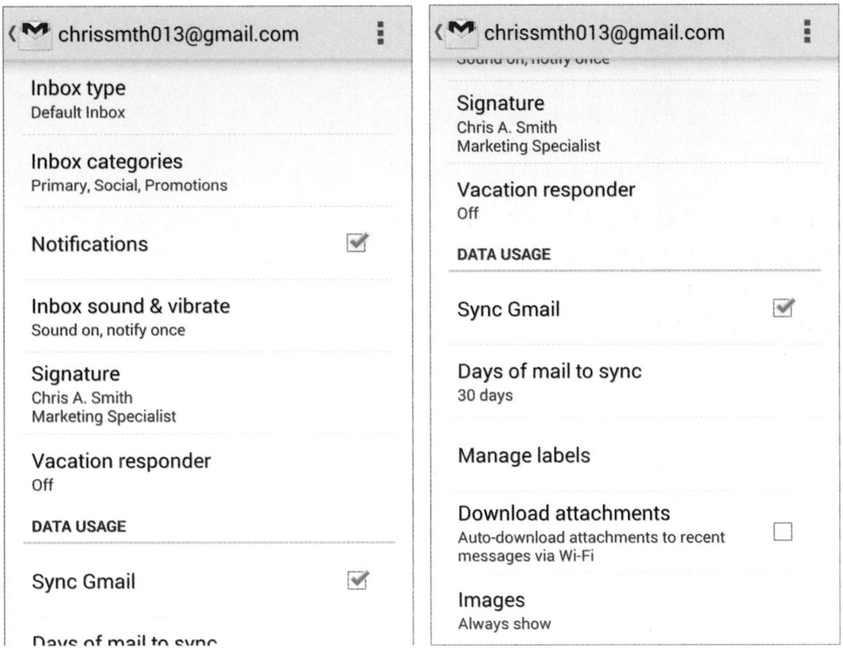

FIGURE 6.4

The account-specific settings screen enables you to configure your Inbox, notifications, sync options, labels, and more.

CONFIGURING YOUR INBOX

Your first choice on an account settings screen is the Inbox type. You can configure it either as a Default Inbox or as a Priority Inbox. Here's what those terms mean:

- **Default Inbox.** A Default Inbox gives you a choice of categories into which you can have it organize your messages. Table 6.1 explains the categories. The Primary category always appears, but you can choose which of the other categories to display.

■ **Priority Inbox.** A Priority Inbox gives you a way to separate your most important messages from the rest. Gmail assesses your incoming messages, decides which are important, and places those in the Priority Inbox.

> 📝 **NOTE** You can train Gmail to recognize important messages for your Priority Inbox. You'll learn how to do this later in this chapter.

Table 6.1   Categories in the Default Inbox

Category	Receives These Messages
Primary	Personal messages, such as from your family and friends; messages that don't fit the other categories you're using; and messages you mark with a star
Social	Messages from your social networks, gaming networks, media-sharing sites, and the like
Promotions	Marketing messages, such as messages containing special offers
Updates	Receipts, bills, statements, and updates
Forums	Messages from mailing lists or online groups to which you subscribe

To choose which categories to use in your Default Inbox, tap the Inbox Categories button and then check or uncheck the boxes on the Inbox Categories screen (see Figure 6.5).

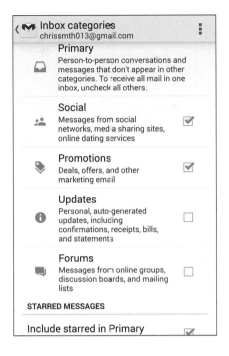

FIGURE 6.5

On the Inbox Categories screen, check the box for each category you want to use in your Default Inbox.

> **NOTE**   By default, the Gmail app places any message you mark with a star in your Primary category. This behavior is normally helpful, but if you don't want it, uncheck the Include Starred in Primary box on the Inbox Categories screen.

If you want to receive notifications when messages arrive in your Inbox, check the Notifications box. You can then tap the Inbox Sound & Vibrate button or the Priority Inbox Sound & Vibrate button and choose options on the Sync & Notify screen (see Figure 6.6). These are the options:

- **Sync Messages.** Tap this button to display the Priority Inbox dialog box (for a Priority Inbox) or the Primary dialog box (for a Default Inbox). You can then tap the Sync: None radio button, the Sync: Last *NN* Days radio button (which shows the number of days you choose in the Days of Mail to Sync dialog box, discussed later in this chapter), or the Sync: All radio button.

> **NOTE** If your device doesn't have a vibration motor, you'll see the Priority Inbox Sound button instead of the Priority Sound & Vibrate button. Similarly, you'll see the Inbox Sound button instead of the Inbox Sound & Vibrate button.

- **Label Notifications.** Check this box to receive notifications for messages with certain labels. This is the overall control for receiving label notifications. You then specify the labels for which to receive notifications as discussed in the section "Managing Your Labels," later in this chapter.

- **Sound.** Tap this button, tap the ringtone you want to use for the notification, and then tap the OK button.

- **Vibrate.** Check this box if you want your device to vibrate to notify you of messages. This box appears only if your device has a vibration motor.

- **Notify for Every Message.** Check this box if you want Gmail to notify you for every incoming message, not just for the first message of a batch.

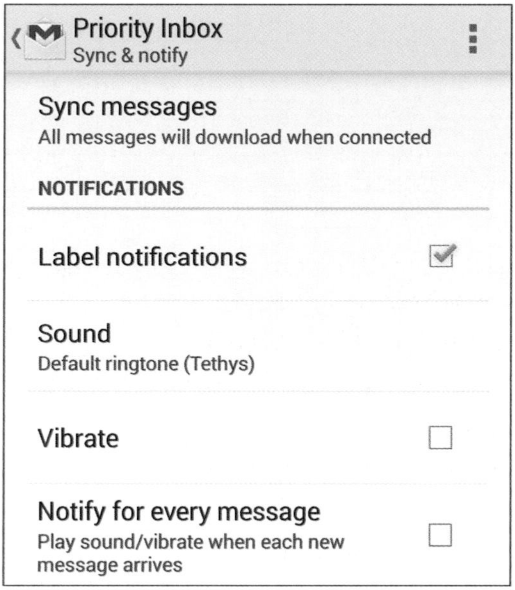

FIGURE 6.6

On the Sync & Notify screen, choose which notifications to receive. You can also choose which messages to sync.

SAVING TIME WITH SIGNATURES

If you need to sign the messages you send from this account in a consistent way, you can create a signature for the account. A signature is text that the Gmail app automatically inserts in each outgoing message—each new message, each reply, and each forwarded message you create.

Tap the Signature button on the account settings screen to open the Signature dialog box. Type in the text—you can create multiple lines by tapping the Enter key—and then tap the OK button.

> **TIP** At this writing, the Gmail app enables you to have only one signature per account. It automatically inserts the signature in every outgoing message; you can't create a signature and turn it off temporarily. If you need more flexibility with signatures, create text shortcuts for the lines you want to have available, such as your position and company or your contact data, and use them to insert custom signatures as needed in your messages.

CREATING A VACATION RESPONDER

The Gmail app includes a built-in Vacation Responder feature that you can set up to respond automatically to incoming messages. Here's how to set up Vacation Responder:

1. Tap the Vacation Responder button on the account settings screen to display the Vacation Responder screen (see Figure 6.7).
2. Tap the Starts button and choose the date.
3. Tap the Ends (Optional) button and choose the end date if necessary.
4. Tap the Subject field and type the message subject.
5. Tap the body text field and type the body text.
6. Check the Send Only to My Contacts box if you want to send the message only to your contacts. Checking this box is often a good idea because it prevents sending vacation messages to promotional messages (unless you've added such senders to your contacts).
7. Set the Vacation Responder switch to the On position.
8. Tap the Done button.

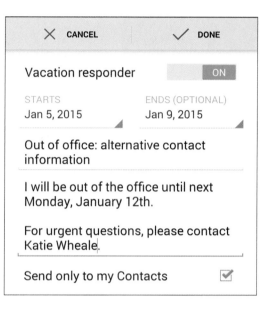

FIGURE 6.7

Set up the Vacation Responder to reply automatically to incoming messages.

CHOOSING WHICH MESSAGES TO SYNC

In the Data Usage section of the account settings screen, choose which messages to sync. Normally, you'll want to check the Sync Gmail box to sync your Gmail messages with the Gmail app on your device. Then tap the Days of Mail to Sync button and use the dial in the Days of Mail to Sync dialog box to set the number of days. Tap the OK button to apply your choice.

MANAGING YOUR LABELS

As you'll know if you've used the service for any length of time, Gmail uses labels instead of folders. So instead of moving a message to a folder for storage, you simply mark it with one or more labels. You can then browse or search by label to find the messages you need.

TIP The advantage of labels over folders is that you can apply multiple labels to an individual message, enabling yourself to locate the message by browsing or searching any of those labels. By contrast, with folders, you can put a message in only a single folder; to get a message into multiple folders, you need to make an extra copy of the message for each folder beyond the first.

To use labels effectively, you'll need to make sure each account has the labels it needs. At this writing, you can't create labels by using the Gmail app on your Android device. Instead, open a browser, log in to your Gmail account, and then create the labels. You can do this on your Android device, but if you have a computer handy, you might want to use that instead.

Here's how to create a new label using your browser:

1. Click or tap the Create New Label link to open the New Label dialog box (see Figure 6.8).

2. Type the name in the Please Enter a New Label Name box.

3. To nest the label under another label (like a subfolder), click or tap the pop-up menu, and then click or tap the existing label. The browser checks the Nest Label Under box automatically, so you don't need to check it manually.

4. Click or tap the Create button.

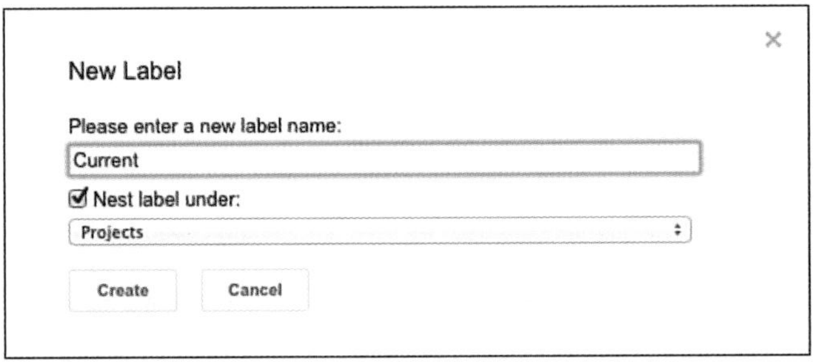

FIGURE 6.8
Use your browser to create a new label in your Gmail account. You can choose to nest the label under an existing label.

After you've customized your list of labels, you can choose notification settings for each label using the Gmail app on your Android device like this:

1. On the account settings screen, make sure you've checked the Notifications check box. If this check box is unchecked, notifications are off for the account as a whole, so you can't set notifications for individual labels.

2. Tap the Manage Labels button to display the Label Settings screen (see Figure 6.9).

3. Tap the label you want to configure. The settings screen for the label appears, and you can choose settings as explained in the section "Configuring Your Inbox," earlier in this chapter.

FIGURE 6.9

On the Label Settings screen, tap the label for which you want to configure notifications.

TRIAGING AND READING YOUR MESSAGES

Now that you've configured your Gmail accounts to your satisfaction, you're ready to deal with your messages quickly and smoothly.

In this section, you learn how to navigate among your accounts and labels, work in the conversation list, and read your messages.

NAVIGATING AMONG YOUR ACCOUNTS AND LABELS

To navigate among your Gmail accounts and your labels, tap the menu button in the upper-left corner of the screen, or tap the Gmail logo or the current mailbox name. In the menu panel that opens, tap the account, the Inbox, or the label that you want to view.

WORKING IN THE CONVERSATION LIST

The conversation list (see Figure 6.10) presents a list of your messages with the newest at the top. You can refresh the conversation list by tapping the conversation list, pulling down the screen a little way, and then releasing the list. Alternatively, tap the Menu button and then tap Refresh on the menu.

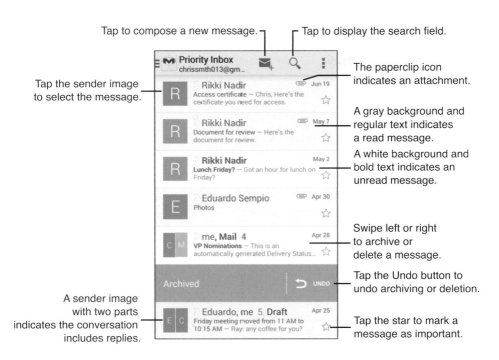

FIGURE 6.10

The conversation list provides an easy-to-navigate list of your messages and conversations.

Each unread message appears with its sender name and subject in boldface against a white background. Each unread message has a gray background, and the sender name and subject appear in regular (nonbold) font.

> **TIP**   The yellow arrow to the left of a message's sender indicates that Google considers the message important. The reason may be that you are the only recipient or that you have marked similar messages as important.

The sender image (or sender initial) square to the left of the sender name gives you a quick way of seeing who the message is from. If the conversation includes replies, the sender image is divided into two rectangles that show the first initial of the last two senders.

> **☑ TIP** If you turn off sender images, you can select a message by tapping and holding it. Doing so turns on Selection mode, and you can then tap other messages to select them.

Tap the sender image square to select the message; the square changes to display a white check mark on a gray square. Selecting a message puts the conversation list into Selection mode, and three buttons for manipulating the selected messages appear at the top of the screen (see Figure 6.11):

- **Archive.** Tap this button to archive the selected messages.
- **Mark as Unread.** Tap this button to mark the selected messages as unread.
- **Move To.** Tap this button to display the Move To dialog box, in which you can tap the label to which you want to move the selected messages.

Also in the conversation list, you can swipe a conversation left or right off the list to archive or delete it, depending on the Archive & Delete Actions setting you chose on the General Settings screen. The Archived bar or Deleted bar appears, confirming the action you've taken with the conversation. You can tap the Undo button at the right end of the Archived bar or Deleted bar if you've gotten rid of the wrong message.

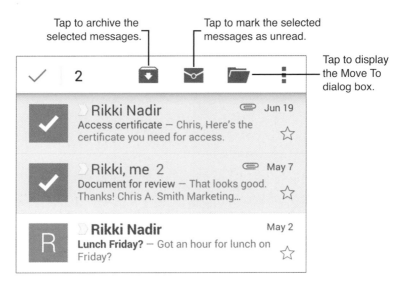

FIGURE 6.11
Use the three buttons at the top of the conversation list to archive the selected messages, mark them as unread, or move them to a folder.

TIP If Gmail identifies an unimportant message as important, select the message, tap the Menu button, and then tap Mark Not Important on the menu. If you do this consistently, Gmail gradually learns which messages are important to you and which are not.

READING YOUR MESSAGES

Tap a message in the conversation list to open it for reading. You can then use the controls shown in Figure 6.12 to take actions with the message:

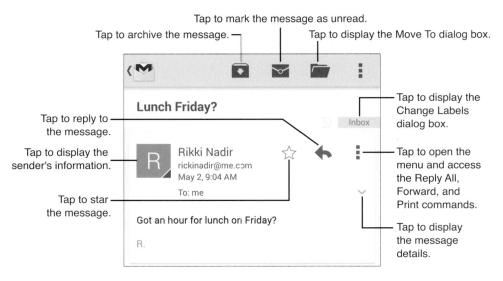

FIGURE 6.12

After opening a message for reading, you can reply to it, forward it, archive it, or move it.

- **Reply to the message.** Tap the Reply button.
- **Reply to all recipients of the message.** Tap the message's Menu button—the Menu button to the right of the sender's name—and then tap Reply All on the menu.
- **Forward the message.** Tap the message's Menu button and then tap Forward on the menu.
- **Print the message.** Tap the message's Menu button and then tap Print on the menu.

- **Delete the message.** Tap the main Menu button and then tap Delete on the menu.
- **Star the message.** Tap the star icon to the left of the Reply button.
- **View the message details.** Tap the Message Details button (the downward arrow below the message's Menu button) to display the From field, To field, and Date field.
- **Change the message's labels.** Tap the current label button above the message's Menu button to display the Change Labels dialog box, check the box for each label you want to apply, and then tap the OK button.
- **Display the sender's information.** If a black triangle appears at the lower-right corner of the sender image, tap the image to display the sender's information. If the triangle doesn't appear, the information isn't available.
- **Archive the message.** Tap the Archive button on the toolbar.
- **Mark the message as unread.** Tap the Mark as Unread button on the toolbar.
- **Move the message to a label.** Tap the Move To button on the toolbar to display the Move To dialog box, and then tap the destination label.

> **NOTE** If the message is part of a conversation, you can tap the Show Quoted Text button to display the quoted text and tap the resulting Hide Quoted Text button to hide it. Tap the Older Messages button to view older messages in the conversation.

WRITING AND SENDING MESSAGES

Gmail makes writing and sending messages easy: Tap the Compose button (the envelope icon with a + sign at its lower-right corner) at the top of the conversation list; fill in the recipient, subject, and message body on the Compose screen; and then tap the Send button, the arrow button to the left of the menu button.

You can also change the account, add Cc or Bcc recipients, and attach files:

- **Choose the account.** If you have set up multiple Gmail accounts, tap the Account pop-up menu and then tap the account to use.

> **NOTE** The Gmail app selects the account you were viewing as the sending account for the message.

- **Add Cc or Bcc recipients.** On a phone, tap the Menu button and then tap the Add Cc/Bcc button on the menu to display the Cc and Bcc fields. On a tablet, tap the +CC/BCC button to the right of the To field to display them. Tap the Cc field or the Bcc field as appropriate, start typing the contact's name or email address, and then tap the contact in the pop-up list of matches.

- **Attach a file to the message.** Tap the Menu button and then tap Attach File on the menu. Use the Open From panel to select the source of the file, such as Images or Videos, and then tap the file to select it. The file appears as a large button showing the file's name. If you need to remove the file, tap the X button.

> **TIP** If you want to label a message you're composing, save it as a draft by either tapping the Menu button and then tapping Save Draft on the menu or by tapping the Back button twice. You can then open the Drafts folder, label the message, and then reopen it so that you can send it.

> **NOTE** If you decide not to send the message, you can discard it. To discard the message, tap the Menu button and then tap Discard on the menu.

LABELING AND ARCHIVING YOUR MESSAGES

To keep your messages in order, you will normally want to label them and archive them.

- **Labeling.** Labeling assigns one or more labels, such as Personal or Work, to the message, enabling you to find it later by browsing through those labels or searching with them. When you label a message, it remains in the same folder, such as your Inbox.
- **Archiving.** Archiving moves a message out of your Inbox.

Between them, labeling and archiving have an effect similar to moving a message to a folder in other email systems. But because you can label and archive messages separately, Gmail gives you more flexibility. The Move To command and Move To dialog box enable you to label and move a message in a single move.

You can label either the message you have open for reading or selected messages in the conversation list by tapping the Menu button and then tapping Change Labels on the menu. The Change Labels dialog box opens (see Figure 6.13), and you can check the boxes for the labels you want to apply, and then tap the OK button.

TIP You can also open the Change Labels dialog box by tapping a label's button on a message you've opened for reading.

NOTE Gmail uses the Inbox label to determine which messages should appear in the Inbox. Removing the Inbox label from a message moves it out of the Inbox; applying the Inbox label to a message makes it appear in the Inbox.

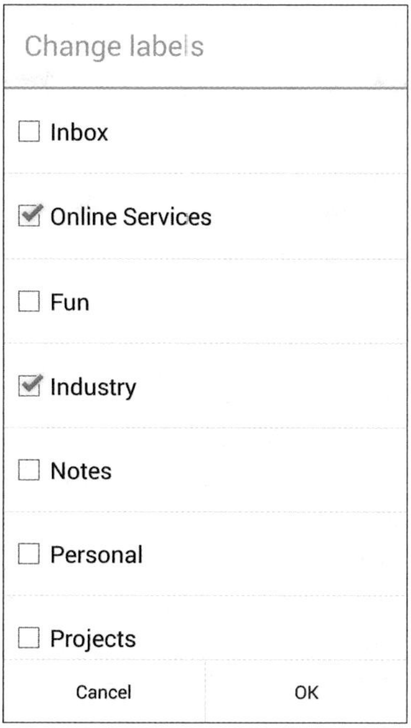

Change labels

☐ Inbox

☑ Online Services

☐ Fun

☑ Industry

☐ Notes

☐ Personal

☐ Projects

Cancel   OK

FIGURE 6.13

Use the Change Labels dialog box to label a message and leave it in its current location.

To archive a message, tap the Archive button at the top of the screen for either a message you have opened for reading or for selected messages in the conversation list.

To label a message and archive it at the same time, tap the Move To button either for the message you have open for reading or the messages you have selected in the conversation list. The Move To dialog box opens (see Figure 6.14), and you can tap the label to which you want to move the message.

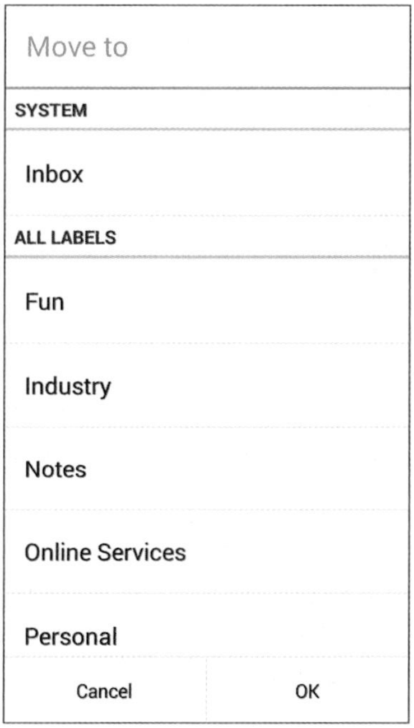

FIGURE 6.14

Use the Move To dialog box to label a message and archive it at the same time.

DEALING WITH PROBLEM MAIL AND PROBLEM SENDERS

If you receive spam or phishing messages, you can report them to Google. With the message either open for reading, or with the message or messages selected in the conversation list, tap the main Menu button and then tap Report Spam or Report Phishing on the menu.

> **TIP** Gmail doesn't give you a way to block specific senders, but you can create filters to put messages from them straight into the Trash. Using a web browser, log in to your Gmail account; if you're using your Android device, you'll need to open the menu and check the Request Desktop Site box. Click or tap the down-arrow button at the right end of the Search box, choose the details in the Filter pane, and then click the Create Filter with This Search button.

> **TIP** For heavier-duty blocking, you can use an e-mail proxy provider that filters your messages for you and permits only those messages that pass your specified criteria to reach you.

SEARCHING FOR MESSAGES

When you need to locate particular messages, you can search for them. You can do a straightforward search using one or more keywords, but you can also use advanced search operators and Boolean operators for more power.

SEARCHING WITH KEYWORDS

To search for messages using keywords, tap the Search icon at the top of the conversation list and type the keywords. If the Gmail app displays a list of suggested matches, tap the appropriate one.

> **TIP** When you use multiple keywords, Gmail search for messages containing them all. For example, if you search for *relocation project*, Gmail searches for messages containing both *relocation* and *project*. To search for an exact phrase, place the keywords in quotation marks—for example, *"relocation project."*

The results list appears, and you can tap the message you want to view.

SEARCHING WITH ADVANCED SEARCH OPERATORS

For more advanced searching, use operators in your searches. Table 6.2 explains the search operators, with examples.

Table 6.2   Advanced Search Operators for Gmail

Search Operator	Meaning	Example
from:	The sender.	from:bill
to:	The recipient.	to:dan@surrealmacs.com
cc:	A Cc recipient.	cc:hr@surrealmacs.com

Search Operator	Meaning	Example
bcc:	A Bcc recipient on messages you have sent.	bcc:hr@surrealmacs.com
subject:	A subject word.	subject:relocation
after: older:	Messages sent or received after the date given.	after:2014/11/11 older:2014/11/11
before: newer:	Messages sent or received before the date given.	before:2015/02/04 from:bill newer:2015/02/20
older_than:	Messages older than the relative date given using days (d), months (m), or years (y).	older_than:6m older_than:1y
newer_than	Messages newer than the relative date given using days (d), months (m), or years (y).	newer_than:7d
label:	The label.	label:money
has:attachment	The message has an attachment.	from:bill has:attachment
filename:	The whole or partial filename of an attachment.	filename:sales.xlsx filename:docx
list:	The mailing list.	list:info@surrealmacs.com
in:	The location.	in:inbox in:trash
in:anywhere	Includes the Spam and Trash folders, which Gmail excludes by default.	from:bill in:anywhere
is:important	Messages that Priority Inbox has marked as important.	from:bill is:important

Search Operator	Meaning	Example
label:important	Messages that Priority Inbox has marked as important.	from:bill label:important
is:starred	The message has a star.	is:starred subject:budget
is:unread	The message status is unread.	is:unread from:bill
is:read	The message status is read.	is:read subject:analysis
has:yellow-star has:red-star has:orange-star has:green-star has:blue-star has:purple-star	The message has a star of the given color.	has:blue-star from:bill
has:red-bang has:yellow-bang	The message has an exclamation point of the given color.	has:yellow-bang
has:orange-guillemet	The message has orange angle-quotes.	has:orange-guillemet
has:green-check	The message has a green check mark.	has:green-check
has:blue-info	The message has a blue info mark.	has:blue-info
has:purple-question	The message has a purple question mark.	has:purple-question
is:chat	The message is a chat message.	is:chat
circle:	Your Google+ circle to which the message's sender belongs.	circle:family subject:Thanksgiving
has:circle	The sender is someone in your Google+ circles.	has:circle subject:park

Search Operator	Meaning	Example
category:	The category that contains the message.	category:social
size:	The minimum messages size in bytes.	size:2000000
larger:	The minimum message size, using abbreviations for numbers (such as M for million bytes).	large:5M
smaller:	The maximum message size, using abbreviations for numbers.	smaller:1M
+	An exact match of the search term.	+result
has:userlabels	The message has user labels applied.	has:userlabels
has:nouserlabels	The message has no user labels applied.	has:nouserlabels
deliveredto:	The message's header contains the address in the Delivered-To line.	deliveredto:info@ surrealmacs.com
rfc822msgid:	The SMTP message ID (found in the message headers).	rfc822msgid: 0059ac168294@ surrealmacs.com

SEARCHING WITH BOOLEAN OPERATORS AND GROUPING

As you saw earlier, when you enter multiple search terms, Gmail searches for messages that contain them all. This is a Boolean AND operator: Searching for *budget spreadsheet 2015* is the equivalent of searching for *budget AND spreadsheet AND 2015*.

You don't need to specify the AND operator, but you can if you want. You can also use the OR operator and the NOT operator:

- **OR.** Use the OR operator to search for one item or another item. For example, *subject:relocation OR subject:planning*.

■ **NOT (–).** Use the NOT operator, represented by the minus sign (–), to specify items you don't want to find. For example, *from:bill –meeting*.

You can use parentheses to group terms together. For example, you can use *subject:(office project)* to messages whose subject lines contain both "office" and "project" (but not necessarily the phrase "office project").

SETTING UP 2-STEP VERIFICATION

To protect your Google account against attackers, you should set up 2-Step Verification for it. This process uses your phone as well as your password to help keep attackers out of your account.

Here's how 2-Step Verification works: Each time you sign in to your Google account using a computer or device on which you haven't signed in before, Google accepts your username and password but then prompts you for a code that it has just sent to your phone. Type in that code, and you can choose whether to authorize that computer or device so that you don't need to enter a code for it again in future.

You can set up 2-Step Verification either using a computer or just your Android device. The following sections explain what to do.

SETTING UP 2-STEP VERIFICATION USING A COMPUTER

If you use a computer as well as your Android device, use the computer to set up 2-Step Verification like this:

1. Open a web browser and go to the Gmail website.
2. Sign in to your Google account by providing your username and password.
3. Click your name or picture in the upper-right corner of the window, and then click Account to display the settings screen for the account.
4. Click the Security tab to display the Security screen.
5. In the Password box, tap the Setup link on the 2-Step Verification line to display the Signing In with 2-Step Verification screen.
6. Tap the Start Setup button.
7. Enter your password, and then click the OK button.
8. On the Set Up Your Phone screen, enter your phone number and select the Text Message (SMS) radio button or the Voice Call radio button, as appropriate.

> **TIP** If you don't know your Android device's phone number by heart, open the Settings app, tap the About Phone button, tap the Status button, and then look at the My Phone Number readout.

9. Tap the Send Code button to send the verification code to your phone (or to receive a phone call).

10. On the Verify Your Phone screen, type in the verification code and click the Verify button.

11. On the Trust This Computer? screen, check or uncheck the Trust This Computer box as needed, and then click the Next button.

> **! CAUTION** Check the Trust This computer box only if this is your own computer or you entirely trust all the other people who use it.

12. On the Confirm screen, click the Confirm button.

Reinforcing Your 2-Step Verification Security

After setting up 2-Step Verification, use the settings on the 2-Step Verification screen to add security mechanisms.

First, go to the Verification Codes tab and click the Add a Phone Number button to add a backup phone in case yours go missing. Then click the Print or Download button in the Backup Codes area to print or download backup codes you can use to get into your account if you have problems with you phone. Backup codes are also useful for travel, when you may have trouble connecting.

Next, click the App-Specific Passwords tab, click the Manage Application-Specific Passwords button, and follow through the process for setting passwords for specific apps, such as Mail apps, that access your Google account.

Last, click the Registered Computers tab and use its controls to configure your list of registered computers. These are computers you can use to manage your account when your phone isn't available, such as when it pits its delicate electronics against gravity or water.

SETTING UP 2-STEP VERIFICATION USING AN ANDROID DEVICE

If you use your Android device on its own, without a computer, you may be able to set up 2-Step Verification directly on the device by using the Google Authenticator app. Open the Play Store app on your device, search for **Google Authenticator**, tap the correct search result, and then install the app. When the installation completes, tap the Open button to open Google Authenticator, and then follow the prompts for choosing the appropriate Google account and setting up 2-Step verification on it.

> ## NOTE
> If Google Authenticator cannot sign you in, it may prompt you to sign in using the web interface instead. Follow the prompts to complete the verification. If Google Authenticator prompts you to continue on a computer instead, do so.

LOGGING IN TO YOUR ACCOUNT WITH 2-STEP VERIFICATION ENABLED

After you enable 2-Step Verification, you need to go through the extra step of verification the first time you log in to your Google account using a computer on which you haven't logged in to your account. Google apps such as Gmail will refuse your password and prompt you to log in using the web-based interface instead.

When you do, the 2-Step Verification dialog box shown in Figure 6.15 appears. The device on which you verified the account receives a text with a six-digit verification code. Type the code, tap the Verify button, and the app will be able to log in.

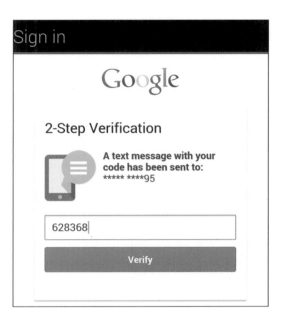

FIGURE 6.15

Type your verification code into the box on the 2-Step Verification screen, and then tap the Verify button.

IN THIS CHAPTER

- Setting up your email accounts
- Sending and receiving messages
- Configuring your accounts to work the way you prefer

7

BECOMING EXPERT WITH THE EMAIL APP

As you read in the preceding chapter, Android includes the Gmail app for connecting to Google's Gmail service. For all other email types, Android provides the Email app.

Using the Email app, you can connect to mail servers running the widely used POP and IMAP protocols as well as to web-based email services (such as Microsoft's Hotmail and Outlook) and to Exchange Server systems.

The Email app is easy to use—after you've set up your accounts in it. Setting up accounts can be tricky, so you'll dig into its details at the beginning of the chapter. You'll then look at how to use the Email app's features to compose, read, and manage your messages. At the end of the chapter, you'll examine how you can configure the general settings and account-specific settings to make the app work the way you prefer.

SETTING UP YOUR NON-GMAIL ACCOUNTS

You can set up an account in the Email app for each non-Gmail account you need to use on your device.

You can set up most accounts using only the email address and password for the account, leaving the Email app's automatic-configuration feature to determine the mail server addresses and security type needed. For other accounts, you may need to know the addresses of the incoming mail server and the outgoing mail server, the security types they use, and whether the outgoing mail server requires you to log in before sending messages.

You should first see if the Email app can set up the account for you. If automatic setup fails, the Email app automatically falls back to manual setup, leaving you to enter the required information for the mail servers.

GATHERING THE INFORMATION NEEDED TO SET UP AN EMAIL ACCOUNT

Before starting to set up your email account, make sure you have the information you need. It's better to have all the information available, and not need all of it when the Email app detects some of the details, than to have to give up partway through and find out the missing pieces of information.

Table 7.1 explains the information you will need and the information you may need, with examples of what each item looks like.

Table 7.1   Information for Setting Up an Email Account

Information	Example	Notes
Email address	csmith@notionalpress.com	
Password	h18Det2!cab0os	The password is case sensitive.
Incoming mail server	imap.notionalpress.com pop.notionalpress.com	The address has periods but no @ sign.
Outgoing mail server	imap.notionalpress.com smtp.notionalpress.com	The address has periods but no @ sign.
Port for incoming mail	110	The port used depends on the mail server type and the security type.

Information	Example	Notes
Security type for incoming mail	SSL/TLS SSL/TLS (Accept All Certificates) STARTTLS STARTTLS (Accept All Certificates)	Most mail servers use SSL/TLS.
Port for outgoing mail	567	The port used depends on the mail server type and the security type.
Security type for outgoing mail	SSL/TLS SSL/TLS (Accept All Certificates) STARTTLS STARTTLS (Accept All Certificates)	Most mail servers use SSL/TLS.

Understanding POP3, IMAP, SMTP, and Exchange

POP3, IMAP, SMTP, and Exchange are four technologies widely used for mail servers. POP3 and IMAP are protocols that email clients (such as the Email app on your Android device) use to communicate with incoming mail servers—the servers from which you receive your messages. SMTP is a protocol used for many outgoing mail servers—the servers that send your messages for you. Exchange is Microsoft's Exchange Server technology for email, scheduling, and calendars.

POP is the acronym for Post Office Protocol, and POP3 is version 3 of Post Office Protocol. IMAP is the acronym for Internet Mail Access Protocol, a newer protocol than POP3. SMTP is the abbreviation for Simple Mail Transfer Protocol, a protocol for sending mail.

The main difference between POP3 and IMAP is that POP3 is mostly designed to download your messages to your email client, removing them from the server, whereas IMAP is designed to enable you to view and manage your messages on the server without downloading it to your email client.

The advantage of IMAP is that, with your messages on the server, you can view and manage them from multiple devices. So if you view a message using your Android device, the message is marked as having been read in your laptop computer's mailbox as well. And if you delete a message on your laptop, it disappears from your Android device's mailbox too.

Your email provider will tell you which account type—POP3, IMAP, or Exchange—to specify when setting up your account. If your email provider gives you the choice between POP3 and IMAP, you'll normally want to choose IMAP for your Android device so that you can access your messages on other computers and devices as well.

Understanding Security Types for Email Accounts

When setting up an email account manually, you need to specify the security type used to secure the connection. Normally, you must choose the right security type to make the email account work at all.

The Email app offers these five security types:

- **None.** This option transmits all data using plain text. You may occasionally need to use this option to check whether an email account is functional. If so, change the security type and password immediately afterward.

- **SSL/TLS.** Secure Sockets Layer (SSL) and Transport Layer Security (TLS) are widely used protocols for securing communications between a computer or device and a server. TLS is based on SSL and is more secure than SSL. SSL and TLS use digital certificates to secure the connection and check that the certificates are valid and issued by a trusted certificate authority (CA). This is the security type you will normally use for an email account.

- **SSL/TLS (Accept All Certificates).** This security type uses SSL and TLS but accepts any digital certificate instead of rejecting certificates that are invalid, out of date, issued by an untrusted certificate authority, or self-signed. (Developers use self-signed certificates for testing code.) You may need to use this security type for some accounts, but accepting all certificates is generally unsafe.

- **STARTTLS.** STARTTLS is a protocol extension that can upgrade an existing insecure connection to a secure connection without changing the port used (as would normally happen). STARTTLS enables servers to make better use of their ports. Despite its name, STARTTLS can use SSL instead of TLS for the secure connection.

- **STARTTLS (Accept All Certificates).** As with SSL/TLS (Accept All Certificates), this security type uses STARTTLS but accepts any digital certificate instead of rejecting certificates that would normally be unacceptable. You may need to use this security type for some accounts or for testing, but accepting all certificates is generally unsafe.

SETTING UP AN EMAIL ACCOUNT

Here's how to set up an account:

1. Open the Email app by tapping its icon on the Apps screen or on a Home screen.

> **NOTE** If you haven't already set up an account in Email, the app displays the first Account Setup screen when you open it.

2. Tap the Menu button and then tap Settings to display the Settings screen (see Figure 7.1).

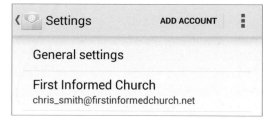

FIGURE 7.1

Tap the Add Account button on the Settings screen to start setting up a new account.

3. Tap the Add Account button. The first Account Setup screen appears (see Figure 7.2).

Account setup

You can set up your account in just a few steps.

csmith@notionalpress.com

• • • • • • • • • • • •

| Manual setup | Next |

FIGURE 7.2

On the first Account Setup screen, you can tap the Next button to try automatic setup or tap the Manual Setup button to retain full control of the configuration.

4. Type or paste your email address in the upper box.

5. Type your password in the lower box.

6. Tap the Next button if you want the Email app to try to set up the account automatically. Otherwise, tap the Manual Setup button to display the second Account Setup screen (see Figure 7.3).

NOTE If automatic setup succeeds, go to step 17. Otherwise, tap the Manual Setup button and continue from step 7.

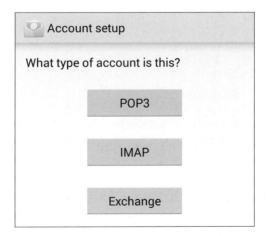

Account setup

What type of account is this?

POP3

IMAP

Exchange

FIGURE 7.3

Specify the account type by tapping the POP3 button, the IMAP button, or the Exchange button on this Account Setup screen.

7. Tap the POP3 button, the IMAP button, or the Exchange button, as appropriate. See the sidebar titled "Understanding POP3, IMAP, SMTP, and Exchange" earlier in this chapter for an explanation of these terms. The next Account Setup screen appears (see Figure 7.4); on a tablet, this screen has the heading Incoming Server Settings.

> **NOTE** The Account Setup screens that appear after this point differ for the different account types. This section shows the IMAP screens and explains the differences in the POP3 screens. You'll learn how to set up an Exchange account in the next main section.

FIGURE 7.4

On this Account Setup screen, enter the server address, choose the security type, and correct the port if necessary.

8. Type the server name, such as imap.notionalpress.com, in the Server box.

9. Tap the Security Type pop-up menu and choose the security type: None, SSL/TLS, SSL/TLS (Accept All Certificates), STARTTLS, or STARTTLS (Accept All Certificates). The Email app enters the normal port for that security type in the Port box.

> **📝 NOTE** Look back to the sidebar titled "Understanding Security Types for Email Accounts" earlier in this chapter for an explanation of the security types.

> **❗CAUTION** Avoid using the None security type or either of the Accept All Certificates security types. Most likely, you should use the SSL/TLS security type.

10. If your email provider has told you to use a different port than the Email app has chosen, type the port number in the Port box. Table 7.2 explains the ports normally used by mail servers.

Table 7.2   Standard Ports for Email Servers

Server Type	Security Type	Port
POP3	None	110
POP3	SSL/TLS	995
POP3	STARTTLS	110 (starts insecure)
IMAP	None	143
IMAP	SSL/TLS	993
IMAP	STARTTLS	143 (starts insecure)
SMTP	None	25
		587
SMTP	SSL	465
SMTP	TLS	587

> **📝 NOTE** For a POP3 server, tap the Delete Email from Server pop-up menu and then tap the Never button or the When I Delete from Inbox button, as appropriate.

11. Tap the Next button. The Email app checks the incoming server and makes sure the account name, password, and security type are valid. If so, the next Account Setup screen appears for you to set up the outgoing mail server (see Figure 7.5). On a tablet, this screen bears the name Outgoing Server Settings.

> **☑ TIP**   If the Couldn't Finish dialog box appears after you tap the Next
> button, it normally means that the information you've provided is wrong. Tap
> the Edit Details button to return to the Account Setup screen you were on, verify
> each piece of information, and correct any mistakes. If you get the same error
> again, check that your Internet connection is working. For example, tap the Home
> button, tap the Chrome icon, and verify that Chrome can load a website.

FIGURE 7.5
*On this Account Setup screen, specify the outgoing server address, security type, port, and
whether to sign in.*

12. Enter the outgoing server's address, such as smtp.notionalpress.com, in the
    Outgoing Server box.

> **☑ TIP**   The Email app automatically fills the SMTP Server box on the Account
> Setup screen for the outgoing mail server with "smtp." and a name derived
> from the incoming mail server name you provided. If your email provider uses a
> different name, you will need to edit the suggested name.

13. Tap the Security Type pop-up menu and then tap the security type: None, SSL/TLS, SSL/TLS (Accept All Certificates), STARTTLS, or STARTTLS (Accept All Certificates). The Email app enters the normal port for that security type in the Port box.

14. If your email provider has told you to use a different port than the Email app has chosen, type the port number in the Port box. Again, look at Table 7.2 for details of the normal ports.

15. If your email provider requires you to sign in to send messages, check the Require Signin box and enter the appropriate username and password in the boxes below.

> **TIP** Your sign-in username may be different from your email address; for example, it may be the portion of your email address before the @ sign (such as csmith for the email address csmith@notionalpress.com). If in doubt, ask your email provider.

16. Tap the Next button. The Email app tries to validate your SMTP settings. If it succeeds, the Account Settings screen appears (see Figure 7.6). On a tablet, this screen has the name Account Options.

FIGURE 7.6

On the Account Settings screen, choose how frequently to check for email, whether to receive notifications, and whether to sync email.

> **TIP** As with the incoming server, if the Couldn't Finish dialog box appears after you tap the Next button on the Account Setup screen for the outgoing server, it normally means that the information you've provided is wrong. Tap the Edit Details button, verify each piece of information, and correct any mistakes.

17. Tap the Inbox Checking Frequency pop-up menu and then tap the frequency with which to check for new messages: Never, Every 5 Minutes, Every 10 Minutes, Every 15 Minutes, Every 30 Minutes, or Every Hour.

18. Check the Notify Me When Email Arrives box if you want the Email app to display a notification when new messages arrive. If new messages arrive in a batch, the app displays a single notification for the batch rather than a separate notification for each message.

19. Check the Sync Email from This Account box to make the Email app sync this account. Normally, you'll want to do this.

20. Check the Automatically Download Attachments When Connected to Wi-Fi box if you want the Email app to download attachments automatically when your device has a Wi-Fi connection instead of a cellular connection. This setting is usually handy unless you often receive large attachments that you don't want to download.

> **NOTE** The Automatically Download Attachments When Connected to Wi-Fi check box appears only on phones and cellular-capable tablets.

21. Tap the Next button. The final Account Setup screen appears (see Figure 7.7).

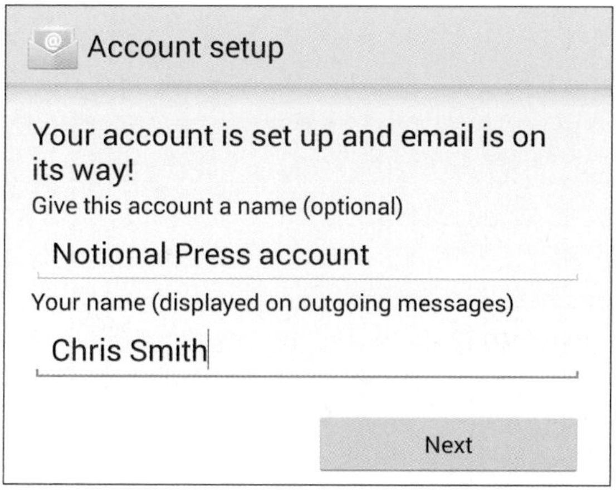

> **Account setup**
>
> **Your account is set up and email is on its way!**
> Give this account a name (optional)
>
> Notional Press account
>
> Your name (displayed on outgoing messages)
>
> Chris Smith
>
> Next

FIGURE 7.7

On the final Account Setup screen, give the email account a descriptive name and enter your name the way you want it to appear on messages you send.

22. In the Give This Account a Name (Optional) box, type a descriptive name for the account. This name is to help you distinguish this account from your other accounts; the more accounts you have, the more important it is to have easily distinguishable names.

23. In the Your Name (Displayed on Outgoing Messages) box, type your name the way you want it to appear on messages you send. For example, you may want your full name to appear, including your middle initial.

24. Tap the Next button. The Settings screen appears, with the new account now on it.

25. Tap the Settings button at the top of the screen or tap the Back button to return to your Inbox.

SETTING UP EXCHANGE SERVER ACCOUNTS

Setting up an Exchange Server account in the Email app works in largely the same way as setting up another account, but you have to jump through several more hoops to set it up. The Email app can set up some Exchange Server accounts automatically with just the email account name and password, but for others, you will need to fill in the server and domain details.

! CAUTION Setting up an Exchange Server account on your Android device requires you to give the Exchange administrator permission to administer your device remotely. The administrator can take a wide range of actions on your device, up to and including remotely wiping it of all its content. Normally, the administrator won't wipe your device unless it goes missing, presumed stolen; however, the administrator *can* wipe the device any time, intentionally or by accident.

If your Android device is one that your company or organization has supplied, this is fine, but you should either avoid storing any personal files on the device or make sure that you have backups of all your personal files elsewhere in case an administrator nukes the device.

If your company or organization allows you to bring your own device (BYOD) to work and set it up to access your Exchange Server account, you need to decide whether having access to your Exchange data is worth the potential loss of your personal data.

GETTING THE INFORMATION NEEDED FOR YOUR EXCHANGE SERVER ACCOUNT

Before trying to set up your Exchange Server account on your device, make sure you have all the information required. Table 7.3 shows the details. Normally, you'll need to get the information from the Exchange Server administrator.

TIP Using the right domain can be crucial to getting your Exchange Server account to work. Exchange Server systems tend to be complex, and it is hard to guess the domain name. What's especially awkward is that you may not need to enter a domain name at all, but usually only the administrator can tell you whether or not to enter it.

Table 7.3   Information for Setting Up an Exchange Server Account

Information	Example	Notes
Email address	csmith@surrealmacs.com	
Password	G43s9PiaPT!	The password is case sensitive.
Domain	CORP	Ask an administrator what the domain is and whether you need to use it.
Security type	SSL/TLS	See Table 7.2, earlier in this chapter, for an explanation of security types.
Client certificate	N/A	Some systems require a digital certificate file provided by an administrator for authentication.
Port	443	The port used depends on the security type.

ENTERING YOUR EXCHANGE SERVER ACCOUNT DETAILS

Here's how to set up your Exchange Server account:

1. Open the Email app by tapping its icon on the Apps screen or on a Home screen.

> ⌇ NOTE   If you haven't already set up an account in Email, the app displays the first Account Setup screen when you open it. Go to step 4.

2. Tap the Menu button and then tap Settings to display the Settings screen.
3. Tap the Add Account button to display the first Account Setup screen.
4. Type or paste your email address in the upper box.
5. Type your password in the lower box.
6. Tap the Next button if you want the Email app to try to set up the account automatically. Otherwise, tap the Manual Setup button to display the second Account Setup screen.

> **✓ TIP** Exchange Server setups can be complex, but the Email app is quite good at detecting server settings, so you may want to try automatic setup. If you need to use a digital certificate for authentication, you must use manual setup.

7. Tap the Exchange button. The Email app tries to retrieve account information from the server. It then displays suggested settings on the second Account Setup screen (see Figure 7.8).

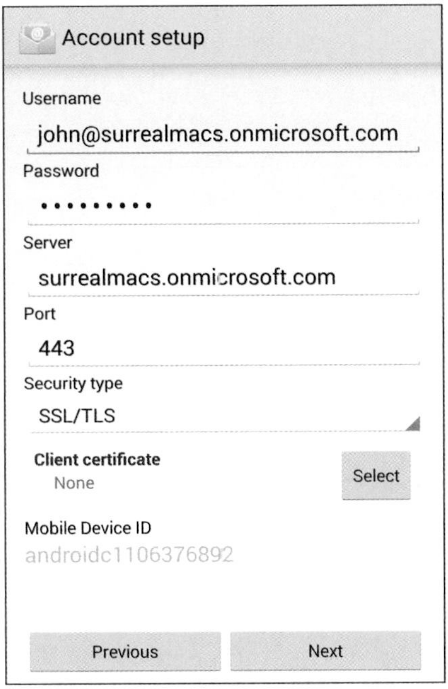

FIGURE 7.8

On the second Account Setup screen, specify the Exchange server name, the security type, and the port. You can also select a client certificate for authentication.

> **✓ TIP** For some systems, you may need to enter in the Username box the domain followed by a backslash and your full email address. For example, if your email address is john@surrealmacs.com, you would enter **surrealmacs.com\ john@surrealmacs.com**. This looks awkward, especially if it's too long to fit in the Domain\Username text box, but it is correct and it does work.

8. Edit the server name in the Server box if necessary.

9. Tap the Security Type pop-up menu and then tap the security type: None, SSL/TLS, or SSL/TLS (Accept All Certificates). The Email app enters the normal port for that security type in the Port box.

> **!CAUTION** Normally, you will use the SSL/TLS security type. Don't use the SSL/TLS (Accept All Certificates) security type, much less the None "security" type.

10. If your Exchange Server administrator has told you to use a different port than the Email app has chosen, type the port number in the Port box.

> **TIP** Exchange Server normally uses port 443 for SSL/TLS and port 80 for no security. These are standard web ports (port 443 for https, giving secure access, and port 80 for open access) because your device is accessing the Exchange Server across the Web.

> **NOTE** If your Exchange Server administrator has given you a digital certificate to use for authentication, tap the Select button to the right of the Client Certificate readout. In the Choose Certificate dialog box that opens, tap the certificate you want to use, and then tap the Allow button. The Client Certificate readout then displays the certificate's name.

11. Tap the Next button. The Email app attempts to validate the server settings. If it succeeds, the Remote Security Administration dialog box opens (see Figure 7.9).

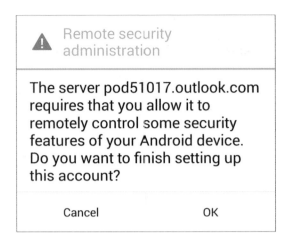

FIGURE 7.9

In the Remote Security Administration dialog box, tap the OK button if you want to proceed with setting up the Exchange Server account.

12. Tap the OK button. The Email app displays the Account Settings screen shown in Figure 7.10.

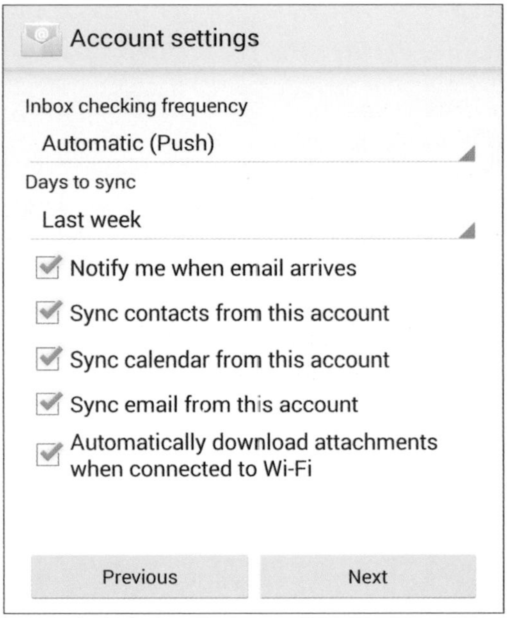

FIGURE 7.10

On the Account Settings screen, choose how often to check email, whether to receive notifications for messages, and which items to sync.

13. Tap the Inbox Checking Frequency pop-up menu and then tap the frequency with which to check for new messages: Automatic (Push), Never, Every 5 Minutes, Every 10 Minutes, Every 15 Minutes, Every 30 Minutes, or Every Hour.

> **TIP** The Push setting for Inbox Checking Frequency causes the mail server to "push" new messages to your device as soon as they arrive instead of waiting for the device to check for new messages. Choose Push to get your messages more quickly at the cost of some battery power.

14. Tap the Days to Sync pop-up menu and choose what to sync: Last Day, Last Three Days, Last Week, Last Two Weeks, Last Month, or All.

15. Check the Notify Me When Email Arrives box if you want the Email app to display a notification when new messages arrive. If new messages arrive in a batch, the app displays a single notification for the batch rather than a separate notification for each message.

16. Check the Sync Contacts from This Account box if you want to sync your contacts to your device. Syncing the contacts is usually helpful.

17. Check the Sync Calendar from This Account box if you want to sync your Exchange Server calendar appointments to your device. This too is usually helpful.

18. Check the Sync Email from This Account box to make the Email app sync this account. Normally, you'll want to do this.

19. Check the Automatically Download Attachments When Connected to Wi-Fi box if you want the Email app to download attachments automatically when your device has a Wi-Fi connection instead of a cellular connection. This setting is usually handy unless you often receive large attachments that you don't want to download.

20. Tap the Next button. The final Account Setup screen appears.

21. In the Give This Account a Name (Optional) box, type a descriptive name for the account—for example, Exchange (Work).

22. Tap the Next button. The Activate Device Administrator? screen appears (see Figure 7.11).

FIGURE 7.11

On the Activate Device Administrator? screen, read the changes an administrator can make to your device remotely. Tap the Activate button if you still want to set up your Exchange Server account.

23. Read the details of what the administrator can do: Erase All Data, Set Password Rules, Monitor Screen-Unlock Attempts, Disable Cameras, and so on.

24. Tap the Activate button if you want to proceed. The Email app activates the device administrator. The Settings screen appears, showing your Exchange Server account.

25. Tap the Settings button at the top of the screen or tap the Back button to return to your Inbox.

DELETING AN ACCOUNT FROM THE EMAIL APP

If you no longer need a particular email account on your device, you can delete it from the Email app. To delete the account, you use the Settings app like this:

1. Open the Settings app.

2. In the Accounts section, tap the button for the account type. For example, to delete an IMAP account, tap the IMAP button. The appropriate screen appears, such as the IMAP screen.

> **NOTE** On some devices, you'll need to tap the Email button, not a button with the account type.

3. In the Accounts list, tap the account name. The Sync screen for the account appears.

4. Tap the Menu button and then tap the Remove Account button. Android displays the Remove Account? dialog box, warning you that removing the account will delete all its messages, contacts, and other data (see Figure 7.12).

5. Tap the Remove Account button. On some devices, you may see a different button, such as a Continue button.

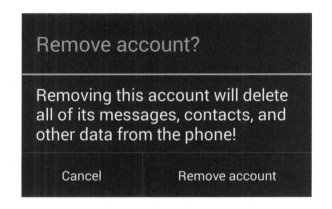

FIGURE 7.12

Tap the Remove Account button in the Remove Account? dialog box to remove an email account from your device.

SENDING AND RECEIVING MESSAGES

By this point, you should have all your non-Gmail email accounts set up in the Email app, so you're ready to send and receive messages. The Email app makes sending and receiving as easy as possible by packing a lot of information and functionality into an apparently straightforward interface.

CREATING AND SENDING A MESSAGE

To create a new message, tap the Compose icon (the envelope icon with a plus sign) at the top of the screen. The Compose screen appears, and you can create the message by making these moves in any order:

- **Choose the account.** If you have set up multiple accounts in the Email app, tap the Account pop-up menu and then tap the account to use (see Figure 7.13).

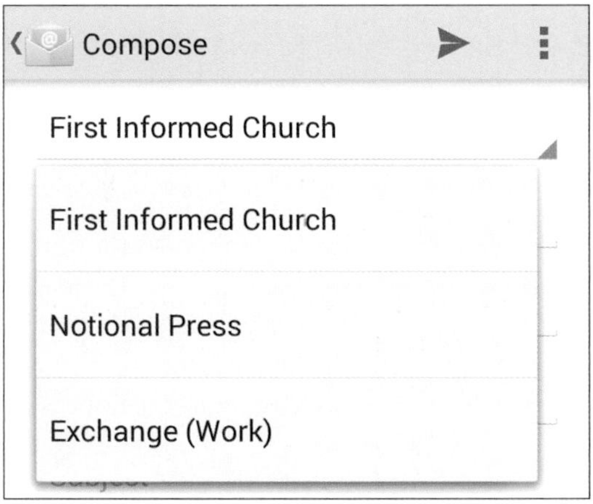

FIGURE 7.13

Open the Account pop-up menu and choose the account from which to send the message.

> **NOTE** When you start a new message from the Inbox for a particular account, the Email app selects that account as the sending account. When you start a message from the Combined View Inbox, the Email app uses the first account in the list.

- **Add To recipients.** Tap the To box and start typing the contact's name or email address; then tap the contact in the pop-up list of matches that appears (see Figure 7.14).

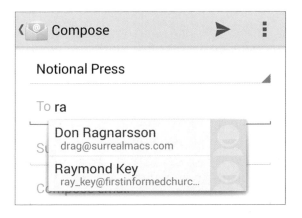

FIGURE 7.14

Start typing the recipient's address, and then tap the address in the pop-up list of matches.

■ **Add Cc or Bcc recipients.** On a phone, tap the Menu button and then tap the Add Cc/Bcc button on the menu (see Figure 7.15) to display the Cc and Bcc fields. On a tablet, tap the +CC/BCC button to the right of the To field to display them. Tap the Cc field or the Bcc field as appropriate, start typing the contact's name or email address, and then tap the contact in the pop-up list of matches.

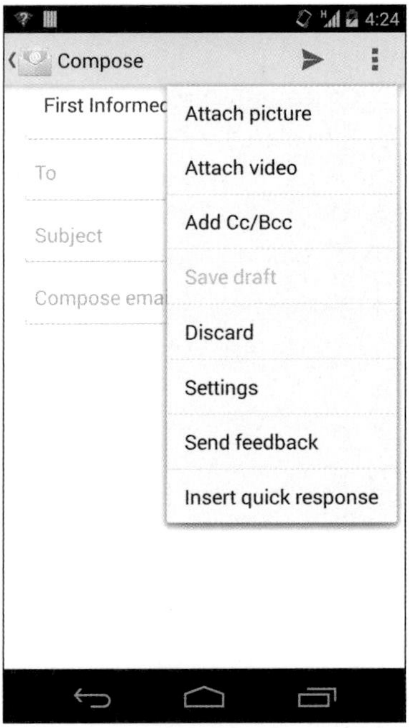

FIGURE 7.15

Tap the Add Cc/Bcc button on the menu if you need to display the Cc and Bcc fields.

> **TIP** If you need to make certain you don't send a message before it is complete, leave the To field (and the Cc field and Bcc field, if you've displayed them) empty until you finish writing the message. If you then tap the Send button by mistake, the Email app gives you a Recipient Error dialog box instead of sending the message.

- **Add the subject.** Tap the Subject field and type or paste the text. Make it brief but descriptive to make sure the recipient can easily see what the message is about.
- **Add the message body.** Tap the Compose Email prompt in the body area and then type or paste in the message text.

> **TIP** When you are sending a message to a list of people who may not know each other, put your address in the To field and all the other addresses in the Bcc field. That way, each recipient sees only your address and her own address, not the addresses of the other recipients.

- **Attach a picture to the message.** Tap the Menu button and then tap the Attach Picture button on the menu. Navigate to the picture and tap it. The picture appears as a thumbnail in the message. A bar across the bottom of the thumbnail shows the filename, its size, and the word *Image* (to help you distinguish it from other file types). The bar also has an X button that you can tap to delete the attachment.
- **Attach a video to the message.** Tap the Menu button and then tap the Attach Video button on the menu. Navigate to the video and tap it. The video appears as a button that includes the filename, the size, and an X button that you can tap to delete the attachment.

> **! CAUTION** The Email app has a 5MB limit on video size. The reason is that many mail servers reject messages with large attachments. If you select a video that will make the message too big, the Email app displays a pop-up message saying "File not attached. 5 MB limit reached" for a moment.

☑ **TIP**   To attach a file other than a picture or a video to a message, you need to start the message from a file-management app rather than from the Email app. Open your file-management app (for example, ES File Explorer), select the file, give the Share command, and then tap Email in the Share Via dialog box. The Email app starts a new message with the file attached. Address and send the message as usual.

Starting an Email Message from the People App

You can quickly start a message in the Email app from the People app. This move is useful when you need to browse the People app to find the relevant contacts.

After you find the contact, tap the contact's picture to display the contact information pop-up panel, tap the Email icon to display the email addresses, and then tap the appropriate address to start a message. If the Complete Action Using dialog box opens, tap the Email button, and then tap the Just Once button or the Always button, as appropriate.

When the message is ready for sending, tap the Send button, the arrow button near the upper-right corner of the screen.

✐ **NOTE**   If you decide not to send the message, you can save it as a draft (as discussed later in this chapter) or discard it. To discard the message, tap the Menu button and then tap the Discard button on the menu.

RECEIVING AND READING MESSAGES

While the Email app is running, it automatically checks for new messages at the frequency you chose in the Inbox Checking Frequency pop-up menu when setting up each account. If you chose the Never setting, or if you need to check immediately, you can check for new messages manually either by pulling down and releasing the conversation list in the Inbox or by tapping the Menu button and then tapping Refresh.

The conversation list (see Figure 7.16) packs a lot of status information into the list of messages:

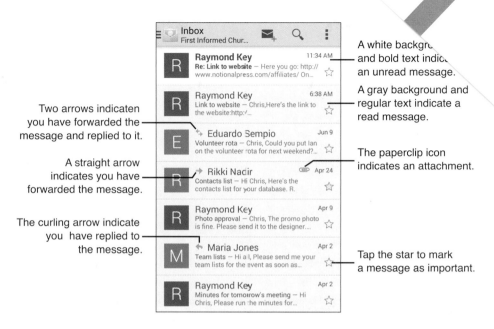

Two arrows indicaten you have forwarded the message and replied to it.

A straight arrow indicates you have forwarded the message.

The curling arrow indicate you have replied to the message.

A white backgr and bold text indic an unread message.

A gray background and regular text indicate a read message.

The paperclip icon indicates an attachment.

Tap the star to mark a message as important.

FIGURE 7.16

The conversation list uses colors, fonts, and icons to indicate message status.

- Unread messages have a white background and bold text on the sender name and subject.
- Read messages have a gray background and regular (nonbold) text.
- A paperclip icon indicates one or more files attached to the message.
- A curling leftward arrow to the left of the sender name indicates that you have replied to the messages.
- A straight arrow pointing right and positioned to the left of the sender name indicates that you have forwarded the message.
- A two-arrow icon, with the arrows pointing left and right, to the left of the sender name indicates that you have both forwarded the message and replied to it.
- You can tap the star outline to mark a message as important, turning the star to gold.

You can scroll up and down to reach other messages.

> **TIP** To search for messages, tap the Search icon at the top of the screen, type your search terms in the Search Email box that appears, and then tap the Search icon on the keyboard. The Results list appears. Tap the Back button to return from the search results to your mailbox.

Tap a message in the conversation list to open it for reading. You can see the message's content and use the controls to manipulate it. Figure 7.17 shows the details.

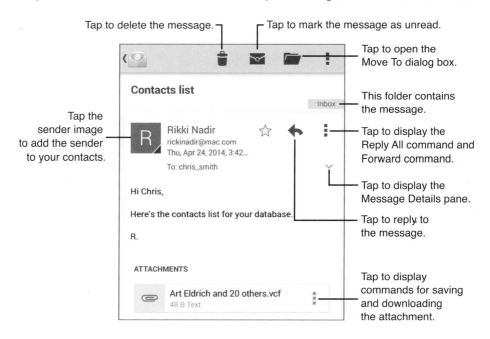

Tap to delete the message.

Tap to mark the message as unread.

Tap to open the Move To dialog box.

Contacts list

This folder contains the message.

Inbox

Tap the sender image to add the sender to your contacts.

Rikki Nadir
rickinadir@mac.com
Thu, Apr 24, 2014, 3:42...
To: chris_smith

Tap to display the Reply All command and Forward command.

Tap to display the Message Details pane.

Hi Chris,

Here's the contacts list for your database.

R.

Tap to reply to the message.

ATTACHMENTS

Art Eldrich and 20 others.vcf
48 B Text

Tap to display commands for saving and downloading the attachment.

FIGURE 7.17

The message screen includes controls for deleting the message, moving it to a folder, or simply replying to it.

- Tap the Delete button (the trash icon) to delete the message.
- Tap the Unread button (the closed envelope icon) to mark the message as unread, even though you have opened it. You might want to mark a message as unread to remind yourself to read it later.
- Tap the Reply button to reply to the message.
- To reply to all recipients on a phone, tap the Menu button within the message, and then tap the Reply All button. On a tablet, tap the Reply All button, the button with a two-headed arrow.

■ To forward the message on a phone, tap the Menu button within the message, and then tap the Forward button. On a tablet, tap the Forward button, the button with the arrow pointing to the right.

■ Tap the sender image or sender letter to add the sender to your contacts.

■ Tap the downward arrow to display the Message Details pane, which shows the sender's name and address, the To address, and the date and time.

■ If the message has an attachment, tap the Menu button on the attachment to display commands for saving and downloading the attachment.

■ Swipe left to display the next message, or swipe right to display the previous message.

When you're ready to return to the Inbox, tap the Back button.

REPLYING TO MESSAGES AND FORWARDING MESSAGES

To reply to a message, tap the Reply button on the message screen. The Email app starts a reply to the message's sender and displays it for you to enter the text.

If the message has multiple recipients and you want to reply to all of them, give the Reply All command: On a phone, tap the Menu button within the message, and then tap the Reply All button; on a tablet, simply tap the Reply All button. The Email app starts a reply to the message's sender, puts all the recipients (apart from you) in the Cc field, and displays the reply for you to enter the text.

TIP When replying to all recipients, you may sometimes want to prune down the list to only those people who really need the reply. To remove an address, touch its button, and then touch the Delete button on the onscreen keyboard.

NOTE If the message had Bcc recipients, you don't see their addresses (other than your own, if you were one of them), and your reply to "all" recipients doesn't go to them.

Apart from what to say in the message (I can't help you with that), you have two choices here:

■ **Quote Text.** Check this box to include the original message in your reply. Including the original is usually helpful because the recipient can look at the original message to remind himself what he wrote. If the original message was long, or if you're replying to a chain of replies, you may want to delete those parts of it that are no longer relevant.

> **NOTE** On some devices, you'll see different controls for quoting text (such as an Original Message check box) and responding inline (such as an Edit Original Message Information button).

- **Respond Inline.** When you check the Quote Text box, the Email app places the insertion point above the quoted text so that you can write your reply in a block at the top of the message. If you want to write your reply between the paragraphs of the quoted message, tap the Respond Inline button.

> **TIP** Responding inline is especially useful when you are addressing (or rebutting) specific points in the original message.

To forward a message, give the Forward command: On a phone, tap the Menu button within the message, and then tap the Forward button; on a tablet, just tap the Forward button. The Email app starts a forwarded message, adding Fwd: to the beginning of the Subject line. You can then address the message, tap the Compose Email prompt, and type whatever text is needed to explain what you're forwarding.

> **NOTE** When forwarding a message, you can tap the Respond Inline button to add your comments in between the paragraphs of the existing message.

SETTING UP AND USING QUICK RESPONSES

To help you write messages quickly and accurately even on the smallest device, the Email app includes a Quick Responses feature. Quick Responses are canned snippets of text that you set up ahead of time and then insert in your messages as needed.

> **TIP** You can create different Quick Responses in each of your email accounts. This enables you to easily respond to different message categories. For example, you might use an informal "Catch you later" response on a personal email account and a more formal request to contact one of your colleagues for advice on a work account.

SETTING UP YOUR QUICK RESPONSES

Here's how to set up your Quick Responses:

1. In the Email app, tap the Menu button and then tap Settings to display the Settings screen.
2. Tap the account whose Quick Responses you want to set up.
3. Tap the Quick Responses button to display the Quick Responses screen (see Figure 7.18).

> **NOTE** If you don't see the Quick Responses button on the Settings screen, look for a button such as Composing and Sending. Tap it and see if the Quick Responses button is on that screen. Not all devices include Quick Responses.

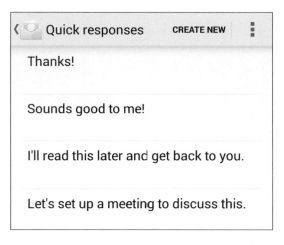

FIGURE 7.18

From the Quick Responses screen, you can create a new Quick Response or edit or delete an existing one.

4. To create a new response, tap the Create New button, type the text in the Quick Response dialog box that opens, and then tap the Save button.

> ✓ **TIP** You can create multiple-line Quick Responses. Just tap the Enter key at the appropriate place to create a new line.

5. To edit or delete an existing Quick Response, tap it. In the Quick Response dialog box that opens, either edit the text and then tap the Save button, or tap the Delete button.

When you finish creating your Quick Responses, tap the Back button three times to return to your Inbox.

USING YOUR QUICK RESPONSES

After setting up your Quick Responses, you can use them in your messages. Tap the Menu button, tap Insert Quick Response to open the Insert Quick Response dialog box, and then tap the Quick Response you want to use.

SAVING AND REOPENING DRAFTS

Sometimes when you're writing a message, you may need to leave it and turn your attention to other email—for example, a message from your boss that requires an instant reply.

When this happens, save the message as a draft by tapping the Back button twice: The first tap hides the onscreen keyboard, and the second saves the message as a draft. A pop-up message appears briefly saying that the message has been saved as a draft.

When you're ready to resume writing the message, tap the button in the upper-left corner of the Inbox or the current mailbox to display the navigation panel, and then tap the Drafts button. The Drafts folder opens, and you can tap the message to open it for editing.

NAVIGATING YOUR MAILBOXES

To navigate among your accounts and mailboxes, tap the button in the upper-left corner of the screen to display the navigation panel (see Figure 7.19), and then tap the account, view, or mailbox you want to view. For example, tap one of the account radio buttons to display the Inbox for that account, or tap the Combined View radio button to display the contents of all your Inboxes.

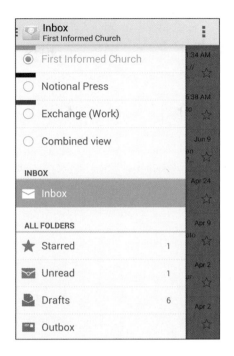

FIGURE 7.19

Use the navigation panel to switch to the account, view, or mailbox you want to display.

After you've chosen what to display, use these moves to work with the messages:

■ **Select messages.** Tap the sender image or sender initial for a message to select it. You can then tap the Delete button (the trash icon) to delete the selected messages or tap the Unread icon or the Read icon to change the messages' status.

■ **Delete a message quickly.** Swipe a message off the list to the left or right. The Deleted bar appears, confirming that you have deleted the message. If you got the wrong victim, tap the Undo button at the right end of the Deleted bar to undo the deletion.

> **NOTE** If swiping a message off the conversation list doesn't work, you need to enable the feature. Tap the Menu button, tap the Settings button, tap the General button, and then tap to check the Swipe to Delete box.

■ **Open a message.** Tap the message to open it for reading.

CHOOSING GENERAL SETTINGS

To get the most out of the Email app, you'll need to configure your accounts to suit your needs. The Email app has plenty of settings you can configure. The settings fall into two categories: General settings that you configure to control how the app itself works and account-specific settings that you can set differently for each account as needed.

Start by tapping the Menu button and then tapping the Settings button to display the main Settings screen. Then tap the General Settings button to display the Settings screen for general settings (see Figure 7.20).

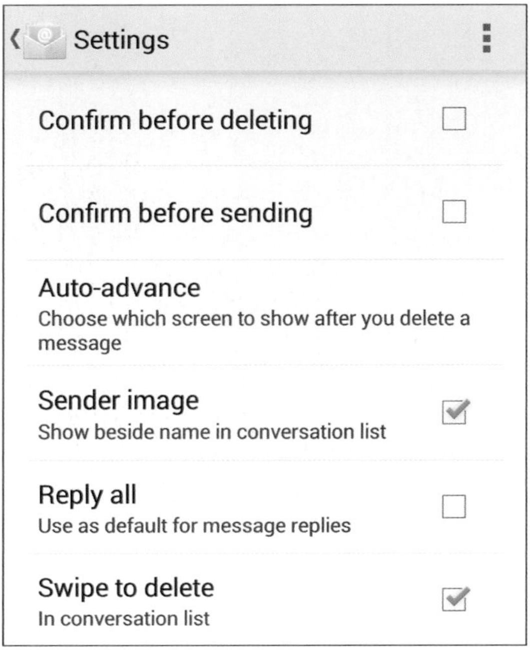

FIGURE 7.20

This Settings screen includes general settings such as confirmations, auto-advance preference, and swiping to delete messages.

NOTE Some devices have different settings, or different arrangements of settings, on the Settings screen. Be prepared to take a few minutes exploring the settings your device offers so that you can make the most of them.

You can choose six settings on the Settings screen:

- **Confirm Before Deleting.** Check this box to make the Email app confirm each deletion.

> ✓ **TIP** The Confirm Before Deleting setting and the Confirm Before Sending setting are useful if you use your device in a crowded or moving setting, such as public transit, where it's easy to tap the wrong button. If you use your device in a stationary setting, you may find the confirmations irksome.

- **Confirm Before Sending.** Check this box to make the Email app confirm the sending of each message.
- **Auto-Advance.** This setting enables you to control which item the Email app displays next after you delete or move a message. Tap the button to display the Set Auto-Advance Preference dialog box and then tap the Newer radio button, the Older radio button, or the Conversation List radio button, as appropriate.
- **Sender Image.** Check this box to make the conversation list display photos for any senders whose mug shots are in your address book.
- **Reply All.** Check this box to use Reply All as the default action for replying to messages that have multiple recipients.

> **! CAUTION** Be careful with the Reply All setting. Usually, it's best to reply to all recipients only manually after due deliberation.

- **Swipe to Delete.** Check this box if you want to be able to delete a conversation from the conversation list by swiping it to the left or right.

CHOOSING ACCOUNT-SPECIFIC SETTINGS

As you read earlier in this chapter, you can choose various settings while setting up an email account on your device. If you need to change any of the settings later, or you want to add an email signature that will enter your details automatically in messages you send, you can work on the settings screen for the account.

To get started, tap the Menu button, tap Settings, and then tap the account name on the Settings screen. The account's settings screen appears (see Figure 7.21), and you can choose the following settings:

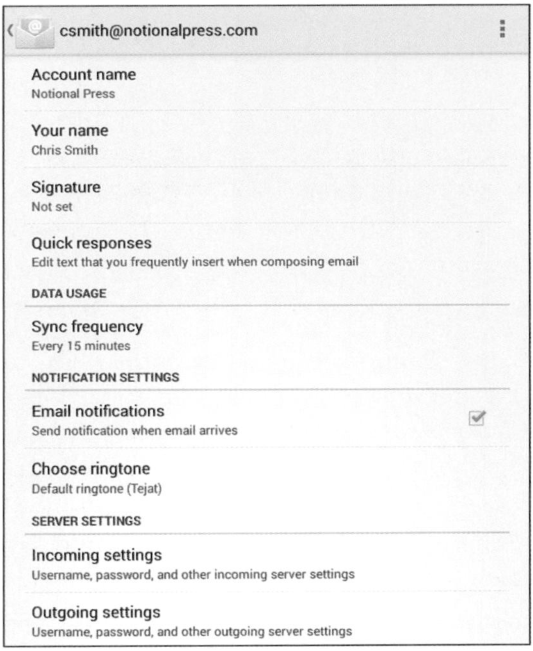

FIGURE 7.21

Use the controls on an account's settings screen to make the account behave the way you prefer.

■ **Account Name.** Tap this button to change the descriptive name for the account.

■ **Your Name.** Tap this button to change the name displayed on messages you send.

■ **Signature.** Tap this button to display the Signature dialog box, in which you can type or paste the text you want the Email app to insert automatically at the end of outgoing messages. You can create multiple lines by tapping the Enter key.

■ **Quick Responses.** Tap this button to set up your Quick Responses, as explained earlier in this chapter.

■ **Sync Frequency.** Tap this button to display the Sync Frequency dialog box, in which you can choose how frequently the Email app checks for mail. If the Push setting is available, choose it if you want to get your messages as soon as possible.

- **Download Attachments**. Check this box to download attachments on recent messages automatically when your device has a Wi-Fi connection.
- **Email Notifications.** Check this box to make the Email app give you a notification when you receive messages.
- **Choose Ringtone.** Tap this button to choose the ringtone used for the email notification.
- **Vibrate.** Check this box to make your device vibrate when the Email app gives you a notification. This check box appears only if your device includes vibration (the tablet shown in Figure 7.21 does not).
- **Incoming Settings.** Tap this button to display the screen for configuring your incoming mail server.
- **Outgoing Settings.** Tap this button to display the screen for configuring your outgoing mail server.

> **NOTE**   As with the general settings, the account-specific settings screen on your device may show different settings, or a different arrangement of settings, than the stock Android screen shown here. Explore the settings available to you so that you know all your options for configuring each account.

IN THIS CHAPTER

- Sharing bookmarks and tabs among your Chrome-enabled devices
- Using Chrome's hidden features
- Configuring Chrome for optimum performance

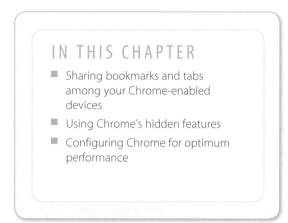

8

BROWSING WITH CHROME

This chapter shows you how to get the most out of Chrome, the Google-built browser that comes with Android. You'll learn how to make the most of Chrome's integration with your Google account to share bookmarks and tabs among your Chrome-enabled devices and to send web pages from Chrome on your desktop computer to Chrome on your Android device for either online viewing or offline viewing.

This chapter will also show you where to find the many clever features hidden in and behind Chrome's apparently straightforward interface. You'll learn how to configure Chrome for best performance and to keep your private information secure, because even the apparently harmless activity of browsing the Web exposes you to a wide variety of attacks.

> ## NOTE
> Some Android devices come with other browsers as well as Chrome or instead of it. For example, most Samsung smart phones and tablets include Samsung's browser, which is usually called Internet but also sometimes called Browser, as well as Chrome. Chrome is free, so if your device doesn't have Chrome, open the Play Store app, search for *google chrome*, and install it.

CHOOSING ESSENTIAL CHROME SETTINGS

To get the most out of Chrome and to protect yourself online, spend a few minutes configuring the app with suitable settings before you use it on the Web.

Launch Chrome by tapping its icon on the Home screen or the Apps screen. Chrome displays the Most Visited tab, from which you can quickly open one of your frequently visited websites. For now, tap the Menu button to open the menu, and then tap the Settings button to display the Settings screen (see Figure 8.1).

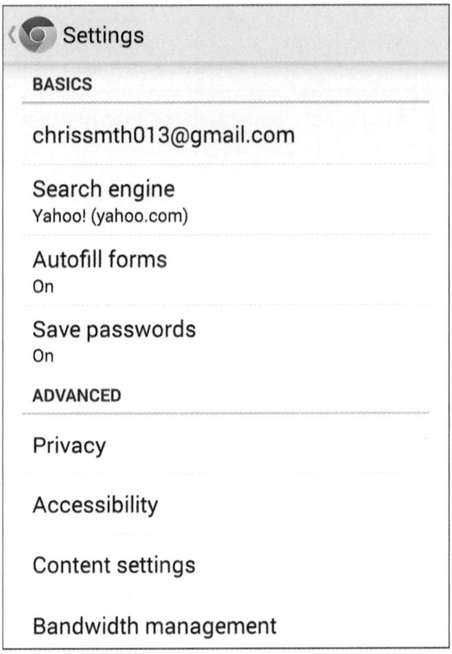

FIGURE 8.1

From the Settings screen, you can change your Google account and search engine; configure the Autofill Forms feature; and choose settings for privacy, accessibility, content settings, and bandwidth management.

CONFIGURING YOUR GOOGLE ACCOUNT

To get Chrome to sync the material you want, you must set it up with your Google account. The first item in the Basics section of the Settings screen is a button that shows the account that Chrome is set up to use. If this is the wrong account, you can change it easily enough; but even if it's the right account, you should make sure it's set to sync the right items. You should also encrypt some or all of the data you're syncing.

So tap the button with the Google account name to display the settings screen for the account (see Figure 8.2).

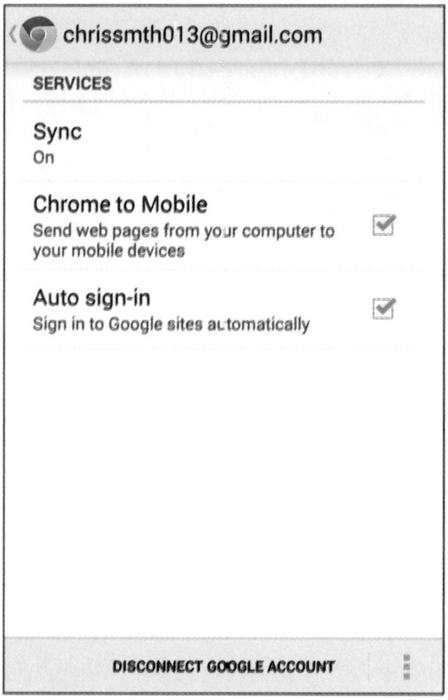

FIGURE 8.2

On the settings screen for your Google account, you can configure syncing, Chrome to Mobile, and Auto Sign-In.

> **NOTE**   If Chrome is using the wrong Google account, tap the Disconnect Google Account button and then tap the Disconnect button in the Disconnect Google Account dialog box that opens. The Settings screen then appears again. Tap the Sign In to Chrome button to display the Google Account dialog box, tap the appropriate account, and then tap the Sign In button.

To set up syncing, tap the Sync button and work on the Sync screen (see Figure 8.3).

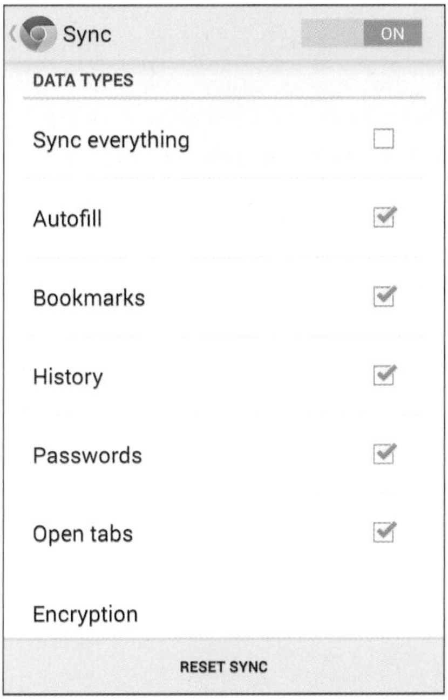

FIGURE 8.3

On the Sync screen, choose which data types to sync with your Google account and whether to apply encryption.

You can turn sync on or off by moving the switch at the top of the screen. Normally, you'll want to keep sync turned on so that you can enjoy its benefits.

Check the Sync Everything check box if you want to sync all the items. This is normally your best move unless you don't want to sync particular items, such as history or passwords. If you want to pick and choose, uncheck the Sync Everything check box, and then check the check box for each item you want to sync:

- **Autofill Forms.** Autofill Forms automatically fills in standard data, such as your address, in web forms. See the section "Setting Up Autofill Forms," later in this chapter, for details.

- **Bookmarks.** Your bookmarks enable you to quickly return to the web pages you mark. You can share bookmarks among the devices on which you use Chrome.

- **History.** Your history contains the list of web pages you've visited using Chrome on your devices.

- **Passwords.** Chrome can store your passwords and enter them automatically for you.
- **Open Tabs.** Chrome syncs the list of open tabs with your Android device, enabling you to pick up your browsing seamlessly on your phone or tablet viewing the same pages you left open on your computer.

Your next move is to set up encryption on what you're syncing. You can encrypt only your passwords if you want, but normally it's best to encrypt all the data you sync.

Tap the Encryption button to display the Encryption dialog box, and then tap the radio button for the setting you want:

- **Encrypt Passwords with Google Credentials.** Tap this radio button to use your Google account credentials to encrypt your synced passwords. At this writing, this radio button is usually dimmed and unavailable; the setting appears to be available only in Chrome on the desktop.
- **Encrypt All with Passphrase.** Tap this radio button to encrypt all your data using a passphrase of your choice that you enter in the Encrypt All with Passphrase dialog box. This is the more secure option. Choose a strong password and commit it to memory. Chrome stores the passphrase on your device and doesn't send it to Google.

> **☑ TIP** To create a strong password, use at least 8 characters and preferably 12 to 20. Combine uppercase and lowercase letters with numbers and symbols (such as $ or %). Avoid using any word or misspelling of a word in any language.

> **! CAUTION** After you encrypt all your synced data using a passphrase, you cannot change to encrypting only passwords unless you completely reset synchronization. To reset synchronization, tap the Reset Sync button at the bottom of the Sync screen, and then follow the prompts.

After choosing your sync options, tap the Back button to return to the settings screen for your Google account. You can then choose two other settings in the Services list:

- **Chrome to Mobile.** Check this box to turn on the Chrome to Mobile extension, which enables you to send a web page from your computer to your Android device. See the section "Using Chrome to Mobile," later in this chapter, for details.

- **Auto Sign-In.** Check this box to allow Chrome to sign you into Google sites automatically.

Tap the Back button on the settings screen for your Google account to go back to the Settings screen.

CHOOSING YOUR SEARCH ENGINE

Chrome can use several different search engines. To choose the one you want, tap the Search Engine button on the Settings screen, and then tap the appropriate button on the Search Engine screen.

The available search engines vary depending on your device's manufacturer and your location. But you'll typically be able to choose from the major engines such as Google, Yahoo!, and Bing.

SETTING UP AUTOFILL FORMS

The Autofill Forms feature enables you to store data you need for filling in online forms, such as your name, address, and credit card details. You set up Autofill Forms by turning it on and adding your profile and any credit cards you want to be able to use easily.

On the Settings screen, tap the Autofill Forms button to display the Autofill Forms screen (shown in Figure 8.4 with a profile and a credit card added). Set the switch to On, and then tap the Add Profile button to display the Add Profile screen. Fill in the data you want to be able to use in the appropriate fields—Full Name, Address Line 1, and so on—and then tap the Save button. Lather, rinse, and repeat until you've set up all the profiles you need.

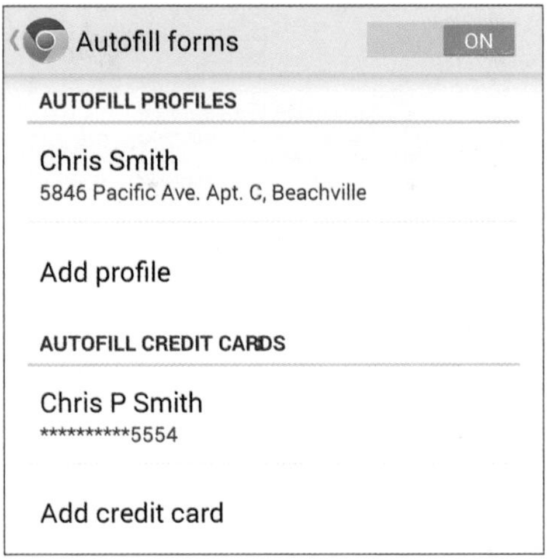

FIGURE 8.4

On the Autofill Forms screen, tap the Add Profile button to start adding your form data.

If you want to save your credit card data, tap the Add Credit Card button to display the Add Credit Card screen, type in the data, and then tap the Save button.

> **NOTE** At this writing, Autofill Forms doesn't enable you to assign descriptive names (such as Capital One Visa or Work MasterCard) to your cards, so you need to be able to identify them by their last four digits.

WORKING WITH THE SAVE PASSWORDS FEATURE

Chrome can save your passwords for websites. This has two advantages: First, you don't have to laboriously type the passwords on your device's onscreen keyboard; and second, you can easily use passwords that are longer, more complex, and more secure.

To set Chrome to save your passwords, tap the Save Passwords button on the Settings screen to display the Save Passwords screen, and set the switch at the top to the On position. Now, when you visit a website and enter your password, Chrome prompts you to allow it to save your password. Tap the Yes button or the Never button, as appropriate; if you want to postpone the decision until next time, tap the X button to close the prompt box.

The Saved Passwords section at the top of the Save Passwords screen lists the sites for which you've saved passwords. To delete a password, tap it, and then tap the Delete button on the Settings screen that appears.

CHOOSING PRIVACY SETTINGS AND CLEARING BROWSING DATA

Chrome includes a handful of privacy settings that you should configure to protect your privacy. From the Privacy screen, you can also clear your browsing data to remove potentially sensitive information.

Tap the Privacy button on the Settings screen to display the Privacy screen (see Figure 8.5). You can then choose these five settings:

- **Navigation Error Suggestions.** This setting controls whether Chrome displays suggestions for web addresses it cannot resolve or reach. For example, if you type in **qupublishing.com** (missing the *e*) instead of **quepublishing.com**, Chrome cannot resolve the address. With Navigation Error Suggestions turned on, Chrome suggests the correct website. With Navigation Error Suggestions turned off, Chrome simply reports that the web page is not available.

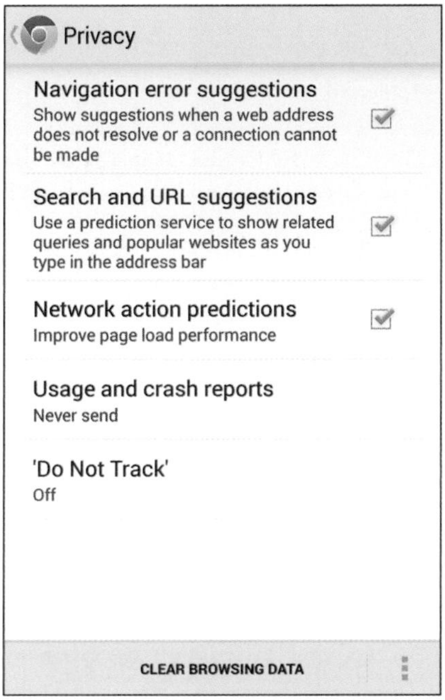

FIGURE 8.5

The Privacy screen includes controls for choosing which suggestions to see and for clearing your browsing data.

- **Search and URL Suggestions.** This setting controls whether Chrome displays suggestions from a prediction service when you type in the omnibox. The suggestions may be helpful, but they could compromise your privacy.

- **Network Action Predictions.** This setting controls whether Chrome looks up the IP addresses of all the links on the current web page so that it can more quickly load the page for whichever link you click.

- **Usage and Crash Reports.** To control whether Chrome sends anonymized reports about your usage of the app and any crashes that occur, tap this button, and then tap the appropriate radio button in the Usage and Crash Reports dialog box: Always Send, Only Send on Wi-Fi, or Never Send. If you want to help Google develop Chrome, Only Send on Wi-Fi is the best choice.

- **'Do Not Track'.** If you want to request that websites not track you, tap this button to display the 'Do Not Track' screen, and then set the switch to the On position.

> **! CAUTION** Some websites don't honor the Do Not Track request, so don't rely on Do Not Track to protect your privacy.

If you want to clear your browsing data, tap the Clear Browsing Data button to display the Clear Browsing Data dialog box (see Figure 8.6). You can then check the box for each item you want to delete:

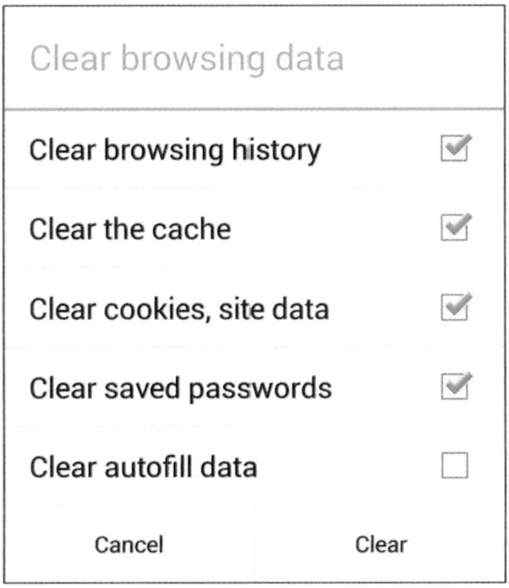

FIGURE 8.6

In the Clear Browsing Data dialog box, check the check box for each item you want to clear, and then tap the Clear button.

- **Clear Browsing History.** Your browsing history is the list of web pages you have visited.
- **Clear the Cache.** The cache contains data that Chrome has stored temporarily to enable itself to quickly load web pages when you return to them.
- **Clear Cookies, Site Data.** Cookies are small text files that web servers store on your device to help them track what you do on their websites. For example, some websites use cookies to implement shopping carts or to give you a quick-access list of products you have browsed recently.

> **TIP**   You can delete data for websites one by one instead of deleting all your cookies and site data. You can also refuse cookies. See the section "Choosing Content Settings," later in this chapter.

- **Clear Saved Passwords.** This setting enables you to get rid of all your saved passwords at once instead of deleting them one by one, as discussed earlier in this chapter.
- **Clear Autofill Data.** This setting deletes your Autofill data. See the section "Setting Up Autofill Forms," earlier in this chapter.

After making your choices, tap the Clear button.

CHOOSING ACCESSIBILITY SETTINGS

If you find the size of text on web pages hard to read, you can use Chrome's Text Scaling feature to enlarge it. Tap the Accessibility button on the Settings screen to display the Accessibility screen, and then drag the Text Scaling slider until the text in the Preview box is the size you want. You can then apply text scaling by double-tapping a paragraph on a web page.

Some websites request web browsers not to let you zoom in on the site. Usually, the reason is that the website designer wants to ensure you view the site at a standard size for artistic reasons. This may make the site unreadable on a small screen even if you have good eyesight.

To deal with this problem, check the Force Enable Zoom check box on the Accessibility screen. Chrome then enables you to zoom in even if the website requests no zooming.

CHOOSING CONTENT SETTINGS

Next, tap the Content Settings button to display the Content Settings screen (see Figure 8.7). "Content Settings" sounds pretty harmless, but the settings here can make a huge difference to your browsing and your security, so take a minute to choose suitable settings.

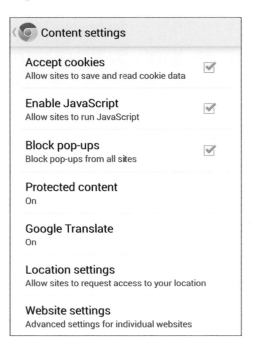

FIGURE 8.7

On the Content Settings screen, you can control cookies, JavaScript, pop-ups, and more.

These are the content settings:

- **Accept Cookies.** Check this box to allow Chrome to accept cookies, the text files that web servers use to track your movements on their sites.

> **!CAUTION** Turning off cookies helps protect your privacy, but it prevents many websites from working properly.

■ **Enable JavaScript.** Check this box to allow websites to run scripts (small programs) written in the JavaScript scripting language. Websites use JavaScript to display dynamic content, such as displaying a moving series of images or news headlines.

> **TIP** JavaScript is different from Java, which is a full-power programming language with capabilities that can threaten a computer's security. Many security experts recommend disabling Java on desktop computers to help avoid problems. Android devices don't normally run Java, so it's not a threat.

■ **Block Pop-Ups.** Check this box to prevent websites from displaying pop-up windows. Blocking pop-ups is a good idea, but you may need to disable pop-up blocking for all the features on some websites to work.

■ **Protected Content.** Some websites provide premium videos that require Chrome to authenticate your device, proving it is authorized to play the videos. To enable Chrome to authenticate your device, tap the Protected Content button and set the switch on the Protected Content screen to On.

> **TIP** If you enable protected content but find that websites cannot authenticate your device, you may need to reset its credentials. To do so, tap the Reset Device Credentials button on the Protected Content screen, and then tap the Delete button in the Confirm Device Credential Deletion dialog box that opens.

■ **Google Translate.** If you want to enable Chrome to use Google Translate to translate pages written in other languages, tap this button and set the switch on the Google Translate screen to the On position.

■ **Location Settings.** To control whether sites can request your location, tap this button, and then set the switch on the Location screen to the On position or to the Off position, as needed.

> **! CAUTION** Setting the switch on the Location screen to the Off position disables Location Services for all apps, not just for Chrome. Normally, it's best to set the switch to the On position and confirm or deny the individual location requests when Chrome displays them. Judge the requests individually: Some websites require your location—for example, to provide information about novel dining experiences within strolling distance—but others are just plain nosy.

■ **Website Settings.** Tap this button to display the Website Settings screen (see Figure 8.8), which displays a list of the websites that have stored data on your device. You can tap a website to display its Settings screen and then tap the Clear Stored Data button to delete the data. Tap the Clear All button in the Clear Stored Data dialog box that opens to confirm the deletion.

Website settings	
https://clients5.google.com	☐
https://maps.google.com	▣
https://plus.google.com	☐
https://support.google.com	☐
www.latimes.com	☐
www.quepublishing.com	☐
assets.rfm.rubiconproject.com	☐
https://www.three.co.uk	☐

FIGURE 8.8

Tap a website to display the screen for clearing its data. The rectangles give a rough idea of how much data each website has stored on your device.

MANAGING BANDWIDTH AND PRELOADING

Chrome can preload web pages linked to the current page so that you can display a page faster when you tap its link. To control whether Chrome preloads pages, tap the Bandwidth Management button on the Settings screen, and then use the options on the Bandwidth Management screen (see Figure 8.9).

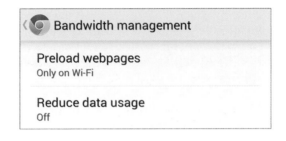

FIGURE 8.9

On the Bandwidth Management screen, choose whether to preload web pages and whether to use the Reduce Data Usage feature.

Tap the Preload Webpages button to display the Preload Webpages dialog box, and then tap the appropriate radio button: Always, Only on Wi-Fi (usually the best choice), or Never.

> **📝 NOTE** On a noncellular device, check or uncheck the Preload Webpages box on the Bandwidth Management screen to control whether Chrome preloads web pages.

> **❗ CAUTION** Preloading web pages can greatly increase the amount of data that Chrome transfers, so you should avoid preloading web pages over a cellular connection unless you have a generous or unlimited data plan.

The second button on the Bandwidth Management screen, Reduce Data Usage, enables you to reduce the amount of data Chrome transfers by having Google's servers compress the web pages you request. To do this, tap the Reduce Data Usage button and then set the switch on the Reduce Data Usage screen to On. Using the Reduce Data Usage feature also turns on Chrome's Safe Browsing system, which helps protect you against malicious web pages and malware.

> **✓ TIP** The Reduce Data Usage feature is well worth trying. However, if you find that it prevents you from accessing premium data services that your carrier provides, turn it off.

BROWSING THE WEB WITH CHROME

Now that you've configured Chrome to suit your device, your eyes, and the way you browse, you're ready to use the app to browse the Web.

NAVIGATING AMONG WEB PAGES

With Chrome open, you can quickly navigate from one web page to another. Figure 8.10 shows Chrome open on a phone with the main controls labeled.

FIGURE 8.10

Chrome hides its browsing power behind a straightforward interface.

Here's how to navigate among web pages:

■ **Type in an address.** Tap the omnibox—the address box at the top of the screen—and type or paste in the address.

> ☑ **TIP** If the address appears as a link in another app, tap the link to open it in Chrome. For example, tap a link in an email message to open the linked page in Chrome. If the address appears but isn't a link, select it, copy it, and then paste it into the Chrome omnibox.

■ **Open a linked page in the same tab.** Tap the link.
■ **Open a linked page in a new tab.** Tap and hold the link, and then tap Open in New tab on the pop-up menu (see Figure 8.11).

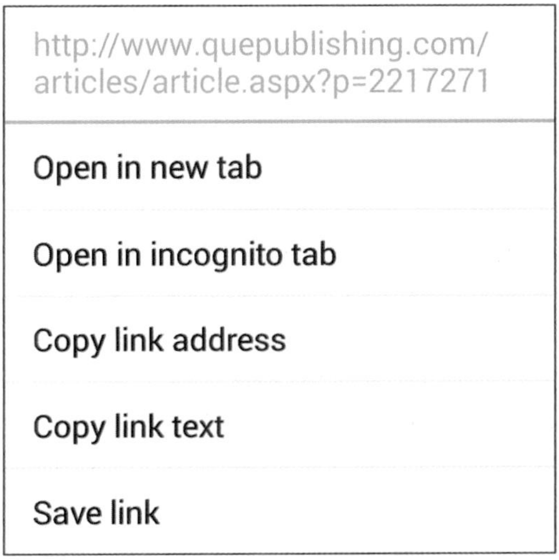

```
http://www.quepublishing.com/
articles/article.aspx?p=2217271

Open in new tab

Open in incognito tab

Copy link address

Copy link text

Save link
```

FIGURE 8.11
From the pop-up menu, you can open a link in a new tab or an incognito tab.

> ☑ **TIP** To reload the current web page, tap the Reload button at the right end of the omnibox. You may want to reload the page to get updated information from it.

Changing Your Default Browser

If your device has multiple browsers installed, you can set one of them as the default browser. Your default browser is the one that opens when you tap a link in another app—for example, a link in an email message.

If you're not sure whether you have a default browser set, tap a link in another app and see what happens. (If you don't have a convenient link, send yourself an email message containing a link.) If a browser opens, that's the default. If the Complete Action Using dialog box opens, showing you a choice of browsers, tap the browser you want to make the default, and then tap the Always button.

If you want to change your default browser, open the Settings app and tap the Apps button to display the Apps screen. Swipe left twice to display the All screen, and then locate the default browser in the alphabetical list. Tap the browser's button to display its App Info screen and then tap the Clear Defaults button.

Now tap a link in another app, and the Complete Action Using dialog box opens. Tap the browser you want to use, and then tap the Always button.

MANAGING AND SWITCHING TABS

Chrome enables you to open multiple web pages at the same time by opening each page in a separate tap. You can open new tabs as needed, switch among your open tabs, and close any tabs you no longer need.

You can open a new tab in a variety of ways:

- **From the menu.** Tap the Menu button and then tap the New tab button.

- **From a link.** Tap and hold the link, and then tap Open in New Tab on the pop-up menu.

- **From the Tabs screen on a phone.** Tap the Tabs button to display the Tabs screen (see Figure 8.12), and then tap the New Tab button. The Tabs button is the icon to the right of the omnibox, the icon showing two page outlines and the current number of tabs.

FIGURE 8.12

Use the Tabs screen on a phone to open new tabs, close existing tabs, or display a different tab.

■ **From the tab bar on a tablet.** Tap the short, blank tab button at the right end of the tab bar.

To manage your tabs on a phone, tap the Tabs button and work on the Tabs screen. Here you can do the following:

■ **Examine a tab.** Tap a tab and drag your finger down to display more of the tab in the tab list.

■ **Display a tab.** Tap the tab to display the web page full screen.

■ **Close a tab.** Tap its X button or swipe it to the right off the list.

■ **Close all tabs.** Tap the menu button and then tap Close All Tabs.

On a tablet, your open tabs appear on the tab bar (see Figure 8.13), and you can simply tap the tab you want to display. To close a tab, tap its X button.

FIGURE 8.13

On a tablet, tap the tab you want to view.

> **TIP** On a tablet, you can drag your tabs into a different order if you want. For example, you may want to group related tabs together for reference.

MAKING THE MOST OF BOOKMARKS

When you want to be able to easily return to a web page, create a bookmark for it. You can store bookmarks on your device, but to get more out of them, you can sync your bookmarks via your Google account, making bookmarks you create on your computer available on your Android device, and vice versa.

CREATING A BOOKMARK

> **NOTE** A bookmark stores only the address of a web page, so when you return to the bookmark, you see the latest version of the page. For example, if you bookmark the home page of a news site, the page will often have changed by the time you return.

To create a bookmark for the current web page on a phone, tap the Menu button and then tap the empty start button in the upper-right corner of the menu. The Add Bookmark screen appears, and you can name the bookmark and assign it to a folder.

To create a bookmark for the current web page on a tablet, tap the empty star button at the right end of the omnibox. The Add Bookmark dialog box opens, and you can name the bookmark and assign it to a folder.

The Add Bookmark screen and then Add Bookmark dialog box work in the same way:

- **Name.** Enter the name for the bookmark in this box. Chrome suggests the web page's title, but you'll usually do better to type a short but descriptive name.

- **URL.** This box shows the web page's address. You can change the address, but if you started from the right page, you shouldn't need to change it.

- **Folder.** This box shows the folder into which Chrome will put the bookmark. To change the folder, tap the button, and then tap the right folder on the Choose a Folder screen or in the Choose a Folder dialog box. You can tap the New Folder button to create a new folder within the current folder.

- **Save.** After naming the bookmark and picking the folder, tap the Save button to save the bookmark.

TIP Bookmarks are great, but if you need to go to a particular web page very frequently, put it on your Home screen. Go to the page in Chrome, tap the Menu button, and then tap Add to Homescreen on the menu. The Add to Homescreen dialog box opens, and you can type the text for the shortcut in the Title box and then tap the Add button.

GOING TO A BOOKMARK

After creating a bookmark, you can go back to the site in moments:

1. Tap the Menu button and then tap Bookmarks on the menu to display the Bookmarks screen.

2. Navigate to the folder that contains the bookmark.

3. Tap the bookmark to go to it.

TIP To delete a bookmark, tap and hold it until the pop-up menu appears, and then tap Delete Bookmark. To edit the bookmark or move it to a different folder, tap and hold the bookmark, and then tap Edit Bookmark on the pop-up menu.

RETURNING TO A TAB YOU RECENTLY CLOSED

To visit a tab you've recently closed, open the Bookmarks screen, and then tap the Recent Tabs button at the bottom. You can then tap the tab you want to reopen.

NOTE On a phone, the Recent Tabs button appears as a folder with two arrows, one pointing up and the other pointing down. On a tablet, the Recent Tabs button bears the text Recent Tabs.

VIEWING YOUR CHROME TABS OPEN ON OTHER DEVICES

If you've chosen to sync your open tabs from other devices that use the same Google account and the Chrome browser, you can easily view those tabs on your Android device. Open the Bookmarks screen, tap the Recent Tabs button at the bottom, and then go to the Other Devices list. Tap the tab for the page you want to see, and you can pick up your browsing where you left off.

RETURNING TO A PAGE YOU VISITED EARLIER

When you want to return to a page that you visited earlier but that you didn't bookmark, you can use your history to find the page quickly. The history is a list of the web pages you have visited, with the most recent page first.

To view your history, tap the Menu button, and then tap History on the menu. The History screen appears. You can browse to find the page you want, or tap the Search History box and type a search term. When you find the relevant history item, tap it to go straight to that page.

NOTE If you've signed in to your Google account, the History screen displays the history from all your devices that are signed in to the same account. This enables you to browse more seamlessly no matter which device you're using.

TIP If your history contains potentially embarrassing items, you can delete them by tapping the X button at the right end of their buttons. If there are too many sensitive items to delete individually, you can clear your history instead. See the section "Choosing Privacy Settings and Clearing Browsing Data," earlier in this chapter, for details.

BROWSING INCOGNITO

Normally, when you browse the Web, your browser adds the web pages you visit to your history list so that you can revisit them if you want. History can be a great way of returning to the past, but at times you may want to turn it off so that you can browse the Web without Chrome saving the details of where you went.

> **! CAUTION** Incognito browsing prevents pages from being added to your history list, but the websites you visit can still track your movements, as can your ISP. Don't assume incognito browsing means anonymity.

When you want to turn off history, open an incognito tab by tapping the Menu button and then tapping the New Incognito Tab button. Chrome displays the tab, using different coloring and the incognito symbol (a head with hat, shades, and turned-up collar) to make clear that the tab is incognito (see Figure 8.14).

FIGURE 8.14

Open an incognito tab when you want to browse without adding the pages you visit to your history.

Chrome keeps incognito tabs separate from regular tabs so that you can easily distinguish the two. Here's how to switch between incognito tabs and regular tabs:

- **Phone.** Tap the Tabs button to display the Tabs screen. Swipe right to move from the list of incognito tabs to the list of regular tabs; swipe left to go from regular tabs to incognito tabs.

- **Tablet.** Tap the Switch Tabs button, the button that appears at the right end of the tab bar.

!CAUTION When you finish using incognito mode, you must close all your incognito tabs to get rid of the details of your incognito browsing session.

REQUESTING A DESKTOP SITE

Many websites offer both a desktop version of web pages and a mobile version. The desktop version of a page is designed for a larger screen and a mouse or similar pointing device, whereas the mobile version of a page is designed for a smaller screen and touch-based controls. As a result, the desktop version and mobile version may differ hugely from one another.

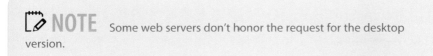 **NOTE** Some web servers don't honor the request for the desktop version.

Normally, when you access a web page using the Chrome browser on your Android device, the web server delivers the mobile version of the page. If that is not what you want, tap the Menu button and then tap Request Desktop Site, checking the box. Chrome reloads the web page, displaying the desktop version this time.

NOTE The Request Desktop Site feature remains turned on for the tab on which you checked the box, but you need to turn it on separately for each new tab you open.

USING CHROME TO MOBILE

The Chrome to Mobile feature enables you to send a web page from Chrome on your computer to your device for either online viewing or offline viewing. Chrome to Mobile is an extension that you install on your computer. You then set up Chrome to Mobile with your mobile device so that you can send pages to the device.

TIP Sending a page for offline viewing can be a great way to carry web pages with you when you don't have an Internet connection or you don't want to burn through your cellular data plan.

NOTE If you don't already have Chrome installed on your computer, install it (for free) from the Chrome Browser page on Google's website, www.google.com/chrome/browser/. After installing Chrome, sign in to it by clicking the Sign In button in the upper-right corner of the screen and then providing your Google account details.

INSTALLING CHROME TO MOBILE ON YOUR COMPUTER

Here's how to install Chrome to Mobile:

1. In Chrome on your computer, display the Settings screen. On Windows, click the Menu button and then click Settings. On the Mac, click the Chrome menu and then click Preferences.

2. Click Extensions in the left column to display the Extensions screen.

3. Click the Get More Extensions link to display the Chrome Web Store.

4. Click the Search box and type **chrome to mobile**.

5. Click the Free button on the Chrome to Mobile result in the Extensions list. The Add "Chrome to Mobile" dialog box opens.

6. Click the Add button. Chrome adds the extension and displays a pop-up message saying it has done so.

SETTING UP YOUR MOBILE DEVICE

After installing Chrome for Mobile, set up your mobile device so that Chrome for Mobile knows about it. Follow these steps:

1. Click the Chrome to Mobile icon at the right end of the omnibox, just to the left of the Bookmark star. The Chrome to Mobile dialog box opens.

2. Click the Connect Your Mobile Device button. The Chrome to Mobile screen appears, listing the permissions that the extension requires.

3. Click the Accept button.

SENDING PAGES TO YOUR DEVICE

After installing Chrome to Mobile, you can send the current web page to your device with just a few clicks. Follow these steps:

1. Click the Chrome to Mobile icon at the right end of the omnibox. A dialog box opens (see Figure 8.15).

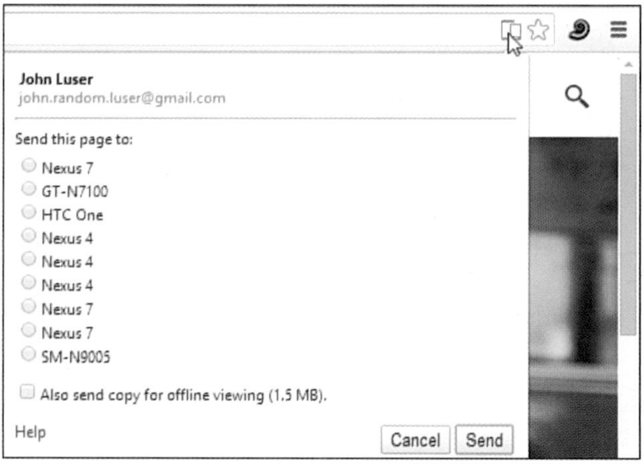

FIGURE 8.15

Click the Chrome to Mobile button, click the radio button for the target device, and then click the Send button.

2. Click the radio button for the device to which you want to send the page.

3. If you want to send an offline copy, check the Also Send Copy for Offline Viewing check box.

4. Click the Send button.

The page opens in a new tab in Chrome on your device, so it's ready for reading when you switch to your device.

☑ TIP Chrome to Mobile also enables you to send a web page from your computer to an iOS device. You'll need to install the Chrome app from the App Store on your iOS device.

9

MAXIMIZING YOUR PRODUCTIVITY

In this chapter, you'll learn how to use your Android device to maximize your productivity. You'll dig into getting Google Now to do your bidding, including setting time- and location-based reminders, and examine how to get around in the Maps app. You'll go through managing your contacts with the People app and managing your schedule with the Calendar app, and then use Google Drive to transfer and sync files. Finally, you'll learn how to print documents from your device as well as other productivity-enhancing moves, such as cordoning off your work files from your personal files and controlling your computer using your Android device.

STREAMLINING YOUR LIFE WITH GOOGLE NOW

Google Now is a powerful tool for locating information that will be helpful to you in your current situation. Google Now automatically displays a series of cards containing information about topics in which you have expressed an interest, such as weather for your current location, listings for the stocks you're tracking, and traffic details for your upcoming appointments. You can find further information by asking questions, either speaking them into your device's microphone or typing them into the Search box.

Google Now predicts your needs and offers information it judges may be helpful to you. You can adjust the information to make it suit your needs better.

Setting Up Google Now

If you haven't used Google Now on your device, you can quickly set it up.

Tap and hold the Home button to display the Google Now circle, and then swipe to the Google button. The Get Google Now screen appears, and you can tap the Next button and then the Yes, I'm In button.

If the Google Now circle doesn't appear when you tap and hold the Home button, you may need to install Google Now. Most devices come with Google Now, but some don't. Tap the Play Store icon on the Home screen, search for *Google search*, and then install the app.

NAVIGATING AND CUSTOMIZING GOOGLE NOW

The Google Now home screen (see Figure 9.1) displays cards containing information.

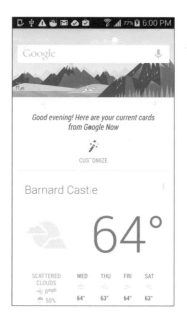

FIGURE 9.1

Google Now displays cards containing information intended to be useful to you.

If you don't want a card, swipe it off the screen. Google Now briefly displays a Done for Now button, with an Undo button that you can tap to recover the card if you swiped it by accident.

Scroll down to see other cards and to reach the controls for customizing Google Now (see Figure 9.2).

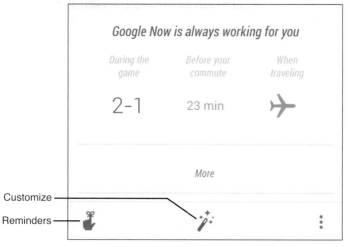

FIGURE 9.2

Tap the Customize button to start customizing Google Now to suit your needs.

CUSTOMIZING GOOGLE NOW TO SUIT YOUR NEEDS

To get the most out of Google Now, you'll want to customize it. To get started, tap the Customize button (the magic wand icon) at the bottom of the Google Now screen; if the Customize button appears at the top of the screen, you can tap it there instead. The Customize Google Now screen appears (see Figure 9.3).

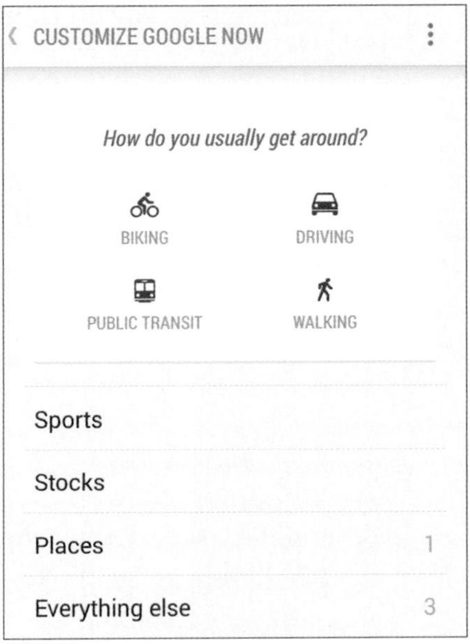

FIGURE 9.3

On the Customize Google Now screen, tap your usual means of getting around, and then use the Sports button, Stocks button, Places button, and Everything Else button to indicate your interests.

When you're setting up Google Now, the How Do You Usually Get Around box may appear. Tap the Biking button, the Driving button, the Public Transit button, or the Walking button, as needed.

In the lower part of the Customize Google Now screen, tap each button in turn and use the resulting screen to start telling Google Now what interests you. For example:

1. Tap the Sports button to display the Sports screen.

2. Tap the Add a Team button.

3. Start typing the name of a team you follow.

4. Tap the correct item in the list of matches that appears. The team's name appears on the Sports screen.

> **TIP** Adding your Work and Home places to the Places screen enables Google Now to provide more accurate commuting times (for example, drive times).

When you return to the Google Now screen, it displays information related to the interests you specified.

CHOOSING SETTINGS FOR GOOGLE NOW

Google Now gives you a wide range of settings that enable you to make it work your way. This section covers the most useful and important settings rather than taking you through every single setting.

To access the settings, tap the Menu button at the bottom of the Google Now screen, and then tap Settings on the menu. The Settings screen appears (see Figure 9.4).

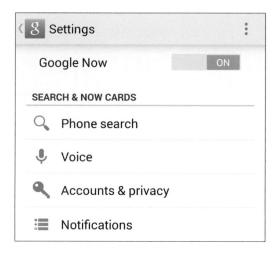

FIGURE 9.4

On the Settings screen, set the Google Now switch to On, and then use the buttons in the Search & Now Cards list to configure Google Now.

The main control here is the Google Now switch, which enables you to turn Google Now off if you don't want to use it. Normally, you'll want to keep this switch set to On.

To control what Google Now searches on your phone or table, tap the Phone Search button or the Tablet Search button, and then check or uncheck the boxes on the Phone Search screen (see Figure 9.5) or the Tablet Search screen.

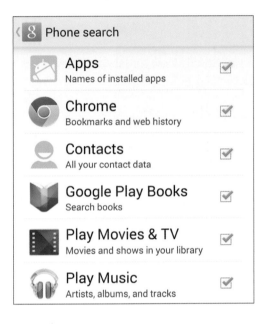

FIGURE 9.5

On the Phone Search screen or the Tablet Search screen, specify what to search by checking or unchecking the boxes.

To configure voice options, tap the Voice button and work on the Voice screen (see Figure 9.6). Here, you can adjust voice search by choosing these settings:

■ **Language.** Tap this button if you need to change the language.

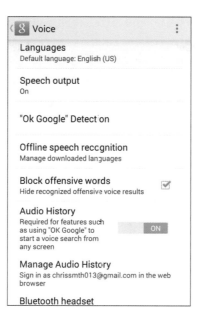

FIGURE 9.6

On the Voice screen, you can turn on or off "OK Google" hotword detection, manage offline speech recognition, and turn on recording through a Bluetooth headset.

- **Speech Output.** Tap this button to display the Speech Output dialog box, and then tap the On radio button, the Hands-Free Only radio button, or the Off radio button, as needed.

- **"OK Google" Detection.** If you want to be able to say "OK Google" to start a voice search from the Home screen or from the Google Search app, tap this button, and then set the "OK Google" Detection switch on the resulting Settings screen to On.

- **Offline Speech Recognition.** Tap this button to display the Download Languages screen. You can then tap the Installed tab to view the list of languages installed for offline speech recognition, tap the All tab to download other languages, or tap the Auto-Update tab to choose settings for updating languages.

> **☑ TIP** Choose the Auto-Update Languages over Wi-Fi Only radio button on the Auto-Update tab of the Download Languages screen. Don't use the Auto-Update Languages at Any Time radio button unless your cellular device has an unlimited data plan.

- **Block Offensive Words.** Check this box to hide any offensive voice results.

- **Audio History.** Set this switch to On to enable yourself to start a voice search from any screen by saying "OK Google."

- **Manage Audio History.** Tap this button to switch to your default browser and go to the screen for managing your Audio History.

- **Bluetooth Headset.** Check this box to enable Google Now to listen to input from your Bluetooth headset.

To change which Google account your device is using for Google Now, and to protect your privacy, tap the Accounts & Privacy button on the Settings screen and choose settings on the Accounts & Privacy screen (see Figure 9.7). These are the options you can choose:

- **Google Account.** Tap this button to switch to another account you've already set up on your device. You can also sign out from your current Google account without switching to another account.

- **Nicknames.** Tap this button to display the Nicknames screen, which shows a list of the nicknames you've created for Google Now.

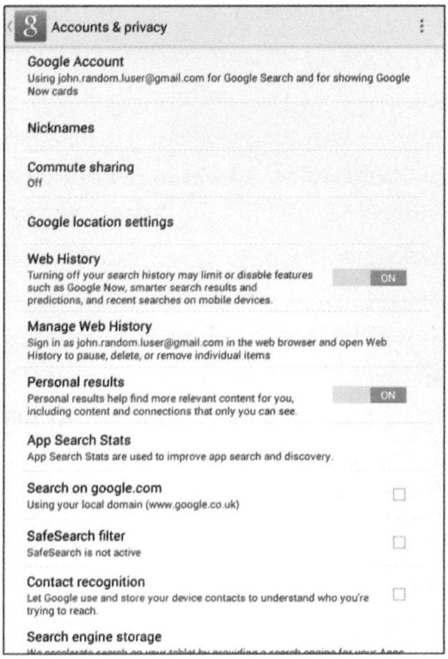

FIGURE 9.7

On the Accounts & Privacy screen, you can change your Google account for Google Now, control your Web History, and choose search options.

Creating Contact Nicknames in Google Now

To help Google Now identify the contacts you want to get in tap with (or ignore), you can create nicknames for them. For example, instead of trying to specify the right Joan out of the dozen Joans among your contacts, you can use the nickname "my wife." This feature isn't available on all devices, but it's well worth trying if your device has it.

To create a contact nickname, open Google Now, say "OK Google" or tap the microphone icon, and then announce the person and the nickname. For example, say "Joan Smith is my wife" or "Alan Jones is the Head Honcho."

The first time you try to create a contact nickname, Android may prompt you to enable the Contact Recognition feature. Do so, and you can then create the contact nickname and start using it.

- **Commute Sharing.** Tap this button to display the Commute Sharing screen. You can then choose which contacts can see your location using Google+ and control whether they see your commute updates.

- **Google Location Settings.** Tap this button to jump to the Location screen in the Settings app, where you can choose the location mode and see which apps have requested your location recently.

- **Web History.** Set this switch to On to allow Google Now to use your recent web browsing and searches to help customize the cards it displays.

- **Manage Web History.** Tap this button to open your History page in your default browser. You can then view the list of your searches on the History page and remove any items you don't want to leave there. Google keeps history for 180 days, and you can delete it at any time.

- **Personal Results.** Set this switch to On to allow Google Search to personalize your search results by using your Web History. This feature should give you more helpful Google Now cards at the cost of some privacy.

! CAUTION Using the Personal Results feature in Google Now causes Google to store more data about what you do on the Web. Given that Google Now aims to provide you with targeted information, this is inevitable, but it's important that you understand you're giving up more privacy. You are the only person who can view this information unless a government agency comes along with a subpoena or a National Security Letter.

■ **App Search Stats *or* Manage History.** Tap this button to display the Manage App History screen. Here, you can uncheck the App History box (it's checked by default) if you want to prevent Google from storing and using links you follow in other apps. You can also tap the Clear App History button to clear your App History. You'd typically do this after unchecking the App History box.

■ **Search on Google.com.** Check this box to search on the main Google.com website. If you uncheck this box, Google searches on the local domain for your geographical region, such www.google.com/au for Australia. If the main Google.com website is your default, this button doesn't appear.

■ **SafeSearch Filter.** Check this box to turn on the SafeSearch Filter feature, which attempts to screen out explicit sexual content.

■ **Contact Recognition.** Check this box to allow Google to store your contacts and use them to interpret your Google Now requests. This feature is usually helpful.

> **! CAUTION**   Checking the Contact Recognition box uploads your device's entire contacts list to Google's servers. Again, this is necessary for the feature to work, but you should understand what's involved.

■ **Search Engine Storage.** You can tap this button to display the Search Engine Storage screen (see Figure 9.8), which enables you to see the apps storing search engine data and the amount of space the data is taking up. You can tap the Clear Now button to clear the contents of the items in the Storage Scheduled for Deletion area.

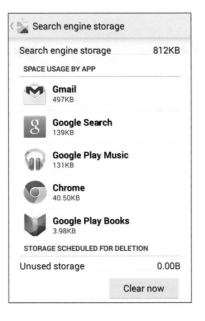

FIGURE 9.8

On the Search Engine Storage screen, you can see the apps that are taking up storage space for search engine data.

> ☑ **TIP** From the Search Engine Storage screen, you can tap an app's button to display the App Info screen for that app. The Storage readout on the App Info screen shows the amount of storage that the app is taking up; you can clear this space by tapping the Clear Data button. The Cache readout shows the amount of data the app has cached. You can delete this data by tapping the Clear Cache button.

> **! CAUTION** Neither the Storage data nor the Cache data on the App Info screen for an app is the same data as that which the Search Engine Storage screen shows the app as holding. Most apps have only a small amount—hundreds of kilobytes or a few megabytes—of search data, and it is seldom worth deleting the data to recover space. But if the data is sensitive, you may want to delete it.

■ **Help Improve Google.** Check this box to allow Google Now to send Google statistics about how you use the app.

To finish configuring Google Now, tap the Notifications button on the Settings screen to display the Notifications screen. Here, you can check or uncheck the Show Updates from Google Now box, set a ringtone for urgent updates, and choose whether to have your device vibrate to signal urgent updates (if your device has a vibration motor).

> **TIP** Set a distinctive ringtone for the "urgent" updates, because they include your reminders, time-to-leave notifications for your appointments, and warnings of unusual traffic conditions as well as public alerts.

ACCESSING GOOGLE NOW FROM THE LOCK SCREEN

To access Google Now directly from the lock screen, tap the up-arrow button at the bottom of the lock screen and drag it up to the Google icon that appears.

You'll need to unlock your device's screen as usual, unless you don't lock it. After you do that, you go straight to the Google Now screen.

WORKING WITH REMINDERS IN GOOGLE NOW

Google Now enables you to create reminders to track things you need to do.

To start working with reminders, display the Reminders screen by tapping the Reminders button at the bottom of the Google Now screen. The Reminders button shows a hand with a finger extended and a piece of string tied around it.

From the Reminders screen, you can start creating a reminder either by tapping the Add a Reminder button and then typing in the details or by saying "Remind me" and the specifics. For example, you could say "Remind me to take the planning spreadsheet to work today at 8 o'clock" to produce the new reminder shown in Figure 9.9.

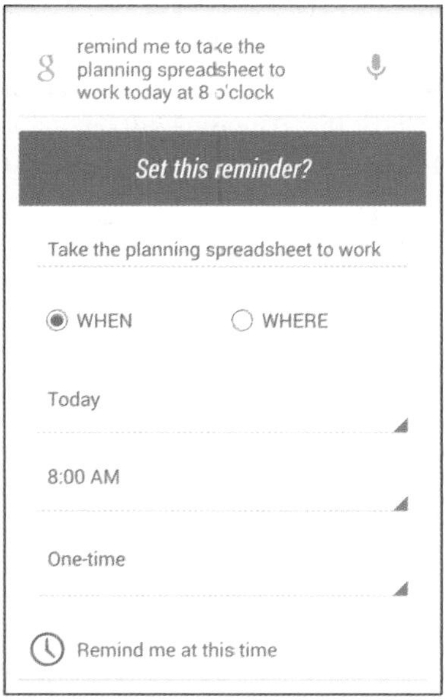

FIGURE 9.9

You can set a reminder in Google Now either by speaking the reminder or by typing its details.

> ✓ **TIP** For a time-based reminder, you can use general times such as "morning," "afternoon," or "evening" as well as specific times. You can also set a timer-based reminder by saying "in five minutes," "in one hour," or a similar phrase.

You can tie a reminder either to a time or to a place. To use a place, tap the Where radio button on the screen for setting a reminder, and then choose the place from the pop-up menu. You can choose a place you've already defined, such as Home or Work, or tap the Set Location button to set a different location.

> ✓ **TIP** You can create a location-based reminder by using a phrase such as "when I get to work" when speaking a reminder.

After you've put all the details in place, tap the Remind Me at This Time button or the Remind Me at This Place button to add the reminder to your list.

> **TIP** If a Google search returns a card that includes a Remind Me on Google Now button, tap that button to set a reminder about that item quickly.

When a time or place triggers a reminder, your device displays a notification. You can tap the reminder to display it in Google Now or tap the Remind Me in 1 Hour button to snooze the reminder.

To delete a reminder, tap it on the Reminders screen, and then tap Delete in the Edit Reminder dialog box.

NAVIGATING WITH MAPS

Google's Maps app enables you to find your location, explore a wide variety of places and optionally share them with others, and get directions from one place to another. You can save map sections for offline access, and you can choose settings to make the app work your way.

MAKING SURE YOU KNOW ESSENTIAL MAPS MOVES

The Maps app is largely straightforward to use after you've grasped the essential moves:

- **Navigate around the map.** Tap and drag to move the map. Flick to move a larger distance, and then tap to slow down the movement if necessary.
- **Choose which map layers to display.** Tap the Menu button to open the menu panel. Then tap the Traffic button, the Public Transit button, the Bicycling button, the Satellite button, or the Terrain button, as needed.

> **NOTE** In Maps, the Menu button is the button with three horizontal lines. On phones, it appears in the lower-left corner of the screen; on tablets, it appears in the upper-left corner for variety.

- **Go quickly to one of your places.** Tap the Menu button to open the menu panel, and then tap Your Places to display the list of your places. Tap the place you want to display in Maps.

> ☑ **TIP**   The Satellite and Terrain layers are mutually exclusive: You can view one or the other, but not both at once. Similarly, you can view only one of the Traffic, Public Transit, and Bicycling layers at a time.

■ **Show your location.** Tap the Location button in the lower-right corner of the screen.

> ✎ **NOTE**   Tap the Google Earth shortcut on the menu panel to switch to the Google Earth app and display the same place you're viewing in Maps.

■ **Turn the map to show the direction your device is facing.** Tap the Location button again. The Location button changes to a compass symbol. The Compass icon appears in the upper-right corner of the screen, with the red needle pointing north.

■ **Zoom in.** Place your finger and thumb together on the screen and pinch apart.

> ☑ **TIP**   You can also zoom by double-tapping. Simply double-tap to zoom in by a zoom increment on the point where you double-tap; double-tap again to zoom further. Double-tap with two fingers to zoom out by increments. You can also double-tap and hold to activate the Zoom feature, and then scroll down to zoom in or scroll up to zoom out.

■ **Zoom out.** Place your finger and thumb apart on the screen and then pinch together. Alternatively, double-tap with two fingers.

■ **Rotate the map.** Place two fingers on the screen and turn them as needed. The Compass icon appears in the upper-right corner of the screen, with the red needle pointing north.

■ **Return the map to north orientation.** Tap the Compass icon.

■ **Search for a place.** Tap the Search box at the top of the screen, and then type or speak your search terms. Tap the icon for the type of result you want: food places, bars, gas stations, and so on. You can search using natural-language queries such as "Mexican restaurants in El Cerrito" or "museums in Albuquerque."

> **TIP** If you want to see all the places Google Maps contains information about in the area you're viewing, type * in the Search box and tap the Search button. Maps displays a red dot for each place. For busy places, this move works best when you've zoomed in a long way.

- **Get directions.** Tap the Directions arrow at the right end of the Search box at the top of the screen, and then specify the start location and the destination. Tap the button at the top of the screen to specify the transit type: driving, public transit, cycling, or walking.

> **TIP** After getting directions, you can specify items to avoid by tapping the Route Options button and then checking the Avoid Highways box, the Avoid Tolls box, or the Avoid Ferries box in the Route Options dialog box.

- **Drop a pin on the map.** Tap and hold where you want to drop a pin. You can then tap the pin's label to display the place info sheet. From here, you can tap the Save button to save the place to your Places list, tap the Share button to share the place with others, or tap the Route button to get directions to the place.

> **NOTE** When you want to remove a pin you've placed on the map, tap elsewhere on the map.

- **Jump into Street View.** Drop a pin for the place (as described in the previous paragraph), tap the pin's label, and then tap the Street View button to go to the place in Street View. You can then look around by tapping and dragging, and move by tapping the white arrows that appear on the road. Tap the Back button when you're ready to leave Street View.

> **TIP** In Street View, tap the screen to display the onscreen controls, and then tap the button with the two curling arrows to make Street View change direction as you turn your device. This feature is great for using Street View to explore the place you're actually in.

SAVING MAPS FOR OFFLINE USE

When you want to be able to access a map even if you have no Internet connection, you can save it for offline use. You can then view the map as needed, update it when your device is online, and delete it when you no longer require it.

SAVING A MAP FOR OFFLINE USE

Here's how to save a map for offline use:

1. Tap the Search box and search for the place.
2. Tap the place name at the bottom of the screen to display the place info sheet.

> ✓ **TIP** If you've browsed to the place rather than searched for it, the place name doesn't appear at the bottom of the screen. To save the map, tap the Search box, tap the Back button to hide the keyboard if necessary, and then tap the Save Map to Use Offline button. You can also tap and hold to drop a pin on the map and then tap the pin's place name to display the place info sheet.

3. Tap the Save Map to Use Offline button. Maps displays the Save This Map? prompt (see Figure 9.10).
4. If necessary, pan and zoom to make the map show the area you want to save.
5. Tap the Save button. Maps displays the Name Offline Map dialog box.
6. Edit the default name (if there is one) for the map as needed, or type a new name.
7. Tap the Save button. The Name Offline Map dialog box closes, and Maps saves the map.

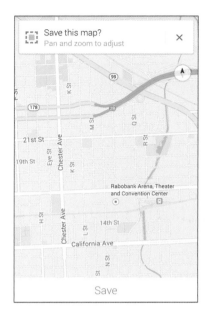

FIGURE 9.10

Pan and zoom the map to the area you want to save for offline use, and then tap the Save button.

DISPLAYING YOUR SAVED MAPS

To display a saved map, tap the Menu button, tap Your Places on the menu panel, and then scroll down to the bottom of the Your Places screen. In the Offline Maps area, tap the map you want to display.

UPDATING, RENAMING, AND DELETING SAVED MAPS

To work with your saved maps, tap the Menu button, tap Your Places on the menu panel, and then tap the View All and Manage button in the Offline Maps box. On the Offline Maps screen that appears, you can tap the Menu button on a map and then tap Rename, Update, or Delete (as needed) on the menu.

> **NOTE** The Maps app automatically deletes your saved maps after 30 days. By updating your maps, you can keep them for longer.

CHOOSING KEY SETTINGS FOR MAPS

If you use the Maps app heavily, spend a few minutes configuring its settings. Tap the Menu button and then tap Settings on the menu panel to display the Settings screen (see Figure 9.11). You can then choose these settings:

- **Switch Account.** Tap this button to switch to another Google account.

- **Edit Home or Work.** To set or change your home address or your work address, tap this button, and then tap the Enter Home Address button (or the Edit Home Address button) or the Enter Work Address button (or the Edit Work Address button).

- **Google Location Settings.** Tap this button to jump to the Location screen in the Settings app, where you can choose the location mode and see which apps have requested your location recently.

- **Location Accuracy Tips.** Tap this button to display the Location Accuracy Tips dialog box, which tells you the Google Location Settings you can choose to improve location accuracy. If you're already using the most accurate settings, Maps displays a message telling you that your location setting is already optimized.

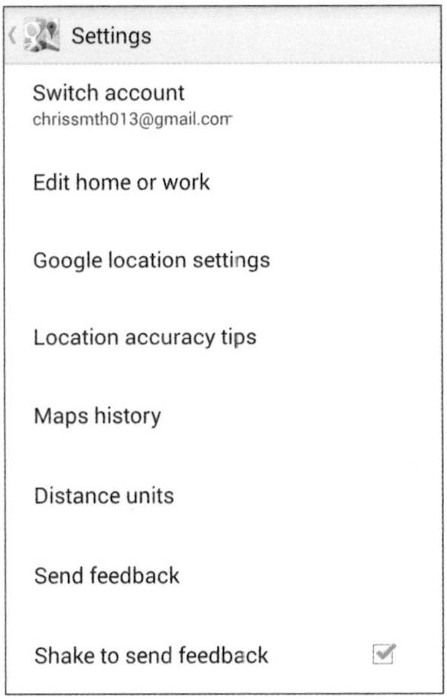

FIGURE 9.11

On the Settings screen in the Maps app, you can edit your home and work addresses, delete indiscretions from your Maps History, and change the distance units.

- **Maps History.** Tap this button to display the Maps History screen, which shows a list of the places you've visited in Maps. You can tap the × icon on the right of a history item to display the Delete dialog box (see Figure 9.12), and then tap the Delete button to delete that item from your Maps History.

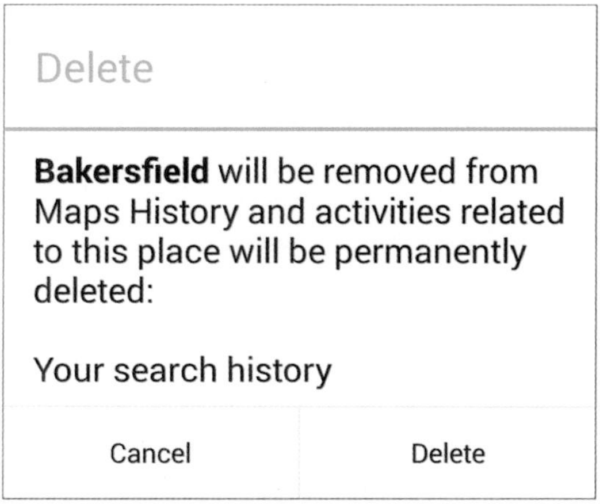

Delete

Bakersfield will be removed from Maps History and activities related to this place will be permanently deleted:

Your search history

Cancel   Delete

FIGURE 9.12

On the Maps History screen, you can delete an item by tapping its × icon and then tapping Delete in the Delete dialog box.

- **Distance Units.** Tap this button to display the Distance Units dialog box. You can then tap the Automatic radio button, the Kilometers radio button, or the Miles radio button, as needed.
- **Send Feedback.** Tap this button to display the Send Feedback screen, on which you can report mapping issues or send feedback either about the app itself or about location features.
- **Shake to Send Feedback.** Check this box if you want to be able to start giving feedback by shaking your device. Tap the Send Feedback button in the Shake to Send Feedback dialog box that opens.

Exploring the Heavens with Google Sky Map

If you enjoy exploring maps on your Android device, download and install the Google Sky Map app. This app is free from the Play Store and provides a fascinating view of the stars and planets.

The app follows the direction your device is pointing, so you can hold it up to the skies and see which heavenly bodies you're gazing at. The Time Travel feature enables you to whizz through time to view the positions of the stars and planets at a particular point, such as the next sunset, next full moon, or the Apollo 11 moon landing.

MANAGING YOUR CONTACTS

Android's People app gives you an easy way to store the information about your contacts. After launching the People app from the Apps screen, you can quickly browse your existing contacts using the Favorites tab, the Contacts tab, and the Groups tab. To navigate among these three tabs, either tap the tab buttons at the top of the screen or swipe left or right.

NOTE On a phone, you can access your contacts through the Phone app as well as through the People app.

TIP If you want to be able to tell from the ringing which of your contacts is phoning you, set a distinctive ringtone for each key contact. To set the ringtone, open the contact, tap the Menu button, and tap Set Ringtone. In the Ringtones dialog box, tap the radio button for the ringtone you want, and then tap the OK button.

ADDING A NEW CONTACT

To add a new contact, tap the New Contact button at the bottom of either the Favorites tab or the Contacts tab. If you have set up multiple accounts, the People app prompts you to choose the account in which to create the contact. You can then fill in the information for the contact, tapping the Add Another Field if necessary to add to the default selection of fields shown, and tap the Done button when you have entered all the available information.

DISPLAYING ONLY THE CONTACTS YOU WANT TO SEE

By default, the People app displays all the contacts you've added to it. If you have many contacts, you may find it helpful to narrow down the display to only those groups you need to see at any particular time.

Here's how to control which contacts appear:

1. Tap the Menu button and then tap Contacts to Display to display the Contacts to Display screen (see Figure 9.13).

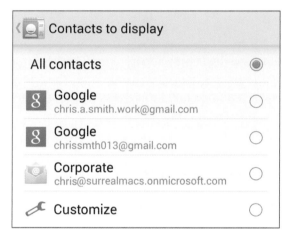

FIGURE 9.13

On the Contacts to Display screen in the People app, you can either tap the radio button for an account or tap the Customize radio button to make a more complex selection.

2. If you want to display all the contacts in a particular account, tap the radio button for that account. If you want to display contacts from multiple accounts, tap the Customize radio button to display the Define Custom View screen (see Figure 9.14).

3. Tap the downward caret to the left of an account's name to expand the account, showing the groups it contains.

4. Check the box for each contact group you want to display.

5. Tap the OK button.

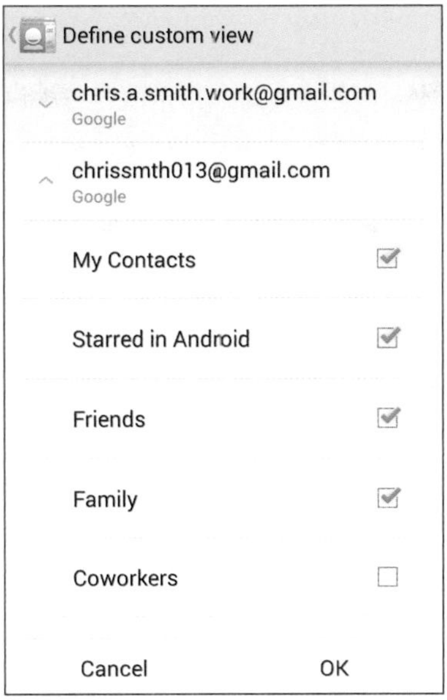

FIGURE 9.14
On the Define Custom View screen, check the box for each contact group you want to include.

NOTE The People app shows Contacts in Custom View or Contacts in *Account* at the top of the screen to indicate that you've restricted the display to only some contacts.

JOINING AND SEPARATING CONTACTS

If you have two or more contact records for the same contact, you can join the records to give a single record containing all the information. Here's how to join contacts:

1. Open one of the contacts.

2. Tap the Menu button and then tap Edit to open the contact for editing.

3. Tap the Menu button and then tap Join to display the contacts list. The Suggested Contacts list at the top shows any contacts that People thinks may be suitable.

4. Tap the appropriate contact. The Contacts Joined readout appears briefly.

5. Tap the Done button to stop editing the contact.

If you find you've joined two contacts by mistake, you can separate them. Open the contact for editing, tap the Menu button, and then tap Separate. The Separate Contact? dialog box appears; tap the OK button to effect the separation.

> **✐ NOTE** If you've joined more than two contacts, the Separate command removes all the joins; you can't separate one of the joined contacts without separating the others as well. So if you need to separate one contact but have two joined, you'll need to join those two contacts again manually.

IMPORTING AND EXPORTING CONTACTS

The People app makes it easy to import contacts from other sources and to export contacts you want to share. To get started, tap the Menu button and then tap Import/Export. In the Import/Export Contacts dialog box (see Figure 9.15), tap the appropriate button:

■ **Import from SIM Card.** If you have contacts stored on your SIM card, you can use this command to import them into the People app.

> **☑ TIP** The Import from SIM Card command is most useful for transferring contacts from your old phone's SIM card to your new phone—providing that the phones take the same size SIM card or that you can get an adapter to make the old phone's SIM card fit in the new phone. If not, export the contacts from the SIM card using the old phone, and then use a different means (for example, your Google account) to put the contacts on the new phone.

■ **Import from Storage.** Use this command to import contacts from either built-in storage or an SD card you've inserted. If you have set up multiple accounts on your device, tap the appropriate account in the Create Contact Under Account dialog box.

■ **Export to Storage.** Use this command to export your contact list to a file that you can then transfer to another device or save for backup. The Export Contacts? dialog box opens, showing the folder and filename of the vCard file to which Android will export the contacts. Tap the OK button to export them.

FIGURE 9.15

The Import/Export Contacts dialog box enables you to import contacts from a SIM card, import contacts from or export them to storage, or share your visible contacts.

> 📝 **NOTE** On some devices, the Import/Export Contacts dialog box also contains the Export to SIM Card command.

■ **Share Visible Contacts.** To share just some of your contacts, restrict the display to just that group using the technique explained in the previous section. Then give this command, select the app or service in the Complete Action Using dialog box, and tap the Just Once button. For example, you can tap the Gmail button to attach the vCard file containing the contacts to a new message in Gmail. You can then address and send the message.

MASTERING YOUR SCHEDULE WITH CALENDAR

The Calendar app gives you an easy way to track your events on your Android device. You can display only those calendars you want to see at a particular time, sync events with your other devices, and share a calendar with other people.

> **TIP** If you haven't already set up all the calendar accounts you want to use, add the missing ones now. In the Calendar app, tap the Menu button and then tap Settings to display the Settings screen. You can then tap the Add Account button and follow the prompts to add another account.

Best of all, you can configure the Calendar app so that it looks and works the way you prefer. Let's start there.

CONFIGURING THE CALENDAR APP

You can customize Calendar's behavior by configuring its settings. To get started, tap the Menu button and then tap Settings. This brings you to the Settings screen, which gives you access to the general settings (which apply across all accounts) and the settings for each account (which affect only that account).

CHOOSING GENERAL SETTINGS

Tap the General Settings button to display the General Settings screen (see Figure 9.16). You can then choose these settings:

■ **Hide Declined Events.** Check this box to display events you've declined instead of displaying only those you've accepted (either definitely or tentatively).

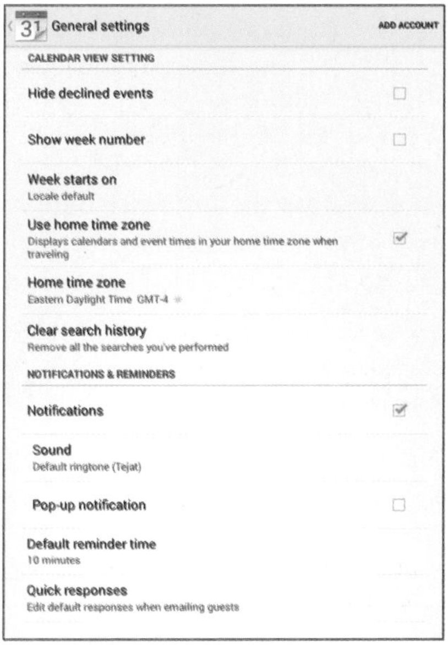

FIGURE 9.16

On the General Settings screen for the Calendar app, you can configure the calendar view and your notifications and reminders.

- **Show Week Number.** Check this box to have Calendar show a readout such as "Week 35" above the month and year.

- **Week Starts On.** Tap this button to display the Week Starts On dialog box, and then tap the Locale Default radio button, the Saturday radio button, the Sunday radio button, or the Monday radio button, to control which day appears at the start of the week.

- **Use Home Time Zone.** Check this box to make Calendar show event times using your home time zone even when you're traveling.

- **Home Time Zone.** If this button shows the wrong time zone, tap it and use the resulting dialog box to select the right time zone.

- **Clear Search History.** Tap this button to clear your search history. There's no confirmation of the clearance.

- **Notifications.** Check this box to allow Calendar to raise notifications.

- **Sound.** Tap this button and use the Sound dialog box to select your notification sound.

- **Pop-Up Notification.** Check this box to enable pop-up notifications.

- **Default Reminder Time.** Tap this button to display the Default Reminder Time dialog box, and then tap the interval you want to use as the default. Your choices range from 1 Minute to 1 Week. You can change the reminder time for any given event.

- **Quick Responses.** Tap this button to display the Quick Responses screen, which contains four canned responses you can send in reply to invitations you receive. To change a quick response, tap it, edit it in the Quick Response dialog box, and then tap the OK button.

> **NOTE** You can't create new quick responses at this writing, so you need to make do by changing the existing four quick responses to suit your needs.

CHOOSING SETTINGS FOR INDIVIDUAL CALENDAR ACCOUNTS

To choose settings for your individual calendar accounts, tap the first account on the Settings screen in the Calendar app. On the Settings screen that appears (see Figure 9.17), check the box for each item that you want to sync, and uncheck all the other check boxes.

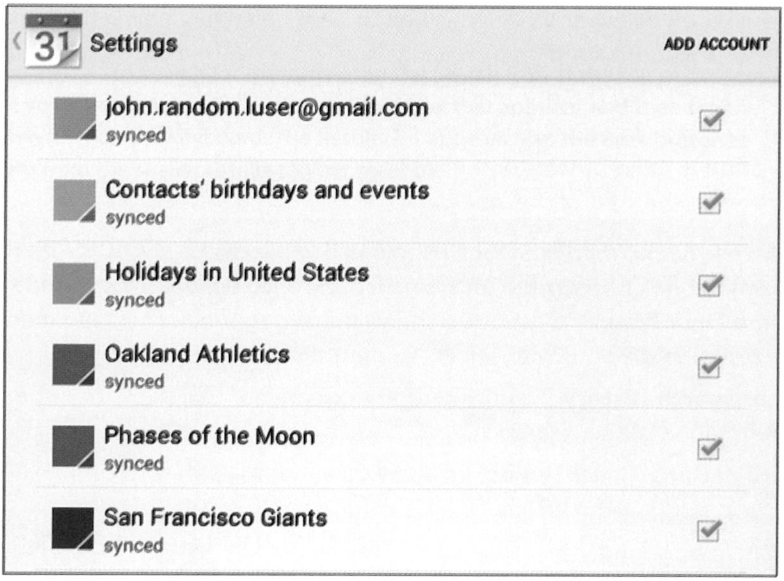

FIGURE 9.17

On the Settings screen for a calendar account, check the box for each item you want to sync.

CHOOSING WHICH CALENDARS TO DISPLAY

Sometimes it's useful to see all your commitments at once, but often you'll find it better to display only some of your calendars so that you can focus on their events. For example, you may want to view only your work calendar so that you can see your work commitments separate from all your other commitments.

To control which calendar the Calendar app displays on a phone, tap the Menu button and then tap Calendars to Display. On the Calendars to Display screen, check the box for each calendar you want to display, and then tap the Back button to return to your calendar.

On a tablet, you can control which calendars the Calendar app displays by tapping the calendars in the list in the lower-right corner of the screen. Tap a calendar once, graying out its button, to hide its contents; tap the button again to display the calendar.

CONTROLLING HOW THE CALENDAR APPEARS

The Calendar app offers four views: Day, Week, Month, and Agenda. The first three views are self-explanatory. The Agenda view displays a list of events for the upcoming days, enabling you to get an overview of your commitments.

On a tablet, the lower-left part of the screen displays a month's calendar in Day view and Week view, giving you an easy way of navigating to other dates. The lower-right part displays a list of the calendars you are using, enabling you to toggle the display of a particular calendar on or off easily.

> **TIP** To hide the month's calendar and the list of calendars on a tablet in Day view or Week view, tap the Menu button and then tap Hide Controls. When you want them back, tap the Menu button again and then tap Show Controls.

CREATING EVENTS

You can create a new event in any of these ways:

- **Manually.** Tap the appropriate time slot in the Calendar, and then tap the + sign that appears.
- **By voice.** Launch Google Now and tell it the event details. For example, say "Create a meeting Monday morning at 10 a.m. with Alice and Bill." Google Now is pretty good about getting the details straight, but if it doesn't, you can fix them on the event sheet that it displays.
- **From an email message.** This approach works only with Gmail in a web browser, not in the Gmail app at this writing. If Gmail automatically underlines an event, move the mouse pointer over it and click the Add to Calendar button that appears.

> **TIP** If you've turned on Google Now, make sure you add the location to each calendar event so that Google Now can display the navigation information and driving time on your cards.

INVITING OTHERS TO AN EVENT

When creating an event to which you want to invite other people, tap the Guests field and enter the invitees. Start typing the first name or email address, and then tap the appropriate result in the list of matches that pops up. The Calendar app adds a button showing the contact's name, and you can start typing the next name.

DEALING WITH INVITATIONS

When you receive an invitation to an event, the Calendar app adds it to your calendar automatically. You can then tap the event to view its details, and then tap the Yes radio button, the Maybe radio button, or the No radio button in the Attending? area to give your response.

SHARING YOUR GOOGLE CALENDARS

Sending invitations works well for individual events, but if you need other people to be able to see every event in a particular calendar, you'll find that sending invitations for each new event grows old fast. Instead, you'll do better to share the calendar. As long as the calendar is a Google one, this is easy to do, but you need to use a web browser rather than the Calendar app at this writing.

Follow these steps to share a Google calendar:

1. Steer your web browser to calendar.google.com and log in if prompted.

2. Click the gear icon in the upper-left corner and then click Settings to display the Calendar Settings screen.

3. Click Calendars at the top of the screen to display the My Calendars list.

4. In the Sharing column, click the link for the calendar you want to share.

5. Click the Person box in the Share with Specific People section and type the email address of the first person with whom you want to share the calendar.

6. Click the Permission Settings pop-up menu and then click the appropriate level of permissions: Make Changes AND Manage Sharing, Make Changes to Events, See All Event Details, or See Only Free/Busy.

7. Click the Save button to make the changes.

> **!CAUTION** Instead of sharing a calendar with specific people, you can check the Make This Calendar Public box to make the calendar appear in public Google search results. Do this only for information you're determined to share with the world at large. If what's important is letting people know when you're available and when you're not, check the Make This Calendar Public box, but then check the Share Only My Free/Busy Information box below it before clicking the Save button to effect the change. Using this setting, people can see when you're free and when you're busy, but they can't see the details of your events.

TRANSFERRING AND SYNCING FILES WITH GOOGLE DRIVE

As you saw in Chapter 2, "Syncing Your Device," you can use Google Drive as an easy way to put files on your Android device, but you'll likely also want to use it for day-to-day file operations as well. In this section, you'll look at how to set up Google Drive, navigate it, choose key settings, and add your documents to it and to your device.

SETTING UP GOOGLE DRIVE

If you're not sure whether the Google Drive app is installed on your device, tap the Apps button on the Home screen and look for the Drive icon. If it's there, tap it to launch the Google Drive app; if not, tap the Play Store icon, search for *Google Drive,* and then install the app.

The first time you launch Google Drive, the app displays the Welcome to Google Drive screen. Swipe up to start reviewing the features. When you finish, the My Drive screen appears (see Figure 9.18).

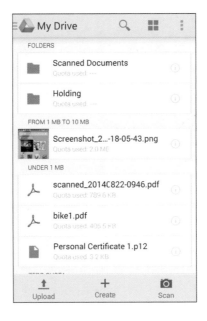

FIGURE 9.18

The My Drive screen gives you quick access to the folders and documents you've stored on Google Drive.

NAVIGATING GOOGLE DRIVE

You can navigate your drive easily using these moves:

■ **Move among the different folders.** Tap the navigation button to display the navigation panel (see Figure 9.19), and then tap the button for the folder you want: My Drive, Incoming, Started, Recent, On Device, or Uploads.

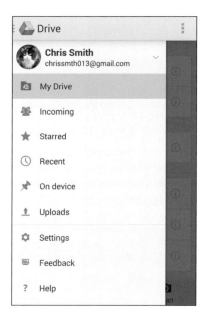

FIGURE 9.19

Use the menu panel to move quickly among the main areas of Google Drive.

■ **Toggle between List view and Thumbnails view.** Tap the Thumbnails button (the four gray squares) or the List button (the four gray dots and horizontal lines) to switch views.

■ **Filter your documents.** Tap the Menu button and then tap Filter By to display the Filter By dialog box. Tap the radio button—Folders, Presentations, Spreadsheets, Text Documents, Images, Videos, and PDF—for the type of item you want to view. Google Drive displays only items of the type you choose. A readout such as Filter: Folders or Filter: Images appears at the top of the screen.

> 📝 **TIP** To remove a filter you've applied, tap the Google Drive logo or the Filter readout, and then tap My Drive on the menu panel.

■ **Sort your documents.** Tap the Menu button and then tap Sort By to display the Sort By dialog box. Tap the radio button—Title, Last Modified, Last Opened by Me, Last Edited by Me, or Quota Used—by which you want to sort, and Google Drive displays the items in that order.

> **TIP**   Sort your documents by Quota Used when you need to see which of them is taking up the most space—for example, when your Google Drive is getting full and you need to free up space.

■ **Open a document or folder.** Tap the thumbnail or the name.
■ **Download a document.** Tap and hold it to display the dialog box of actions for the document (see Figure 9.20), and then tap the Download a Copy button.

bike1.pdf
Send
Move to...
Keep on this device
Open with
Send link
Download a copy
Rename
Print
Remove

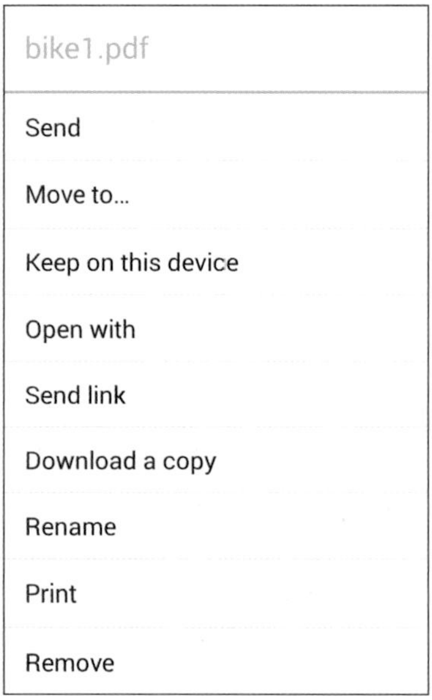

FIGURE 9.20

In the dialog box for a document, tap the Download a Copy button to download the document to your device.

- **View information for a document or folder.** Tap the Info (i) button on the thumbnail or the name button.
- **Search for a document or folder.** Tap the search icon at the top of the screen and type your search terms.

CONFIGURING THE CACHE, ENCRYPTION, AND DATA USAGE

To get the best out of Google Drive, you should configure the cache, turn on encryption, and make sure the app transfers files via the cellular connection only if you want it to. Tap the Navigation button to display the menu panel, and then tap Settings to display the Settings screen (see Figure 9.21). You can then choose these settings:

- **Documents Cache.** Tap the Cache Size button to display the Cache Size dialog box, and then tap the radio button—25 MB, 50 MB, 100 MB, or 250 MB—for the cache size to use. If you use Google Drive extensively, set the Documents Cache to 250 MB (the maximum amount) to allow the app to cache plenty of data. Google Drive caches data so that it can provide it quickly on demand, without needing to download it from the Internet.

> **NOTE** You can tap the Clear Cache button in the Documents Cache area of the Settings screen for Google Drive to clear all your currently cached documents. Normally, you'd do this only if some documents have become corrupt and won't open or sync.

- **Encryption.** Check the Enable Encryption box to encrypt your Google Drive documents on your device. If you have encrypted your Android device as a whole, you don't need to enable encryption in the Google Drive app, but you can if you want.
- **Data Usage.** Check the Transfer Files Only over Wi-Fi box if you want to prevent Google Drive using cellular data on your phone or cellular tablet.

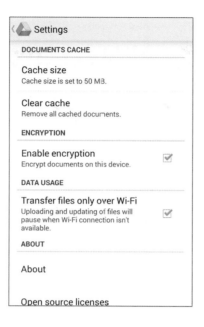

FIGURE 9.21

On the Settings screen for Google Drive, set the cache size and enable encryption. On a phone, you may want to restrict the app to using Wi-Fi.

> **! CAUTION** If you need your Google Drive files to be up to date all the time, uncheck the Transfer Files Only over Wi-Fi box, but keep a close eye on your data plan to make sure you don't go over your limits.

CREATING A FOLDER

Here's how to create a folder on Google Drive:

1. From the My Drive screen, navigate to the folder in which you want to create the new folder.
2. Tap the Create (+) button to display the Create dialog box.
3. Tap the Folder button to display the Folder Name dialog box.
4. Type the name for the folder.
5. Tap the OK button.

Google Drive creates the folder and displays its contents—nothing so far. You can then upload documents to the folder, create new documents in it, or scan documents to it.

ADDING DOCUMENTS TO GOOGLE DRIVE

You can quickly add documents to Google Drive in three ways. First, navigate to the folder in which you want to place the documents. Then take the appropriate action:

- **Upload the document.** Tap the Upload button, navigate to the file, and then tap it. Google Drive starts the upload automatically.

- **Create a new document.** Tap the Create (+) button to display the Create dialog box; tap the Document button, the Spreadsheet button, or the Presentation button, as needed; and then create the document in the Docs module that opens. Tap the check box when you finish editing the document. Then tap the Docs button to close the document.

- **Scan the document.** If your device has a rear camera, tap the Scan button. Line up the document and tap the blue button to photograph it, and then use the cropping tools to crop the document as needed. You can tap the Type button and then tap the document type—None, Black & White, Color, or Color Drawing—on the Type pop-up menu. If you want to rename the document, tap the default name, type the new name, and then tap the OK button. Tap the check mark when the document is ready for upload to Google Drive.

KEEPING DOCUMENTS ON YOUR DEVICE

To keep a specific document on your device, tap the Info (i) button on the file to display the Information screen, and then set the Keep on Device switch to On.

> **TIP** From the Information screen, you can also share a file, send it to others, rename it, move it to a folder, or print it.

Separating Work from Play on Your Device

If you use your Android device for both work and play, you may wish there were a way to keep your work files separate from your personal files. Google is working on such a feature, called Android for Work, for the next version of Android (Lollipop), but as of this writing, you need a third-party solution.

At this point, the best option is the Divide app from the company called Divide. Google purchased Divide (the company) in May 2014, so it seems likely that Android for Work will be based on Divide.

Divide creates a "work container" in which you do your work. You use this container to log in to a Mobile Device Management system rather than logging in with your device as a whole. That may sound abstruse, but consider this example: To connect to an Exchange Server system, you must give the administrator permission to wipe (erase) your device entirely. If you connect using your device, the administrator can wipe all its software; but if you connect using your work container, the administrator can erase the container, not the device.

PRINTING DOCUMENTS

Even if you take your Android device with you everywhere, you may still need to print documents from it sometimes—for instance, so that you can show them to other people without having to hand over your device.

You have four main choices for printing from Android:

- Print to a Wi-Fi printer or Bluetooth printer that supports Android.
- Print to an HP printer using the HP Print Service Plugin.
- Print to a cloud printer. A *cloud printer* is one that connects directly to the Web, receives your print jobs from the Google Cloud Print server, and prints them.
- Print through your existing printer courtesy of your computer, Chrome, and your Google account.

PRINTING TO LOCAL PRINTERS

To print to a local printer, you'll need a printer that directly supports Android.

As you'd imagine, for a Wi-Fi printer, you'll need to connect your device to the same Wi-Fi network. Similarly, for a Bluetooth printer, make sure Bluetooth is enabled on your device, and pair the device with the printer.

If the app from which you want to print has a Print command, give that command, and work through the resulting dialog boxes or screens. For example, in Gmail, open a message for reading. To print the message, tap the message's Menu button (not the main Menu button for the app) and tap Print. In the dialog box that opens, tap the printer, choose other options such as the copies and paper size, and tap the Print button.

If the app from which you want to print doesn't have a Print command, you'll need to use a third-party printing app. One example is PrinterShare, which you can download for free from the App Store. To print with such an app, you launch the app and use its controls to select the document you want to print. You can then choose which printer to use, select other options for printing, and send the document to the printer.

PRINT TO AN HP PRINTER USING THE HP PRINT SERVICE PLUGIN

The HP Print Service Plugin is a software component that comes preinstalled on some Nexus, Samsung, and HP Android devices. This plugin enables those Android devices to print to a wide range of HP inkjet and laser printers.

If your device has the HP Print Service Plugin installed, you can connect to a supported HP printer either via a wireless network or directly (if the printer supports direct wireless connections). Once connected, you can print to the printer.

PRINTING TO CLOUD PRINTERS

Google's overarching printing solution for its apps and devices is Cloud Print, an Internet-based service with which you can register a printer. To print using Cloud Print, you install the Google Cloud Print app or an equivalent app on your device, which enables your device to connect to printers registered on Cloud Print.

! CAUTION Printing via Cloud Print raises moderate security concerns, because each document you print has to be sent across the Internet to Google's servers so that it can then be transmitted to the printer. The documents you print are not private. Google keeps a copy of each document temporarily but deletes it when the print job is complete.

To print to a cloud printer, you open the document in the usual app you use for it and then give the Print command. Apps use different locations for the Print command, but you can usually find it easily. For example, in Google Docs, tap the Menu button, tap Share & Export, and then tap Print.

> **TIP** If no cloud printer is available, you can "print" from your device by saving the document to Google Drive. You can then print the document from there afterward.

PRINTING ON YOUR EXISTING PRINTER

To print on your existing printer that doesn't directly support Android, you need to install third-party software on your device. You may also need to install software on your computer to make the printer visible on the network.

The specifics depend on the software, but here's an example using the PrinterShare app, which is pretty straightforward. To set up printing with PrinterShare:

- Install the PrinterShare app on your Android device and use it to open the document you want to print.
- If the printer is connected to a Mac, you open System Preferences, go to the Sharing pane, and turn on Printer Sharing for the printer you want to use.
- If the printer is connected to a Windows PC, you install the PrinterShare app from the PrinterShare website (http://printershare.com).

You can then print to the printer from your Android device. PrinterShare provides its software for free but charges you to actually print. You can print a test page for free to make sure PrinterShare is a viable option for you.

Controlling Your Computer from Your Android Device

If you want to do even more with your Android device, set it up to control your computer. This move is great both for when you're at home and don't want to go to the next room and for when you're at home and you need to access your computer at work without the commute.

To control your computer from your Android device, you typically need to install and run a server app on your computer and a client app on your device. The server app receives an incoming connection from the client and transfers data back and forth. The client app receives the data from the server, displays it for you (so that you can see what's happening on your computer's screen), and transmits your finger movements and your keystrokes to the server.

Various combinations of software are available, but these are the four most promising at this writing:

- **Splashtop.** Splashtop (www.splashtop.com) consists of a client app called Splashtop, which you install on the remote device (in this case, your Android device), and a server called Streamer, which you install on your PC, Mac, or Linux box. Splashtop comes in various different editions, such as Personal, Business, and Classroom.

- **LogMeIn.** LogMeIn (www.logmein.com) is a service that enables you to connect remotely to your PC or Mac across either a local network or the Internet. Using one of the LogMeIn client apps, such as the LogMeIn for Android app, you can use your Android device to control your PC or Mac after you have connected to it.

- **Remote Desktop Connection.** If your computer has one of the "business" versions of Windows, such as the Professional or Ultimate versions, you can turn on the Remote Desktop feature and connect to your computer using a Remote Desktop client app. Start with the Microsoft Remote Desktop app for Android, which is free, and move on to other apps if you find it doesn't meet your needs.

- **VNC client.** Virtual Network Computing (VNC) is a feature for remotely viewing and controlling other computers. VNC consists of a server app and a client app. OS X includes a built-in VNC server that you can enable by checking the Screen Sharing box in the Sharing pane in System Preferences. You can then connect your Android device using a VNC client such as VNC Viewer from RealVNC Limited, which is available for free from the App Store.

USING A CHROMECAST DEVICE

Google's Chromecast device provides easy way to display the content from your Android device on a large screen, such as an HDTV or a monitor. The Chromecast device is the size of a large (and swollen) thumb that connects to the HDTV or monitor via an HDMI port. Your Android device connects to the Chromecast device via Wi-Fi and plays content on it.

> ⟨🖉 **NOTE** The device is simply called "Chromecast"—but the app you use to configure the device and to start casting your screen to it is also called "Chromecast." So, this section uses the terms *Chromecast device* and *Chromecast app* for clarity.

Android plays content on the Chromecast device in two ways, depending on what the content is:

■ **Remote control.** If the media file is online, Android causes the Chromecast device to connect to the file. If the media file is on your device, Android transfers the media file to the Chromecast device. Android then uses remote control to play back the file on the Chromecast device.

■ **Streaming.** The Android app you're using plays the media file but streams the playback to the Chromecast device, which displays the video content and outputs the audio content.

SETTING UP A CHROMECAST WITH YOUR ANDROID DEVICE

You can set up your Chromecast device using your Android device or another device or computer. This section contains instructions for setup using your Android device.

> ⟨🖉 **NOTE** On a computer, take your web browser to www.chromecast.com/setup and follow the instructions.

1. On your Android device, go to the Play Store and install the free Chromecast app.
2. After installation, open the Chromecast app. The Chromecast app automatically searches for available Chromecast devices that need setting up. It then displays the Found screen showing your Chromecast device (see Figure 9.22).

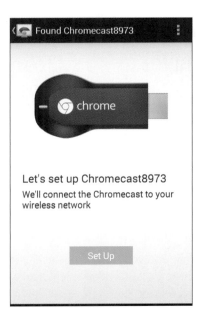

FIGURE 9.22

On the Found screen showing your Chromecast device, tap the Set Up button.

3. Tap the Setup button and follow through the setup process until the Chromecast app displays the Change the Name of Your Chromecast screen (see Figure 9.23).

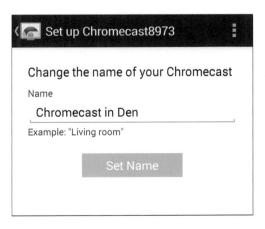

FIGURE 9.23

Type the name you want to assign your Chromecast device, and then tap the Set Name button.

4. Type the name you want to give the Chromecast device and then tap the Set Name button. The Chromecast app displays the Connect Chromecast to Your Wi-Fi screen (see Figure 9.24).

FIGURE 9.24

Use the controls on the Connect Chromecast to Your Wi-Fi screen to connect your Chromecast device to your wireless network.

5. Tap the Wi-Fi Network pop-up menu and then tap the network you want to use.

6. Tap the Password field and then type the password.

7. Tap the Set Network button. The Sweet! You Are Ready to Cast screen appears (see Figure 9.25).

> **NOTE** At this point, the Chromecast device connects to the Internet and checks automatically for updates. If it finds an update, it downloads and installs it. You'll see a message and progress readout on your TV screen while this is happening. During the update, the Chromecast device reboots. You don't need to do anything at this point—just wait until the Chromecast screen appears again on your TV.

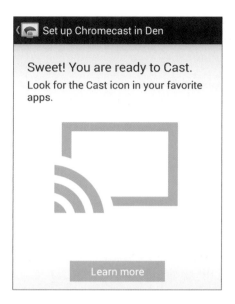

FIGURE 9.25

When you see the Sweet! You Are Ready to Cast screen, you can start using your Chromecast device.

CASTING YOUR SCREEN TO THE CHROMECAST DEVICE

When a Chromecast device is available to your Android device, apps that support Chromecast display the Cast icon. For example, the YouTube app displays the Cast icon near the Menu button, as you can see in Figure 9.26.

FIGURE 9.26

Tap the Cast icon in an app to connect to a Chromecast device.

Tap the Cast icon to display the Connect to Device dialog box (see Figure 9.27), and then tap the Chromecast device you want to use.

FIGURE 9.27

In the Connect to Device dialog box, tap the Chromecast device you want to use.

Android connects to the Chromecast device, and the Chromecast device begins playing back the content (see Figure 9.28).

FIGURE 9.28

You can use your Android device to control playback on the Chromecast device.

PLAYING MUSIC TO THE CHROMECAST DEVICE

You can also use the Chromecast device to play music through the speakers connected to your HDTV or monitor. This can be great for sharing music with your friends or with your neighbors.

If the music file is stored online, Android causes the Chromecast device to stream it from the online site. If the music file is stored on your device, the device transfers the audio to the Chromecast device, and the Chromecast device then plays it back.

For example, in the Play Music app, tap the Cast icon to display the Connect to Device dialog box, and then tap the Chromecast device's name. The Play Music transfers the music file to the Chromecast device and enables remote control, so you use the playback buttons in the Play Music app to control playback on the Chromecast device.

> **NOTE** After you've started the music playing on the Chromecast device, you can close the Play Music app\ (or even shut down your Android device) without the music stopping, because the Chromecast device is playing it. Closing the app (or shutting down your device) isn't helpful unless you need to convince someone that Android isn't streaming the audio to the Chromecast device.

10

MAKING THE MOST OF PHONE AND MESSAGING

In this chapter, you learn how to get the most out of the standard Phone app that comes with Android phones. You then dig into how to get the most out of Google's Hangouts app, including messaging and audio and video chats.

BECOMING EXPERT WITH THE PHONE APP

Open the Phone app by tapping the Phone icon on the Home screen or on the Apps screen. You can then quickly start making calls, review recent activity, or choose settings to configure the Phone app.

> 📝 **NOTE** Many manufacturers customize the Phone app heavily, so your phone may have a substantially different look and layout than the Phone app shown here. Your phone may also have extra features added, but the essential features should be the same.

MAKING CALLS THE EASY WAY

When you first open the Phone app, it displays a screen showing any recent activity plus the Speed Dial list (see Figure 10.1). From here, you can take the following actions:

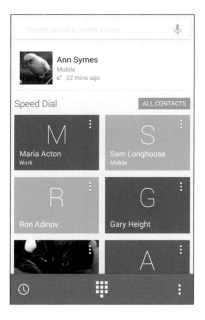

FIGURE 10.1

At first, the Phone app displays recent calls and the Speed Dial list.

- ■ Tap the Search box at the top and search for a contact or a number.
- ■ Tap a recent item to call that number.
- ■ Tap a tile in the Speed Dial list to call that contact. If the contact has multiple numbers, the Choose Number dialog box opens (see Figure 10.2). Check the Remember This Choice box if you want to use this particular number in the future, and then tap the number to call.

> **✓ TIP** The Speed Dial list shows those of your Favorites in the People app that have one or more phone numbers. To add a contact to the Speed Dial list, open the contact in the People app and tap the Favorite star. To remove a contact from the Speed Dial list in the People app, open the contact and tap the Favorite star to remove it. To remove a contact from the Speed Dial list in the Phone app, tap and hold the contact, and then drag it to the Remove button that appears at the top of the screen. Doing this also removes the contact from the Favorites list.

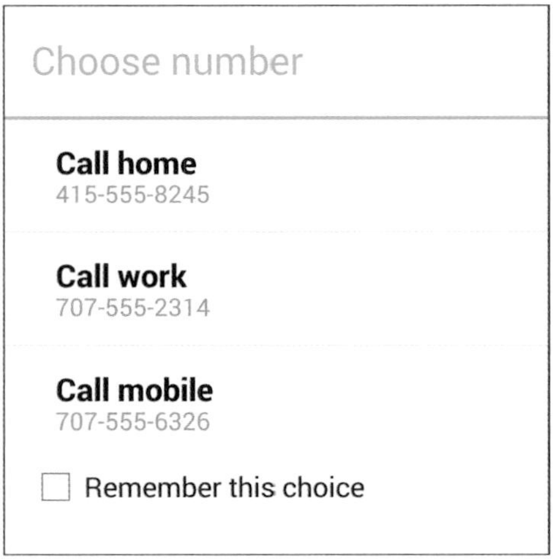

Choose number

Call home
415-555-8245

Call work
707-555-2314

Call mobile
707-555-6326

☐ Remember this choice

FIGURE 10.2

If the contact has multiple numbers, tap the appropriate one in the Choose Number dialog box.

■ Tap the Menu button on a tile to display other calling options, such as sending an instant message instead.

> **✓ TIP** You can also place phone calls from the People app or from other apps that display contact information that includes phone numbers. If in doubt, try tapping the phone number and see what happens.

■ Tap the All Contacts button to display the All Contacts screen so that you can browse all your contacts.

> **NOTE** In either the Phone app or the People app, you can tap the Menu button and then tap Clear Frequents to clear the Frequently Contacted list. This is the list that appears below the Favorites list in the People app. It is separate from the Speed Dial list in the Phone app. On some phones, you can clear the list only from the Favorites tab of the Phone app.

SAVING TIME WITH THE CALL LOG AND HISTORY

You can often save time and effort by using the call log, which tracks your incoming and outgoing calls. KitKat refers to the call log as History, whereas older versions of Android refer to it as Call Log; some phones call it Recent. Either way, it's easy to use: Tap the button with the clock icon in the lower-left corner of the Phone app, and the History screen (or the Call Log screen, or the Recent screen) appears.

> **TIP** Place your vital contacts on the Home screen so that you can get in touch with them quickly. Open the contact in the People app or in the Phone app, tap the Menu button, and then tap Place on Home Screen.

The All tab (see Figure 10.3) on the History screen appears at first. Here, a green arrow shows an outgoing call, a red arrow shows an incoming call you missed or ducked, and a blue arrow shows an incoming call you took. You can tap the Missed tab to restrict the list to calls you missed.

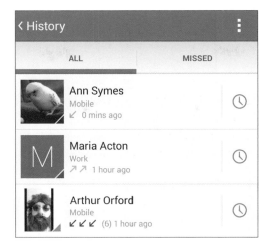

FIGURE 10.3

Use the History screen or Call Log screen to return missed calls or to follow up with people you are trying to reach.

You can tap the Call Details icon (the clock icon) on the right side of a button on the History screen to display the Call Details screen (see Figure 10.4). On some phones, you may need to tap in the middle instead. Here you can view the list of recent contacts and also take these actions:

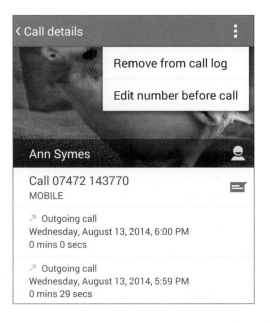

FIGURE 10.4

Display the Call Details screen when you need to see the details of your calls with a contact.

- **Call the contact.** Tap the appropriate Call button—for example, the Mobile number.

> **TIP** In Samsung TouchWiz, you can swipe right from the Call Log to call the contact's default number. For balance, you can also swipe left from the Call Log to start an instant message.

- **Edit the contact's number and then place the call.** Tap the Menu button and then tap Edit Number Before Call. For example, you may need to add a dialing prefix, a pause, or a wait to the number.
- **Remove the call from the call log.** Tap the Menu button and then tap Remove from Call Log.

> **TIP** When you've worked your way through the call log, clear it by tapping the Menu button and then tapping Clear Call Log.

DIALING WITH THE SMART DIALER

To dial with the Smart Dialer, tap the Dialer button at the bottom of the screen and then tap the buttons to dial. You can also take the following actions:

- **Dial a contact.** As you dial, the Phone app displays contacts with matching numbers at the top of the screen. Tap the contact you want to dial.
- **Add a two-second pause.** Tap the Menu button and then tap Add 2-Sec Pause.
- **Add a wait.** Tap the Menu button and then tap Add Wait.

MAKING MULTIPERSON CALLS WITH THE PHONE APP

The Phone app enables you to easily make multiperson calls: You simply place the initial call as usual and then add other calls one by one as needed.

> **NOTE** The maximum number of participants in a call depends on your carrier rather than on your phone. If you need to find out the limit, ask your carrier's support department.

To add a call, tap the Add Call button on the right of the control bar at the bottom of the call screen (see Figure 10.5). The Dial to Add a Call screen appears, and you can dial the call by using the Dialer or the History screen.

> **TIP** Tapping the Add Call button puts the first caller on hold, so it's a good idea to tell that person you're about to disappear temporarily.

Add Call

FIGURE 10.5

Tap the Add Call button to start turning a single-person call into a multiperson call.

After the new person you've called answers, exchange pleasantries, tell the person you're about to drop him in a multiperson call, and then tap the Merge button (see Figure 10.6) to merge the calls.

Merge

FIGURE 10.6

Tap the Merge button to merge the new call into the existing call.

After you merge the calls, the Phone app displays the Conference Call screen, replacing the participants' pictures with a group picture of smiling but otherwise faceless characters (see Figure 10.7). You can now add other calls if necessary (tap the Add Call button as before) or just talk, but you can also chat privately to individuals or drop people from the call.

FIGURE 10.7

Tap the Manage Conference button on the Conference Call screen when you need to speak individually to participants or to drop people from the call.

To manage the call like this, tap the Manage Conference button and work on the Manage Conference Call screen (see Figure 10.8). Here you can tap the arrow button to speak to a participant privately or tap the End Call button to drop that participant from the call.

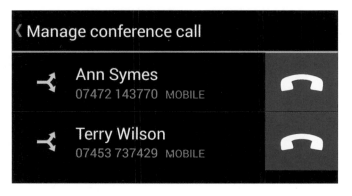

FIGURE 10.8
Using the Manage Conference Call screen, you can speak to a participant individually or hang up on a participant.

TAKING CALLS—OR AVOIDING THEM

When you receive a phone call, you can take it, decline it, or send a text response.

TAKING OR DECLINING A CALL

When you receive a call, your phone displays the calling number if it's available and any associated contact name and picture. The circle containing a phone receiver and the expanding concentric circles around it (see Figure 10.9) give a visual cue that the phone is ringing in case you've suppressed the sound.

FIGURE 10.9

When a call comes in, your phone displays the number (if available) and any associated contact name and picture.

Tap the receiver icon to display the available actions (see Figure 10.10). You can then drag the receiver to the green icon on the right to accept the call or to the red icon on the left to decline it.

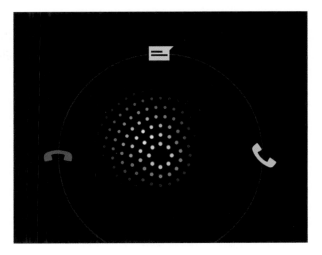

FIGURE 10.10

Drag to the green icon to take the call or to the red icon to decline it. Drag up to the Quick Response icon to send a Quick Response.

SENDING A TEXT RESPONSE TO A CALL

When you receive a call you can't take or don't want to take, you can send one of your Quick Responses back as a text. Drag the call circle straight up to the Quick Response icon, and then tap the response you want to use in the Quick Response dialog box that opens (see Figure 10.11).

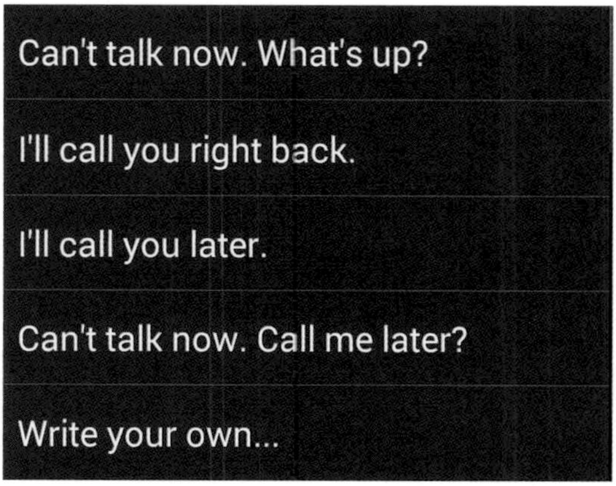

Can't talk now. What's up?

I'll call you right back.

I'll call you later.

Can't talk now. Call me later?

Write your own...

FIGURE 10.11

Tap the Quick Response you want to send, or tap Write Your Own, type the response, and then tap the Send button.

CONFIGURING THE PHONE APP TO WORK YOUR WAY

To get the most out of the Phone app with minimal effort and frustration, spend a few minutes configuring it to work your way. Open the Phone app, tap the Menu button, and then tap Settings to display the Settings screen (see Figure 10.12).

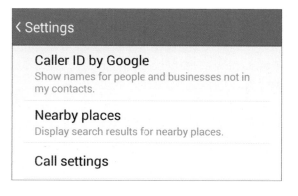

< Settings

Caller ID by Google
Show names for people and businesses not in my contacts.

Nearby places
Display search results for nearby places.

Call settings

FIGURE 10.12

From the Settings screen in the Phone app, you can turn on Caller ID by Google, view search results for nearby places, or display the Call Settings screen.

TURNING ON CALLER ID BY GOOGLE

First, turn on the Caller ID by Google feature to help identify as many incoming calls as possible. To do so, tap the Caller ID by Google button on the Settings screen, and then set the Caller ID by Google switch on the resulting screen to On.

> ### NOTE Some phones don't offer the Caller ID by Google feature.

The Phone app displays caller information for a call from any number listed in your contacts in the People app unless the caller has blocked Caller ID or there's another problem. For example, the call may be routed internationally or through a calling service. Caller ID by Google enables the Phone app to display information for callers who are not among your contacts in the People app.

CHOOSING WHETHER TO USE THE NEARBY PLACES FEATURE

On the Settings screen, you can tap the Nearby Places button to display the Settings screen that contains information about the Nearby Places feature. You can then set the Nearby Places switch to On or Off, as needed. Nearby Places uses your location (as determined by your device's GPS, by its cellular connection, or by known wireless networks nearby) to add nearby places from Google's database to your search results.

> ### NOTE Only some phones have the Nearby Places feature.

From the Settings screen for Nearby Places, you can tap the View Location Settings button to jump to the Location screen in the Settings app. Here you can set the Location switch to Off if you want to turn off location reporting. You can also tap the Mode button and choose High Accuracy, Battery Saving, or Device Only on the Location Mode screen.

DISPLAYING THE CALL SETTINGS SCREEN

After choosing settings for the Caller ID by Google and Nearby Places feature, tap the Call Settings button on the Settings screen to display the Call Settings screen (see Figure 10.13). Here you find most of the options for configuring the Phone app.

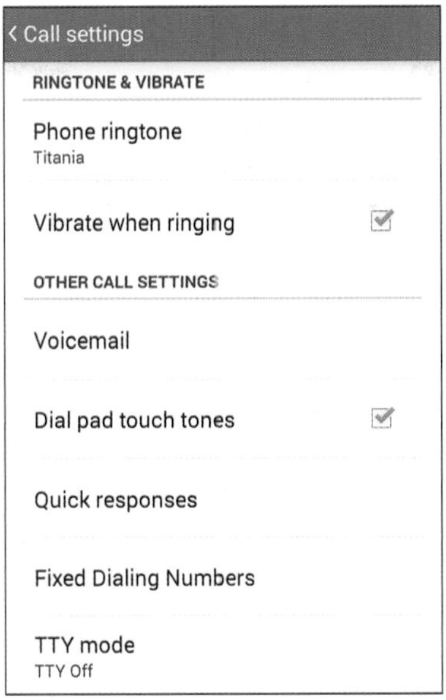

FIGURE 10.13

From the Call Settings screen, you can configure the Phone app's default ringtone and vibration, set up Quick Responses and Fixed Dialing Numbers, and configure Internet calling.

CHOOSING RINGTONE, VIBRATE, VOICEMAIL, AND TOUCH TONES SETTINGS

The top part of the Call Settings screen has four essential settings:

- **Phone Ringtone.** Tap this Phone Ringtone button to set the default ringtone—the ringtone that plays when the calling number isn't a contact to whom you've assigned a default ringtone or the calling number isn't available.

- **Vibrate When Ringing.** Check this box if you want your phone to vibrate when it's ringing.

- **Voicemail.** Tap this button to display the Voicemail screen. Here, you can tap the Service button to choose the voicemail service (such as your carrier); tap the Setup button to set up the Voicemail feature with the appropriate phone number; tap the Sound button to choose the Voicemail notification sound; and check or uncheck the Vibrate check box as needed.

- **Dial Pad Touch Tones.** Check this box to have Android play touch tones as you dial numbers.

TAILORING YOUR QUICK RESPONSES TO YOUR NEEDS

The Phone app provides four preset Quick Responses, such as "I'll call you right back" and "Can't talk now. Call me later?" You can edit them by tapping the Quick Responses button on the Call Settings screen and then working on the Edit Quick Responses screen. Tap a Quick Response to open it for editing, type the text you want in the Quick Response dialog box, and then tap the OK button.

> **NOTE** As of writing, you can't add extra Quick Responses. If you want to restore the Quick Responses to their default text, tap the Menu button on the Edit Quick Responses screen and then tap Restore Defaults.

LIMITING OUTGOING CALLS WITH FIXED DIALING NUMBERS

The Fixed Dialing Numbers (FDN) feature enables you to limit the phone to call only specific numbers you save to the SIM card. You might want to set up Fixed Dialing Numbers on a phone you give to a child.

> **NOTE** The Fixed Dialing Numbers feature is available only on phones that use the Global System for Mobile Communications (GSM) standard. If your phone uses the Code Division Multiple Access (CDMA) standard, Fixed Dialing Numbers isn't available.

> **! CAUTION** To set up the FDN feature, you may need to get a PIN2 number from your carrier. PIN2 is a secondary PIN, separate from your unlocking PIN or your encryption passcode (or PIN), used to secure the Fixed Dialing Numbers list against unauthorized access.

Here's how to set up Fixed Dialing Numbers:

1. Tap the Fixed Dialing Numbers button on the Call Settings screen to display the Fixed Dialing Numbers screen (see Figure 10.14).

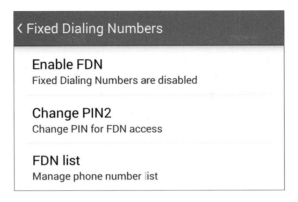

FIGURE 10.14

To limit outgoing calls to specific numbers, set up the FDN list and then enable the FDN feature on the Fixed Dialing Numbers screen.

2. Tap the FDN List button to display the FDN List screen. You can then tap the Menu button and tap Add Contact to add a contact to the list. You'll need to type the contact name and phone number manually; you can't add this information directly from the People app.

3. After you've set up the FDN list, tap the Enable FDN button on the Fixed Dialing Numbers screen. In the Enable FDN dialog box, type the PIN2, and then touch OK.

Choosing a TTY Mode to Help with Hearing Problems

If you have hearing problems, you can use the TTY Mode setting on the Call Settings screen to turn on a particular teletypewriter mode on your Android device. Tap the TTY Mode button to display the TTY Mode dialog box, and then tap the appropriate radio button: TTY Off (the default setting), TTY Full (for full teletypewriter features), TTY HCO (for Hearing Carry-Over functionality), or TTY VCO (for Voice Carry-Over functionality).

SETTING UP CALL FORWARDING

To set up Call Forwarding, tap the Call Forwarding button on the Call Settings screen to display the Call Forwarding Settings screen. Here you can choose these four settings:

- **Always Forward.** When you need to forward all calls, tap this button, enter the number in the Always Forward dialog box, and then tap the Enable button.

> **NOTE** Some phones and carriers don't provide call forwarding. Others provide only some forwarding features, such as an All Incoming Calls button and an Unanswered button.

- **Forward When Busy.** Tap this button to display the Forward When Busy dialog box, change the number if necessary, and then tap the Update button.

> **NOTE** The Forward When Busy, Forward When Unanswered, and Forward When Unreachable features are normally enabled and go to your voicemail service by default. You can redirect them as needed—for example, to a work colleague or a family member. You can also tap the Disable button in the feature's dialog box if you need to disable the feature.

- **Forward When Unanswered.** Tap this button to display the Forward When Unanswered dialog box, change the number if necessary, and then tap the Update button.
- **Forward When Unreachable.** Tap this button to display the Forward When Unreachable dialog box, change the number if necessary, and then tap the Update button.

CONFIGURING CALLER ID AND CALL WAITING

To configure Caller ID and Call Waiting, tap the Additional Settings button on the Call Settings screen. On the Additional Settings screen, tap the Caller ID button, and then tap the Network Default radio button, the Hide Number radio button, or the Show Number radio button in the Caller ID dialog box (see Figure 10.15).

> **NOTE** Some phones name the Caller ID controls differently, such as Caller ID Readout. Other phones and carriers provide neither Caller ID nor Call Waiting.

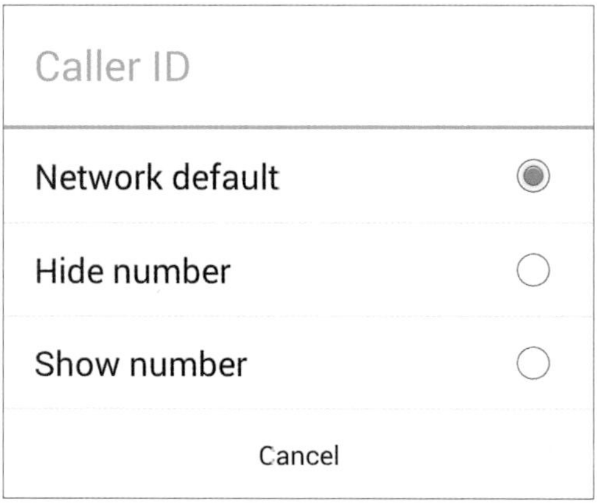

Caller ID	
Network default	●
Hide number	○
Show number	○
Cancel	

FIGURE 10.15

In the Caller ID dialog box, choose whether to show your number when calling, hide it, or go with the network default setting.

> **CAUTION** Don't use the Network Default setting for Caller ID unless you know what it does. If you're not sure, ask your carrier or place a call to another mobile phone you can see to find out what the default setting for standard calls is.

> **TIP** In the United States, you can override your Caller ID blocking for a call by dialing *82 before the number. If you've turned on Caller ID, you can block it for a call by dialing *67 before the number. Other countries use different numbers for blocking and releasing.

On the Additional Settings screen, check the Call Waiting box if you want Call Waiting to notify you of incoming calls when you're already in a call.

CONFIGURING INTERNET CALLING

Use the buttons in the Internet Call Settings section at the bottom of the Call Settings screen to set up your Internet calling accounts and to specify when to use them.

> **NOTE** Some phones and carriers don't offer Internet calling.

Tap the Accounts button to display the Internet Calling (SIP) Accounts screen. You can then add an Internet calling account by tapping the Add Account button at the bottom of the screen, filling in the account's details on the SIP Account Details screen, and then tapping the Save button.

> **NOTE** SIP is the acronym for Session Initiation Protocol, the Internet protocol used for Internet calls.

On the Internet Calling (SIP) Account screen, check the Receive Incoming Calls box if you want your device to listen for incoming calls. Be aware that turning on this feature reduces your device's battery life.

Back in the Internet Call Settings section of the Call Settings screen, tap the Use Internet Calling button to display the Use Internet Calling dialog box, and then tap the appropriate option button: For All Calls When Data Network Is Available, Only for Internet Calls, or Ask for Each Call.

SETTING CUSTOM RINGTONES FOR IMPORTANT CALLERS

If you want to be able to distinguish your important callers easily, set a custom ringtone for each of them like this:

1. Open the contact in either the Phone app or in the People app.
2. Tap the Menu button and then tap Set Ringtone to display the Ringtones dialog box.
3. Tap a ringtone to listen to it.
4. After you've made your choice, tap the OK button.

> **TIP** If you tire of your device's built-in ringtones, you can download plenty more from the Internet. Alternatively, use an app such as Ringtone Maker from Big Bang (available free from the Play Store) to create custom ringtones from key sections of your favorite songs.

BLOCKING AND SCREENING CALLS

The great thing about having an Android phone is that anyone can call you at any time.

The bad thing about having an Android phone is that anyone can call you at any time.

To keep peace of mind and your privacy, you'll probably want to send some contacts' calls directly to voicemail, either sometimes or always. You may want to block some calls completely to prevent specific people (or specific phone numbers) from calling you. You may also want to screen your calls so that you can choose which to take and which to leave.

SENDING A CONTACT'S CALLS DIRECTLY TO VOICEMAIL

To send all of a contact's calls to voicemail, open the contact from the People app or the Phone app, tap the Menu button, and then check the All Calls to Voicemail box.

BLOCKING CALLS

Sending a contact's calls to voicemail is straightforward. Blocking calls isn't. But here are four things you can do:

■ **Have your carrier block specific numbers.** If you're being plagued by calls from a particular phone number, you can ask your carrier to block it. Setting up the blocking is a hassle, but the blocking is effective.

> **TIP** If you are being troubled by telemarketing calls in the United States, you can register your phone number on the National Do Not Call Registry (www. donotcall.gov). The listing takes up to 31 days to become effective; and not all telemarketers respect the Registry, but many do. If you're in another country, see if it has a similar registry or body.

- **Use a call-blocker app.** When you need to block calls from specific numbers, look at apps such as Call Control or Extreme Call Blocker. These apps let you choose which calls to take and which to avoid.
- **Use an app such as Do Not Disturb.** The Do Not Disturb app from Cabooze Software enables you to suppress phone calls, Short Message Service (SMS) messages, and other interruptions either on a schedule you define (for example, to allow you to sleep at night) or for a period of time (for example, two hours starting now). You can allow interruptions from specific people or for emergency calls. Do Not Disturb offers a two-week trial that enables you to test the features included in the premium version. After the trial, you must either pay for the premium version ($1.99) or give up on some of the more attractive features.

TIP The forthcoming version of Android, Lollipop, has a full-fledged Do Not Disturb feature.

- **Turn on Airplane mode.** When you need total peace and quiet, open the Quick Settings panel and tap the Airplane Mode button to silence all communications.

NOTE Some phones have a Blocking mode that you can use to block all calls. For example, Samsung phones have a Blocking mode that enables you to block incoming calls, turn off notifications, or turn off the alarm and timer—or all three features.

SETTING A SIM CARD LOCK

As you know, Android enables you to secure your phone or tablet against intrusion by setting a screen lock, such as a PIN or a password, and to secure your data by encrypting it. But a phone also has another point of vulnerability: Anyone who can get one-on-one time with the phone can remove the SIM card, insert it in another phone, and run up charges on your tab.

! CAUTION To set a SIM card lock, you will need to know the PIN Unlock Key, or PUK, for your SIM. Normally, you get the PUK from your carrier. For example, if your phone is on AT&T, log in to myAT&T, click Wireless, click Phone/Device, and then click Unblock SIM Card to get the PUK. On Verizon, log in to My Verizon, click About My Device, and then use the My PIN and Unblocking Key (PUK) controls.

To minimize the damage from someone filching your SIM card, you can lock it. Follow these steps:

1. Open the Settings app.
2. Tap the Security button to display the Security screen.

NOTE Depending on your phone, you may need to take different steps here. For example, you may need to display the Security & Screen Lock screen or tap the button to assign a SIM PIN.

3. Tap the Set Up SIM Card Lock button to display the SIM Card Lock Settings screen.
4. Check the Lock SIM Card box. The Lock SIM Card dialog box opens.
5. Type the SIM PIN.
6. Tap the OK button.

TIP After enabling the SIM card lock, tap Change SIM PIN on the SIM Card Lock Settings screen and set a new SIM for security.

Adding Phone Calling to a Tablet with Google Voice

If you have a tablet rather than a phone, and you're in the United States, consider adding the Google Voice app to it so that you can use the Google Voice telecommunications service. The app is free and the cost is minimal: Domestic and outbound calls from the United States and Canada are free, and calls from elsewhere cost $0.01 per minute. The main limitation is that the service is available only to Google account holders in the United States.

To get the Google Voice app, fire up the Play Store app, tap the Apps button, and then search for *Google voice*. Tap the right result, tap the Install button, and then review the extensive list of permissions that the app requires.

You first need to sign up for Google Voice. Open a web browser, either on your Android device or (easier) on a computer, and go to www.google.com/voice. Sign in with your Google account, and then go through the signup process for Google Voice. You need to verify your application using an existing U.S. phone number to prove that you're in the United States rather than maintaining a virtual presence through a virtual private network (VPN).

CHATTING, TALKING, AND CONFERENCING VIA HANGOUTS

Google's Hangouts app and Hangout service enable you to chat via text, via audio, or via audio and video across either a Wi-Fi connection or a cellular connection. Google has been developing Hangouts aggressively, has recently integrated Google Talk and Google Messenger into Hangouts, and has made Hangouts the default app for text messaging in Android KitKat and later versions.

> **NOTE** Android may let you choose between Messaging and Hangouts as your default messaging app.

Hangouts makes all three kinds of chat as simple as possible, but the underlying technologies are far from simple. Because of this, it's vital to configure your Hangouts account or accounts correctly so that you can get the most out of this app. You should also be aware of the wide range of configurable options that Hangouts offers, even if you choose to leave many of them set to their default settings.

> **NOTE** Google syncs your hangouts automatically across your devices that are logged in to the same Google+ account on Hangouts. This means that you can start a hangout on your phone, pick it up on your tablet, and then finish it on your computer.

GETTING AN ACCOUNT

To start using Hangouts, you need a Google account. Chances are that you have set up your Google account on your device already, because you can't get far on Android without a Google account. But if you use multiple Google accounts on your device, you may need to set up another account at this point.

> **TIP** To get the most out of Hangouts, sign up for the Google+ service. With Google+, you can get up to nine people in a video chat in Hangouts; without Google+, you can have only yourself and one other person.

GETTING STARTED WITH HANGOUTS

To get started with Hangouts, tap the Hangouts icon on the Apps screen. If it's not there, open the Google folder and tap the Hangouts icon there.

> **NOTE** The first time you launch Hangouts on a phone, the app prompts you to confirm your phone number. After you do this, Hangouts prompts you to turn on SMS so that you can send text messages. Tap the Turn On SMS button if you want to do this; it's usually helpful. If you want to postpone this decision, tap the Maybe Later button.

The first time you launch Hangouts, it displays the Share Device, Call Status, and Mood dialog box. Tap the OK button if you want to share all three items.

Otherwise, tap the Settings button to display the Share Your Status screen (see Figure 10.16), and then choose settings:

- **Set Your Mood.** Tap this button, and then tap the icon. You can set your mood quickly afterward by opening the menu and then tapping Set Mood.
- **Device.** Check this box to allow others to see which device you're using.
- **In Call.** Check this box to let others see when you're in a video call or an audio call.

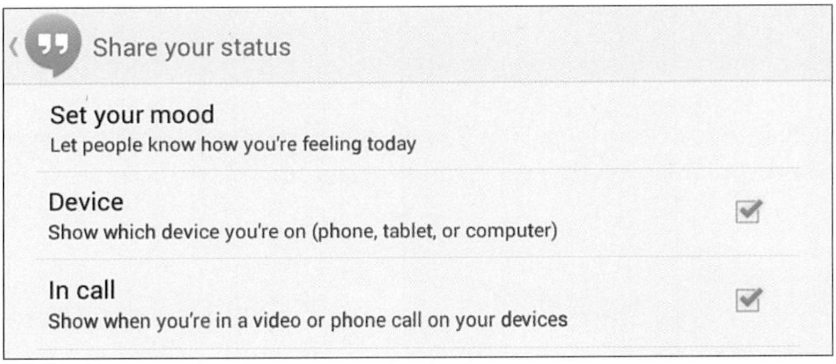

FIGURE 10.16

On the Share Your Status screen, choose which information you want to share with other people on Hangouts.

Tap the Back button at the top of the Share Your Status screen to go back to the main Settings screen, which lists your Google accounts and Google+ accounts. You can then configure Hangouts as described in the next section.

MAKING HANGOUTS COMFORTABLE FOR YOU

From the main Settings screen, tap your account name to display the settings screen for the account (see Figure 10.17). You can then choose settings using these controls:

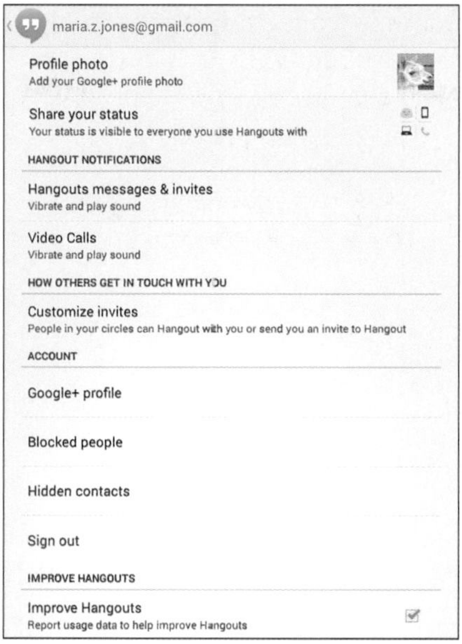

FIGURE 10.17

Use the main Settings screen in Hangouts to set your profile photo, choose notifications, and manage your profile and contacts.

- **Profile Photo.** Tap this button to set your profile photo for Hangouts.
- **Share Your Status.** Tap this button to display the Share Your Status screen, shown in Figure 10.16, earlier in this chapter.
- **Hangouts Messages & Invites.** Tap this button to display the Hangouts Messages & Invites screen. You can then check the Notifications box to receive notifications, tap the Sound button to choose the sound for incoming Hangouts messages and invitations, and check the Vibrate box to have your device vibrate (if it has a vibration motor).
- **Video Calls.** Tap this button to display the Video Calls screen. This screen has the same options as the Hangouts Messages & Invites screen (discussed in the preceding bullet).
- **Customize Invites.** Tap this button to display the Customize Invites screen (see Figure 10.18). Here you can tap either a circle or the Everyone Else button to open a dialog box for configuring invitations, and then tap either the Hangout with You radio button or the Invite Only radio button.

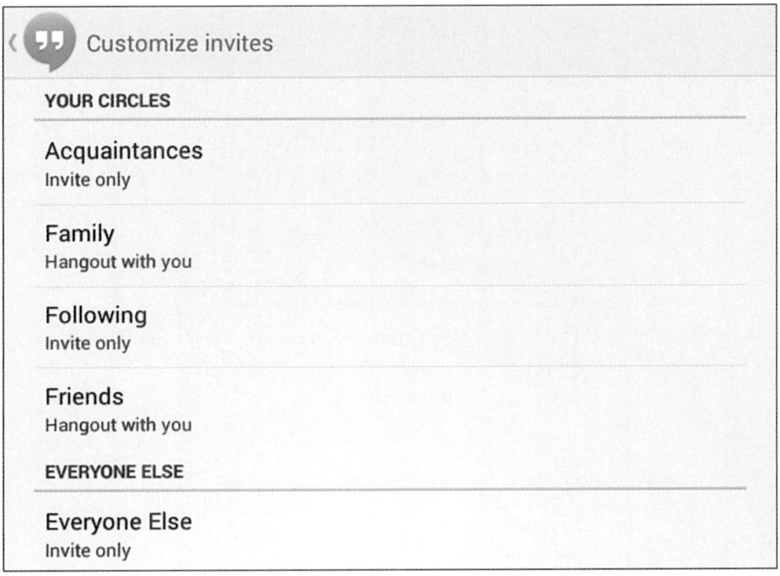

FIGURE 10.18

On the Customize Invites screen, tap the circle for which you want to customize invitations, or tap the Everyone Else button.

- **Google+ Profile.** Tap this button to open your Google+ profile in either the Google+ app or in a browser.

- **Confirm Phone Number.** On a phone, tap this button to confirm the phone number to use for calls and SMS messages. (This button doesn't appear in Figure 10.18, which shows a tablet.)

- **Blocked People.** Tap this button to display the Blocked People screen, which shows a list of the people you have blocked. Tap the Unblock button for anybody you want to reprieve.

- **Hidden Contacts.** Tap this button to display the Hidden Contacts screen, which shows a list of the contacts you have hidden. Tap the Unhide button to hide a contact.

- **Sign Out.** Tap this button to sign out of Hangouts.

- **Improve Hangouts.** Check this box to allow your device to send data to Google about how you use Hangouts so that Google can improve the app and the service.

CONFIGURING SMS IN HANGOUTS

If you're going to use SMS in Hangouts, spend a few minutes choosing suitable settings. Tap the SMS button on the Settings screen to display the SMS screen. Figure 10.19 shows the top part of the SMS screen.

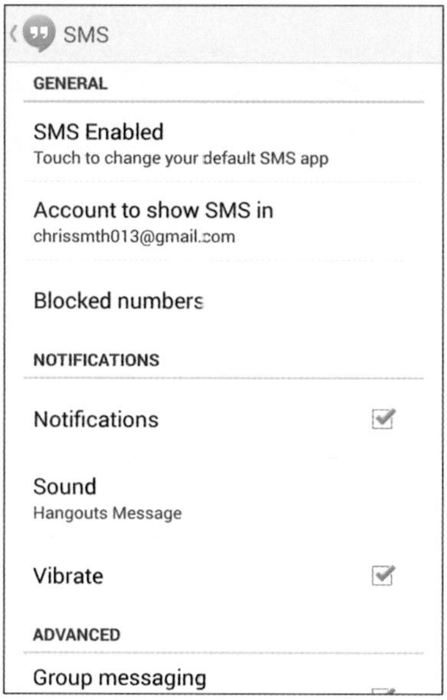

FIGURE 10.19

On the SMS screen in Hangouts, select your default SMS app and choose notifications.

Here you can choose the following settings:

- **SMS Enabled.** Tap this button to go to the Wireless & Networks screen in the Settings app. Here you can tap the Default SMS App button and choose a different SMS app (if you have installed one) in the Default SMS App dialog box.

> **NOTE** On some devices, such as the Nexus 5, Hangouts is the default text-messaging app. You can't uninstall Hangouts, but you can install a third-party messaging app and make it the default app instead of Hangouts. See the section "Sending Messages in the Hangout," later in this chapter, for information about other messaging apps.

- **Account to Show SMS In.** This button shows the Google account in Hangouts in which SMS messages sent to your Android phone will appear (if you have multiple accounts set up on it). To change the account, tap this button and then tap the appropriate Google account in the Select SMS Account dialog box.

- **Blocked Numbers.** Tap this button to display the Blocked People screen, which shows a list of people whose phone numbers you've blocked. Tap the Unblock button to unblock a number.

- **Notifications.** Check this box to receive SMS notifications.

- **Sound.** Tap this button to choose the sound to play when an SMS message arrives in Hangouts.

- **Vibrate.** Check this box to have your phone vibrate when an SMS message arrives in Hangouts.

- **Group Messaging.** Check this box to have Hangouts use Multimedia Messaging Service (MMS) instead of SMS to send a single message to multiple recipients.

- **Delete Old Messages.** Check this box to have Hangouts automatically delete old messages when your phone runs out of space. This feature is helpful unless you must keep your old Hangouts messages.

- **Delivery Reports.** Check this box to request a delivery report for each SMS message. You receive the delivery reports only if the recipient has allowed Hangouts to send them.

- **Auto Retrieve MMS.** Check this box to have Hangouts automatically retrieve MMS messages sent to your phone. This feature is usually helpful.

- **Roaming Auto-Retrieve.** If you check the Auto Retrieve MMS box, you can check this box to have Hangouts retrieve MMS messages automatically when you are roaming. You may want to turn this feature off unless you have a generous data plan.

- **Wireless Alerts.** Tap this button to display the Cell Broadcasts screen in the Settings app, which shows a list of emergency alerts broadcast on the cellular network.

- **Access Point Names.** Tap this button to display the APNs screen. Here, you can tap the radio button for the APN you want to use. If the right APN doesn't appear, tap the Add (+) button and use the Edit Access Point screen to add the APN.

> **! CAUTION** Normally, it's best not to change the APN your phone is using unless your carrier's support staff tells you that you need to. APN is the abbreviation for Access Point Name, the identifier for the gateway by which a phone connects to the cellular network.

- **Enable Merged Conversations.** Check this box to allow Hangouts to merge SMS hangouts from a particular contact with other hangouts from the same contact.

COMMUNICATING VIA HANGOUTS

After you've set up Hangouts, communicating is largely straightforward—as soon as you know your way around the interface.

OPENING A NEW HANGOUT OR AN EXISTING HANGOUT

When you open Hangouts, the app displays the list of current hangouts (see Figure 10.20). A *hangout* is a chat session whose list of participants is saved, so you can easily return to chatting with the same person or group of people. Hangouts saves text chat history as well, so you can go back to previous chats.

> **✅ TIP** If you've set up Hangouts for multiple Google accounts, you can switch from one account to another by tapping the pop-up button at the top of the screen and then tapping the account you want to use.

To start a new hangout, tap the + button to display the New Message screen, and then either type in the contact name, email address, phone number, or circle; or tap the person in the People You Hangout With list or the Phone Contacts list.

Tap the pop-up menu to change the account.

Tap to start a new hangout.

The SMS badge shows this account has SMS enabled.

Tap an existing hangout to open it.

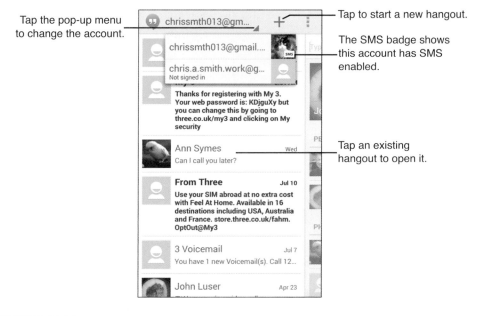

FIGURE 10.20

Hangouts displays your current hangouts so that you can easily return to them.

SENDING MESSAGES IN THE HANGOUT

After you've opened a hangout, you can chat with the other people in it. For a text chat, simply type the message in the message box at the bottom of the screen (see Figure 10.21) and then tap the Send button to send it.

To switch to another type of chat, tap the appropriate icon at the top of the screen. The choices available depend on the device and the communications technology you're using. For example, in Figure 10.21, you can tap the phone icon to the left of the Menu button to place a phone call.

> **❗CAUTION** Any SMS messages you send via Hangouts go across the cellular network and count against your data allowance. Look for the SMS indicator at the left end of the message box if you're not sure whether this hangout is using SMS or the Internet.

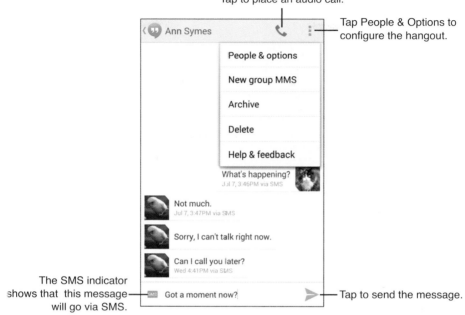

Tap to place an audio call.

Tap People & Options to configure the hangout.

The SMS indicator shows that this message will go via SMS.

Tap to send the message.

FIGURE 10.21

After opening a hangout, you can chat, switch to another chat type, or configure the hangout.

> **TIP** If you want to stop recording the history for a non-SMS hangout, tap the Menu button in the hangout and then tap Turn History Off.

CONFIGURING THE HANGOUT

To configure the hangout, tap the Menu button, and then tap People & Options to display the People & Options screen (see Figure 10.22). Here you can take the following actions:

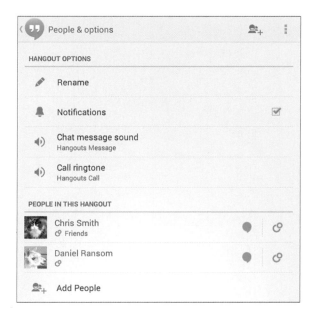

FIGURE 10.22

On the People & Options screen for the hangout, you can add other participants, rename the hangout, or choose options to make the hangout easy to identify.

- **Add people to the hangout.** Tap the Add People button to display the Add People screen. You can then add participants from the People You Hangout With list or the Phone Contacts list or by typing in the contact name, email address, phone number, or circle.

- **Add a participant to a circle.** Tap the Circles icon on the right of the participant's button in the People in This Hangout list to display the Add to Circles panel. You can then check the box for the circle or circles to which you want to add the participant.

- **Block a participant.** You can block someone who is participating in a hangout via SMS by tapping the Block *Name* button on the People & Options screen for the hangout. Tap the Block button in the Block dialog box that opens (see Figure 10.23). Blocking prevents the person from contacting you directly, and you no longer receive notifications about the person's messages. The person still appears in any group hangouts of which you're both members.

TIP To unblock a contact, tap the New Message button to display the New Message screen, and then tap the contact in the Phone Contacts list. Hangouts displays a message saying that you've blocked the contact. Tap the Unblock button to remove the blocking. Tap the Back button if you don't want to start a new hangout with the contact.

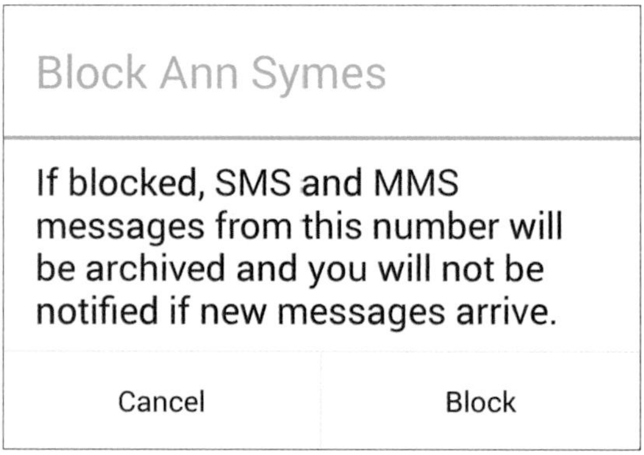

Block Ann Symes

If blocked, SMS and MMS messages from this number will be archived and you will not be notified if new messages arrive.

Cancel	Block

FIGURE 10.23
You can block a participant who is using SMS to connect to the hangout.

- **Rename the hangout.** Tap the Rename button, type the new name in the Rename Hangout dialog box, and then tap the Save button.

- **Enable or disable notifications for the hangout.** Check or uncheck the Notifications box.

- **Set a distinctive chat message sound.** Tap the Chat Message Sound button and browse for a suitable sound.

- **Set a distinctive call ringtone.** Tap the Call Ringtone button and select a ringtone you will be able to identify easily.

TIP You can hide a contact from the People You Hangout With list by tapping and holding until the Contact Options dialog box opens, and then tapping Hide Contact. To get a hidden contact back, go to the main Hangouts screen, tap the Menu button, and then tap Settings. On the Settings screen, tap the account for which you hid the contact. Tap the Hidden Contacts button to display the Hidden Contacts screen, and then tap the Unhide button for the appropriate contact. The contact then reappears in the People You Hangout With list.

MERGING HANGOUTS

If you've checked the Enable Merged Conversations box on the SMS screen in Hangouts Settings, Hangouts automatically merges your SMS messages from a particular contact with your other Hangouts messages from that contact.

TIP If you need to separate the SMS messages from the rest of the hangout, tap the Menu button in the hangout and then tap Un-Merge SMS.

Troubleshooting the Merging of Hangouts

If you've checked the Enable Merged Conversations box on the SMS screen, but SMS messages from a contact appear in a separate hangout from other messages from that contact, you may need to edit the contact's record to get the conversations to merge. In either the People app or the Phone app, open the contact's record, tap the Menu button, and then tap Edit. Make sure that the contact record has both the right phone number (for SMS messages) and the right email address; if not, add the missing information. Save the changes.

Often, the problem is that you have two separate contact records, one with the phone number and the other with the email address. When this happens, open one of the contacts for editing, tap the Menu button, and then tap Join. Select the second contact record, and then tap the Done button.

ARCHIVING A HANGOUT

When you've finished using a hangout for now, you can archive it. Archiving the hangout removes it from your Hangouts list and places it in the Archived Hangouts list, where you can access it again if you need to.

To archive a hangout, swipe it off the Hangouts list to the left or right. The Hangout Archived pop-up message appears briefly at the bottom of the screen, with an Undo button that you can tap to undo the archiving if it was a mistake.

 **TIP** You can also archive a hangout by tapping and holding it in the Hangouts list until Hangouts switches to selection mode, and then tapping the Archive icon (the folder icon) at the top of the screen. Alternatively, after going into Selection mode, tap other hangouts to add them to the selection, tap the Menu button, and then tap Delete.

To return to a hangout you've archived, tap the Menu button and then tap Archived Hangouts. On the Archived Hangouts screen, tap the hangout.

DELETING A HANGOUT

When you no longer need a hangout, you can delete it:

1. Tap and hold the hangout in the Hangouts list until Hangouts switches to Selection mode.

2. Tap the Delete icon (the trash icon) at the top of the screen. The Delete Hangout dialog box opens (see Figure 10.24).

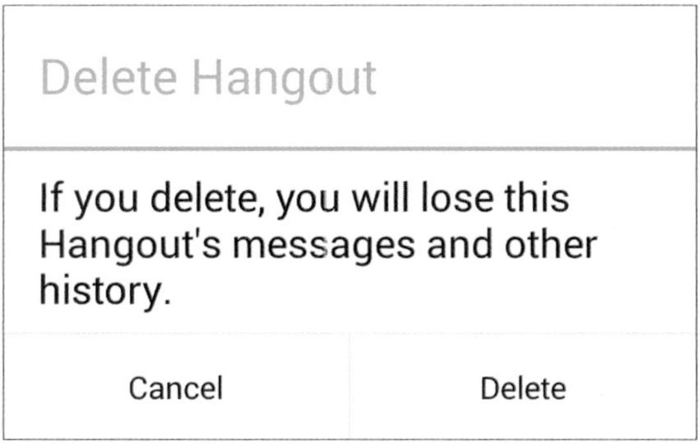

Delete Hangout

If you delete, you will lose this Hangout's messages and other history.

| Cancel | Delete |

FIGURE 10.24

Tap the Delete button in the Delete Hangout dialog box to delete the hangout, its messages, and its history.

3. Tap the Delete button.

TIP To delete multiple hangouts, go into selection mode and select the appropriate hangouts. Then tap the Menu button and tap Delete.

IN THIS CHAPTER

- Configuring the Camera app to shoot your way
- Taking photos and capturing video
- Editing photos
- Capturing screenshots on your device

11

EXPLOITING CAMERA, PHOTOS, AND VIDEOS

Always in your hand if not in your pocket or your bag, your Android device is perfectly positioned to take photos and videos of anything interesting you encounter.

Most Android phones have both a front (screen-side) camera for taking shots and footage of yourself and your surroundings and a rear camera for shooting the rest of the world.

In this chapter, you'll explore how to get the most out of your device's cameras. That means configuring the Camera app to take the types of photos and videos you want, using the app's features to actually capture those shots and footage, examining your photos and videos, and editing your photos as needed. You'll also examine how to capture screenshots showing what's on your device's screen.

GETTING GREAT PHOTOS WITH THE CAMERA APP

In this section, you'll explore the Camera app, configure it to suit your needs, and then give its various modes a good workout.

> **NOTE** This section shows screens from the Nexus 5, Google's flagship phone, which runs the Google Camera app. Many phone and tablet manufacturers provide a custom camera app instead of Android's default. If your device has a different camera app, use the suggestions in this section for exploring the features that your device's app offers. See Chapter 14, "Using Samsung TouchWiz," for coverage of the Camera app on Samsung devices. See Chapter 15, "Using HTC Sense," for coverage of the Camera app on HTC devices.

> **TIP** You can install the Google Camera app on any device that is running KitKat. The app is free from the App Store and is well worth trying. If your device is running KitKat but has an older version of the stock Camera app, update to Google Camera to get the features described here.

OPENING THE CAMERA APP AND NAVIGATING ITS INTERFACE

Tap the Camera icon on the Home screen (it's usually there) or on the Apps screen to open the Camera app. The app has a stripped-down, uncluttered user interface, as you can see in Figure 11.1, which shows the Camera mode, the mode you use to take regular photos.

FIGURE 11.1

The Camera in Camera mode, for taking regular photos. Tap the three horizontal dots (…) to display the options.

> **✓ TIP** If you have an early-model Nexus 7, which has a front camera but no rear camera, download and install the Camera Nexus 7 app. This app gives you access to the device's camera, which otherwise you can access only through apps such as Hangouts.

Swipe right to display the Modes list (see Figure 11.2), which enables you to switch among the app's five modes: Photo Sphere mode, Panorama mode, Lens Blur mode, Camera mode, and Video mode.

FIGURE 11.2

Swipe right and then tap the camera mode you want to use.

With the Modes list open, you can also tap the Settings icon to access the Settings screen.

ACCESSING THE CAMERA FROM THE LOCK SCREEN

To enable you to take photos quickly without messing about authenticating yourself, recent versions of Android let you access the Camera app directly from the lock screen. If the Camera icon appears in the lower-right corner of the lock screen, swipe left to display the Camera app.

You can then take photos as usual by tapping the Shutter button. Swipe right to display the Mode list if you want to change to a different mode, such as Video or Panorama. After taking a photo (or video), you can swipe left to display it for viewing.

For security, the Camera app restricts you to taking photos and videos and viewing what you've just taken since the device was locked. So you can determine whether you've shot what you need or whether you need to keep shooting. After you swipe past the first photo or video you took, a lock screen icon appears. You can then unlock your device to view other photos.

Similarly, after displaying a photo or video, you can tap the Photos icon in the upper-left corner to jump to the Photos app, but to get there, you must unlock your device.

> **NOTE** KitKat considers the camera on the lock screen to be a shortcut rather than a widget. This means that you can't remove the camera from the lock screen by unchecking the Enable Widgets box on the Security screen in the Settings app.
>
> The only way to remove the camera shortcut is to replace the lock screen. You can find various lock screen replacements in the App Store.

CONFIGURING THE CAMERA APP TO SUIT YOUR NEEDS

To get the most out of the Camera app, spend a few minutes configuring it to suit your needs. In the Camera app, swipe right to display the main controls, and then tap the Settings icon in the lower-right corner to display the Settings screen (see Figure 11.3).

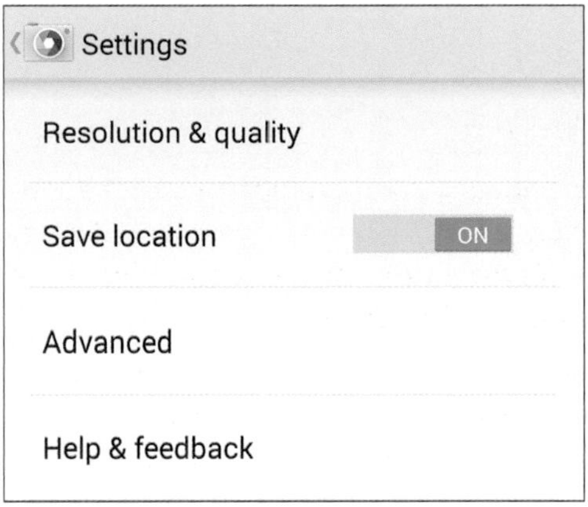

FIGURE 11.3

From the Settings screen for the Camera app, you can choose resolution and quality settings, turn on or off saving the location in photos, and visit the Advanced screen.

CHOOSING RESOLUTION AND QUALITY SETTINGS

Tap the Resolution & Quality button on the Settings screen to display the Resolution & Quality screen (see Figure 11.4). You can then choose the following settings:

- **Back Camera Photo.** Tap this button to open the Back Camera Photo dialog box, and then tap the radio button for the resolution you want.

> **✓ TIP** When setting the Back Camera Photo resolution and the Front Camera Photo resolution, you'll normally want to use the highest resolution available. This means that the big decision is whether to go for the 4:3 aspect ratio or the 16:9 (widescreen) aspect ratio. Typically, the 4:3 aspect ratio uses all of the camera's resolution, whereas the 16:9 resolution lops off the outer parts of the long sides. So unless you specifically need the widescreen format, you're usually better off shooting in the 4:3 format and then cropping the photos as required.

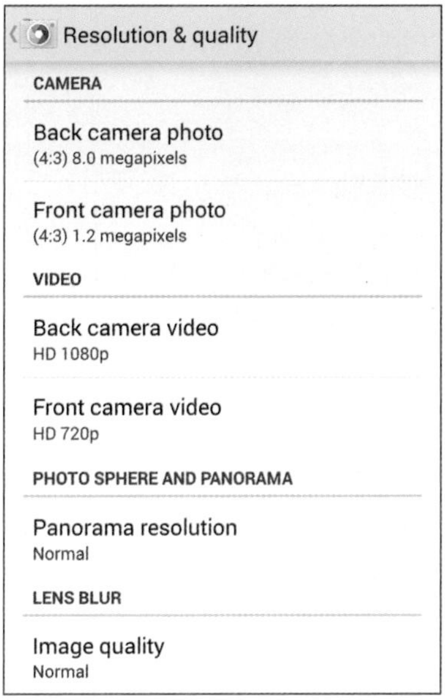

FIGURE 11.4

On the Resolution & Quality screen, set the resolution for shooting photos and videos with your device's cameras.

■ **Front Camera Photo.** Tap this button to open the Front Camera Photo dialog box, and then tap the radio button for the resolution you want.

> **NOTE** The resolutions available for Back Camera Photo, Front Camera Photo, Back Camera Video, and Front Camera Video vary depending on your device's cameras.

■ **Back Camera Video.** Tap this button to open the Back Camera Video dialog box, and then tap the radio button for the video resolution to use.

> **TIP** You can down-resolve video as needed after shooting it, but doing so takes much more effort than down-resolving a photo. So it's a good idea to set the video resolution you'll normally want. If your device is short of space, shooting video at a lower resolution can help you avoid running out altogether.

> **NOTE** Some camera apps offer the CIF format for shooting video. CIF is the acronym for Common Intermediate Format, a standard video format that uses 352×288-pixel resolution. This resolution is very low by today's standards, so use it only if you're certain that it's what you need.

■ **Front Camera Video.** Tap this button to open the Front Camera Video dialog box, and then tap the radio button for the video resolution to use.
■ **Photo Sphere and Panorama.** Tap this button to open the Panorama Resolution dialog box, and then tap the High radio button, the Normal radio button, or the Low (Fastest) radio button, as needed.

> **TIP** To get the best Photo Sphere and panorama photos, tap the High radio button in the Panorama Resolution dialog box and use a tripod to keep your device steady while taking the photos.

■ **Image Quality.** To control the resolution the Lens Blur feature uses, tap this button to display the Image Quality dialog box, and then tap the Normal radio button or the Low (Fastest) radio button, as needed.

> **! CAUTION** The Low (Fastest) setting in the Image Quality dialog box uses 1024×768 resolution for the Lens Blur feature to give quicker response time. This setting is sometimes useful when you need the speed, but 1024×768 resolution is quite low. So usually it's better to use the Normal setting, which uses the resolution you set in the Back Camera Photo dialog box.

CHOOSING WHETHER TO SAVE THE LOCATION IN YOUR PHOTOS

Back on the main Settings screen for the Camera app, set the Save Location switch to On or Off to control whether the Camera app saves the location in photos you take.

Saving the location enables you to sort your photos by locations, which is great for browsing and organizing your photos. The disadvantage of saving the location is that it enables anyone with whom you share the photo to see exactly where you took it. If you post photos online, this may be a privacy concern.

> **TIP** You can remove location information from a photo by using an app such as PhotoInfo Eraser or Pixelgarde Free, both of which you can download for free from the Play Store.

CHOOSING ADVANCED SETTINGS

Tap the Advanced button on the Settings screen to display the Advanced screen, and then choose from the available settings. At this writing, there's only one: You can set the Manual Exposure switch to On if you want to be able to control the exposure manually from the Settings bar.

TAKING REGULAR PHOTOS

By this point, whether you've carefully chosen settings to suit your needs or you've decided to stick with the defaults, you should be ready to take photos. This section covers regular photos, the kind you'll likely want to take most of the time. The following sections cover the specialized photo types: Photo Sphere photos, panorama photos, and photos using the Lens Blur feature.

SWITCHING TO THE REGULAR CAMERA

If the Camera app doesn't display the regular Camera feature when you open the app, swipe right to display the Modes list, and then tap Camera.

ZOOMING, FOCUSING, AND SHOOTING

To take a quick photo, aim the camera lens at your subject, and then tap the Shutter button.

> **TIP**   You can press either the Volume Up button or the Volume Down button to take a photo.

To zoom in, place your finger and thumb (or two fingers) together on the screen and then pinch apart. To zoom back in, place your finger and thumb apart on screen and then pinch together.

To focus, tap the point on which you want to place the focus. The Camera app displays a focus icon briefly (see Figure 11.5) to indicate that it is adjusting the focus.

Tap the point where you want to focus.

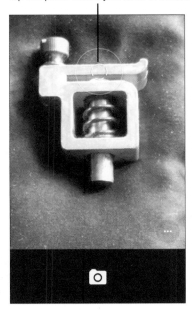

FIGURE 11.5

Tap the point on the photo where you want to place the focus.

Eliminating Camera Shake

Camera shake—the camera moving while the shutter is open—can ruin a photo by making it blurred. The smaller and lighter the camera you're using, the easier it is to get camera shake when taking photos. With one of today's featherweight phones, getting camera shake is easier than falling off a log.

Some devices have automatic image stabilization for photos. But even so, you may need to use other means to steady your device when taking photos, especially when the light is low or when you have zoomed far in.

If you're taking photos of still subjects, a tripod remains the most effective means of stabilization. Where a tripod is impractical, try a monopod or a chest brace. You can also use a foot strap, which you slip around your foot and then hold the device under tension by pulling upward. To use any of these options, you'll need a tripod mount for your device.

When you have no hardware beyond your device, stabilize your position by using an available solid object, such as a tree, a building, or a vehicle. You may also be able to reduce camera shake by, instead of tapping the Shutter button to take a photo, tapping and holding the Shutter button while you line up the shot, and then releasing it when you're ready to take the photo. This trick doesn't work if your device has a Burst mode and you've enabled it, because tapping and holding the Shutter button takes a burst of photos instead.

USING THE TIMER, GRID, HDR, AND FLASH

To choose settings for taking photos, tap the button with three horizontal dots (…) in the lower-right corner of the screen. The Camera app displays the settings bar (see Figure 11.6), and you can choose the following settings:

■ **Manual Exposure.** Tap this icon to display the Manual Exposure bar (see Figure 11.7), and then tap the exposure you want: −2, −1, 0 (the default), +1, or +2.

TIP Use the −1 exposure setting for backgrounds that are too bright for the automatic exposure control; use the −2 setting for extremely bright backgrounds, such as snow in sunshine. Use the +1 setting for a background that is too dark, and the +2 setting for photographing black cats in a coalmine at night.

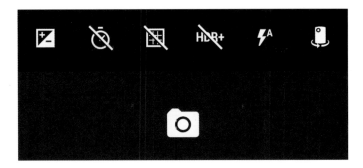

FIGURE 11.6

From the settings bar, you can control exposure, the timer, and the flash; turn on the grid or HDR; and switch between the rear camera and the front camera.

> **NOTE** The Manual Exposure icon appears on the settings bar only if you have set the Manual Exposure switch on the Advanced screen to On.

FIGURE 11.7

On the Manual Exposure bar, tap the exposure value to use for the photo.

- **Timer.** Tap this icon to cycle through the three settings: No delay, 3 seconds, and 10 seconds.
- **Grid.** Tap this icon to toggle the grid on or off. Many people find the grid useful for composing their photos. You can use the grid simply to help make sure that vertical objects are upright and horizontal objects are level on the screen, or you can use it to help you compose your photos according to the Rule of Thirds, a compositional guideline for placing your subjects in photos.

> **☑ TIP** If you search online for *rule of thirds*, make sure you get the rule about photography rather than the rule about driving (one third of your gas supply is for the outward journey, one third for the return journey, and the last third for safety).

■ **HDR+.** Tap this icon to toggle the HDR feature. HDR stands for High Dynamic Range. It helps improve the color and lighting balance of your photos, and sometimes adds more detail, by taking a series of shots in rapid succession and merging them into a single photo.

When to Use HDR and When Not To

HDR is a great feature in the Camera app and a great addition to your photography arsenal, so you'll probably want to use it often—but don't use it all the time.

Use HDR when you're taking photos of still subjects, such as landscapes, buildings, or still lifes (peaches, grapes, optional dead pheasant). Keep your device as steady as possible to make sure that each of the shots has the same alignment and contents, enabling Camera to merge them successfully. Use a tripod or other steadying device when you can, especially when shooting in low light.

Don't use HDR for anything involving movement, such as sports, children, or candid photos. You can't use HDR for any photos that need the flash, because the Camera app disables the flash when you turn on HDR.

> **☑ NOTE** Some cameras don't support HDR mode. Many support it on the rear camera but not on the front camera.

■ **Flash.** Tap this icon to cycle among the three flash settings: On (the lightning-bolt symbol), Automatic (the lightning-bolt symbol with an A to its right), and Off (the lightning-bolt symbol with a diagonal line through it).

> ⎘ **NOTE**   Turning on HDR disables the flash and timer. It also disables Manual Exposure control (if you have set the Manual Exposure switch on the Advanced screen to On).

> ⎘ **TIP**   Set the Flash feature to On when you need to force Camera to use the flash when it normally would not, such as when you need the flash to light up the shadowed face of a subject positioned in front of a bright background. Set Flash to Off when you need to be discreet or when you'll get a better effect with the ambient light.

■ **Switch Cameras.** Tap this icon to switch from the rear camera to the front camera or vice versa.

> ⎘ **NOTE**   The capabilities of the front camera depend on the device, but a typical front camera has no flash and cannot use the HDR feature.

After selecting the settings you want, compose your photo and tap the Shutter button to take it.

REVIEWING YOUR PHOTOS QUICKLY

To see the photo or photos you've just taken, swipe left from the main Camera screen. The photo appears (see Figure 11.8), and you can share it, edit it, or delete it by tapping the three icons at the bottom of the screen.

Open in the Photos app.

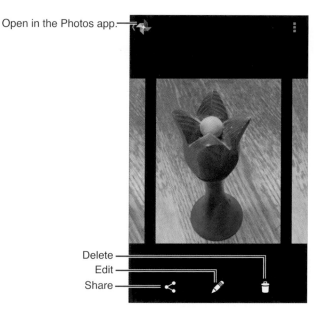

Delete
Edit
Share

FIGURE 11.8

After displaying a photo for viewing in the Camera app, you can share it, delete it, edit it, or view it in the Photos app.

You can view the information for a photo by tapping the Menu button and then tapping Details. The Details dialog box opens (see Figure 11.9), showing you a wide range of information from the date, time, and location; through the photo's resolution and orientation; whether the flash was used; and the focal length, aperture, exposure time, and ISO rating.

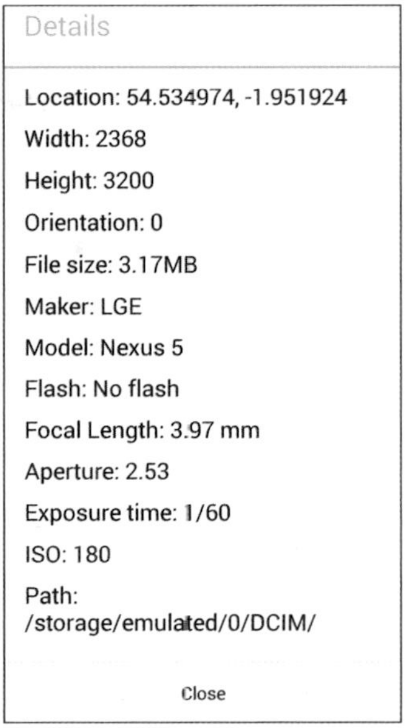

Details
Location: 54.534974, -1.951924
Width: 2368
Height: 3200
Orientation: 0
File size: 3.17MB
Maker: LGE
Model: Nexus 5
Flash: No flash
Focal Length: 3.97 mm
Aperture: 2.53
Exposure time: 1/60
ISO: 180
Path: /storage/emulated/0/DCIM/
Close

FIGURE 11.9

Open the Details dialog box to see a photo's location, resolution, aperture, exposure time, and other details.

Tap the Close button when you've seen enough.

Swipe right to go back to the Camera screen so that you can take more photos.

Improving Your Photos Using Tripods and Lenses

If you need to be able to keep your phone or tablet steady while taking photos, attach it to a tripod. All you need is a tripod mount for the device. Many of these are spring-loaded clips with a hole at the bottom threaded to receive a standard tripod screw—very simple, but effective as long as they're strong enough. You can use any standard tripod, from a table-top toy to a professional monster.

Search online using terms such as *smartphone tripod mount, tablet tripod mount,* or *flexible tripod mount,* and you'll find plenty of options, usually starting from the price of a disappointing cup of coffee. Or see what your local electronics store can offer.

You can expand your photo-taking repertoire greatly by adding lenses to your phone or tablet. Many clip-on or stick-on lens sets are available that enable you to add macro, wide-angle, or fish-eye capabilities to your phone or tablet. These are straightforward to use, although you need to position them carefully to get the best effect. Both clip-on and stick-on lenses usually require you to remove any case from your device.

You can also get telephoto lenses and zoom lenses. Because these are typically bigger than macro, wide-angle, and fish-eye lenses, they need firmer fixing, such as a case with a lens mount built into it. This arrangement enables you to swap lenses easily and make sure the lenses are positioned correctly for the camera, so it's helpful if you use lenses a lot. But you have to remove any case from your device for these lenses as well.

TAKING PHOTO SPHERE PHOTOS

The Photo Sphere feature enables you to create panoramic photos that pan up and down as well as from side to side. These can be a lot of fun to view. The Camera app does a fine job of stitching together the component photos into a whole, but while you can take Photo Sphere photos and get reasonable results, it helps to use a tripod with a smooth panning mechanism so you can keep the central point of the sphere the same.

In the Camera app, swipe right to display the Modes list, tap Photo Sphere, and then follow the prompts for aiming the lens. The Camera app displays white dots to indicate the areas you can go to next; when you track to a dot, it turns blue, as you see in Figure 11.10; and when you hold steady on a dot, Camera captures that section of the picture.

FIGURE 11.10

Move the white circle over the blue dot to continue capturing the Photo Sphere.

When you finish capturing the area for the Photo Sphere, tap the check mark.

TAKING PANORAMA PHOTOS

The Panorama feature enables you to take regular panorama photos—long, flat panoramas—but also vertical, square, and rounded panorama photos.

In the Camera app, swipe right to display the Modes list, and then tap Panorama. If you want to change the type of panorama, tap the three horizontal dots (…) and then tap the panorama type. Tap the Shutter button, and then follow the dots.

When you finish capturing the panorama, tap the check mark.

TAKING PHOTOS WITH THE LENS BLUR FEATURE

The Lens Blur feature enables you to make a subject stand out more from the background. Lens Blur works with both the rear camera and the front camera on many devices, so you can use it for taking self-portraits as well as taking photos of other subjects.

> **TIP** Lens Blur is mostly useful for close-up photos, such as portraits of people or pictures of objects, in which your subject is positioned in front of a background whose main features are some distance between them. For example, if you're taking a photo of your significant other in the park, you can use Lens Blur to make sure that the background is blurred to draw attention to the subject.

To use Lens Blur, take the photo and then move the device up to enable the Camera app to record information about the depth of objects in the picture. After taking the photo, you can adjust the amount of blur as needed. Follow these steps:

1. Swipe right on the main Camera screen to display the Modes list.

2. Tap Lens Blur to switch to Lens Blur mode.

3. Optionally, tap the three horizontal dots to display the options bar, and then tap the options you want. Only two are available: You can toggle the display of the grid, and you can switch between the rear camera and the front camera.

4. Line up your shot and tap the Shutter button. Camera takes the initial photo and prompts you to move the device upward (see Figure 11.11).

FIGURE 11.11

Raise your phone or tablet slowly following the Lens Blur feature's prompts and the arrow on the screen.

> **NOTE** If the light is low, Camera warns you of this and instructs you to move the device slowly.

5. Slowly raise your device, following the tracking arrow and keeping the subject centered in the frame, until Camera displays a check mark.

6. Swipe left to see the photo. You may have to wait while Camera processes the Lens Blur effect.

7. Tap the Lens Blur button (the shutter symbol, second from the left) to display the controls for editing the blurring.

8. If necessary, tap the point to which you want to move the focus.

9. Drag the slider to the left or right as needed. The left screen in Figure 11.12 shows a photo with a small amount of lens blur. The right screen shows the same photo with blurring turned up all the way.

FIGURE 11.12

Drag the slider on the Lens Blur screen to adjust the amount of blurring.

10. Tap the Done button when you are satisfied with the result.

> **☑ TIP**   If you need to move the camera faster than the Lens Blur feature will allow in order to get your shot, go back to the Resolution & Quality screen in the Camera app's settings, tap the Image Quality button, and then tap the Low (Fastest) radio button. This setting reduces the image resolution to 1024×768, so be aware you're sacrificing many pixels to get the extra speed.

EDITING YOUR PHOTOS

It's great if you can get your photos perfect when shooting them, but chances are that you'll need to edit many of your shots to get them just the way you want. Your Android device provides easy-to-use editing tools that enable you to make anything from subtle tweaks to wholesale changes.

To edit a photo from the Camera app, swipe left from the screen for whichever camera mode you've been using, swipe further left as needed until you reach the right photo, and then tap the Edit button to open the photo for editing in the Photos app.

> **! CAUTION**   Many Android devices include multiple apps that can edit photos. So the first time you tap the Edit button for a photo in the Camera app, Android displays the Complete Action Using dialog box to let you decide which app to use. To follow these examples, tap Photos. If you want to use Photos for all your editing, tap the Always button; if you want to keep your options open, tap the Just Once button.

Alternatively, you can tap the Photos button in the upper-left corner of the screen to open the Photos app. You can then browse the photos and start any editing directly in the Photos app.

The Photos app contains a wide range of editing tools that range from basic moves (such as cropping and rotating photos) to more advanced moves (such as Tilt-Shift). These tools work in largely the same way, but some have extra features that you can switch to.

Here are the basic moves for using the editing tools:

1. Open the photo you want to change.

2. Tap the Edit button to turn on Editing mode.

3. Tap the appropriate tool button at the bottom of the screen. Figure 11.13 shows the first screen's worth of buttons in landscape orientation.

FIGURE 11.13

Tap the button for the appropriate editing tool, such as Crop or Tune Image.

4. You use the tool's controls to manipulate the photo. For example, on the Rotate screen, tap the photo and drag to straighten the photo (as shown in Figure 11.14), or tap the Rotate Left button or the Rotate Right button to rotate it 90 degrees at a time.

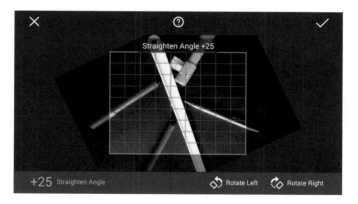

FIGURE 11.14

On the Rotate screen, tap the photo and drag to straighten it.

> **TIP** For some editing tools, you can tap and hold the Toggle Original button in the middle of the toolbar at the top to display the original photo momentarily so that you can check the effect of the changes you've made.

5. Tap the check mark to keep the changes you've made or the cross to discard them.

So far, so easy. But many of the editing tools have options to which you can switch by tapping and holding the screen and then sliding your finger to the item you want to select. Here's an example with the Tune Image tool:

1. Tap the Tune Image button at the bottom of the screen to display the Tune Image screen. As you can see in the left screen in Figure 11.15, the Tune Image tool selects the Brightness option first, so the Brightness readout appears in the lower-left corner of the screen.

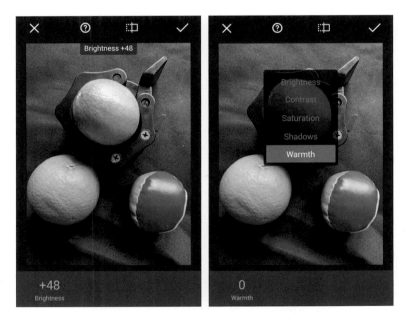

FIGURE 11.15

In the Tune Image tool, tap and slide your finger horizontally to adjust the brightness (left). Tap, hold, and slide your finger vertically to switch among the options (right).

2. Tap the photo and slide your finger horizontally if you want to adjust the brightness. The current setting appears both at the top of the screen and on the Brightness readout.

3. Tap the photo and slide your finger vertically to switch to another option: Contrast, Saturation, Shadows, or Warmth. The Warmth readout replaces the Brightness readout.

4. Tap the photo and slide your finger horizontally to adjust the warmth.

5. Switch to another option and adjust it as needed.

Many of the tools have a Style button that gives you access to a selection of predefined styles. For example, when you tap the Style button in the Retro Lux tool, you can choose from the lighting mixes shown at the bottom of the screen in Figure 11.16.

FIGURE 11.16

Tap the style you want to use, and then tap the down-arrow button to hide the Style list.

After choosing the style you want, tap the down-arrow button at the right of the Style list to hide the list again.

SHOOTING VIDEOS

The Camera app makes it easy to shoot videos. Simply open the app, swipe right to display the Modes list, and then tap Video to switch to video mode.

> **NOTE** When you switch to video mode with your device in portrait orientation, the Camera app displays an animated symbol in the middle of the screen suggesting that you turn it to landscape orientation. If you ignore this symbol and start shooting in portrait orientation, the symbol goes away.

Video mode typically offers three options: displaying or hiding the grid, turning the flash on or off, and switching between the rear camera and the front camera.

After you've made those choices, tap the Shutter button to start shooting video. You can zoom in or out as needed by pinching outward or pinching together. Tap the Shutter button again when you're ready to stop filming.

> **TIP** While shooting a video, you can capture a still photo by tapping the screen.

CAPTURING SCREENSHOTS

Sometimes it's useful to capture what's on the screen of your Android device so that you can use it to amaze your friends or confound your carrier's tech support—or simply refer to it yourself later.

You can capture the screen on any stock Android device by pressing the Power button and the Volume Down button at the same time and holding them for a moment. This maneuver may be awkward until you get the hang of it, so it's worth practicing a few times before you need it. When you get it right, the screen gives a flash and displays a smaller version of what's onscreen, framed with a white border like an old-style photo, so you'll know you've captured the screen.

Android stores the screenshots in a folder called Screenshots inside the Pictures folder, so you can access them easily using any file browser.

> **TIP** If you need to shoot a lot of screens on Android, install the Android SDK from the Android Developer website (http://developer.android.com), run the Monitor app, and use the Screenshot feature to capture screens. This method has the advantage of saving the screens directly to your computer. It's also useful for those (relatively few) screens you can't capture using the Power-and–Volume Down keypress.

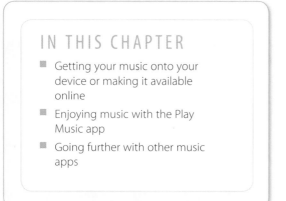

ENJOYING YOUR MUSIC EVERYWHERE

One of the great things about your device is that you can use it to enjoy high-quality music through headphones or speakers everywhere you go.

But should you put the music files on your device, or should you stream them across the Internet? Should you do both? And how do you get your existing music files, such as those on your CDs, onto your device? What format and compression should you use to get as much music as possible on your device at as high a quality as you need, and how can you make it sound as good as possible?

In this chapter, you'll learn about the Play Music app. Stock Android devices come with this app, which provides plenty of features for playing back music either stored on your device or streamed across the Internet. You'll also learn about some of the other music apps you may want to try on your device. Finally, you'll discover options for dealing with the space problems that music addiction tends to bring to Android devices.

UNDERSTANDING YOUR OPTIONS FOR LISTENING TO MUSIC ON YOUR DEVICE

You have three main options for listening to music on your device:

- **Put your own music on your device and play it back from the device.** This is what you might call the old-school approach, but it remains simple and effective, and many people prefer it. The two disadvantages are that you need to get the music files, and your device must have enough space to hold them—plus all the other files you need to carry with you, not to mention preferably leaving several gigabytes free for you to shoot the next viral video.

- **Stream music from an online service.** Various online services (Spotify, Pandora, and so on) enable you to stream music from their servers across your Internet connection and play the music on your device. On the plus side, you can access a wide variety of music that you don't own and you don't need to store the music files on your device. The disadvantage is that you may need to pay for the online service (typically via a subscription), and you always need an Internet connection to be able to play the music.

- **Put your music online, stream it, or store it on your device.** You can combine the two preceding approaches by putting your music collection online using a service such as Google's Play Music or Apple's iTunes Match. You can then either stream the music when you have a suitable Internet connection or put specific songs on your device so that you can play them anywhere, even when you don't have an Internet connection. The advantage of this approach is that you can play your music on a variety of devices (usually up to a set number of devices). The disadvantage is that you may need to pay for the service, and you need an Internet connection when streaming music.

GETTING YOUR MUSIC ONTO YOUR DEVICE

You can transfer your music files onto your device by using the techniques discussed in Chapter 2, "Syncing Your Device":

- **Windows 8.** Use File Explorer to copy files.
- **Windows 7 and earlier versions.** Use Windows Explorer to copy files.
- **OS X.** Use Android File Transfer or another app to copy files.

> **📝 NOTE** If you're going to use Google's Play Music service, you don't necessarily have to put music on your device, because you can simply stream it all instead. Skip ahead to the section "Getting the Most out of the Play Music App" to read about streaming with the Play Music app. The same goes for other streaming services: You don't need to put the music on your device.

Alternatively, if your device takes an SD card, you can copy the music files to the SD card using your computer and then insert the SD card in your device.

> **✅ TIP** If your device doesn't take an SD card, you can copy the files to a USB On-the-Go drive and connect it to your device's micro-USB port. You can then either play the files from the drive or use a file-management app to copy them to the Music folder or another convenient folder.

> **📝 NOTE** Android's default file system includes a folder called Music, which is the central repository for music files. To keep your device's file system neatly organized, you may want to put your music files here. But you can also store them in other folders, because Android automatically makes all music files available to music-player apps, no matter which folder the files are in. If your device has limited built-in storage but enables you to add an SD card, putting your music on the SD card is usually the best approach.

UNDERSTANDING WHICH MUSIC FORMATS YOUR DEVICE CAN PLAY

Android can play music in the following formats:

- **MP3.** Technically, MP3 stands for "MPEG-1 Audio Layer III" or "MPEG-2 Audio Layer III," where MPEG stands for Moving Pictures Expert Group, so it's no surprise that people simply use the abbreviation. MP3 is a lossy audio format (see the nearby tip) that sounds okay for music at bit rates of 128Kbps and pretty good at higher bit rates, such as 256Kbps or 320Kbps.

☑ **TIP** Audio formats use either lossless compression or lossy compression to reduce the amount of space needed for an audio file. *Lossless compression* retains the full audio quality, whereas *lossy compression* loses some of the details—preferably the details that the human ear would normally miss anyway because they're masked by other sounds. Lossy compression is adjustable, so you can choose the quality, but typically it can compress audio far more than lossless compression.

✐ **NOTE** Audio encoders use several settings to determine the quality and—indirectly—the file size. The key setting is the *bit rate*, which is the number of bits (individual pieces) of data per second. The bit rate can be either constant or variable. Variable bit rate (VBR) gives better quality than constant bit rate (CBR) at the same bit rate because it can use the bits more intelligently to store the data.

- **AAC.** Advanced Audio Coding (AAC) is a lossy audio format that provides slightly better quality than MP3. AAC is technically superior to MP3 and is Apple's preferred format for lossily compressed audio, but MP3 is more widely used.
- **OGG.** Ogg Vorbis (variously referred to as "Ogg," "Vorbis," and "Ogg Vorbis") is a lossy audio format that delivers similar quality to MP3 and AAC at similar file sizes. At this writing, Ogg Vorbis is not widely used.

✐ **NOTE** Ogg Vorbis and FLAC are open-source formats, which means that anyone can use them without paying licensing fees. By contrast, MP3 and AAC are both proprietary formats that require the payment of licensing fees. Usually, the manufacturers of the devices pay these fees, so you, as the user of a device, don't need to pay.

- **FLAC.** Free Lossless Audio Codec (FLAC) is a lossless compression format. FLAC delivers full-quality sound, but its files are large. Therefore, it is not a good choice for an Android device unless the device has plenty of storage, or you are happy to carry only a small amount of music with you.

- **PCM/WAV.** Pulse Code Modulation (PCM) and Waveform Audio File Format (WAVE or WAV, after the three-letter file extension) are uncompressed audio formats. This means they deliver full-quality audio, but the file sizes are huge, so you wouldn't normally want to use them on an Android device. These formats also don't have containers for the tag information in which the other formats store the artist, album, song name, and so on, so the only way to identify PCM and WAV files is by their filenames.

> **NOTE** The preceding formats are built into Android. Some apps may support other music formats, but you're generally better off sticking with the main ones.

> **TIP** Opinions vary, but normally, you're best off using MP3 or AAC for audio files on your Android device. If possible, spend some time listening to MP3 files and AAC files encoded at 128Kbps and higher bit rates to decide the minimum level of quality you need. Listen to the songs on both your Android device and on your computer (if you use one), and listen through both headphones and speakers.

GETTING YOUR CDS ONTO YOUR ANDROID DEVICE

If you have CDs containing songs you want to play on your device, you'll need to create digital files from the CDs. This process is called *ripping*, and you can perform it with many different apps on computers.

At this writing, iTunes is arguably the best free app for ripping audio files from CDs. iTunes comes built into OS X, so if you have a Mac, you already have iTunes installed. If you have Windows, you can download iTunes for free from Apple's website, www.apple.com/itunes/download/.

Here's how to configure iTunes with suitable settings for ripping your CDs:

1. Open the Preferences dialog box by pressing Ctrl+, (Ctrl+comma) in Windows or Cmd+, (Cmd+comma) on the Mac.

2. Click the General button on the tab bar to display the General pane.

3. In the When You Insert a CD pop-up menu, choose Show CD.

4. Check the Automatically Retrieve CD Track Names from Internet box.

5. Click the Import Settings button to display the Import Settings dialog box. Figure 12.1 shows the Import Settings dialog box in Windows.

FIGURE 12.1

In the Import Settings dialog box for iTunes, choose the encoder and setting for the file format you want.

6. Open the Import Using pop-up menu and click the encoder to use. Normally, you'll want to choose either AAC Encoder or MP3 Encoder.

7. Open the Setting pop-up menu and click the setting to use. The settings available depend on the encoder. For example, for AAC, you can choose High Quality (128Kbps), iTunes Plus, or Spoken Podcast. For MP3 Encoder, you can choose Good Quality (128Kbps), High Quality (160Kbps), or Higher Quality (192Kbps). To get other—or higher—quality on either MP3 Encoder or AAC, click Custom and work in the AAC Encoder dialog box or the MP3 Encoder dialog box (see Figure 12.2). Figure 12.2 shows the MP3 Encoder dialog box in Windows.

! CAUTION Use the Spoken Podcast setting only for spoken-word audio. It uses high compression that makes music sound horrible.

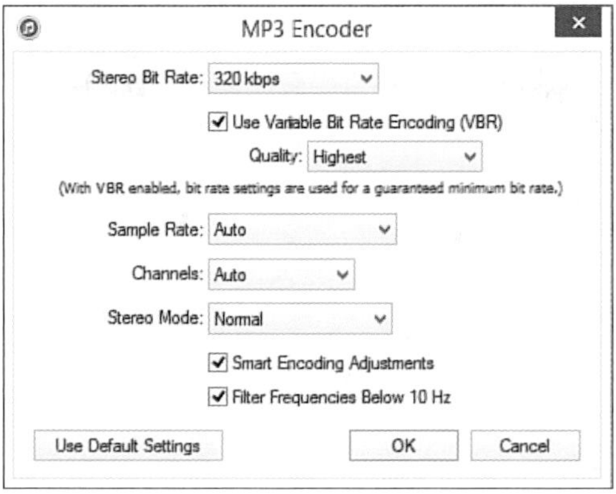

FIGURE 12.2

For high quality on your audio files, choose custom settings in the MP3 Encoder dialog box or the AAC Encoder dialog box.

TIP For highest quality of AAC and MP3 files, choose the 320Kbps setting in the Stereo Bit Rate pop-up menu, leave the Sample Rate pop-up menu and Channels pop-up menu set to Auto, and check the Use Variable Bit Rate Encoding (VBR) box.

For MP3 Encoder, choose Highest in the Quality pop-up menu, choose Normal in the Stereo Mode pop-up menu, and check both the Smart Encoding Adjustments box and the Filter Frequencies Below 10 Hz box.

For AAC Encoder, check the Use High Efficiency box, but uncheck the Optimize for Voice box.

8. Check the Use Error Correction When Reading Audio CDs box. Using error correction slows down the ripping process a little but helps avoid getting skips and crackles in your audio files.

9. Click the OK button to close the Import Settings dialog box.

CAUTION Don't choose the Apple Lossless Encoding option in the Import Settings dialog box in iTunes. This format is great for Apple devices (such as iPhones, iPads, and Macs), but most Android devices don't play it.

10. Click the OK button to close the Preferences dialog box.

> ### NOTE
> In Windows, you can use Windows Media Player to rip CDs to MP3 files. Windows Media Player uses Microsoft's Windows Media Audio file format by default, so you need to change the settings. Click the Organize menu and then click Options to open the Options dialog box, click the Rip Music tab, and then open the Format drop-down list and choose MP3. Drag the Audio Quality slider to set the bit rate you want, and then click the OK button.

> ### TIP
> If you want to create Ogg Vorbis files or FLAC files in Windows, use an app such as Total Audio Converter, which you can download from many software sites online. There's a 30-day trial, after which the app costs $19.90. The Audacity audio editor app (free from http://audacity.sourceforge.net) can also export audio in both Ogg Vorbis and FLAC formats. The easiest way to create Ogg Vorbis files or FLAC files on the Mac is by using XLD, which is available for free from various software sites.

After you've chosen your import settings, you can insert a CD in your computer's optical drive and rip it. Assuming you checked the Automatically Retrieve CD Track Names from Internet box, iTunes downloads the CD's details from the Gracenote database on the Internet and displays the results.

At this point, you can simply click the Import CD button to start importing the songs. But before you do, it's usually a good idea to look through the details that iTunes has retrieved and correct any errors. The Gracenote database contains an impressive amount of information, but it has many typos and other errors.

If any item of the CD info as a whole is wrong, click the CD Info button and use the CD Info dialog box to change it. This dialog box contains fields for the artist, composer, album title, disk number (for example, disk 1 of 2), genre, and year. You can also check the Compilation CD box if this CD is a compilation by different artists.

> ### CAUTION
> Check the Compilation CD box in the CD Info dialog box only if the CD is a compilation by different artists, not a compilation from the works of a single artist. Checking this box makes iTunes store the file in the folder called Compilations instead of in the artist's folder. When the CD is by a single artist, store the files in the artist's folder, where you can find them easily.

To change the information for an individual track, you can click a field twice to open it for editing. Pause between the clicks so that iTunes doesn't receive a double-click, which starts the track playing. For more extensive changes, right-click or Ctrl+click the track name and then click Get Info to display the Information dialog box, which gives you access to a wide range of fields for the track.

> **✓ TIP** When importing CDs, you'll often need to change the genre allocated to the music. Music fans can argue all day long about exactly which genre any given track belongs to, and iTunes and other apps enable you to assign a genre to each track rather than having to assign the genre at the album level (so that each track must have the same genre). To keep your music library straight and enable you to find the types of music you want easily, assign the genre that you will find most useful, no matter what genre other people suggest.

> **✐ NOTE** Samsung provides the Kies app for managing many of its devices, including most Samsung Android devices. You can import your music files into Kies and then sync them from there to your Samsung device. You can download Kies from http://www.samsung.com/in/support/usefulsoftware/KIES/JSP. For Windows, you must establish whether Kies (the older version) or Kies 3 (which is newer) is compatible with your device, so check the devices listed before you download the software.

TRANSCODING EXISTING FILES

If you have music files in formats that your device can't play, you have two options: Either install an app that can play back the files, or transcode the files to a supported format so that you can play them with your existing app.

Usually, transcoding the files is the better option, because it enables you to use your preferred music player for all your music. If the files in question are lossless, you can transcode them to another lossless format without losing quality or transcode them to your preferred lossy format with the normal loss in quality. Transcoding lossy files to another lossy format sacrifices more audio quality—you get any defects the first lossless format produced plus any defects the transcoding adds—but usually produces acceptable results. (If the results aren't acceptable, you can delete the transcoded files and figure out a plan B.)

In Windows, iTunes can transcode WMA files to a format such as MP3 or AAC. Otherwise, you'll need an app such as Total Audio Converter for Windows or XLD for the Mac.

SYNCING SONGS DIRECTLY WITH DOUBLETWIST

If you use iTunes to manage your music, you can use the free doubleTwist app to sync songs directly between iTunes and your Android device. Syncing directly can save you time and effort over syncing manually, so it's well worth a try. doubleTwist is also a music-playback app for Android; you can use it instead of the Play Music app or other playback apps.

Here's how to set up and use doubleTwist:

1. On your Android device, open the Play Store app and download the doubleTwist Music Player app from the Apps section. This app is free.

!CAUTION In Windows, the doubleTwist Setup Wizard recommends you install AVG PC TuneUp, a free trial version of a commercial app. Unless you actually want to install this app, you must uncheck the I Accept the Terms of the AVG PC TuneUp End User License Agreement and Privacy Policy and Want to Install AVG PC TuneUp box on the Install AVG PC TuneUp screen.

2. On your Mac or PC, go to the doubleTwist website (www.doubletwist.com) and download the doubleTwist Music Player app by clicking the Download for PC link or the Download for Mac link. Follow through the installation procedure as usual.

TIP In Windows, the final screen of the doubleTwist Setup Wizard contains two check boxes—the Launch doubleTwist box and the Always Run on Startup box—that are checked by default. Launching doubleTwist now is usually helpful, but you may want to uncheck the Always Run on Startup box so that you can run doubleTwist manually.

3. Connect your device to your Mac or PC via USB.

> 📝 **NOTE** On the Mac, OS X warns you that doubleTwist is from an unidentified developer and verifies that you want to run it. Click the Open button if you want to use the app. doubleTwist then requests access to your contacts. You'll probably want to deny this request by clicking the Don't Allow button.

4. Drag your music from your library to your device in the Devices list in the sidebar. You can also drag photos and videos to your device.

> 📝 **NOTE** If you want to sync your music via Wi-Fi, pay for the upgrade to the doubleTwist AirSync feature.

GETTING THE MOST OUT OF THE PLAY MUSIC APP

The Play Music app is the app Google provides for enjoying music on mobile devices. Play Music can play music stored on your phone or device, but its most compelling feature is its ability to stream songs stored online. You can store 20,000 songs in your Google account. And if you subscribe to Google Music, you can also listen to any of the millions of songs in the Google Music catalog.

> ✅ **TIP** If your device doesn't have the Play Music app installed, open the Play Store app, search for **play music**, and then install the app. It's free.

GETTING STARTED WITH PLAY MUSIC

To get started with Play Music, tap the Play Music icon on the Home screen or on the Apps screen. The first time you launch the Play Music app, you need to decide between standard use (tap the Use Standard button) or signing up for a trial subscription (tap the Try All Access button). You may want to start with standard use, which enables you to upload 20,000 of your songs to Google Play and listen to them on your devices.

After you've made that decision, the Listen Now screen appears (see Figure 12.3). This is one of the four main screens in the Play Music app: Listen Now, My Library,

Playlists, and Instant Mixes. To navigate among the screens, tap the Menu button to display the menu panel (see Figure 12.4), and then tap the screen you want to display.

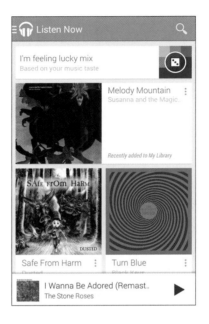

FIGURE 12.3

The Listen Now screen gives you access to your recent music and to recommendations. To navigate to other areas of Google Play, tap the Listen Now heading or the Menu button to its left to display the menu panel.

If your device contains songs, you can start playing them by navigating to one of them and tapping it. For example, on the Listen Now screen, tap an album to open it, and then tap the song you want to play.

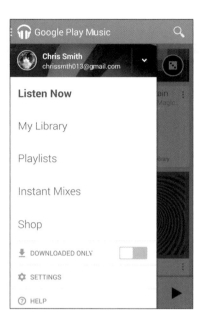

FIGURE 12.4

On the menu panel, tap the button for the area of Google Play Music that you want to use, or tap the Settings button to display the Music Settings screen.

SETTING UP AN ACCOUNT

If you've set up a Google account on your Android device, the Play Music app automatically uses that account. If necessary, you can switch to another account by following these steps:

1. Tap the Menu button to display the menu panel.

2. Tap Settings to display the Music Settings screen.

3. In the General section, tap the Google Account button to display the Select an Account screen.

4. Tap the existing account to use, or tap the Add Account button and follow through the resulting screens to set up a new account.

SYNCING YOUR 20,000 SONGS TO PLAY MUSIC

If you plan to sync songs to Google Play so that you can play them back with the Play Music app on your device, download and install the Google Music Manager app from https://music.google.com/music/listen#manager_pl. Click the Download Music Manager button to download the app's distribution file, and then install it by double-clicking the file in Windows or by dragging the app's file from the disk image to the Applications folder on OS X.

After installing Music Manager, open it from the Start screen or Start menu (in Windows) or from Launchpad on the Mac. The Music Manager setup routine runs, and you can configure the app by doing the following:

1. On the Sign In with Your Google Account screen, sign in using the Google account you will use for music on your computer and your device.

2. On the What Would You Like to Do? screen, select the Upload Songs to Google Play radio button and click the Continue button.

3. On the Where Do You Keep Your Music Collection? screen (see Figure 12.5), select the iTunes radio button, the Music Folder radio button, or the Other Folders radio button, as appropriate. If you select the Other Folders radio button, click the Add Folder button and add the folders to the list box. Click the Continue button when you're done.

FIGURE 12.5

On the Where Do You Keep Your Music Collection? screen, specify the folders you want Music Manager to search for music to upload to your Google Play account.

4. On the screen that asks whether you want to automatically upload songs you add to your selected folders in the future, click the Yes button or the No button, as appropriate. Uploading the songs automatically can be helpful, but you may want to perform quality control on your computer first to avoid loading turkeys into your Google Play account.

5. Follow through the remaining screens until the Your Music Is Being Added screen appears. You can then click the Go to Music Player button to open the online music player in your default web browser or click the Close button to close the Music Manager setup routine without opening the online music player.

> **NOTE** Uploading your songs will likely take hours or days, depending on how many songs you're uploading and how fast your Internet connection is. You can pause the upload at any time by giving the Pause command from the Music Manager icon in the notification area in Windows or toward the right end of the menu bar in OS X. From the pop-up menu, you can also click Go to Music Player to display the music player in your browser.

BUYING SONGS FROM THE PLAY STORE

The Play Music app makes it easy for you to buy music from the Play Store. From within the Play Music app, you can get to the Music section of the Play Store in a couple of ways:

- **Go to the Home screen of the Music section.** In the Play Music app, open the menu panel and then tap Shop. The Shop button is dimmed if you have set the Downloaded Only switch (which you'll learn about shortly) to On.

- **Go to a particular artist.** Tap the menu button for an artist, album, or song, and then tap Shop This Artist on the menu.

In each case, the Play Music app switches you over to the Play Store app. If you prefer, you can simply start with the Play Store app by tapping its icon on the Home screen or on the Apps screen. On the Home screen of the Play Store, either tap the Music button to start browsing music, or simply search by the name of the artist, album, or song you're looking for.

You can preview a song by tapping the Play button to its left. When you find a song you want to buy, tap its price button and then follow through the payment process.

> **TIP** If you'd like some free music, look at the Free Music area on the Home page of the Music section of the Play Store. You can tap the More button to display the Free Music screen, which shows all the free songs. These songs are genuinely free, but you still have to specify your means of payment and tap the Buy button to approve the payment of $0.00.

NAVIGATING THE PLAY MUSIC APP

The Play Music app has four main areas:

- **Listen Now.** The Listen Now screen provides quick access to the music you've added recently, music you've played recently, and music that Google Play recommends for you (if you have a subscription). You can tap the I'm Feeling Lucky Mix button at the top to create a custom mix of songs. If you've set the Downloaded Only switch to On, the Shuffle All button appears instead of the I'm Feeling Lucky Mix button.

- **My Library.** The My Library screen (see Figure 12.6) enables you to browse the music in your music library by genres, by artists, by albums, or by songs. Tap the tab by which you browse. Tap the menu button for an item (such as a song) to display the menu of actions you can take with it, such as Play Next or Go to Artist.

> **NOTE** The songs in your music library are those you've loaded onto your device and those you've uploaded to the Play Music service. You can download songs from the Play Music service and store them on your device so that you can play them directly from the device without streaming. We'll look at how to do this a little later in this chapter.

- **Playlists.** The Playlists screen contains three categories of playlists. The Recent Playlists category contains playlists you've created or edited recently. The Auto Playlists category contains playlists that the Play Music app maintains for you, such as the Last Added playlist and the Free and Purchased playlist, to give you easy access to particular categories of music. The All Playlists category shows all the playlists you've created.

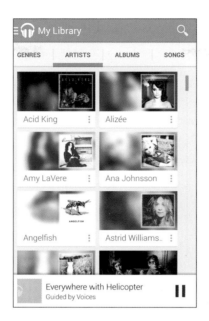

FIGURE 12.6

On the My Library screen, tap Genres, Artists, Albums, or Songs. You can then browse your music or start it playing.

■ **Instant Mixes.** The Instant Mixes screen enables you to create and enjoy mixes of songs that the Play Music app assembles for you. The My Mixes tab contains mixes you've created, and you can tap the Create New Instant Mix to start creating a new instant mix based on a song you select. The Recommended tab contains mixes that the app recommends for you.

You navigate among these areas by opening the menu panel and then tapping Listen Now, My Library, Playlists, or Instant Mixes.

The menu panel also contains three more commands (plus the Help command and the Send Feedback command):

■ **Shop.** Tap this command to go to the Music section of Google Play in the Play Store app.

■ **Downloaded Only.** Tap this switch, turning it from gray (off) to orange (on), to set the Play Music app to display only the music on your device. You'd do this when your device doesn't have an Internet connection or when you don't want to use up your cellular allowance by streaming music.

■ **Settings.** Tap this command to display the Music Settings screen. You'll look at this in the section "Configuring the Play Music App," later in this chapter.

PLAYING SONGS

To play a song, navigate to it and then tap it. Here's an example:

1. Tap the Artists button to display the Artists screen.

2. Tap the artist to display the list of albums.

3. Tap the album to display the list of songs from the album.

4. Tap the song you want to play. A playback indicator showing three moving vertical bars appears (see Figure 12.7).

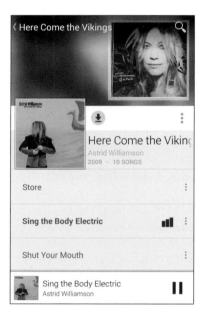

FIGURE 12.7

Tap the song you want to play. The playback indicator appears.

From here, you can tap another song to play it, or tap the Now Playing button at the bottom of the screen to display the Now Playing screen (see Figure 12.8). You can easily control the music:

Tap to display the track list.

Tap to open the menu.

Tap to rate the song.

Drag the Playhead to move through the song.

Tap to toggle shuffle on and off.

Tap to cycle through Repeat Off, Repeat All, and Repeat One.

FIGURE 12.8

From the Now Playing screen, you can drag the Playhead to move quickly through the song, turn on repeat or shuffle, rate the song, and display the track list.

- Use the playback controls to pause or resume playback, fast-forward or rewind, or skip to the next song or go back to the previous song.
- Drag the Playhead to scrub quickly through the song.
- Tap the Repeat button to cycle through Repeat Off, Repeat All, and Repeat One.
- Tap the Shuffle button to toggle shuffling on or off.
- Tap the thumbs-up icon to like the song or the thumbs-down icon to dislike it.
- Tap the Track List button to display the track list. You can then tap another song to start it playing.
- Tap the Menu button to display the menu, which contains commands such as Start Instant Mix, Play Next, Add to Playlist, Go to Artist, Go to Album, Remove from Queue, and Shop This Artist.

> ☑ **TIP**   The queue contains the list of songs that will play next. You can add a song to the queue by opening the menu and then tapping Add to Queue. (If the song is already on the queue, the Remove from Queue command appears on the menu instead of the Add to Queue command.) To clear the current songs from the queue, tap the Menu button on the Now Playing screen and then tap Clear Queue. To save the contents of the queue as a playlist, tap the Menu button, and then tap Save Queue. In the Add to Playlist dialog box, you can either tap an existing playlist to add the queue's contents to it or tap New Playlist to create a new playlist.

> ✎ **NOTE**   If you lock your device while music is playing or Android locks it after the Sleep interval you have set, the music continues to play. Android displays playback controls on the lock screen enabling you to pause and resume the music without unlocking your device. You can also skip to the next song, return to the beginning of the current song, or go back to the previous song.

DOWNLOADING SONGS

The Play Music app shows both the songs that are actually on your device and those that are stored online in your Google Play library. When you start to play a song that isn't on your device, the Play Music app streams it across your device's Internet connection.

When you don't have a Wi-Fi connection, you may want to turn off streaming music so as not to use your cellular data plan. Tap the Menu button to display the menu panel and then set the Downloaded Only switch to On to make the Play Music app show only the songs that are on your device and that you can play without streaming. The app displays a gray bar saying Downloaded Only near the top of the screen to remind you that you've restricted the library.

You can download songs from your Google Play library to your device as needed—preferably over a Wi-Fi connection. Tap the Albums button to display the albums screen, navigate to the album you want to download, tap the Menu button, and then tap Download.

DELETING SONGS FROM YOUR DEVICE AND YOUR LIBRARY

If you don't like a song, you can delete it. You may also want to delete songs if your device becomes too full and you need to clear some space on it.

Because the Play Music app shows you both the songs actually on your device and those in your Google Play library, you need to be careful when deleting songs.

If the song is part of an album you've downloaded from your Google Play library, you'll usually do best to remove the album from your device. This keeps the album in your Google Play library, so you can play it again via streaming any time.

To remove an album, go to the album's screen, tap the album's Menu button, and then tap Remove Download. In the confirmation dialog box (see Figure 12.9), tap the Remove button; you can check the Don't Ask Me Again box first if you want to suppress this confirmation in the future.

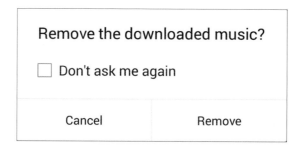

FIGURE 12.9

To free up space on your device, you can remove a downloaded album, leaving the songs available in your Google Play library.

You can also simply delete a song by going to the song, tapping its Menu button, and then tapping Delete. What happens then depends on whether you've copied the song to your device directly or it is in your Google Play library:

- **Song copied to your device.** A delete confirmation dialog box opens showing the song's name (see Figure 12.10). Tap the OK button to delete the song.

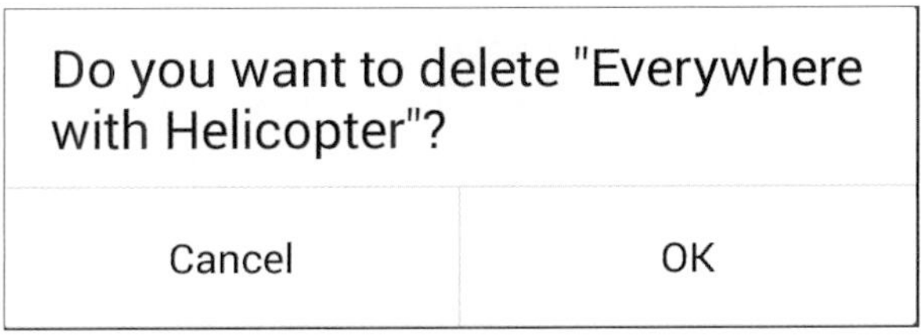

> Do you want to delete "Everywhere with Helicopter"?
>
> | Cancel | OK |

FIGURE 12.10

This type of delete confirmation dialog box indicates the song is one that you've copied to your device.

■ **Song in your Google Play library.** The Delete from Library? dialog box opens (see Figure 12.11). You can tap the OK button to delete the song, but normally it's best to tap the Cancel button and then use the Remove Download command to remove the downloaded album, leaving the songs in your Google Play library.

> Delete from Library?
>
> **I Wanna Be Adored (Remastered)**
> **The Stone Roses**
>
> This song will no longer be available from your Google Play library on any device.
>
> | Cancel | OK |

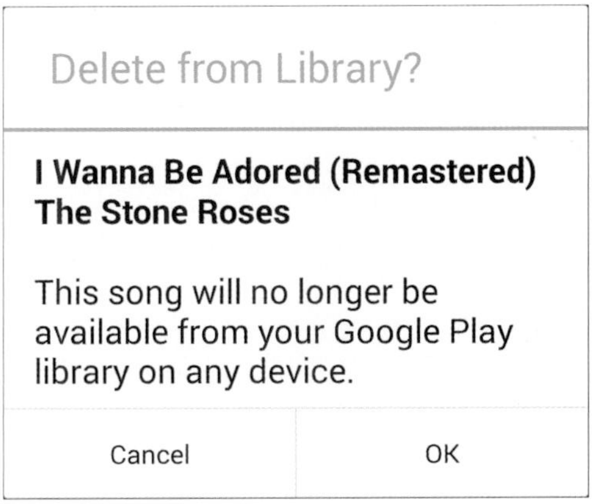

FIGURE 12.11

The Delete from Library? dialog box checks that you want to remove the song from your Google Play library, not just from your device.

CONFIGURING THE PLAY MUSIC APP

Like most apps, the Play Music app offers a variety of settings that you can customize to make the app work your way. To configure it, open the menu panel, tap Settings, and then work on the Music Settings screen (see Figure 12.12).

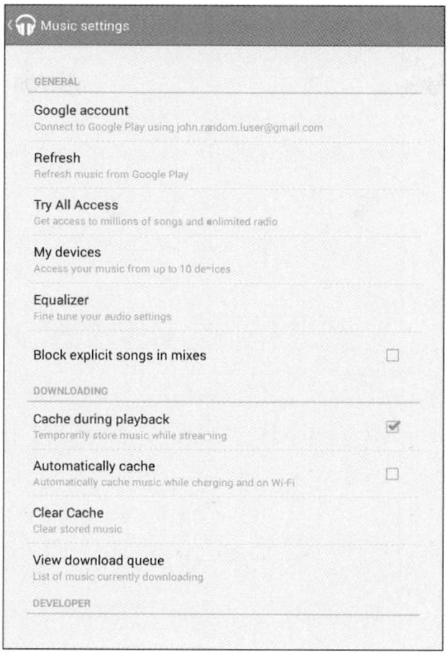

FIGURE 12.12

The Music Settings screen enables you to manage your devices, control downloading and caching, and access the Equalizer.

> **TIP** If you play streaming music with the Play Music app, it's important to configure your streaming and caching settings to make sure you don't go through data allowance unintentionally.

The Music Settings screen has three sections: General, Downloading, and Developer. Here's what you can do with the General settings:

- **Google Account.** Tap this button to display the Select an Account screen. You can then select the account you want to use for Google Play Music.

- **Refresh.** Tap this button to refresh the list of music from Google Play. You'd want to do this after uploading songs from your computer to Google Play.

- **Try All Access.** Tap this button to start setting up a 30-day trial of access to all the music on Google Play. When the trial ends, continuing all access costs $9.99 per month.

- **My Devices.** Tap this button to display the My Devices screen, which lists the devices you're using for Google Play Music. You can use up to 10 devices at a time. To stop using a device, tap the × icon on the right of its button, and then tap the Deauthorize button in the Deauthorize Device dialog box (see Figure 12.13).

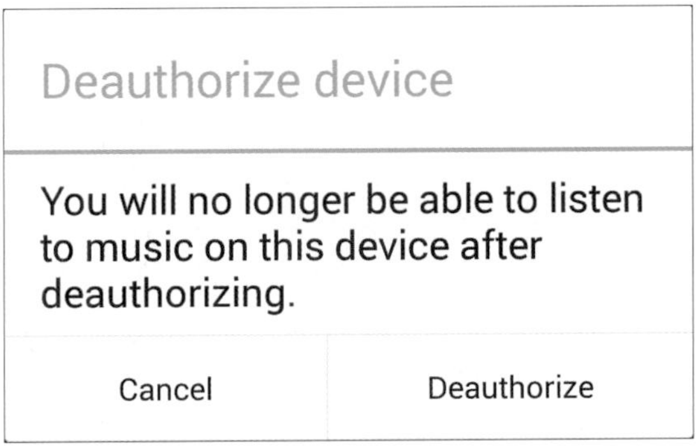

FIGURE 12.13
You can deauthorize a device that you no longer want to use with Google Play Music.

- **Equalizer.** Tap this button to choose Equalizer settings. You'll look at how to do this a little later in this chapter.

- **Block Explicit Songs in Mixes.** Check this box to prevent Play Music from including in mixes any songs that are marked as Explicit. This setting doesn't ensure complete sanitization of the music, but it's pretty solid—although it seems to block the occasional "explicit" instrumental.

These are the Downloading settings you can choose:

- **Cache During Playback.** Check this box to enable the Play Music app to *cache* (store) data temporarily while streaming music. Caching helps prevent interruptions, so it's usually helpful. Turn caching off only when your device is crammed full of data.

- **Automatically Cache.** Check this box to allow the Play Music app to cache data only while your device is on Wi-Fi and when it's charging. This check box is available only when you've checked the Cache During Playback box.

- **Clear Cache.** Tap this button to delete all the cached music. Normally, you'd want to do this only to reclaim the space the cached music is occupying.

- **Download via Wi-Fi Only.** (Cellular-capable devices only.) Check this box to prevent your device from downloading music across the cellular network. If you've got a meager data plan, it's a good idea to keep this box checked.

- **View Download Queue.** Tap this button to display the Download Queue screen so that you can see which songs the Play Music app is currently downloading.

> **NOTE** The Developer section of the Music Settings screen contains to the Open Source Licenses button, which you can tap to see the details of the open-source licenses that the app uses, and the Music Version button, which displays the app's version number. You might need the version number when reporting or troubleshooting a problem with the app.

CREATING PLAYLISTS

The Play Music app makes it easy to create playlists containing only the songs you want to hear and in your preferred order. You can start creating a playlist from any song in your library. You can also quickly add songs to an existing playlist.

Here's how to create a playlist:

1. Navigate to the song or other item you want to put in the playlist.
2. Tap the item's Menu button and then tap Add to Playlist on the menu. The Add to Playlist dialog box opens (see Figure 12.14).

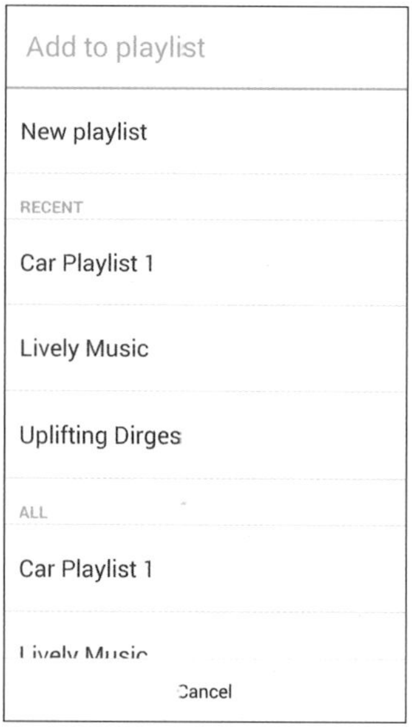

Add to playlist

New playlist

RECENT

Car Playlist 1

Lively Music

Uplifting Dirges

ALL

Car Playlist 1

Lively Music

Cancel

FIGURE 12.14

From the Add to Playlist dialog box, tap New Playlist to start a new playlist, or tap the existing playlist to which you want to add the item.

3. Tap New Playlist. The New Playlist dialog box opens (see Figure 12.15).

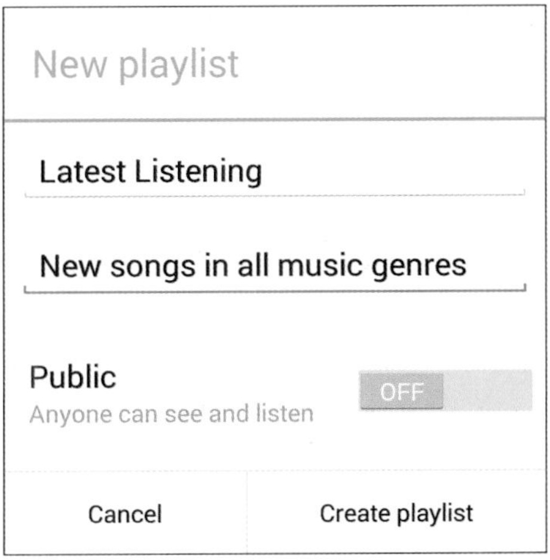

New playlist

Latest Listening

New songs in all music genres

Public
Anyone can see and listen   OFF

Cancel   Create playlist

FIGURE 12.15

In the New Playlist dialog box, type the name and description for the playlist and decide whether to make it public.

4. Type the name and description for the playlist.

> **TIP**   The description is to help you identify the playlist from others with similar names, so it's a good idea to type something clear, no matter how redundant it seems now.

5. Set the Public switch to On if you want to make the playlist visible to other people on Google Play.

6. Tap the Create Playlist button.

Now that you've created the playlist, you can add other songs—or other items, such as an album or artist—to it by tapping each item's Menu button, tapping Add to Playlist, and then tapping the playlist's name in the Add to Playlist dialog box.

To play back a playlist, open the menu panel and tap Playlists to display the Playlists screen. You can then tap the playlist to open it and tap a song to start it playing.

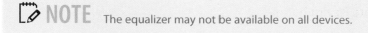 **TIP** To change a playlist you've created, display the playlist. You can then drag a song up or down the playlist using the handle on the left side. To remove a song from the playlist, swipe it off to the left or to the right.

IMPROVING YOUR MUSIC WITH THE EQUALIZER

To make the music to which you listen sound as good as possible through your headphones or speakers, it's a good idea to use the equalizer built into the Play Music app. You can either apply an existing equalization, such as Folk or Heavy Metal, or create a custom equalization that suits your ears and your headphones or speakers.

TIP If you often listen to music using your Android device, consider getting a headphone amplifier to improve the sound. A headphone amplifier is a small device that enables you to adjust the sound balance or turn up the volume.

TURNING ON THE EQUALIZER

Connect your headphones or speakers and set some music playing so that you can hear the effects of the changes you make. Then open the menu panel, tap Settings to display the Settings screen, and then tap Equalizer. On the Equalizer screen (see Figure 12.16), set the switch to On, enabling the other controls.

NOTE The equalizer may not be available on all devices.

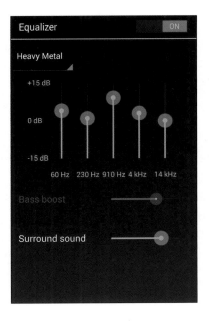

FIGURE 12.16

Set the Equalizer switch to On, pick an equalization from the pop-up menu, and then adjust the Bass Boost and Surround Sound as needed.

> **NOTE** The Bass Boost and Surround Sound features are available only if your device has the audio hardware needed for them.

You can then tap the pop-up menu and tap the preset equalization you want to apply: Normal, Classical, Dance, Flat, Folk, Heavy Metal, Hip Hop, Jazz, Pop, Rock, or FX Booster.

> **NOTE** The Flat equalization has all the sliders at their midpoints, giving 0 decibel (dB) adjustment. This equalization has the same effect as turning the Equalizer off except that you can adjust the Bass Boost and Surround Sound settings (if your device supports them). The Normal equalization gives a slight boost to the lowest (60Hz) and highest (14kHz) frequencies to punch up the sound a little.

Now drag the Bass Boost and Surround Sound sliders to tweak the sound to how you prefer it.

CREATING A CUSTOM EQUALIZATION

The Equalizer's presets offer a good range of equalizations, but if none meets your needs, you can create a custom equalization. Apply the existing equalization that sounds best to you, and then drag the frequency sliders to improve the sound. As soon as you adjust one of the sliders, Play Music selects the User item in the pop-up menu.

> **NOTE** You can also start creating your custom equalization by opening the pop-up menu and tapping User. This enables you to start with all the sliders at their midpoints.

When you've set up the equalization you want, tap the Back button twice to return to your music.

Add an Equalizer to Android Versions Before Jelly Bean

Android versions before Jelly Bean (Android 4.1) come without an equalizer. You can find various equalizers on the App Store—some of them free, others paid. The app called Equalizer from Smart Android Apps, LLC is a good place to start.

USING OTHER MUSIC APPS

Play Music can be great, but you can use a huge number of other Android apps to play music on your device. This section introduces you to three apps for identifying music you hear and three streaming services for exploring music and radio.

THREE APPS FOR IDENTIFYING MUSIC

These apps enable you to identify music easily:

- **Shazam.** Shazam is a free app that can automatically identify a song by listening to a snippet of it playing. Shazam enables you to share your music and TV discoveries via Facebook and Google+, but you can ignore these features if you don't need them.

- **SoundHound.** SoundHound is a free app that can automatically identify a song by listening to it being played nearby or by your humming the tune.
- **TrackID.** Also free, TrackID enables you to identify songs within range of your device's microphone. TrackID gives you access to artist biographies and links to music videos on YouTube.

THREE STREAMING SERVICES

If you like listening to a wide variety of music, try these three streaming services:

- **Spotify.** Spotify gives you access to a huge amount of music via streaming. You can browse through top lists or new releases, explore genres and moods, or simply search using keywords. The basic Spotify service is free and supported by ads. You can upgrade to the Premium service to get ad-free listening.
- **Pandora.** Pandora is a music-streaming service that plays selections based on the artists you choose. You can rate the songs that Pandora plays to tune the selections toward what you like. Pandora enables you to find information about the music played and to purchase it from various sources. Pandora also includes other features, such as enabling you to set alarm clocks and providing personalized radio recommendations.

> **NOTE** At this writing, Pandora is available only in the United States, Australia, and New Zealand because of licensing constraints. To access Pandora from other countries, you need to use a VPN connection to one of these three countries.

- **TuneIn Radio.** TuneIn Radio is an online radio station that offers more than 100,000 real radio stations and millions of on-demand programs and podcasts. TuneIn Radio is a free service, but you can pay for the TuneIn Radio Pro upgrade if you want to be able to record radio to your device so that you can listen to it later.

> **! CAUTION** Streaming audio can take up a huge amount of bandwidth if you use it frequently. If you use streaming audio over the cellular network, keep a close eye on your data usage to make sure you don't rack up charges.

13

STAYING IN TOUCH VIA SOCIAL NETWORKING

Your Android device is great for keeping in touch with your contacts via social networking no matter where you go—or where they go. In this chapter, you'll learn how you can make the most of Facebook and Twitter on your device.

Both apps are largely straightforward to use, especially if you are familiar with how the two services work. But both have serious implications for your privacy, so it's essential that you configure them suitably. In particular, you should secure your Facebook account by setting up two-factor authentication and your Twitter account by applying login verification.

GETTING SERIOUS WITH FACEBOOK

If you're on Facebook, you'll probably want to use your Android device to keep up with your friends' latest news and to post your own.

Facebook makes it easy to share your information—too easy, many would say. You'll have no difficulty posting, liking,

or commenting, so we'll concentrate on the other side of the equation: how to configure Facebook so that you're sharing only what you want to share, and no more.

Most Android devices include the Facebook app, but if yours doesn't, go to the Play Store and download it. You'll then need to log in using your account.

MAKING THE RIGHT DECISION WHEN LOGGING IN

When you're logging in, the big decision comes on the Contacts Sync screen (see Figure 13.1), where you need to tap the right radio button out of these three:

- **Sync All.** Tap this radio button to sync data about all of your Facebook friends to your contacts on your Android device. This approach may mean adding many contacts to your device.

- **Sync with Existing Contacts.** Tap this radio button to sync data about only those Facebook friends who already have a contact record on your device. This is often the best option.

- **Don't Sync.** Tap this radio button to keep your Facebook friends separate from the contacts on your Android device, even if some of them are the same people.

FIGURE 13.1

When logging in to Facebook, choose which of your Facebook information to sync to the contacts on your Android device.

Tap the Sync button or the Done button—whichever button appears on the Contacts Sync screen after you have selected the radio button you want—to implement your choice.

GETTING AND CONFIGURING FACEBOOK MESSENGER

Until summer 2014, the Facebook apps for Android and other mobile platforms (such as Apple's iOS) enabled you to send messages from within the app. But in summer 2014, Facebook started requiring you to use its separate Facebook Messenger app for sending messages. At this writing, there's no way around using Messenger unless you're prepared to give up sending messages on Facebook.

GETTING FACEBOOK MESSENGER

If the Facebook app prompts you to get the Facebook Messenger app, tap the Get App button and follow through the process of downloading and installing it from the Play Store.

NOTE Facebook Messenger requires a daunting set of permissions, including Identity, Contacts/Calendar, Location, Photos/Media/Files, Camera/Microphone, and Device ID & Call Information. These permissions are necessary for the many functions that Facebook Messenger provides, such as taking selfies and videos and sharing them with your contacts.

CAUTION Installing Facebook Messenger causes Samsung devices to display the Potential Threat Alerts dialog box, which warns you that the app is authorized to access Messages. This looks like a problem, but it is not: If you want to be able to use Facebook Messenger, you need it to be able to send and receive messages.

After installing Facebook Messenger, tap the Open button on the Play Store screen to open the app. (If you've left the Play Store screen, go to the Apps screen and tap the Messenger icon there to open Facebook Messenger.)

On the Welcome to Messenger screen, tap the Continue button. Next, the Text Anyone in Your Phone screen appears (on a phone). You can either tap the Sync Contacts button to sync all your contacts continuously with Facebook, enabling you to see which of them are on Messenger (and, optionally, get in touch with them) or tap the Not Now button.

Whichever choice you make here, the What Number Can People Use to Reach You? screen appears. Make sure that the correct phone number appears, and then tap the OK button. (If you don't want to provide your phone number at this point, tap the Not Now button and then tap the Skip button in the Skip Phone Number? dialog box that opens to nag you for the phone number.)

> ## NOTE
> Facebook doesn't make the phone number you specify on the What Number Can People Use to Reach You? screen available to other people. Instead, it enables people who already have this phone number for you to contact you on this number.

Next, the Confirming Your Phone Number screen appears while Facebook sends you a confirmation code via instant message. Normally, Facebook Messenger receives this message automatically (because you gave it permission to access your messages) and dismisses the Confirming Your Phone Number screen. If not, type in the confirmation code manually and tap the Continue button.

> ## CAUTION
> Facebook also sends you an email confirming that it has added this phone number to your account. If you receive one of these emails without adding a phone number to your account, open your browser, go to www.facebook.com/hacked, and click the My Account Is Compromised button. Don't click the Secure Your Account link in the Facebook message about confirming your phone number because fraudsters can make convincing replicas of both the message and the Report Compromised Account page on Facebook's website.

> ## NOTE
> If the Secure Your Account dialog box opens at this point, click the Continue button.

On the You're on Messenger! screen, tap the Continue button to start using Facebook Messenger.

NAVIGATING THE FACEBOOK MESSENGER INTERFACE

Now that you have Facebook Messenger up and running, you'll find your way around easily. As you can see in Figure 13.2, Facebook Messenger has four tabs:

- **Recent.** Tap this tab to see recent activity. You can tap a chat to display it, or tap the New Message button to start a new message.

- **Groups.** Tap this tab to display your list of groups. You can create a new group by tapping one of the New Group placeholders or by tapping the New Group button in the lower-right corner.

- **Contacts.** Tap this tab to display the Contacts screen. This screen has two tabs: the Messenger tab and the Active tab. Tap the Messenger tab to display your list of contacts. Tap the Active tab to display your active chats.

- **Settings.** Tap this tab to display the Settings screen. See the next section for details.

FIGURE 13.2

On the Recent screen, you can tap a chat to open it, or tap New Message to start a new message.

CHOOSING SETTINGS FOR FACEBOOK MESSENGER

To make Facebook Messenger work the way you want, tap the Settings icon on the tab bar and work on the Settings screen (see Figure 13.3). These are the settings you can choose on the main screen:

▪ **Facebook Chat.** Check this box to enable Facebook chat. Normally, you'll want to do this.

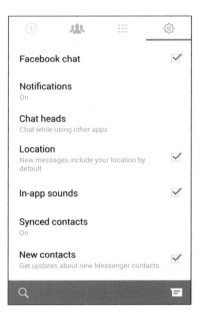

FIGURE 13.3

Review the settings for Facebook Messenger to make sure they're suitable for you.

▪ **Notifications.** Tap this button to display the Notifications screen. There are a bunch of these screens, and you'll learn about them in the next section.

▪ **Chat Heads.** Tap this button to display the Chat Heads screen. Here, you can set the Chat Heads switch to On if you want to use Chat Heads or to Off if you don't. You can also set the two options discussed in the nearby note.

> **NOTE** If you use Chat Heads, you can check the Hide When Using Apps That Take Up the Full Screen box to remove Chat Heads when you're using a full-screen app (such as a game). You can check the Start Conversations from the Notification Tray box to enable yourself to start a conversation in Facebook Messenger by tapping the Chat Heads notification in the Notifications panel.

■ **Location.** Check this box if you want new messages you send to include your location unless you remove it.

> **! CAUTION** Including your location in new messages is great for letting your friends know where you are, but if it raises any concerns about your security, uncheck the Location box and add your location manually to only those messages that need it.

■ **In-App Sounds.** Check this box to allow Facebook Messenger to play sounds.

■ **Synced Contacts.** This button shows whether Facebook Messenger is currently syncing your contacts. To change your setting, tap this button and then tap the OK button in the Synced Contacts dialog box.

> **NOTE** Turning off syncing removes all your phone's contacts from Facebook Messenger.

■ **New Contacts.** Check this box if you want to receive updates about new Facebook Messenger contacts.

CHOOSING NOTIFICATIONS SETTINGS FOR FACEBOOK MESSENGER

You can choose the following settings on the Notifications screen for Facebook Messenger (see Figure 13.4):

■ **Notifications.** Set this switch to Off if you want to suppress all notifications temporarily.

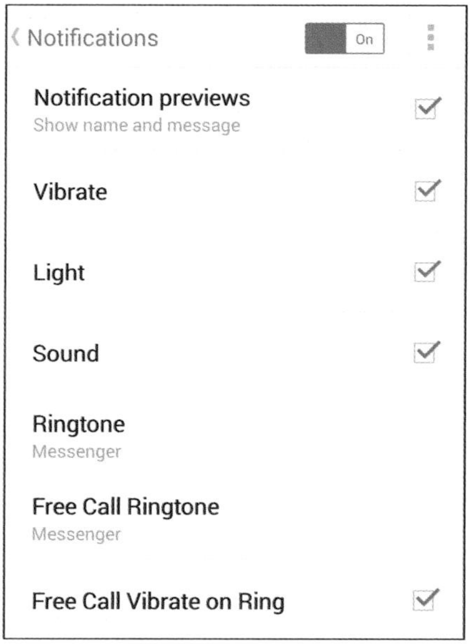

FIGURE 13.4

On the Notifications screen for Facebook Messenger, you can choose whether to view notification previews and whether to use vibration, light, and sound for notifications.

■ **Notification Previews.** Check this box to display previews of the friend's name and the message. These previews are usually handy unless you get too many of them.

■ **Vibrate.** Check this box to have your device vibrate when you receive a notification. This setting is available only on devices that have a vibration motor.

■ **Light.** Check this box to have your device pulse the notification light when you have a notification.

■ **Sound.** Check this box to have your device play a sound when you receive a notification.

■ **Ringtone.** Tap this button, select the ringtone in the Ringtone dialog box, and then tap the OK button.

> **TIP** The Free Call Ringtone setting enables you to use a different ringtone to identify free calls from paid calls.

- **Free Call Ringtone.** Tap this button, select your preferred free call ringtone in the Ringtone dialog box, and then tap the OK button.
- **Free Call Vibrate on Ring.** Check this box if you want your phone to vibrate when you get a free call. This setting is available only on devices that have a vibration motor.

MAKING FACEBOOK WORK YOUR WAY

Facebook has a large number of settings that you can configure to make the Facebook app and the Facebook platform work your way. The default settings tend to be configured in ways that suit Facebook, so you'd be wise to spend a few minutes understanding what the settings do and configuring them to suit your needs.

REACHING THE SETTINGS

To reach the settings, tap the More button on the right side of the main toolbar. This brings you to the More screen, which starts with your profile picture and your Favorites list. Scroll down past the Apps list, the Feeds list, the Groups list, and the Pages list, and you'll find the Help & Settings section.

CHOOSING APP SETTINGS

To get started choosing settings, tap the App Settings button to display the Settings screen (see Figure 13.5).

You can choose these settings in the General Settings section:

- **Facebook Chat.** Tap this button to toggle Facebook Chat on or off.
- **Refresh Interval.** Tap this button to display the Refresh Interval dialog box, and then tap the appropriate radio button: 30 Minutes, 1 Hour, 2 Hours, 4 Hours, or Never.

> **☑ TIP** Set a longer refresh interval—or Never—to reduce the amount of battery power and data that Facebook takes.

- **Messenger Location Services.** Tap this button to display the Location dialog box, and then check or uncheck the Location Is On box. Tap the OK button to close the dialog box.

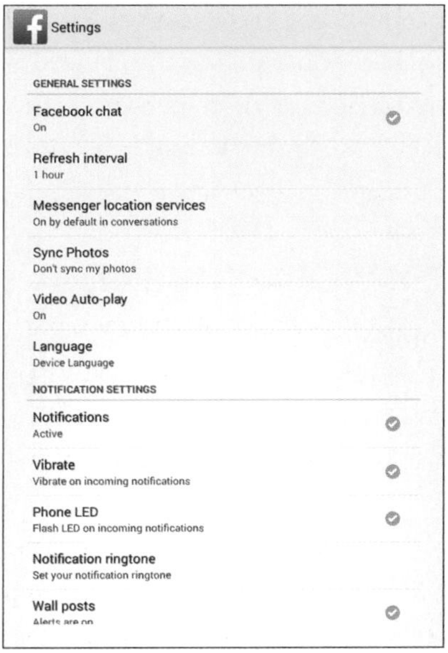

FIGURE 13.5

The main Settings screen includes vital settings such Facebook Chat, the Refresh Interval, and the notifications you receive.

- **Sync Photos.** Tap this button and use the Photo Syncing screen to choose which photos and albums to sync.
- **Video Auto-Play.** Tap this button to display the Video Auto-Play dialog box, and then tap the appropriate radio button: On, Wi-Fi Only, or Off.

> **❗CAUTION** Select the On radio button for Video Auto-Play only if you have a generous or unlimited data plan.

- **Language.** To change the language, tap this button, and then tap the appropriate radio button in the dialog box that opens. The default setting is Device Language, which works well for general purposes.

You can choose these settings in the Notification Settings section:

- **Notifications.** Check this box to make notifications active and to make all the other settings in the Notification Settings section available.
- **Vibrate.** Check this box to make your device vibrate to signal an incoming notification. This works only if your device has a vibration motor.

- **Phone LED.** Check this box to have the phone LED flash to let you know there are incoming notifications.
- **Notification Ringtone.** Tap this button to display the Notification Ringtone dialog box, tap to select a distinctive ringtone, and then tap the OK button.
- **Wall Posts.** Check this box to receive an alert when someone defaces your wall.
- **Messages.** Check this box to enable messages.
- **Comments.** Check this box to receive alerts when people post comments.
- **Friend Requests.** Check this box to receive alerts when you receive friend requests.
- **Friend Confirmations.** Check this box to receive alerts when you receive friend confirmations.
- **Photo Tags.** Check this box to receive alerts for events.
- **Event Invites.** Check this box to receive alerts for event invites.
- **Application Requests.** Check this box to receive alerts for application requests.
- **Groups.** Check this box to receive alerts for changes to groups.
- **Lock Screen Notifications Settings.** Check this box to see notifications on the lock screen.

The Chat Heads section of the Settings screen has only one button, the Messenger Settings button. Tap the button to jump to the Chat Heads screen of settings in the Facebook Messenger app.

MANAGING YOUR NEWS FEED

To manage your news feed, tap the Manage News Feed button on the More screen, and then work on the Manage News Feed screen. Here, you can tap the Follow button to start following someone or tap the Following button to stop following someone. (There's one button on each news feed item. The button displays either "Follow" or "Following," as appropriate.)

CHOOSING ESSENTIAL PRIVACY SETTINGS

To maintain as much privacy as you want while sharing your information on Facebook, you must make sure that you choose suitable privacy settings. This section concentrates on the most important settings—those that will make the greatest difference.

OPENING THE PRIVACY SHORTCUTS SCREEN

You can configure the absolute minimum of privacy settings from the Privacy Shortcuts screen. Here's how to display the Privacy Shortcuts screen:

1. In the Facebook app, tap the More button to display the More screen.

2. In the Help & Settings section, tap the Account Settings button to display the Settings screen.

3. Tap the Privacy Shortcuts button to display the Privacy Shortcuts screen (see Figure 13.6).

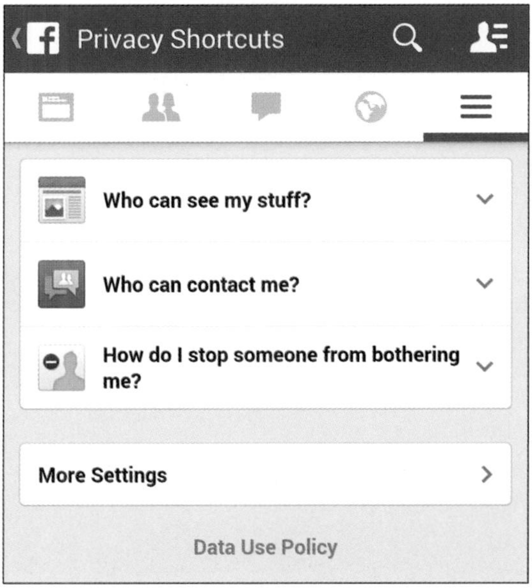

FIGURE 13.6

The Privacy Shortcuts screen gives you access to the three most important privacy settings, plus a More Settings button for those times when you want to dig into the Privacy settings.

NOTE Depending on your device and your region, you may see a different screen (such as the Privacy screen) instead of the Privacy Shortcuts screen.

CONTROLLING WHO CAN SEE YOUR POSTS

On the Privacy Shortcuts screen, tap the Who Can See My Stuff? heading to display its contents (see Figure 13.7).

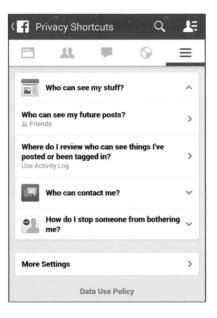

FIGURE 13.7

On the Privacy Shortcuts screen, expand the Who Can See My Stuff? section, and then tap the Who Can See My Future Posts? button.

Tap the Who Can See My Future Posts? button to display the Select Audience screen (see Figure 13.8). You can then tap the appropriate button: Public, Friends, Only Me, or a specific group.

> **! CAUTION**　Share your posts with the Public audience only if you are certain that you want to share everything you post on Facebook with anybody in the world, both now and forever onward. Sharing your posts with the Friends audience is usually a much better choice.

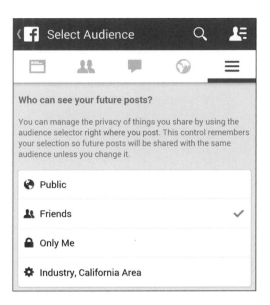

FIGURE 13.8

On the Select Audience screen, tap the button for the group with which you want to share your posts.

REVIEWING AND SANITIZING YOUR ACTIVITY LOG

Tap the Back button to return to the Privacy Shortcuts screen, and then tap the Where Do I Review Who Can See Things I've Posted or Been Tagged In? button. The Facebook app displays the Activity Log screen (see Figure 13.9).

TIP You can also go straight to the Activity Log screen by tapping the Activity Log button in the Help & Settings section of the More screen.

Tap the Filter button to display the Activity Log Options screen (see Figure 13.10), and then tap the button for the item type you want to view. The Activity Log screen appears again, this time showing the items of the type you chose.

NOTE You can filter by a long list of item types, from Your Posts, Posts You're Tagged In, and Photos all the way through Likes, Comments, and Friends to Questions, Location History, and Apps.

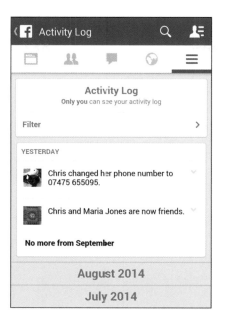

FIGURE 13.9

On the Activity Log screen, tap the Filter button to display the Activity Log Options screen.

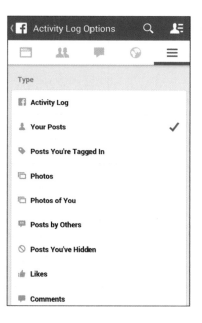

FIGURE 13.10

On the Activity Log Options screen, tap the button for the item type you want to view on the Activity Log screen.

Tap a downward-caret button to display a menu of actions you can take with it. For example, on a friend announcement (see Figure 13.11), you can tap the Hide from Timeline button or the Unfriend button.

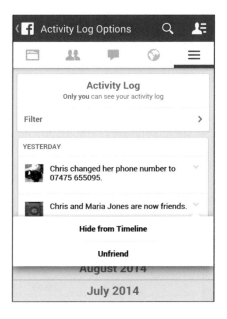

FIGURE 13.11

Tap the downward-caret button on an item to display actions you can take with it.

CONTROLLING WHO CAN CONTACT YOU

To control who can contact you, tap the Who Can Contact Me? button on the Privacy Shortcuts screen to display its contents (see Figure 13.12).

In the Whose Messages Do I Want Filtered into My Inbox? box, tap the Basic Filtering button or the Strict Filtering button, as needed.

> **TIP** If you're getting too many unwanted messages in your Inbox, try turning on Strict Filtering. By and large, this setting allows only your friends to send you messages, but Facebook also lets through some other messages that it has high confidence you will want. If you turn on Strict Filtering, visit your Other Messages folder periodically to make sure you're not filtering out messages you want.

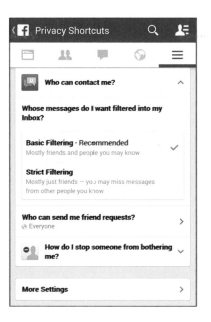

FIGURE 13.12
Expand the Who Can Contact Me? section on the Privacy Shortcuts screen to display the options for controlling who can contact you.

Next, tap the Who Can Send Me Friend Requests? button to display the Select Audience screen, and then tap the Everyone button or the Friends of Friends button, as needed.

> **NOTE** Friends of Friends is the sensible choice for friend requests except for a Facebook account that you use to maintain a public presence. For example, if you have a Facebook account for your band, you'd probably want to allow friend requests from everyone.

BLOCKING A PERSON WHO IS BOTHERING YOU

If someone is harassing you on Facebook, you can block that person. Follow these steps:

1. Tap the How Do I Stop Someone from Bothering Me? button on the Privacy Shortcuts screen to display the section's controls (see Figure 13.13).

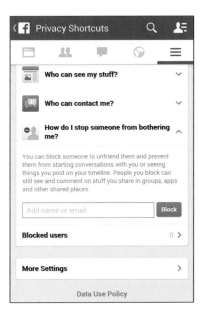

FIGURE 13.13

You can block someone from contacting you by typing his name or email address and then tapping the Block button.

2. Type the offender's name or email address in the Add Name or Email box.

3. Tap the Block button. The Privacy Shortcuts displays a list of matches (see Figure 13.14).

4. Tap the Block button for the person you want to block. The Block Users screen appears (see Figure 13.15), making clear that the person will not be able to see items you post on your timeline, tag you, invite you to events or groups, start conversations with you, or add you as a friend.

> **TIP** If you're not certain which of the list of matches on the Privacy Shortcuts screen is the person you want to block, tap the person's name to display her profile.

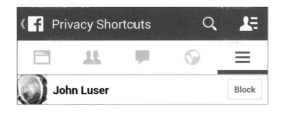

FIGURE 13.14

In the list of matches, tap the Block button for the person you want to block.

5. Tap the Block button to block the person.

> **NOTE** Blocking someone with whom you're a currently a friend also unfriends that person.

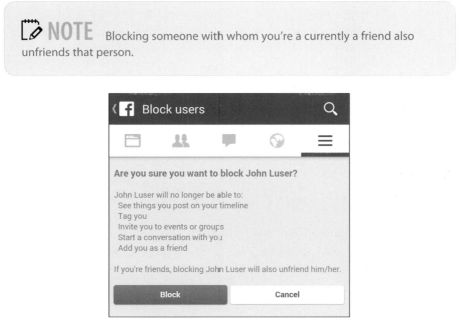

FIGURE 13.15

Tap the Block button on the Block Users screen to implement the blocking.

> **TIP** To manage your blocked list, tap the Blocked Users button at the bottom of the How Do I Stop Someone from Bothering Me? section on the Privacy Shortcuts screen. On the Block Users screen, you can review the Blocked Users list, and tap the Unblock button to unblock someone if necessary.

> **NOTE** If you run into abusive content, spam, or policy violations, tap the Report a Problem button on the More screen and follow through the procedure for reporting the problem to Facebook.

SECURING YOUR FACEBOOK ACCOUNT WITH TWO-FACTOR AUTHENTICATION

As you know, the default means of authentication (proving your identity) to Facebook is entering your user ID and password. This is one-factor authentication and gives you only a modest amount of security. To help prevent anyone hacking into your account, you can set up two-factor authentication so that you have to enter a code each time you log in to Facebook from an unknown device.

> **TIP** Please do set up two-factor authentication to secure your account. It takes minimal time and effort and provides pretty good protection against hacking.

SETTING UP TWO-FACTOR AUTHENTICATION

Here's how to set up two-factor authentication:

1. In the Facebook app, tap the More button to display the More screen.
2. In the Help & Settings section, tap the Account Settings button to display the Settings screen.
3. Tap the Security button to display the Security Settings screen (see Figure 13.16).

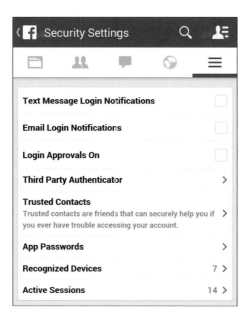

FIGURE 13.16

On the Security Settings screen, check the Login Approvals On box to start setting up two-factor authentication.

4. Check the Login Approvals On box. The Facebook app prompts you to re-enter your password (see Figure 13.17).

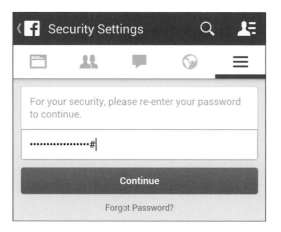

FIGURE 13.17

Re-enter your password to authenticate yourself.

5. Type your password.

6. Tap the Continue button. The first Login Approvals screen appears (see Figure 13.18).

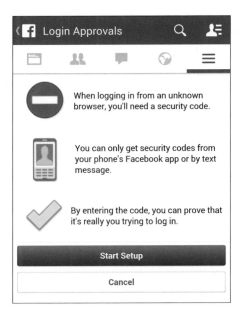

FIGURE 13.18

On the first Login Approvals screen, tap the Start Setup button.

7. Tap the Start Setup button. The second Login Approvals screen appears (see Figure 13.19), showing the phone number to which Facebook will text a code to confirm.

> **NOTE** If necessary, tap the Change Phone Number button and use the Set Up Security Code Delivery screen to add your mobile phone number to your Timeline.

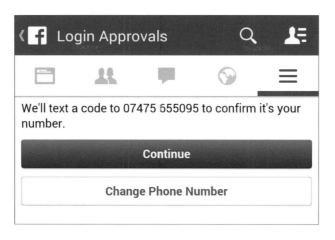

FIGURE 13.19

On the second Login Approvals screen, verify the phone number or tap the Change Phone Number button to provide a different phone number.

8. Tap the Continue button. The third Login Approvals screen appears (see Figure 13.20), prompting you to enter the confirmation code that Facebook has texted to your phone.

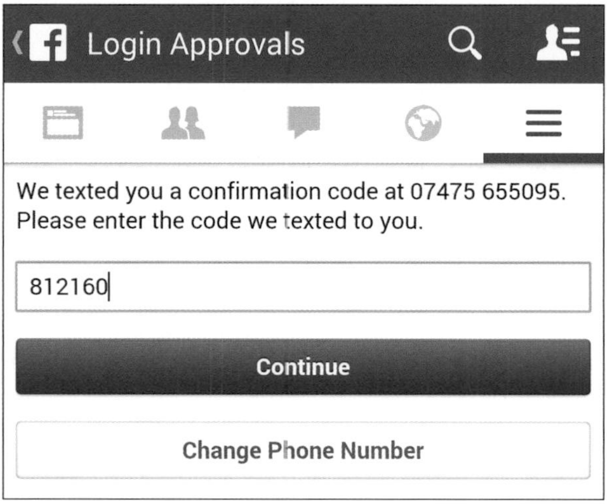

FIGURE 13.20

Enter the confirmation code that Facebook has texted you, and then tap the Continue button.

9. Type in the code.

10. Tap the Continue button. The final Login Approvals screen appears (see Figure 13.21).

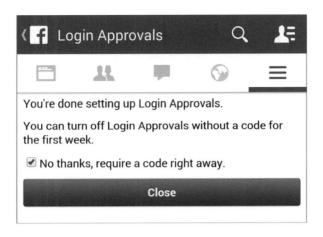

FIGURE 13.21

On the final Login Approvals screen, check the No Thanks, Require a Code Right Away box to tighten your security immediately.

11. Check the No Thanks, Require a Code Right Away box to decline Facebook's offer to let you turn off Login Approvals without a code for the first week.

12. Tap the Close button. The Security Settings screen appears again.

> **NOTE** Facebook now sends you an email notifying you that Login Approvals is now activated.

LOGGING IN WITH A CODE

Now that you've turned on Login Approvals, you'll need to enter a code when you log in from a different device. The Facebook app displays the Login Approval Required dialog box (see Figure 13.22) to let you know.

Tap the OK button, enter the code when you receive it in a text, and then tap the Continue button to log in.

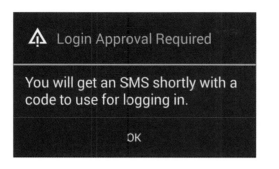

FIGURE 13.22
The Facebook app displays the Login Approval Required dialog box when you try to log in from a different device.

Creating Your Own Login Approval Code

If you need to log in to Facebook using a different device, but your phone isn't able to receive text messages, you can use the Code Generator to generate a code.

Tap the More button to display the More screen, and then tap the Code Generator button in the Help & Settings section. The Code Generator screen appears, showing a numeric code that changes every 30 seconds. Type in the code on the device that requires Login Approval, and then tap the Continue button.

USING MULTIPLE FACEBOOK ACCOUNTS ON THE SAME DEVICE

Android's Settings app includes a feature for setting up a Facebook account on your device. To get started, you open the Settings app, tap the Add Account button in the Accounts section, and then tap the Facebook button on the Add an Account screen. Android then walks you through the process of setting up the account.

This feature enables you to set up only one account on your device. If you go back to the Settings app and try to add another Facebook account, you get the message "Only one Facebook account is supported."

USING MULTIPLE ACCOUNTS BY LOGGING OUT AND LOGGING IN

The simplest way to use multiple Facebook accounts on your device is to log out of the account you've been using and then log in to the account you want to use next.

> **NOTE** The Facebook app is set up to keep you logged in all the time so that you can share your news and views easily and receive updates from your friends and anyone else you have allowed to contact you. So normally you don't need to log out unless you want to unhook yourself from Facebook for a while or you need to change accounts.

Here's how to log out from Facebook:

1. Tap the More button to display the More screen.

2. Tap the Log Out button (at the bottom of the screen). The Log Out dialog box opens (see Figure 13.23).

3. Tap the Log Out button. Facebook logs you out and displays the Log In screen.

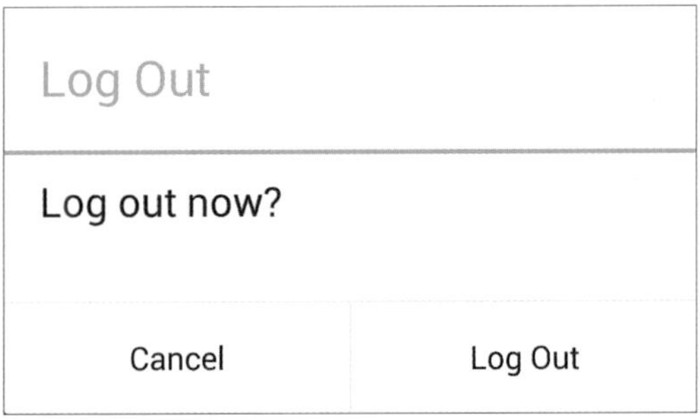

Log Out

Log out now?

Cancel   Log Out

FIGURE 13.23

Tap the Log Out button in the Log Out dialog box to log out of Facebook—for example, when switching from one account to another.

Now that you've logged out of the account you were using, you can log in to the next account you want to use.

> **NOTE** If you've implemented two-factor authentication on the account to which you're logging in, you'll also need to enter a Login Approval code. This is the code from a text that Facebook sends to your phone or a code that you generate using the Code Generator on your phone.

USING MULTIPLE ACCOUNTS BY USING A BROWSER

Another way of using multiple Facebook accounts is to open a browser, go to the Facebook website (www.facebook.com), and log in. You can log in using a different Facebook account than you're using in the Facebook app.

The advantage of this method is that you can be logged in to two or more accounts at once. The disadvantage is that some of the accounts are using the browser interface instead of the Facebook app, which is normally easier to use on a mobile device.

TIP If you need to use multiple Facebook accounts from within the same app, look at Friendcaster from OneLouder Apps. This free app (that offers in-app purchases, as usual) enables you to set up multiple accounts and switch among them. You set up your main account first, making it your primary account. To switch accounts, tap the Settings button (the cog icon), tap Accounts, and then tap the account you want to use.

REMOVING YOUR FACEBOOK ACCOUNT FROM YOUR DEVICE

If you no longer need to use a particular Facebook account on your device, you can remove it.

! CAUTION Removing a Facebook account from your device deletes all its messages and other data from your device. It also deletes all the contact information from Facebook.

First, log out of the Facebook app if it's running. Tap the More button, tap the Log Out button, and then tap Log Out in the Log Out dialog box.

Next, close the Facebook app. Tap the Recent Apps button, and then swipe the Facebook app off the list to the left or right.

Last, remove your Facebook account. Open the Settings app and tap the Facebook button in the Accounts section to display the Sync screen. Tap the Menu button, tap Remove Account, and then tap the Remove Account button in the Remove Account dialog box (see Figure 13.24).

FIGURE 13.24

Tap the Remove Account button in the Remove Account dialog box to remove your Facebook account and all its data from your device.

MAKING THE MOST OF TWITTER

If you enjoy using Twitter, you'll want to fully exploit it on your Android device. Twitter is pretty straightforward compared to Facebook, but you should still spend some time configuring the settings to suit your needs and avoid any unpleasant surprises. You'll probably want to implement the login verification feature to secure your account against unauthorized access.

SIGNING IN TO TWITTER

The first time you run the Twitter app, you sign in to your Twitter account. If you don't have an account, tap the Create My Account button on the Welcome to Twitter screen to create an account using your Gmail address.

On the Sign In screen (for an existing account) or the Success screen (for an account you've just created), you need to pay attention to the check box called Upload My Address Book and Use My Phone Number to Connect Me with Friends and Send Me Text Updates. This box is checked by default, so you'll need to uncheck it if you don't want to upload all your contacts to Twitter.

> **TIP** If you do leave the Upload My Address Book check box checked, go through the list on the Invite Friends screen and uncheck the boxes for any who won't appreciate an invitation to join you on Twitter. Alternatively, tap the Skip button to skip sending invitations altogether.

After you sign in, the Twitter app prompts you to let it use your current location to "customize your experience" (see Figure 13.25)—in other words, to include location-specific information in what it shows you.

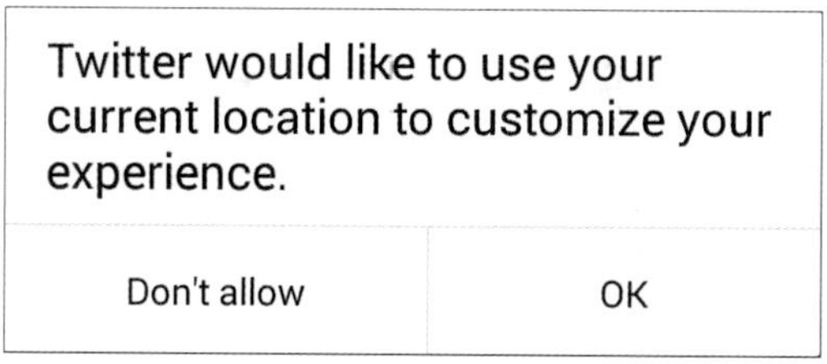

Twitter would like to use your current location to customize your experience.	
Don't allow	OK

FIGURE 13.25

Tap the OK button in this dialog box if you want to allow Twitter to use your location.

> **TIP** You can change Twitter's access to your location information afterward by checking or unchecking the Location box on the General screen in the app's settings.

NAVIGATING THE TWITTER APP

After you've finished setting up the app, you'll see your Home screen (see Figure 13.26).

These are the main screens of the Twitter app:

■ **Home.** The Home screen displays a list of tweets for you to browse. At the top of the screen, the Who to Follow list suggests other people you may want to follow.

> **TIP** The Home screen is at the top level of the Twitter app, so you tap the Back button to go back to it after navigating to another screen.

■ **Notifications.** This screen displays updates when people follow you, retweet your tweets, make you a favorite, or mention you.

■ **Messages.** This screen displays your private messages.

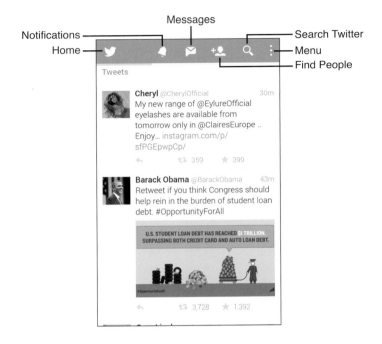

FIGURE 13.26

From the Home screen, you can quickly navigate to other areas of the Twitter app.

> ✎ **NOTE** When the Messages screen is empty, you can tap the Import Contacts button on the screen to upload your contacts to Twitter so that it can help you find friends and suggest users you may want to follow.

- **Find People.** On this screen, you can browse people on the Suggested tab or use the Popular tab to browse by topics (such as Music, Sports, or Entertainment). You can also tap the Search icon to display the Search field, and then search by keywords.
- **Search Twitter.** Use this screen to search Twitter using keywords.

CONFIGURING THE TWITTER APP

Compared to Facebook, Twitter has refreshingly few settings, but there are enough to make a big difference to your Twitter experience.

Tap the Menu button, and then tap Settings to display the Settings screen (see Figure 13.27).

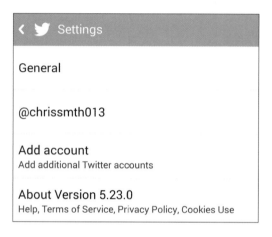

FIGURE 13.27

From the Settings screen, you can choose General settings, choose account-specific settings, and add other accounts.

CHOOSING GENERAL SETTINGS

Start your configuration of the Twitter app by choosing General settings. These settings apply to all your Twitter accounts. Tap the General button on the Settings screen to display the General screen (see Figure 13.28). You can then choose these settings:

- **Sound Effects.** Check this box to enable sound effects.
- **Font Size.** Tap this button to display the Font Size dialog box and then tap the radio button for the font size you want.
- **Image Previews.** Check this box if you want to display image previews. The previews are usually helpful for making tweets more comprehensible, but you may want to turn them off if you have a slow Internet connection.
- **Location.** Check this box to allow the Twitter app to use your location to customize the information it displays to you.

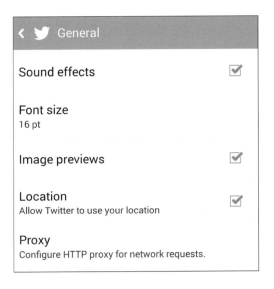

FIGURE 13.28

The General screen includes the font size, image previews, and proxy settings.

- **Proxy.** Tap this button to display the Proxy screen (see Figure 13.29). You can then check the Enable HTTP Proxy box to turn on proxying, tap the Proxy Host button and specify the hostname or IP address of the proxy server, and tap the Proxy Port button and enter the port number for the proxy server in the Proxy Port dialog box.

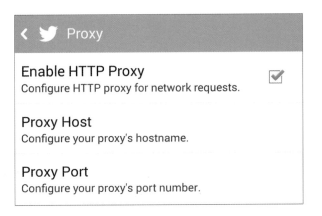

FIGURE 13.29

Use the Proxy screen to turn on proxying for Twitter and to specify the details of the proxy server.

> **NOTE** A *proxy server* fulfills and redirects Internet requests. You may need to configure a proxy if your employer or organization blocks Twitter.

When you finish choosing settings on the General screen, tap the Back button to return to the Settings screen.

CHOOSING SETTINGS FOR AN ACCOUNT

Now tap your first Twitter account on the Settings screen to display its settings screen (see Figure 13.30).

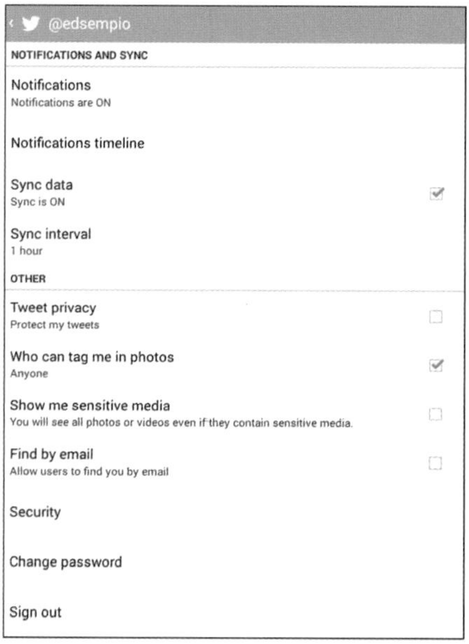

FIGURE 13.30

On the settings screen for an account, you can configure your notifications, privacy, and security.

These are the settings you can configure in the Notifications and Sync section:

■ **Notifications.** Tap this button to display the Notifications screen (see Figure 13.31). You can then check the Vibrate box, the Ringtone button, and the Notification Light box to specify what feedback you receive for a notification. In the Notification Types section, choose which notification types to receive.

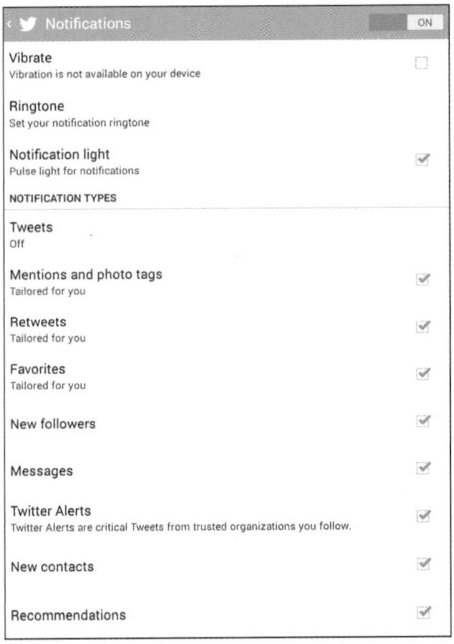

FIGURE 13.31

On the Notifications screen for an account, you can choose which types of notification to receive and which items to receive them for.

> **NOTE** For the Mentions and Photo Tags type, the Retweets type, and the Favorites type, you can not only check or uncheck the box but also tap the button to display a dialog box that gives you a choice of three radio buttons: Tailored for You, From Anyone, or Off.

■ **Notifications Timeline.** Tap this button to display the Notifications Timeline screen (see Figure 13.32). You can then check the box for any timeline filter you want to apply to notifications.

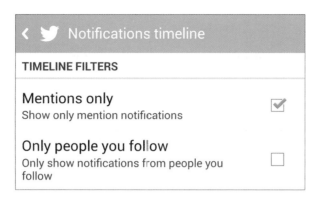

FIGURE 13.32

On the Notifications Timeline screen, check the box for each timeline filter you want to apply.

- **Sync Data.** Check this box to sync your Twitter data.
- **Sync Interval.** If you check the Sync Data box, tap this button to display the Sync Interval dialog box, and then tap the sync interval to use, such as 15 Minutes.
- **Tweet Privacy.** Check this box to protect your tweets, enabling you to control who is able to view them.
- **Who Can Tag Me in Photos.** Tap this button to display the Who Can Tag Me in Photos dialog box, and then tap the Anyone radio button, the Only People I Follow radio button, or the Off radio button, as needed.
- **Show Me Sensitive Media.** Check this box if you want to see photos or videos deemed sensitive (in other words, offensive to some people).
- **Find by Email.** Check this box to enable people to find your Twitter name via your email address.
- **Find by Phone Number.** Check this box to enable people to find your Twitter name via your phone number.
- **Security.** Tap this button to implement login verification. You'll learn how to do this a little later in this chapter.
- **Change Password.** If you need to change your password, tap this button and work on the Change Password screen. As usual, you need to provide your current password to prove that you know it.
- **Sign Out.** If you want to sign out of Twitter, tap this button and then tap the OK button in the Sign Out dialog box that opens.

! CAUTION Signing out of Twitter removes all your Twitter data from your Android device. So normally you won't want to sign out. Instead, just leave the Twitter app running so that you can access it quickly as needed, or close the app if you don't want to use it for a while.

ADDING OTHER TWITTER ACCOUNTS

The Twitter app enables you to add multiple accounts to your device and use them alongside each other. To add an account, tap the Add Account button on the Settings screen, enter the details on the Sign In screen that appears, and then tap the Sign In button.

! CAUTION On the Sign In screen on a phone, make sure you check or uncheck the box called Upload My Address Book and Use My Phone Number to Connect Me with Friends and Send Me Text Updates. This box is checked by default, so you'll need to uncheck it if you don't want to upload all your contacts to Twitter. If you do upload all your contacts, work through the list on the Invite Friends screen and uncheck the box for any contact who will not welcome an invitation to connect with you on Twitter.

SECURING YOUR TWITTER ACCOUNT WITH LOGIN VERIFICATION

To protect your Twitter account against being hacked, you should set up login verification on it. Here's how to do that:

1. Tap the Menu button, and then tap Settings to display the Settings screen.
2. Tap the account you want to configure. The settings screen for the account appears.
3. Tap the Security button to display the Security screen (see Figure 13.33).
4. Check the Login Verification box. The Login Verification dialog box opens (see Figure 13.34), making sure that you know that you will need this device to sign in to Twitter.

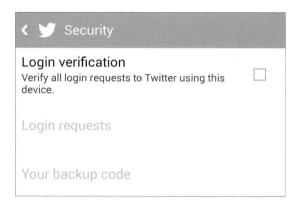

FIGURE 13.33

On the Security screen, check the Login Verification box to start setting up login verification.

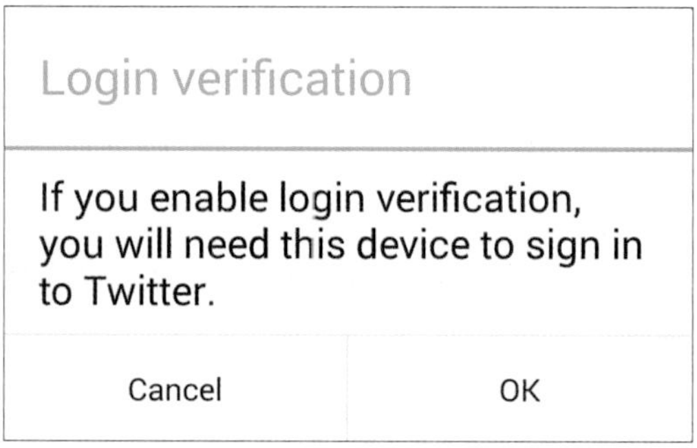

Login verification

If you enable login verification, you will need this device to sign in to Twitter.

Cancel   OK

FIGURE 13.34

Tap the OK button in the Login Verification dialog box.

5. Tap the OK button. The Your Backup Code dialog box opens (see Figure 13.35), offering to take a screenshot of your backup code and store it in your Android Gallery app.

> **❗CAUTION** Taking a screenshot is a good way to store your backup code—but only as long as nobody else can view the photos in the Gallery app. If you take the screenshot, be sure to use a secure means of locking your device. It is also a good idea to encrypt your device.

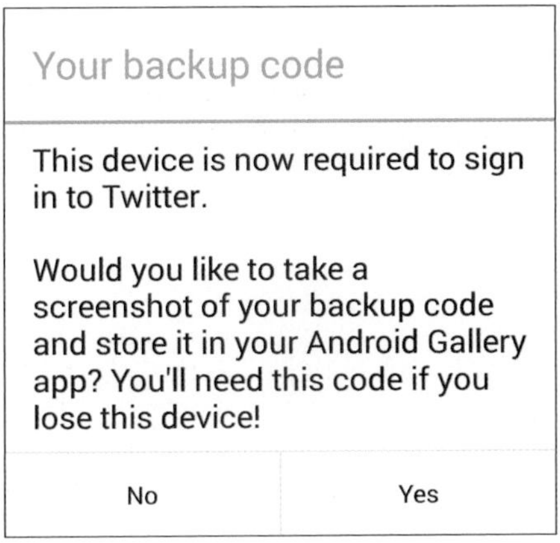

Your backup code

This device is now required to sign in to Twitter.

Would you like to take a screenshot of your backup code and store it in your Android Gallery app? You'll need this code if you lose this device!

No	Yes

FIGURE 13.35

Tap the Yes button in the Your Backup Code dialog box if you want to take a screenshot of your backup code.

6. Tap the Yes button or the No button, as appropriate. The Your Backup Code screen appears (see Figure 13.36).

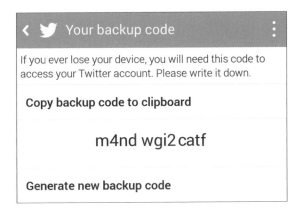

FIGURE 13.36

Memorize or write down the code that appears on the Your Backup Code screen. You can also tap the Copy Backup Code to Clipboard button to copy the code and paste it elsewhere.

7. Memorize the code or write it down.

8. Tap the Back button three times to leave the Settings screens and return to the Twitter screen you were using.

TIP On the Security screen, you can tap the Login Requests button to review the login requests that have been made for your Twitter account.

NOTE Now that you have applied login verification to your account, any login attempt displays the Verify Login screen prompting you for the login code. Type in the code that Twitter has just texted to you, and then tap the Send button. Once the login request is approved, you can start using the Twitter app.

USING MULTIPLE TWITTER ACCOUNTS

When you've set up multiple accounts in the Twitter app, you can easily switch from account to account by tapping the current account name on the Tweet screen. In the Accounts dialog box that opens (see Figure 13.37), tap the account to which you want to switch.

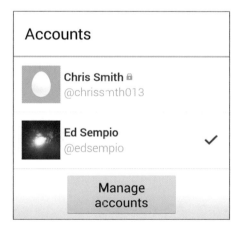

FIGURE 13.37

To switch the account you're using, tap the current account name to display the Accounts dialog box, and then tap the account you want to use.

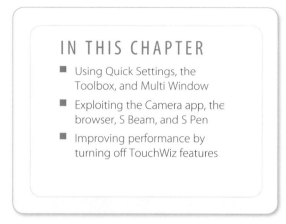

14

USING SAMSUNG TOUCHWIZ

Most Samsung Android devices come with Samsung's TouchWiz skin. TouchWiz is a heavy skin that makes a huge difference to the way that devices look and work, all the way from the Home screen and the Quick Settings panel to the Internet browser app and the Camera app.

In this chapter, you'll take a whirlwind tour of the main features of TouchWiz, concentrating on what you need to know to use your device effectively.

> **! CAUTION** Samsung has a vast number of different devices, ranging from miniature phones to colossal tablets, and these devices run many different versions of TouchWiz. This chapter covers Android 4.4 (KitKat) running on typical Samsung hardware, but your device may well have some differences. If so, explore the commands available to see if Samsung has put the features described here in a different place.

GETTING UP TO SPEED WITH TOUCHWIZ ESSENTIALS

In this section, you get up to speed on the essentials of the TouchWiz interface, including its custom buttons, how you navigate the Home screen and the Apps screen, and the gestures you can use to control your device.

Should You Create a Samsung Account?

Samsung's software heavily encourages you to create a Samsung account both while setting up your Android device and afterward. A Samsung account is free, and you can set up one in moments, but it's worth evaluating whether you need an account rather than simply going ahead.

The main point of a Samsung account is to enable you to store certain data online and sync it among your devices. Inevitably, storing that data in a Samsung account gives Samsung information about you and the ways in which you use your Android device.

Some of Samsung's apps, such as the S Health app and the S Translator app, require you to have a Samsung account in order to use the app at all. Other apps don't require a Samsung account to use the app but do require an account for some features. For example, the Internet app enables you to sync your browsing across your computers and devices by using your Samsung account. If you don't need to use apps such as S Health, and if you don't need to sync data in apps such as the Internet app, you may not need to get a Samsung account.

USING THE BUTTONS IN TOUCHWIZ

Instead of the default Android set of three soft buttons (the Back button, the Home button, and the Recent Apps button, looking from left to right), Samsung devices have a physical Home button located below the screen. On current devices, the Recent Apps soft button appears to the left of the Home button, and the Back soft button appears to the right.

NOTE Samsung devices designed for Android Jelly Bean (4.1 and 4.2) and older versions have a Menu soft button to the left of the physical Home button and the Back soft button to the right of the Home button.

The Home button works as usual—but with one added feature:

- **Press.** Displays the Home screen panel you were using last. Press again to display your main Home screen panel.
- **Press and hold.** Opens Google Now.

> NOTE Samsung devices that don't have a Recent Apps button require you to press and hold the Home button to display the Recent Apps screen, not to open Google Now.

- **Double-press.** Opens S Voice, Samsung's voice-driven assistant.

NAVIGATING THE HOME SCREEN

In TouchWiz, the Home screen (see Figure 14.1) consists of a horizontal series of panels among which you navigate by swiping left or right. Some versions of TouchWiz include My Magazine as the leftmost Home screen panel by default.

FIGURE 14.1

The TouchWiz Home screen is a series of panels among which you can move by swiping left or right.

> **NOTE** My Magazine is a feature that provides a personalized set of current information based on the interests you exhibit. To customize My Magazine, open it, tap the Menu button, tap Settings, and then check the boxes for the topics you want to see. If you don't find My Magazine useful, you can turn it off, as you'll see in a moment.

> **TIP** In some versions of TouchWiz, the Home screen panels work as a carousel. That is, you can swipe left or right to switch among the panels as usual, but when you reach the last panel or the first, you can swipe again to wrap around to the first panel or the last.

CUSTOMIZING YOUR HOME SCREEN

To start customizing your Home screen, pinch inward with two fingers on it. TouchWiz opens the Home screen for customization (see Figure 14.2). You can then make these changes:

FIGURE 14.2

Pinch inward with two fingers to open the Home screen for customization.

- **Rearrange the Home screen panels.** Tap the thumbnail for a panel and then drag it to where you want it.

> **NOTE** On some versions of TouchWiz, opening the Home screen for customization displays the thumbnails of all the Home screens on the screen at once, but not the Wallpapers, Widgets, and Home Screen Settings buttons. On these versions of TouchWiz, you can rearrange the Home screen panels using the same techniques as described here. To change the wallpaper, or to add apps, widgets, and folders, tap and hold open space on the Home screen, and then tap the appropriate button in the Home Screen dialog box that opens.

- **Remove a Home screen panel.** Tap the thumbnail for the panel and then drag it up to the Remove icon. When the Remove icon turns red, release the thumbnail.
- **Add a Home screen panel.** Scroll the thumbnails all the way to the left, and then tap the + button on the last panel.

> **NOTE** You can have up to seven Home screen panels on TouchWiz.

- **Change the wallpaper.** Tap the Wallpapers button to display the Set Wallpaper dialog box. Tap the Home Screen button, the Lock Screen button, or the Home and Lock Screens button, as appropriate. On the screen that appears, select the wallpaper, and then tap the Set Wallpaper button.
- **Add a widget.** Tap the Widgets button to display the Widgets screen. Navigate to the widget, tap and hold its icon until the Home screen panel thumbnails appear, and then drag the icon to the panel and position where you want it to appear.
- **Choose Home screen settings.** Tap the Settings button to display the Home Screen Settings screen. Here you can tap the Transitions Effects button to select a transition effect or uncheck the My Magazine box to remove the My Magazine feature from the Home screen.

When you finish customizing the Home screen, tap the Back button to hide the customization options again.

USING GESTURES TO CONTROL YOUR SAMSUNG DEVICE

Samsung has built a large number of gestures into TouchWiz to give you options for interacting with your device. The gestures are well worth knowing about even if you choose not to use them. Some gestures work for both phones and tablets, but others are specific to phones.

The following list explains the gestures:

- **Air Browse or Air Gesture.** Wave your hand above the phone's front sensor to give a command. For example, wave your hand over the sensor from right to left to perform the air equivalent of a left swipe on the screen. This feature's name varies depending on the version of TouchWiz.

> **NOTE** The selection of gestures available depends on the device you have and the version of TouchWiz it's running, so you may need to spend a few minutes roaming through the Settings app to learn about all the gestures you can use.

> **TIP** To enable or disable the gestures, work on the Motions and Gestures screen or the Motions screen in the Settings app (depending on the version of TouchWiz).

- **Air View.** Hover your finger over an item onscreen to display a preview of information about it. For example, hold your finger over an event in the S Planner calendaring app to display details of the event.
- **Direct Call.** Pick up the phone to call the contact you have currently displayed in the Phone app or the Contacts app.
- **Smart Alert.** Pick up the device to view the calls and messages you have missed.
- **Zoom.** When browsing photos in the Gallery app, tilt the device away from you to zoom out on the current photo, or tilt it toward you to zoom in. When you get the hang of it, this gesture is more useful than it sounds.
- **Browse an Image.** When you've zoomed in on a photo, you can display different parts of it by turning the device this way and that.
- **Mute/Pause.** You can mute the current music or an incoming phone call by turning the device over and laying it facedown. In theory, you can also pause

music by putting your palm—or a convenient flat object—over the device's screen, but this gesture seldom works in my experience.

■ **Palm Swipe to Capture or Capture Screen.** This feature also appears as the Palm Motion check box on the Motion Control screen in some versions of TouchWiz. Swipe across the screen from right to left or from left to right using the side of your hand to capture what is onscreen. (The side of your hand is the fleshy part below the palm, between your little finger and your wrist.) This gesture may feel awkward at first, but it usually works.

> **TIP** If your device is running too slowly, you may need to turn off some gestures and other features. See the section "Improving Performance by Turning Off TouchWiz Features," later in this chapter, for details.

CUSTOMIZING THE APPS SCREEN

To launch an app that's not on your Home screen, you touch the Apps button to display the Apps screen as usual, and then touch the app's icon.

> **TIP** In TouchWiz, the Apps screen panels are on a carousel, so after you swipe to the last panel (or the first), you can swipe again to wrap around to the first panel (or the last).

If you have many apps, you may want to customize the Apps screen so that you can find those you want more easily. Here's what you can do:

■ **Create a folder.** Tap the Menu button and then tap Create Folder. In the Create Folder dialog box that opens, type the name for the folder and tap the + button to display a screen of apps with a check box on each. Check the box for each app you want to add to the folder, and then tap the Done button.

■ **Change the view.** Tap the Menu button and then tap View As or View Type, depending on the version of TouchWiz. In the View As dialog box or the View Type dialog box, tap the radio button for the view you want. Depending on the version of TouchWiz, your choices may be among Customizable Grid, Alphabetical Grid, and Alphabetical List; or between

Custom and Alphabetical Order (see Figure 14.3). If you choose Customizable Grid or Custom, tap the Menu button again, tap Edit, and then drag the icons into the order you want. Tap the Back button when you finish.

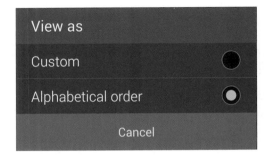

FIGURE 14.3

You can switch the Apps screen between alphabetical order and a custom order.

■ **Uninstall or disable apps.** You can uninstall any app you've installed. You cannot uninstall any of the built-in apps, but you can disable them instead. Tap the Menu button and then tap Uninstall/Disable Apps. A black circle containing a red – sign appears on the upper-right corner of each app. Tap this circle to display the Uninstall Application dialog box (for an app you've installed) or the Disable Application dialog box (for a built-in app). You can then tap the Uninstall button or the Disable button, depending on the dialog box. Tap the Back button when you finish.

> **✓ TIP**   To get back the apps you've disabled, tap the Menu button, and then tap Show Disabled Apps. To get back the apps you've hidden, tap Show Hidden Apps. On the resulting screen, check the box for each app you want to enable or unhide, and then tap the Done button.

■ **Hide apps you don't want to see.** Tap the Menu button and then tap Hide Apps. Check the box for each app you want to hide, and then tap the Done button.

> **✎ NOTE**   Only some versions of TouchWiz enable you to hide apps. If your version doesn't, create a folder instead and park the unwanted apps in it.

WORKING WITH QUICK SETTINGS AND SETTINGS

TouchWiz customizes the Quick Settings panel and the Settings app heavily, so if you're used to stock Android, you're in for some changes—and some welcome improvements.

USING THE NOTIFICATIONS PANEL AND THE QUICK SETTINGS BAR

When you want to see your notifications, pull down from the top of the screen with one finger. The Notifications panel opens (see Figure 14.4), showing the list of notifications, which you can navigate as usual:

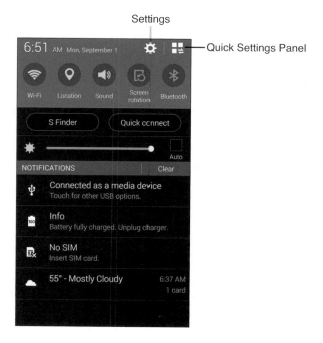

FIGURE 14.4

In TouchWiz, the Quick Settings bar appears at the top of the Notifications panel, giving you access to essential settings.

- **Open the app that raised the notification.** Tap the notification.
- **Expand the notification.** If the notification contains extra information, tap it and draw your finger down to expand it. For example, you can expand a Gmail notification about multiple messages to display details of the messages.

- **Remove a notification.** Swipe left or right to remove the notification from the list.
- **Clear all notifications.** Tap the Clear button.
- **Open the Settings app.** Tap the Settings button.
- **Display the Quick Settings panel.** Tap the Quick Settings panel button.

TouchWiz adds a Quick Settings bar across the top of the Notifications panel to give you even faster access to the settings you use most. Here's how to use the Quick Settings bar:

- **Turn a feature on or off.** Tap the button for the feature. If the button doesn't appear on the first section of the Quick Settings bar, scroll left as needed.
- **Display a feature's screen in the Settings app.** Tap and hold the button for the feature until the related screen appears.
- **Customize the Quick Settings bar.** Open the Quick Settings panel (discussed next) and tap the Edit button to display the Notification Panel screen (see Figure 14.5). You can then check or uncheck the Brightness Adjustment box to control whether the Brightness slider appears, tap the Recommended Apps and use the Recommended Apps screen to control

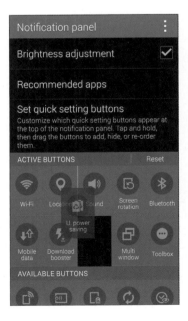

FIGURE 14.5

On the Notification Panel screen, choose Brightness Adjustment and Recommended Apps settings, and then drag the Quick Settings buttons into your preferred order.

whether the recommended apps list appears (and which apps it contains), and use the Active Buttons area to set up the list of buttons you want to have in the Quick Settings bar and the order in which they appear. You can add a button to the Quick Settings bar by dragging it from the Available Buttons list to the Active Buttons list. Similarly, drag a button from the Active Buttons list to the Available Buttons list to remove that button from the Quick Settings bar.

USING THE QUICK SETTINGS PANEL

When you want access to the full range of Quick Settings, open the Quick Settings panel (see Figure 14.6). You can open it either by dragging down from the screen with two fingers or by opening the Notifications panel and then tapping the Quick Settings icon.

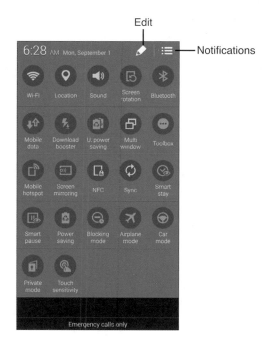

FIGURE 14.6

From the Quick Settings panel, you can turn a feature on or off by tapping its button, or display the related screen in Settings by tapping and holding the button.

Tap a button in the Quick Settings panel to turn the feature on (so that its icon appears in green) or off (the icon appears in gray).

Tap and hold a button in the Quick Settings panel to display the screen on which the feature appears in the Settings app.

NAVIGATING THE SETTINGS APP

The Settings screen in stock Android is arguably a bit plain, with its straightforward list of settings and its monochrome icons. Perhaps to compensate, TouchWiz goes over the top with a heavily customized Settings screen that features colorful icons—and, in some versions, multiple ways to view them.

CHOOSING BETWEEN GRID VIEW AND LIST VIEW

In some versions of TouchWiz, you can choose whether to display the Settings screen in Grid view (shown on the left in Figure 14.7), List view (shown on the right in Figure 14.7), or Tab view (shown in Figure 14.8):

- **Grid view.** This view displays large icons laid out in a grid pattern, separated by type into sections such as Quick Settings, Network Connections, Connect and Share, and Sound and Display. You can collapse and expand sections by tapping their headings.

- **List view.** This view shows a long list of settings broken up into sections by headings, starting with the Quick Settings section. You can't collapse the sections, so you may need to scroll way down. Alternatively, tap the Search icon and search for the setting you need.

- **Tab view.** This view divides the settings onto different tabs, which you navigate by tapping the appropriate tab button at the top of the screen. The tabs depend on the version of TouchWiz, but may include Quick Settings, Connections, and Device.

TIP   You can customize the Quick Settings section of the Settings screen to put the icons you find most useful at the top of the screen (or on the first tab in Tab view). Open the Settings app, tap the Menu button, and tap Edit Quick Settings. You can then check the box for each item you want (up to a maximum of 12 items) and tap the Save button to save the changes.

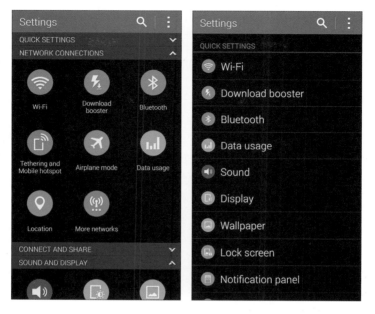

FIGURE 14.7
Some versions of TouchWiz offer Grid view (left) and List view (right) for the Settings screen as well as Tab view.

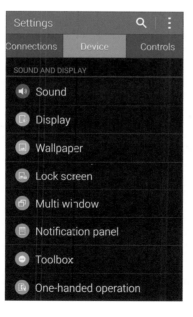

FIGURE 14.8
Other versions of TouchWiz offer only Tab view.

FINDING THE SETTINGS YOU NEED

The Settings app in TouchWiz contains so many settings that it can be hard to find those you need. When you need a major feature, the quickest way to access it is often to open the Quick Settings panel and then tap and hold the relevant icon.

Alternatively, open the Settings app (using whichever technique you prefer) and tap the Search button at the top. Start typing a keyword, and you'll get a screen full of matches (see Figure 14.9). You can then tap the right setting to display the screen that contains it.

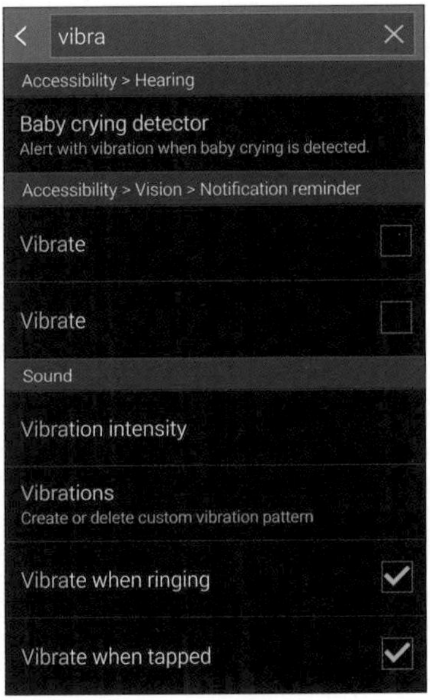

FIGURE 14.9

Use the Search feature in Settings to locate the settings you need by keyword.

USING THE TOOLBOX

Some versions of TouchWiz include a feature called the Toolbox that enables you to put up to five of your most-needed apps just a couple of taps away from use. Here's how to use the Toolbox:

■ **Turn on the Toolbox.** Either open the Notifications panel and tap the Toolbox icon on the Quick Settings bar, or open the Quick Settings panel and tap the Toolbox icon. The Toolbox appears as a gray circle containing three horizontal dots; after a few seconds of inactivity, it fades to become less conspicuous.

> ☑ **TIP**   You can reposition the Toolbox as needed. Just tap the gray circle and drag it to where you want it onscreen.

■ **Open the Toolbox and launch an app.** Tap the gray circle to open the Toolbox (see Figure 14.10), and then tap the app you want to launch.

FIGURE 14.10

To launch an app from the Toolbox, tap the gray circle and then tap the app's icon.

■ **Edit the Toolbox.** Tap and hold the Toolbox icon, and then drag it to the Edit icon that appears at the top of the screen. On the settings screen for the Toolbox that appears, check the box for each app you want to include (up to five apps) and then tap the Save button.

■ **Remove the Toolbox.** Tap and hold the Toolbox icon, and then drag it to the Remove icon that appears at the top of the screen. Alternatively, either open the Notifications panel and tap the Toolbox icon in the Quick Settings bar, or open the Quick Settings panel and tap the Toolbox icon there.

USING MULTI WINDOW

TouchWiz includes a Multi Window feature that enables you to split the screen between two apps. They can be two different apps or two instances of the same app. Only some apps work in Multi Window—those that appear in the Multi Window panel.

Multi Window is great for tablets, where you have enough screen space to use the apps productively alongside each other, but some phones also offer Multi Window. You can turn Multi Window off if you don't need it.

Here's how to use Multi Window:

■ **Display the Multi Window panel.** Tap and hold the Back button until the panel appears on the left side of the screen (see Figure 14.11).

> **NOTE** If you don't use the Multi Window panel for a few seconds, the panel disappears, leaving only a > button on the left of the screen. You can tap this button to open the Multi Window panel. Tap the corresponding < button to close the Multi Window panel.

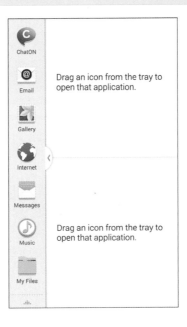

FIGURE 14.11

Tap and hold the Back button to display the Multi Window panel, and then tap the first app you want to launch.

- **Open the apps.** Tap the first app (scroll down as needed) and then drag it into the pane in which you want it. Tap the second app and drag into the other pane.

> **TIP** If you frequently use the same apps together, create a pair of apps so you can open them more easily. Open the apps and arrange them in the panes the way you want. Tap the > button to open the Multi Window panel, and then tap the up-arrow button at the bottom. On the menu section that appears, tap the Create button. In the Create Window Group dialog box, edit the suggested name for the pair—the app names—and then tap the OK button. The pair of apps then appears at the top of the list in the Multi Window panel.

- **Work in the apps.** With the apps open (see Figure 14.12), you can work in the apps much as usual—except that you have only half the amount of space for each. A white line appears around the active app. Tap the other app when you need to make it active.

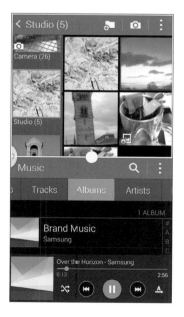

FIGURE 14.12

After opening the apps in Multi Window, you can work in them as usual.

- **Resize the window panes.** Tap the white dot or blue dot on the line between the panes and drag it up or down, or left or right, as needed.
- **Switch the window panes.** Tap the white dot or blue dot to display the control buttons (see Figure 14.13), and then tap the Switch Windows button, the icon with the two arrows.

FIGURE 14.13

The Multi Window menu enables you to switch the window panes, copy text or an image from one window to another, or close a pane.

TIP Some versions of Multi Window include other control buttons, such as a Full Screen button for expanding the current pane to take up all the screen.

- **Copy text or an image from one window to another.** Tap the pane that contains the content, so that a white outline or blue outline appears around it. Tap the white dot or blue dot to display the control buttons, and then tap the Copy button, the icon with a dotted rectangle and a plus sign. Tap the paragraph or the image and drag it to the other window until it snaps into place.

- **Close a window pane.** Tap the pane you want to close, so that a white outline or blue outline appears around it. Tap the white dot or blue dot to display the control buttons, and then tap the Close button (the X button).

- **Hide the Multi Window panel.** When you finish using the Multi Window panel, tap and hold the Back button until the panel disappears.

UNDERSTANDING THE SAMSUNG HUB, S APPS, AND SAMSUNG APPS

Samsung provides a wide range of apps for its Android devices. Some of the apps come preinstalled, whereas others are available for free download. As usual, the specifics depend on the device you're using and the version of TouchWiz it's running. This section summarizes the apps briefly so that you're clear what's what.

- **Samsung Hub.** Most Samsung devices come with the Samsung Hub app, which is designed as a one-stop shop for audio, video, and other media files. On older versions of TouchWiz, you'll see separate apps: Music Hub, Video Hub, and so on. These apps require a Samsung account.

- **GALAXY Apps.** Formerly Samsung Apps, this app gives you access to Samsung's App Store for its mobile devices. You can browse using the Best Picks tab, the For GALAXY tab, or the Top tab, which offers "top" categories such as New, Most Downloaded, or Price: Low to High. Many of the apps are free, but others you must pay for.

> **！CAUTION** If the Samsung Apps app displays the Updates screen, you may need to tap the Update button to update it before you can use it. (Tapping the Update Later button often opens a Notice dialog box telling you that Samsung Apps will close if you don't update it now.) Updating Samsung Apps is a good move, but make sure your device is connected to a Wi-Fi network rather than using a cellular connection.
>
> On the Updates screen, don't check the box called I Want to Keep Samsung Apps Up to Date at All Times. This May Result in Additional Charges unless you have an unlimited data plan or a Wi-Fi–only device. Instead, use the Update button to update Samsung Apps manually as needed.

- **S Voice.** S Voice is a voice-driven assistant that you can ask for information in the same way that you can ask Google Now.

- **S Note.** S Note is a note-taking app designed for the Galaxy Note series. It includes handwriting and drawing features for the S Pen stylus.
- **Memo.** Memo is a straightforward note-taking app for devices that don't have the S Pen. You can enter text using the keyboard, and you can insert existing pictures or new photos you take.
- **S Planner.** S Planner is a calendar app that can sync data with various calendar accounts including Google Calendar and the calendar feature of Exchange Server.
- **S Health.** S Health is a health-management app that you can use to track your fitness goals and weight, calculate your nutritional needs and how you attempt to fulfill them, and measure activity using a pedometer and other features. If your device has a heart-rate sensor, you can use it to measure your heart rate. Note that you must remain "still and quiet," and the results are "not for medical or clinical use," which arguably reduces their worth.

> **TIP**   Two things here. First, S Health requires a Samsung account (as does S Translator, discussed next). Second, when creating your profile in S Health, check the Hide My Profile Information from Other S Health Users box on the Create Profile screen unless you are certain that you want to share your information.

- **S Translator.** S Translator is a translation app that enables you to translate words and phrases quickly between various languages including English, French, German, Spanish, Russian, and Korean. You can either type a phrase or speak it.

USING THE CAMERA APP'S EXTRA FEATURES

Samsung devices include a heavily customized Camera app. This section tells you what you need to know to get the most out of this app.

> **TIP**   Because of the complexity of the Camera app, it's a good idea to spend some time working through the settings and modes to find out which are useful to you and which you can safely ignore.

MASTERING THE ESSENTIALS OF THE CAMERA APP

After launching the Camera app by tapping its icon on the Home screen or the Apps screen, you can take photos quickly. Here are the essentials of the Camera app (see Figure 14.14):

- **Zoom in or out.** Place your finger and thumb on the screen and pinch apart to zoom in or pinch together to zoom in.

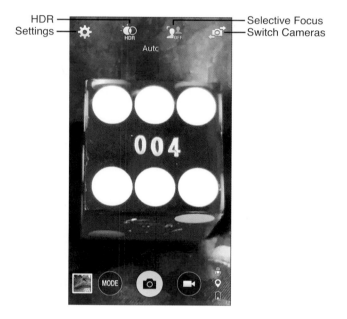

FIGURE 14.14

From the main Camera screen, you can access the Settings screen, turn on HDR or Selective Focus, or simply take a photo or a video.

> **TIP** You can open the Camera app from the lock screen by tapping the Camera icon in the lower-right corner and swiping upward. If the Camera icon doesn't appear on the lock screen, open the Settings app, tap the Lock screen button, and then check the Camera Shortcut box.

- **Focus.** Tap the point on the screen where you want to focus.
- **Take HDR photos.** Tap the HDR icon at the top of the screen so that the HDR (High Dynamic Range) readout appears instead of the Off readout.
- **Take Selective Focus photos.** Tap the Selective Focus icon at the top of the screen and follow the prompts.

> **NOTE** The Selective Focus feature enables you to adjust the focus on the photo after you take it. Selective Focus requires the subject of the photo to be positioned in the foreground with an appreciable distance between it and the background. Only some devices have Selective Focus.

- **Switch to the front camera.** Tap the Switch Cameras button to switch from the rear camera to the front camera; tap again to switch back.

MAKING THE MOST OF THE CAMERA MODES

The Samsung Camera app includes a large number of different modes to help you take various kinds of shots. Different versions of the Camera app have different modes, but your device likely offers some (maybe most) of the following modes—and maybe a bunch more modes:

- **Auto.** Use this mode for general shooting—in other words, when you don't have a good reason to use any of the other modes.
- **Beauty Face.** Use this mode for taking portraits of individual people you want to make look good at the expense of reality. Beauty Face detects the face in the shot and attempts to improve it by enlarging the eyes and removing blemishes. Results vary.
- **Shot & More.** This mode has a group of submodes based on taking a series of shots in rapid succession and then using some or all of them. The submodes are Best Photo, Best Face, Drama Shot, Eraser, and Panning Shot. When you tap the Shutter button in Shot & More mode, the Camera app takes a burst of photos. It then displays the list of submodes so that you can select which to use out of those that are available. Depending on what you have photographed, only some of the submodes are available. For example, the Best Photo submode enables you to select which photos to keep from the burst; and the Best Face submode enables you to select the best version of each person's face in a group shot and merge them into a single photo.

> NOTE In some versions of TouchWiz, the Camera app lists the Shot & More modes separately as Best Photo, Best Face, and Drama Shot.

- **Panorama.** Turn on this mode when you want to take a panorama photo such as a landscape. The Camera app displays arrows to guide your movements of the camera.
- **Virtual Tour.** This mode enables you to create an interactive visual tour of a room or a building. The Camera app displays arrows and prompts to guide you where to point the lens, and takes photos automatically when it is pointing the right way.
- **Dual Camera.** This mode enables you to position a photo or video of yourself (taken on the front camera) on the picture or video you're taking with the rear camera.

> TIP Tap the Manage Modes button on the Modes panel to display the Manage Modes screen, on which you can uncheck the box for any mode you want to remove from the Modes panel. Tap the Done button when you finish. Tap the Download button on the Modes panel to download other modes for free from the GALAXY Apps service.

SETTING THE CAMERA TO TAKE THE PHOTOS AND VIDEOS YOU WANT

The Camera app's modes are great for quickly taking substantially different types of photos, but you'll also want to dig into the settings that the Camera app offers in order to get exactly the photos you want.

Different versions of the Camera app not only have different settings but also lay them out in different ways. Typically, you tap the Settings button (the gear icon) to open the Settings panel. Figure 14.15 shows the top part of the Settings panel on a Galaxy S 5; you scroll down to display further settings.

FIGURE 14.15

The Camera app on Samsung devices offers many customizable settings.

These are the settings that your device may offer:

- **Picture Size.** Normally, you'll want to shoot at the highest resolution available unless you need a different aspect ratio, such as 4:3 instead of 16:9.

- **Burst Shots.** Tap this button to toggle burst shooting on or off. Burst shooting is great for action, children, and pets, but turn it off if you find you trigger it unintentionally.

- **Picture Stabilization.** Tap this button to toggle stabilization on or off. Stabilization can be a big help for getting good photos in low light conditions if you don't use a tripod or other means of holding the camera steady. Turning on picture stabilization may disable other features, such as ISO adjustment.

> **TIP** If you find that your device's Camera app takes too long to snap a photo, turn off the Picture Stabilization feature. This feature may be on by default, and it adds a delay before the Camera app can take a photo.

- **Face Detection.** Tap this button to toggle face detection on or off.
- **ISO.** Tap this button to adjust the light sensitivity of the cameras' sensors. It's best to use the Auto setting unless you need to make the camera more sensitive—for example, to shoot moving subjects in low light.

> **! CAUTION** The higher the ISO value you use, the more likely it is that you'll get "noise"—incorrectly colored dots or areas—in your photos.

- **Metering Modes.** Tap this button to switch among the light-metering modes. Your choices are typically Center-Weighted (the default), Matrix, and Spot.

> **TIP** Use Center-Weighted light metering when your subject is in the middle of the photo. Use Matrix light metering when you need to balance the light across the photo as a whole. Use Spot light metering when you will tap the point in the photo where you want to measure the light.

- **Tap to Take Pics.** Tap this button to toggle on or off the feature that enables you to take photos by tapping the screen. This feature is useful when you're shooting in conditions too bright to see the controls onscreen easily, but it's less useful when you're trying to adjust the focus and exposure for a shot— each tap on the screen takes a photo.
- **Selective Focus.** Tap this button to turn on the Selective Focus feature. Normally, it's easier to tap the Selective Focus button at the top of the screen.
- **Video Size.** Tap this button to display the Video Size dialog box, and then tap the video size you want.

> **! CAUTION** Use the UHD (3840×2160-pixel) video size only when you need the highest resolution, because the footage takes up a huge amount of storage space. UHD resolution is four times higher than Full HD (1920×1080-pixel) resolution.

- **Recording Mode.** Tap this button to display the Recording Mode dialog box, which enables you to choose among available recording modes. The modes depend on the camera; you should always have a Normal mode (the default); you'll usually have a Limit for MMS mode for taking short, small videos suitable for sending in MMS messages; and you may also have a Slow Motion mode, a Fast Motion mode, and a Smooth Motion mode.
- **Video Stabilization.** Tap this button to toggle video stabilization on or off. It's a good idea to use video stabilization if you're not using a tripod or other support to keep your device steady.

> **NOTE** Video stabilization may not be available at the highest resolution your camera supports.

- **Audio Zoom.** Tap this button to toggle audio zoom on or off. When audio zoom is on, zooming in on a subject also zooms the audio in that direction.
- **Effects.** Tap this button to display the Effects list, which enables you to apply an effect to the photo you're shooting. Tap the No Effect "effect" to remove the current effect.
- **Flash.** Tap this button to cycle through the three Flash states: On, Auto, and Off.
- **Timer.** Tap this button to display the Timer dialog box, and then tap the delay you want: Off, 2 Sec, 5 Sec, or 10 Sec.
- **HDR (Rich Tone).** Tap this button to toggle HDR on to get a better color and lighting balance. Normally, it's easier to tap the HDR button at the top of the screen.
- **Location Tags.** Tap this button to turn location tagging on or off.

> **TIP** Adding location data enables you to sort your photos by locations and see exactly where each photo was taken. But if you share your photos with others, the location data may be a threat to your privacy.

- **Storage Location.** Tap this button to switch between storing the photos and videos you take on your device's built-in storage and storing them on an SD card you have inserted.

■ **Review Pics/Videos.** Tap this button to toggle the review feature, which automatically displays each photo or video you take so that you can see if it is good enough. Review is useful for leisurely shooting, but turn it off when you are shooting live action.

■ **Remote Viewfinder.** Tap this button to display the Remote Viewfinder dialog box, which enables you to allow another Samsung device to view and control what the camera on your device is seeing. In the Remote Viewfinder dialog box, tap the Easily Connect via NFC button or the Wi-Fi Direct Settings button, as needed, and then follow the prompts to set up the remote viewing and control.

■ **White Balance.** Tap this button to display the White Balance dialog box, and then tap the Auto radio button, the Daylight radio button, the Cloudy radio button, the Incandescent radio button, or the Fluorescent radio button, as needed.

> **TIP** Use the Auto setting for White Balance unless you find that it's not dealing well with the light. In this case, tap the radio button for the predominant lighting type. Use the Cloudy setting for shooting outdoors in the shade on sunny days as well as when it is actually cloudy.

■ **Exposure Value.** Tap this button to display the Exposure Value slider, which you can adjust either by dragging the slider button or by tapping the – button at the left end or the + button at the right end.

> **TIP** Increase the exposure if the picture looks too dark with automatic exposure control. For example, if you're photographing a person positioned in front of a bright background such as a beach and the ocean, you may need to increase the exposure to avoid having the subject's face in shadow. Decrease the exposure if the picture looks light and washed out.

■ **Grid Lines.** Tap this button to display the grid lines onscreen, which you can use to compose your photos and videos.

■ **Volume Key.** Tap this button to display the Set the Volume Key To dialog box, and then tap the Take Pictures radio button, the Record Video radio button, or the Zoom radio button, as needed.

- **Voice Control.** Tap this button to toggle the Voice Control feature on or off. Voice Control enables you to take a shot by saying one of four control words: "Cheese," "Shoot," "Smile," or "Capture." Voice Control is good for group shots including yourself or for self-portraits using the rear camera.

- **Reset Settings.** Tap this button to reset the Camera's settings to their default values.

BROWSING WITH SAMSUNG'S INTERNET BROWSER

Most Samsung devices include Samsung's browser, which is usually called Internet but also sometimes called Browser and is usually set as the default browser with a shortcut on the Home screen. We'll call it "the Internet app" here for clarity. The Internet app is pretty easy to use and offers standard features such as bookmarks, history, and private browsing (which it calls Incognito mode).

GRASPING THE ESSENTIALS OF THE INTERNET APP

The Internet app has a straightforward interface, as you can see in Figure 14.16.

> **NOTE** The Internet app hides its controls by default as soon as you leave the top of a page to which you've navigated, but you can display them at any time by tapping the screen and dragging your finger down a short way.

You can go to a web page by tapping the address box, typing the address, and then tapping the Go button on the keyboard; or by following a link on another page.

You can navigate back to the previous page by tapping the Back button. After you've gone back, you can tap the Forward button to go forward again.

You can tap a link to open its page in the same window, or tap and hold to display a dialog box of actions. You can then tap the Open in New Window command to open the linked page in a new window.

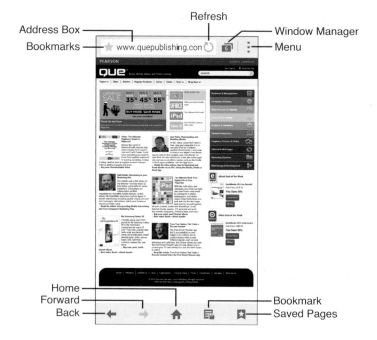

Address Box

Bookmarks

Refresh

Window Manager

Menu

Home
Forward
Back

Bookmark
Saved Pages

FIGURE 14.16

The Internet app has a straightforward interface with an address box, Back and Forward buttons, a Home button, and a Bookmarks button.

📝 **TIP**   Many web pages attempt to detect whether the browser you're using is on a mobile device or a full-bore computer and display mobile versions of pages for mobile devices. To request the desktop version of the current page, tap the Menu button and then check the Desktop View box. This setting persists for the current window until you either uncheck the Desktop View box or close the window.

Switching from the Internet App to Chrome

If the Internet app doesn't suit you, use Chrome instead. Many Samsung devices include Chrome, so look on the Apps screen or in the Google folder to see if it's there. If not, open the Play Store app and download it.

You'll then want to stop the Internet app from being your default browser. With the Internet app running, open the Recent Apps screen, tap and hold the Internet icon, and then tap App Info. On the App Info screen for the Internet app, tap the Clear Defaults button.

Now set Chrome as your default browser. Go to your email app, find a link in a message, and tap it. In the Complete Action Using dialog box that opens, tap the Chrome button, and then tap the Always button. After you've done this, Chrome always opens when you tap a link in another app.

SAVING PAGES AND READING THEM LATER

When you don't have time to read an interesting page you've found, tap the Menu button and then tap Save Page. You can then go to your Saved Pages list by tapping the Saved Pages icon at the bottom of the screen and tap the page to open it.

TIP Saving a page saves it in its current state, so when you return to it, you see the page as it was when you saved it. By contrast, when you return to a bookmark, you see the latest version of the page. Save a page instead of creating a bookmark when you need to be able to refer to the page as it was.

To delete a saved page, tap and hold until the Internet app goes into Selection mode and selects it. You can then check or uncheck the boxes for other saved pages as needed and tap the Delete button (the Trash icon) to delete them.

RETURNING TO WEB PAGES WITH BOOKMARKS

The Internet app makes it easy to bookmark web pages and then return to them. You can add a bookmark like this:

1. Go to the page you want to bookmark.

2. Tap the Bookmarks button (the bookmark icon with a star on it) to display the Bookmarks screen.

> **NOTE** In some versions of the Internet app, the Bookmarks button appears at the bottom of the screen. In others, it appears at the top of the screen.

> **TIP** In some versions of the Internet app, you can tap the Menu button and then tap Add Bookmark to start creating a bookmark for the current page. You may also be able to tap the gray star icon to the left of the address in the address box.

3. Edit the bookmark's name to something short and easily identifiable.
4. Choose the folder in which to save the bookmark.
5. Tap the Save button.

To go to a bookmark, tap the Bookmarks button to display the Bookmarks screen, navigate to a different folder if necessary, and then tap the bookmark for the page you want to view.

> **TIP** You can change the order of your bookmarks by tapping the Menu button on the Bookmarks screen, tapping Change Order, and then using the dotted handles to drag the bookmarks into the order you want. Tap the Done button when you finish.

OPENING MULTIPLE WINDOWS AND NAVIGATING AMONG THEM

Like any decent browser, the Internet app enables you to open multiple windows so that you can have multiple pages open at the same time. You can switch from window to window as needed and close any window that you no longer require.

You can open a new window in either of these ways:

■ Tap and hold a link, and then tap Open in New Window in the dialog box that opens.

■ Tap the Window Manager button (the icon to the right of the address box at the top of the screen, which shows the current number of windows) to display the Window Manager screen, and then tap the New Window button in the upper-right corner.

Figure 14.17 shows the Window Manager screen, which you also use to navigate among windows and close windows.

Tap + to open a new window.

Tap - to close a window.

Tap a thumbnail to display the window.

FIGURE 14.17

On the Window Manager screen, tap the – button to close a window, or tap the window whose contents you want to display.

LOADING YOUR FAVORITE PAGES ONTO THE QUICK ACCESS SCREEN

Some versions of the Internet browser include a Quick Access feature that you can use to get to your favorite pages quickly. To add a page to the Quick Access screen, open the page, tap the Menu button, and then tap Add to Quick Access. On the screen that appears, edit the name in the Title box as needed and then tap the Save button.

You can then tap the Windows button to display the Window Manager screen, tap the + button to display the Quick Access screen, and then tap the icon for the page you want to display.

ADDING A WEB PAGE SHORTCUT TO YOUR HOME SCREEN

When you need to be able to access a particular web page quickly, add a shortcut for it to your Home screen. Go to the page, tap the Menu button, and then tap Add Shortcut to Home Screen (or Add Shortcut to Home in some versions of the Internet app).

BROWSING INCOGNITO

When you want to browse without adding the trail of pages you visit to your history, tap the Menu button and then tap Incognito mode. The Internet app opens an Incognito mode tab that stores the details of the pages you visit only during the Incognito mode session (so that you can navigate back and forward as needed) and then disposes of them.

When you no longer need to use Incognito mode, close the Incognito mode tab.

SYNCING OPEN PAGES THROUGH A SAMSUNG ACCOUNT

The Internet app enables you to sync your open web pages across your computers and devices by signing in to your Samsung account on each computer or device.

To sign in to your Samsung account on your Samsung device, tap the Menu button in the Internet app, and then tap Settings. On the Settings screen, tap the Account button in the Basics section, and then follow the prompts to sign in.

SHARING VIA S BEAM

As well as the standard Android Beam feature, Samsung devices include a feature called S Beam. S Beam is basically Android Beam on mild steroids and is available only on Samsung devices. When S Beam works, it can transfer large files more quickly than Android Beam can.

> **NOTE** S Beam uses Near Field Communication (NFC) to set up a Wi-Fi Direct connection between the devices, enabling faster data connections than Android Beam, which uses NFC to set up a Bluetooth connection. (Wi-Fi Direct is faster than Bluetooth.) S Beam usually takes longer to establish a connection than Android Beam does, but not enough to worry about.

To use S Beam, make sure Android Beam is on. On many Samsung devices, you can turn Android Beam on and off quickly by tapping the NFC icon on the Quick Settings panel; on some devices, the S Beam icon appears on the Quick Settings panel by default, and you can turn on both S Beam and Android Beam (if it is off) by tapping the S Beam icon.

If NFC or S Beam does not appear on the Quick Settings panel on your device, you can either customize the Quick Settings panel to add the icons or use the controls in the Settings app instead. In Tab view, you'll find the NFC button in the Connect and Share section of the Connections tab.

> **TIP** If you just want to be able to share files easily via beaming, turn on both NFC (standard Android Beam) and S Beam. Bring your Samsung device back to back with the device to or from which you want to beam content, and let the devices sort out which type of beam to use.

MAKING THE MOST OF THE GALAXY NOTE'S S PEN

The Samsung Galaxy Note series of oversized phones and tablets include the S Pen pointing device. The S Pen is a short stylus with which you can tap objects and draw onscreen more accurately than with your finger. You can still use your finger whenever you want. The S Pen also has a control button that you press to access other features.

Removing the S Pen from its holder wakes the Galaxy Note if it's sleeping, so you don't need to press the Power button or the Home button.

> ☑ **TIP**   The bane of having a stylus is losing it. To help you avoid this, turn on the S Pen Keeper feature: Open the Settings app, tap the Controls tab, tap the S Pen button, and then check the S Pen Keeper box on the S Pen screen. Now, when you leave the S Pen behind and start moving away, the Galaxy Note warns you that the S Pen is missing. Be warned that this feature works only with the screen off. If the screen is on, you can escape from the S Pen without the Galaxy Note protesting.

Here are three neat moves you can perform with the S Pen:

- **Write an Action Memo.** Press and hold the S Pen button and tap the screen twice. The Action Memo window appears above whichever screen is currently displayed, and you can scribble a note and then tap the Save button (the check mark). Action Memo stores the quick memo with your other memos, which you can access through the Action Memo app (which you can run from the Apps screen).

> ☑ **TIP**   The Galaxy Note screens are pressure sensitive, so the harder you press with the S Pen, the heavier the line it draws. Go easy with this feature. When you need thicker lines in the S Note app, tap the Pen Settings button and then adjust the Line Weight slider to give the line you want without digging holes in the screen.

- **Capture a screenshot.** Line up what you want to capture onscreen. Press and hold the S Pen button, and then tap the S Pen to the screen and hold it still for a second. The screen flashes and the Galaxy Note plays a shutter sound as it takes the photo. The screenshot then appears full screen with a control bar at the top. You can then annotate or crop the screen and tap the Save button to save it.

- **Air Command.** By default, when you remove the S Pen from its holder, the Galaxy Note displays the Air Command pop-up panel (see Figure 14.18). You can then tap Action Memo to start an action memo, tap Scrap Booker to draw around an area on the screen that you want to add to your scrap book, tap Screen Write to capture the screen and then write on the capture, tap S Finder to search using the S Finder feature, or tap Pen Window to draw a window in which you can then open an app (from a selection the Galaxy Note automatically offers you) to work with it on top of the current app.

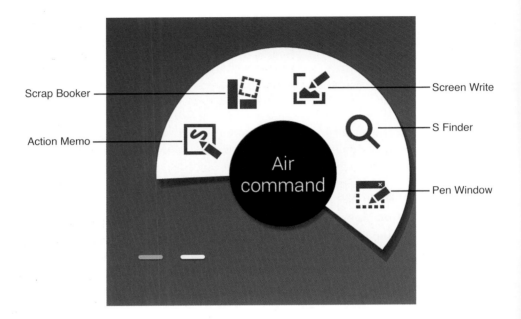

FIGURE 14.18

The Air Command pop-up panel gives you access to five useful S Pen features.

> **TIP** You can also display the Air Command pop-up panel by pressing the button on the S Pen.

IMPROVING PERFORMANCE BY TURNING OFF TOUCHWIZ FEATURES

If your Galaxy Note is running slowly, you may be able to improve performance by turning off some of the TouchWiz features.

- **Strip useless widgets off the Home screen.** Like most Android devices, Samsung's phones and tablets seem convinced that the more widgets on the Home screen, the fuller your life will be. But the widgets can slow down your device, so getting rid of any you don't need can improve performance.

> **TIP** If your Samsung device is running slower than usual, try restarting it: Press and hold the Power button until the Device Options dialog box appears, and then tap the Restart button. As with most computers and devices, restarting your Samsung device can clear up any number of slowdowns and niggling problems.

- **Turn off Multi Window.** You can turn off Multi Window temporarily by tapping and holding the Back button. But if you don't want to use Multi Window at all, open the Settings app, tap the Device tab, and then set the Multi Window switch to Off.

- **Close any apps you're not using.** Tap the Recent Apps button, scroll up to the top, and swipe any apps you're not using off the list. This could hardly be easier to do, but it can give you an appreciable performance boost.

> **TIP** Another way to speed up your Samsung device is to replace the default TouchWiz launcher with another launcher. See Chapter 3, "Customizing Your Device," for a discussion of alternative launchers.

- **Turn off gestures you don't need.** As you saw earlier in this chapter, Samsung's gestures for controlling your device are clever and can be helpful. But if you don't use some of the gestures, or if you don't use any, don't waste processor power trying to track your movements. Open the Settings app and locate the options for controlling gestures. Where you find these depends on the version of TouchWiz. In Tab view, tap the Controls tab, and then tap the Motions and Gestures button (if it appears) or the Motions button. You can then turn off gestures such as Direct Call, Smart Alert, Mute/Pause, or Browse an Image, depending on the version of TouchWiz.

- **Turn off S Voice access via the Home button.** Unless you find accessing S Voice by pressing and holding the Home button highly convenient, turn off this feature and access S Voice from the Apps screen instead. Press and hold the Home button one last time to access S Voice; then tap the Menu button and tap Settings. On the Settings screen, uncheck the Open via the Home Key box in the Wake-Up section.

> **TIP**   Turning off S Voice access via the Home button makes TouchWiz display the Home screen more quickly when you press the Home button because it doesn't have to wait to see if the press is a press-and-hold move.

Turning Off Developer Animations on TouchWiz

Samsung TouchWiz includes several animation settings that you can turn off on the Developer Options screen in the Settings app. You may want to try turning off these animations if you're trying to get the best performance out of your Samsung device.

First, you may need to make the Developer Options icon available, because it's hidden by default. Open the Settings app and locate the About Device icon, either in the System section of the long-screen version of Settings or at the bottom of the General tab in the tabbed version of Settings. If the Developer Options icon doesn't appear just before the About Device icon, tap the About Device to display the About Device screen, go to the Android Version button, and tap that button three times. A readout appears, saying you are four steps from becoming a developer; tap the button four more times, and you'll see a message that Developer Options have been turned on. Tap the Back button to return to the Settings screen.

Now tap the Developer Options button to display the Developer Options screen and scroll down to the Drawing section. You can now tap the Window Animation Scale button to display the Window Animation Scale dialog box, and then tap the Animation Is Off radio button to turn off the animation. Repeat the move with the Transition Animation Scale button and the Animator Transition Scale button to turn these animations off as well.

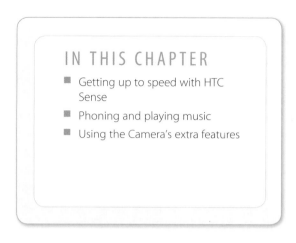

15

USING HTC SENSE

If you have an HTC device, the chances are high that it's running the HTC Sense skin. This thick skin makes HTC devices look and behave in a substantially different way to standard Android devices.

In this chapter, you'll look at the ways in which HTC Sense differs from standard Android, how you can navigate quickly and effectively in the skin, and how you can make the most of its many features.

TAKING A FIVE-MINUTE TOUR OF THE ESSENTIALS

HTC Sense makes a wide range of changes to essential Android navigation. This section tells you what you need to know about the soft buttons, the long screens, the tabbed screens, the three-finger gestures, and more.

UNLOCKING YOUR PHONE

To unlock your phone, swipe up on the lock screen. If you have an unlock method set, the phone then prompts you for it. For example, the keypad appears so that you can type in your PIN.

> **TIP** Some HTC devices have a fingerprint reader on the back and enable you to set up one or more fingerprints to unlock the device. As long as you don't need to protect that part of the back of your phone with a case, this unlock method is easy and moderately secure.

GETTING THE HANG OF THE SOFT BUTTONS

Instead of the three soft buttons—the Back button, the Home button, and the Recent Apps button—that stock Android devices use, HTC Sense uses two: the Back button on the left and the Home button on the right.

The Back button works as normal: You tap it to go back to the screen you were on previously, or to cancel out of a dialog box from which you don't want to proceed.

> **TIP** Here's a little difference in HTC Sense that makes a big difference: When you're navigating within an app that uses < buttons to return to the previous screen, such as in the Settings app, you must actually tap the < button to go back instead of tapping either the button or the screen's name next to it. This means you must tap the button more precisely than on stock Android. As usual, you can tap the Back soft button instead.

With the Home button, you can use four moves:

- **Tap.** This displays the Home screen, as usual.
- **Double-tap.** This displays the Recent Apps screen.
- **Tap and hold.** This launches Google Now, as usual.
- **Tap and swipe up.** This also launches Google Now, just for variety.

NAVIGATING THE LONG SCREENS

Unlike the Apps screen on standard Android, which divides into panels among which you can scroll or swipe horizontally, the Apps screen on HTC Sense scrolls vertically. You can swipe up or down to move to the next screen's worth of apps (assuming that the Apps screen contains enough apps to fill the screen).

> **TIP** Tap the status bar to jump to the top of the Apps screen or the Settings screen.

HTC Sense also customizes the Settings screen. Unlike some skins, which divide the settings into tabs for easy navigation, HTC Sense keeps the Settings screen as a single long list, as it is in stock Android, but breaks up the categories differently.

NAVIGATING THE TABS

Many of HTC's custom apps include screens with multiple tabs arranged horizontally. You can navigate among these tabs in three ways:

- **Swipe left or right.** This is usually the quickest way.
- **Tap the current tab, and then tap the target tab on the pop-up menu.** Figure 15.1 shows an example in the Music app.
- **Tap the target tab.** Only two or three tab buttons appear at a time, so this means of switching tabs is often less convenient than the others.

> **TIP** You can control which tabs appear and in which order by tapping the Menu button and tapping Edit Tabs. On the screen that appears, uncheck the box for any tab you want to remove; then tap the handles on the right side and drag the tabs into your preferred order. Some apps have tabs that you cannot hide, such as the Phone tab and the People tab in the Phone app.

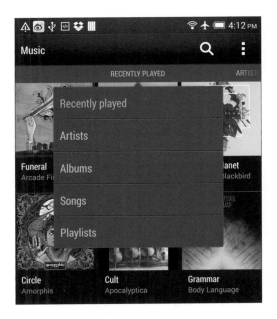

FIGURE 15.1

In tabbed apps such as the Music app, you can navigate among tabs by swiping left or right, by tapping the current tab and then tapping the target tab on the pop-up menu, or by tapping another tab's name.

GETTING TO GRIPS WITH THE THREE-FINGER GESTURES

HTC Sense supports most of the gestures you can use in stock Android, such as the tap-and-hold gesture, the double-tap gesture, the pinch-inward gesture and the pinch-outward gesture, and so on. But HTC Sense also enables you to use two three-finger gestures:

- **Three-finger swipe.** Swipe up the screen with three fingers to display the Choose a Device bar for selecting a device on which to play your music or display your photos or videos. When you're done with the device, swipe down the screen with three fingers to disconnect from the device.

- **Three-finger tap.** Tap the screen with three fingers in the HTC Car app to activate Voice Command mode.

NAVIGATING AND CUSTOMIZING THE QUICK SETTINGS PANEL

HTC Sense makes substantial changes to the Quick Settings panel (see Figure 15.2). You open the Quick Settings panel by either tapping the Quick Settings button at the upper-right corner of the Notifications panel or by dragging down or swiping down with two fingers from the top of the screen.

Edit button

FIGURE 15.2

In HTC Sense, you use the buttons on the Quick Settings panel to turn features on or off. You tap the individual Menu buttons to access the Settings screens.

Each button in the Quick Settings panel is for turning the feature on or off or for quickly adjusting its settings. For example, you tap the Wi-Fi button to turn Wi-Fi on or off, and you tap the Brightness button to cycle among the preset brightness levels.

As you can see in Figure 15.2, many of the buttons have a small Menu button in the lower-right corner. You tap this Menu button to display the screen for the feature in the Settings app. For example, tapping the Menu button on the Bluetooth button on the Quick Settings panel displays the Bluetooth screen in the Settings app.

To make the Quick Settings panel easy to use, customize the panel by tapping the Edit button and then working on the Quick Settings screen (see Figure 15.3):

■ **Move an item to a different position.** Tap the item's handle and drag the item up or down the list.

■ **Hide an item.** Tap the item's handle and drag the item to the Hidden Items section of the list.

■ **Display a hidden item.** Tap the item's handle and drag the item from the Hidden Items section of the list to the upper section.

■ **Stop editing.** Tap the Done button.

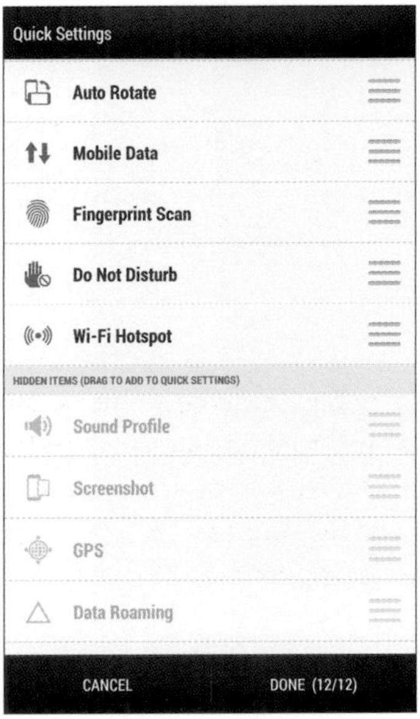

FIGURE 15.3
You can edit the contents of the Quick Settings panel by dragging items to different positions or to the Hidden Items section.

SETTING UP THE LOCK SCREEN ON YOUR HTC PHONE

If you don't apply a means of screen security, you simply swipe upward on the lock screen to unlock your phone.

HTC Sense offers four standard means of unlocking—Face Unlock, Pattern, PIN, and Password—plus fingerprint unlocking on some models. You can apply a means of unlocking by opening the Settings app, tapping the Security button, and then tapping the Screen Lock button.

When you first set up a means of screen security, HTC Sense displays the Lock Screen Previews dialog box (see Figure 15.4), prompting you to hide message previews and missed call previews from your lock screen. Tap the OK button if you want to implement this security measure; tap the Cancel button if you don't mind the possibility of other people seeing this information.

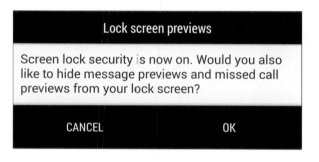

FIGURE 15.4

HTC Sense enables you to hide message previews and missed call previews from your lock screen.

This prompt is handy, but if you want to configure the lock screen exactly the way you want it, tap the Notification Settings button in the Lock Screen section of the Security screen. The Notification screen appears (see Figure 15.5), and you can check or uncheck the five boxes—Phone, Voice Mail, Text Messages, Emails, and Calendar—to control what notifications the lock screen shows and what it suppresses.

> **TIP** To tighten up security on your HTC phone, you can make it display the Security screen on waking rather than displaying the lock screen. To do this, check the Bypass Lock Screen on Wake box on the Security screen in the Settings app.

If you want to be able to control your music from the lock screen, check the Music Playback box in the Lock Screen section of the Security screen. Displaying the music controls on the lock screen is usually helpful.

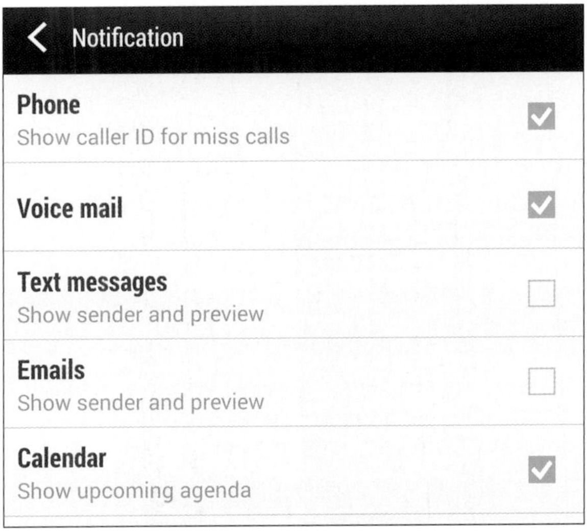

‹ Notification	
Phone Show caller ID for miss calls	☑
Voice mail	☑
Text messages Show sender and preview	☐
Emails Show sender and preview	☐
Calendar Show upcoming agenda	☑

FIGURE 15.5

On the Notification screen, choose which notifications you want the lock screen to show.

> **TIP**   If you're brave enough to let your child use your HTC phone, you can use Kid Mode to limit the damage that the little darling can wreak. Kid Mode creates a virtual sandbox that enables your child to play her favorite games without being able to access any of your data. To get started, put a bombproof case on your pride and joy, and then tap the Kid Mode icon on the Apps screen.

MAKING THE MOST OF THE HOME SCREEN

In HTC Sense, the Home screen consists of a series of panels among which you can swipe horizontally. As you swipe, a narrow bar appears momentarily at the bottom of the screen with a blue line to indicate which of the Home screens you're currently on.

In HTC Sense, the Home screen includes HTC BlinkFeed, a feature that displays tiles containing the latest information from the social networks and news sources you choose. Figure 15.6 shows BlinkFeed.

FIGURE 15.6

HTC BlinkFeed displays a customizable selection of feeds from news sources and social networks.

> **TIP** To update HTC BlinkFeed with the latest information, tap the screen, pull down a short way for a moment, and then release it.

As you'd imagine, you tap a tile in HTC BlinkFeed to display the full story or topic. On the resulting screen, you can either read the topic—the straightforward approach—or tap the Read Later button to add it to your reading list.

> **TIP** After you use the Read Later command to add items to your reading list, the Reading List button appears near the top of the slideout menu in HTC BlinkFeed. Tap this button to display the Reading List screen, and then tap the item you want to read.

At the bottom of the Home screen is the launch bar, which contains shortcuts to your key apps.

CUSTOMIZING HTC BLINKFEED

To make the HTC BlinkFeed feature useful to yourself, you'll want to customize it. HTC BlinkFeed can display a wide range of different information, ranging from the hottest stories to stories that focus tightly on your interests.

> **TIP** If you don't want to use HTC BlinkFeed, tap and hold on one of the regular Home screens (not the HTC BlinkFeed screen) until it switches to Customization mode. You can then tap the BlinkFeed On button in the upper-left corner to turn off BlinkFeed. Tap the resulting BlinkFeed Off button if you want to turn HTC BlinkFeed back on later.

REMOVING AN ITEM FROM HTC BLINKFEED

To remove an item from HTC BlinkFeed, tap and hold the item until the Actions dialog box opens, and then tap the Remove button.

ADDING AN ITEM TO HTC BLINKFEED

Here's how to add an item to HTC BlinkFeed:

1. In HTC BlinkFeed, swipe right to display the slideout menu.
2. Tap the + button to display the Topics & Services screen (see Figure 15.7).

> **NOTE** If a screen appears showing the Connect with Facebook button and the I'll Select Interests on My Own button, tap the appropriate button. The Topics & Services screen then appears.

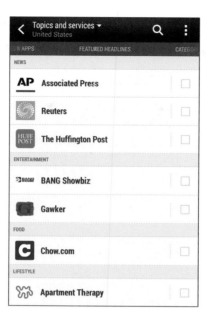

FIGURE 15.7

On the Topics & Services screen, check the box for each item you want to add to HTC BlinkFeed.

> **TIP** For some services, you can choose which regional edition to get. Tap the pop-up menu button at the top of the screen, and then tap the locale or region you want.

3. Swipe left or right, or tap the tabs at the top of the screen, to display the tab you want. The tabs are Services & Apps, Featured Headlines, Categories, and Custom Topics.

4. If the item you want has a check box, check the box to add that item. If the item has no check box, it's a category of items, so you can tap the button to display a screen showing the items. You can then check the box for each item you want.

5. Tap the Home button to go back to the Home screen. HTC BlinkFeed updates to show the items you selected.

> **TIP** You can quickly post to your social networks from HTC BlinkFeed. Swipe right to display the slideout menu, tap the Menu button, and then tap Compose to display the Post To dialog box. Tap the social network to which you want to post, compose your post using the usual techniques, and then tap the Post button.

Customizing Your Highlights Topics

The Highlights feed in HTC BlinkFeed displays the latest status updates and the top trending articles from your feed sources. You can customize the Highlights feed to show only those items from particular sources.

In HTC BlinkFeed, open the slideout menu by swiping right; then tap the Menu button and tap Settings to display the Settings screen. Tap the Choose Highlights Topics button to display the Choose Highlights Topics screen, and then uncheck the boxes for any topics you don't want to see in the Highlights feed. (All the boxes are checked by default.)

PUTTING WHAT YOU NEED ON YOUR HOME SCREENS

You can quickly customize your Home screens with the items you find most useful. Tap an open space on one of the Home screens to pop up the customization screen (see Figure 15.8).

From here, you can customize the Home screens like this:

- **Add a Home screen.** Tap the + sign at the right end of the Home screen thumbnails at the top.
- **Remove a Home screen.** Tap and hold the Home screen's thumbnail, and then drag it to the Remove button that appears at the top of the screen.
- **Reorder the Home screens.** Tap and hold the thumbnail of the Home screen you want to move, and then drag it to where you want it.
- **Change your main Home screen.** Tap the Home screen that you want to have appear first, and then tap the Set as Home button.

FIGURE 15.8

You can quickly customize your Home screens with the widgets, apps, and shortcuts you need.

 **TIP** The house symbol appears on the thumbnail for the main Home screen.

- **Turn BlinkFeed off.** Tap the BlinkFeed On button.
- **Add a widget, app, or shortcut.** Select Widgets, Apps, or Shortcuts in the pop-up menu, and then scroll the list of those items to the one you want. Tap and hold the item, and then drag it to the appropriate Home screen thumbnail.

When you finish customizing the Home screens, tap either the Back button or the Home button.

GETTING MORE OUT OF THE STATUS BAR

The right end of the status bar displays the current time in your chosen format. To display the day and date, tap and hold the status bar for a moment; lift your finger when you're done.

If you need to manage your battery power closely, add the battery level readout (for example, 84%) to the status bar for quick reference. To do so, open the Settings app, tap the Power button in the Phone section, and then check the Show Battery Level box.

!CAUTION Some HTC phones include an option called Fast Boot, which you can enable or disable by checking or unchecking the Fast Boot box on the Power screen in the Settings app. As its name suggests, this option makes the phone shut down and start up more quickly—so it seems like a good thing.

The only problem—and it's a doozy—is that the Fast Boot option prevents you from performing a factory reset on your phone if you run into trouble. If your phone is still working well enough for you to open the Settings app, you can simply disable the Fast Boot option. But if you forget your password, you will not be able to perform a factory reset to recover your device.

If you use the Fast Boot option, be sure to activate your phone on the Android Device Manager website (www.google.com/android/devicemanager). After you've done this, you can use the website to reset your phone in this situation. (Otherwise, you will need to have HTC reset it for you.) If you don't want to do this, turn off the Fast Boot option.

NAVIGATING THE APPS SCREEN

As usual, you tap the Apps button on the Home screen to display the Apps screen. The launcher bar remains visible at the bottom of the screen, but the middle button changes from the Apps button to a Home button that you can press to return to the Home screen.

To make the Apps screen easier to navigate, you can sort it the way you prefer, hide apps you don't want to see, and change the grid size.

SORTING THE APPS YOUR WAY

To sort the list of apps, display the Apps screen and pull down a little way at the top. A toolbar appears containing the Sort pop-up menu, the Search icon, the Play Store shortcut, and the Menu button.

Tap the Sort pop-up menu, and then tap the sort type you want:

- **Alphabetical.** This straightforward sort at least makes it easy to find your apps by name.

- **Most Recent.** This sort makes Android put the apps you've used most recently at the top of the list, where they should be easier to locate. The Most Recent sort works well if you usually run the same apps, but if you run many apps, you may find the most recent ones aren't the ones you want.

- **Custom.** This sort enables you to drag the app icons into the order you find most useful. After choosing Custom, tap and hold an icon until the screen shrinks (see Figure 15.9). You can then drag the icon to where you want it.

> **TIP** You can drag the icon to the upward-caret icon at the top to go up a screen's worth of apps or to the downward-caret icon at the bottom to go down a screen's worth.

FIGURE 15.9

If you select Custom in the Sort pop-up menu, you can tap and drag the app icons to exactly where you want them on the Apps screen.

> ☑ **TIP**   You can quickly create an app shortcut on the Home screen. Tap and hold the app's icon on the App screen, and then drag it to the Shortcut icon that appears in the upper-left corner of the screen.

HIDING THE APPS YOU DON'T WANT TO SEE

By default, the Apps screen displays an icon for each app you install on your device. This feature is handy because it enables you to launch the apps easily. But if you've installed some apps you don't want to see on your Apps screen, you can hide them; when you want them back again, you can unhide them.

Here's how to hide and unhide apps:

1. On the Apps screen, pull down a little way from the top to display the toolbar.

2. Tap the Menu button and then tap Hide/Unhide Apps. A check box appears on the lower-right corner of each app's icon.

3. Check the box for each app you want to hide.

4. Tap the Done button. The apps that you hid disappear.

> ☑ **TIP**   The Manage Apps item on the Apps screen's menu displays the Apps screen in the Settings app. Here, you can view the lists of your downloaded apps, apps on the SD card (if your device has a card), running apps, or all apps; and you can tap an app's button to display the App Info screen for that app.

CHANGING THE GRID SIZE

If you want more apps or fewer apps on the Apps screen at the same time, try changing the grid size. Follow these steps:

1. On the Apps screen, pull down a little way from the top to display the toolbar.

2. Tap the Menu button and then tap Grid Size to display the Grid Size dialog box.

3. Tap the 3×4 radio button or the 4×5 radio button, as needed.

PHONING AND GESTICULATING

HTC Sense includes a custom Phone app that makes placing and taking calls easy. You can also answer calls—or decline them—using gestures.

GETTING AROUND THE PHONE APP'S FIVE TABS

The Phone app displays five tabs, among which you can navigate by swiping left or right, using the pop-up panel from the current tab, or tapping another tab:

- **Call History.** This tab displays the calls you've received. You can tap the menu on the left side of the toolbar and then tap the filter you want: All Calls, Incoming Calls, Outgoing Calls, Missed Calls, or Recent Calls.

> **TIP** You can delete some or all calls from your call history by displaying the Call History tab, tapping the Menu button, and then tapping Delete Call History. On the Delete from Call History screen, check the box for each item you want to delete, and then tap the Delete button.

- **Phone.** This tab displays your last caller at the top, in case you need to call that person back, plus a keypad for dialing numbers. When you start dialing a phone number, the app displays matches from your contacts (see Figure 15.10). You can then tap the contact to complete dialing, tap the contact-card icon to display other means of getting in tap with the contact, tap the Matches button to display other contacts with matching numbers, or simply keep dialing.

- **Favorites.** This tab contains the contacts you have designated Favorites by adding them to the Favorites group.

> **TIP** Favorites are handy, but for anybody you call all the time, create a Speed Dial entry. Open the contact record, tap the Menu button, and then tap Set Speed Dial. On the Speed Dial screen, tap the Number button and choose the number, and then tap the Location button and tap the speed-dial number in the Select Location dialog box. Tap the Save button to save the change. You can then call that phone number by tapping and holding the assigned number on the keypad on the Phone screen.

Touch the Matches button to see other matches

Touch the contact's card to see other contact options

FIGURE 15.10

When dialing a number, you can dial the contact shown, open the contact's card, or tap the Matches button to see other matches.

- **People.** This tab displays a list showing your contacts from the People app. You can narrow down the list by tapping the pop-up button in the upper-left corner and then using the resulting pop-up panel to specify which accounts and groups to include.

- **Groups.** This tab displays a list showing your groups from the People app. You can open a group for viewing or tap the Menu button and then tap Edit Groups to edit the list of groups.

USING GESTURES WHEN YOUR PHONE RINGS

HTC Sense enables you to use gestures to answer your phone when it rings:

- **Answer the call.** Lift the phone, look at the screen to see who is calling, and then move the phone to your ear.

- **Lower the ringing volume.** When the phone rings, pick it up to reduce the ringing volume. If this doesn't work, open the Settings app, tap the Sound button to display the Sound screen, and then check the Quiet Ring on Pickup box.

> **TIP** While you're on the Sound screen in Settings, check the Pocket
> Mode box if you want your phone to ring more loudly when it's in your pocket or
> in a bag. (The phone rings more loudly for an incoming call any time the sensors
> detect the phone is surrounded.)

■ **Mute the call.** Turn your phone facedown. This move works best if your phone
is lying faceup on a flat surface, but you can also use it when holding your
phone if you don't mind having the back of the phone face you for a while.

ENJOYING MUSIC WITH THE SENSE MUSIC APP

HTC Sense includes a custom Music app that has a swipe-based user interface and
strong playback features. Tap the Music icon on the Apps screen to launch the Music
app. You can then navigate among the five tabs by swiping left or right, using the
pop-up menu from the current tab, or tapping another tab's name, as usual.

The following five tabs appear at the top level of the Music app:

■ **Recently Played.** This tab (see Figure 15.11) displays albums you've played
recently and ones you've added recently.

FIGURE 15.11

The Music app has five tabs, including the Recently Played tab and the Artists tab, at the top level.

- **Artists.** This tab displays an alphabetical list of artists.

> ☑ TIP   You can get the latest artist photos available for your artists from the Gracenote music database service by tapping the Menu button and then tapping Update Artist Photos.

- **Albums.** This tab displays a grid showing the covers of the albums from which the songs on your device come. You can sort the albums either by the album name or the artist name. To change the sort, tap the Menu button and then tap Sort by Artist Name or Sort by Album Name. (These commands replace each other, so only one of them appears on the menu at any time.)
- **Songs.** This tab displays an alphabetical list of the songs on your device.

> ☑ TIP   You can easily share a song from the Music app. Tap the song's Menu button and then tap Share to display the Share dialog box, which shows the song's name in its title bar. You can then tap the Share Music Info button to share the song's details via Facebook, Twitter, Gmail, or other means; or tap the Share File button to share the song file via means such as Bluetooth, Dropbox, Google Drive, Messages, or Gmail.

- **Playlists.** This tab displays a grid of your playlists, including the Recently Played smart playlist and the Recently Added smart playlist that the Music app automatically provides for you.

Each item has its own menu button that you can tap to display a dialog box of actions for the item. For example, the dialog box for a song includes actions such as Add to Playlist and Add to Queue.

Creating Ringtones Easily from Your Songs

The HTC Music app makes it easy to use a song as a ringtone or to create a ringtone from a song. Navigate to the song you want to use, tap its Menu button to display the Actions dialog box, and then tap Set as Ringtone. In the Set as Ringtone dialog box, you can tap the Phone Ringtone button to use the song as your default phone ringtone, tap the Contact Ringtone button to use it as the ringtone for a particular contact, or tap the Trim the Ringtone button to display the Ringtone Trimmer screen.

After selecting the appropriate part of the song on the Ringtone Trimmer screen, tap the Set As button to display a smaller version of the Set as Ringtone dialog box. You can then tap the Phone Ringtone button or the Contact Ringtone button, as needed.

TIP If you already use Google Play Music, go to the Apps section of the Play Store and install the Play Music app on your HTC phone. You can then play the music you have stored online as well as the music on your phone.

USING THE CAMERA'S EXTRA FEATURES

HTC Sense includes a heavily customized Camera app that offers you a wide variety of features and settings. This section covers the camera's essentials, the configuration options for a typical HTC phone, and the two headline features: dual capture mode and HTC Zoe.

NOTE Many HTC phones include the camera technology that HTC has branded as UltraPixel. Unlike most camera technologies, which have sought to increase the pixel count to improve image quality, UltraPixel uses fewer pixels to get a better picture. HTC claims that because the pixels on UltraPixel sensors are larger, they can capture more photons while the camera's shutter is open, thus giving better results in low light.

UltraPixel shots look great on a phone's screen and look pretty good on larger screens. But because the pixel count is substantially lower than that of most directly competing cameras, photo quality deteriorates rapidly if you enlarge the photos a lot or if you crop them. So when you're using an UltraPixel camera, it is even more important than usual to compose your photos tightly so that they need only minimal cropping. For distant subjects, sticking or clipping a telephoto lens on your HTC phone gives better results than using digital zoom.

SHOOTING WITH THE CAMERA APP

You can quickly get going with the Camera app: Just tap the Camera icon on the Home screen, and your phone displays the Viewfinder screen showing what the rear camera is seeing (see Figure 15.12). You can then tap the Take Photo button to take a photo or the Take Video button to take a video. Alternatively, tap the Filters button to apply a filter to the preview in the Viewfinder before you take a photo or a video.

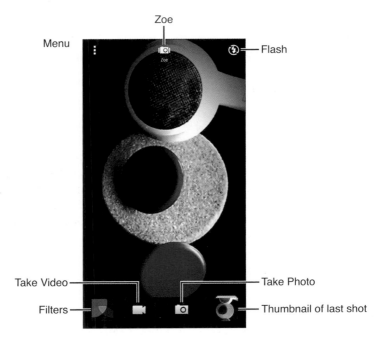

FIGURE 15.12

The HTC Camera app gives you instant access to the Zoe feature, to the flash, and to the filters. You can start taking either a photo or video by tapping a button.

> **NOTE** On many HTC phones, you can tap and hold the Take Photo button to take a burst of photos.

> **☑ TIP**   On the lock screen, slide up the Camera icon to go straight to the Camera app without unlocking your phone.

Tap the Flash button to cycle among the three settings—Auto, On, and Off—as usual. Use the On setting when you need to force the flash to fire to light the foreground against backlighting. Use the Off setting when flash is indiscreet or forbidden. Use the Auto setting the rest of the time.

You can pinch outward to zoom in and pinch inward to zoom out as usual. To quickly switch between the main camera and the front camera, swipe either left or right in the Camera app.

Tap a point on the screen to focus and meter the light there.

> **☑ TIP**   To lock Automatic Exposure and Auto-Focus at a particular point, tap and hold that point until the "AE and AF locked" readout appears. You can then compose the shot as needed, maintaining the focus and exposure you chose. This capability is great for action shots: Before your kid comes running past you, focus on a point the right distance away, and lock the focus. You'll then be ready to shoot when she reaches the right point.

> **☐ NOTE**   After a few minutes of inactivity, the Camera app displays a blank screen and the prompt "Tap the screen to activate the camera." This lets you get back to shooting more quickly than Android's standard Camera app, which returns you to the Home screen after a similar period of inactivity.

CONFIGURING THE CAMERA APP TO TAKE THE PHOTOS YOU WANT

The Camera app has a huge number of settings that you access by tapping the Menu button on the Viewfinder screen and working in the pop-up panel, the top part of which appears in Figure 15.13. Some of these settings are self-explanatory, but others are more complex, so let's quickly go through them.

FIGURE 15.13

To configure the Camera app, tap the Menu button and then work in the pop-up panel.

CHOOSING SETTINGS IN THE CAMERA SECTION

The Camera section of the pop-up panel contains the Camera setting, which enables you to switch between the main camera (the rear camera) and the front camera.

CHOOSING THE PHOTO CAPTURE MODE AND VIDEO CAPTURE MODE

To help you shoot good-looking pictures in different lighting conditions, the Camera app provides 11 photo capture modes. There are 4 main modes, one of which has 6 submodes, as explained in the following list:

■ **Scene.** Use this mode for shooting regular photos. That means all photos that are not night photos, High Dynamic Range (HDR) photos, or panoramas. Choose the Normal submode for standard photos. Choose the Portrait submode for photos featuring people in which you want to smooth the look of the skin, giving a more flattering look. Choose the Landscape submode for pictures of landscapes and scenery. Choose the Backlight submode when your subject is backlit and you want to avoid the subject being too dark; with this setting, Camera balances the light metering on the assumption the middle of the screen is backlit. Choose the Text submode to maximize the contrast and definition when you are taking a photo of a text document. Choose the Macro submode for close-up shots.

- **Zoe.** Use this mode to shoot a series of photos combined with a short video. We'll look at the Zoe feature later in this chapter.
- **Night.** Use this mode for shooting photos in low light.

> ☑ **TIP** Use a tripod, monopod, or other means of steadying your phone when using Night mode. This mode slows down the shutter speed and boosts the ISO (the film sensitivity), so it's doubly important to keep the phone steady while shooting. When you have no means of support, you may be able to take the photo more steadily by using the self-timer than by tapping the Take Photo button.

- **Sweep Panorama.** Use this mode for shooting panorama photos.
- **Dual Capture.** Use this mode to superimpose a picture from the front camera on the picture from the rear camera. For example, you can enhance (or sully) a beautiful landscape by adding a selfie to it. We'll look at this feature later in this chapter.
- **Anti-Shake.** Use this mode to enable yourself to get a steady picture in circumstances in which you might otherwise get camera shake, such as when you're in motion or the light is low.
- **HDR.** Use this mode when you need to increase the dynamic range of a photo.

> ☑ **TIP** If you notice the sky looking too white or the rest of the frame too dark when you're lining up the photo, try switching to HDR. HDR takes multiple exposures and combines them to improve the dynamic range; it's slower than taking regular photos, so use it for stationary subjects, not for moving subjects.

Similarly, the Camera app provides four submodes of the Scene mode for video:

- **Normal.** Use this mode for standard video shooting.
- **Slow Motion Video.** Use this mode to shoot slow-motion video. The Camera app shoots twice as many frames and then plays them back at normal speed, so the motion lasts twice as long as real time.
- **Fast HD (60 fps).** Use this mode to shoot video at double-speed to capture movement more accurately without blurring. Fast HD is great for shooting sports, kids, and other mobile subjects.

! CAUTION Both Slow Motion Video and Fast HD take up twice as much space as regular video, so they can eat through your device's storage faster than teenagers through pizza.

- **Video HDR (Full HD).** Use this mode to improve the lighting and color balance on videos you're shooting in tricky light.

NOTE For Video HDR, the Camera app shoots at twice normal speed, varying the exposure for each pair of frames. It then combines each pair of frames into a single frame that should have better lighting and color balance.

CHOOSING OTHER SETTINGS

The Settings section of the pop-up panel contains the remaining settings for the Camera app:

- **Self-Timer.** Tap this button and then tap + or – to adjust the number of seconds.
- **Crop.** Tap this button and then tap the cropping you want: Wide, Regular, or Square.
- **Video Quality.** Tap this button and then tap the video quality you want: Full HD (1920×1080), HD (1280×720), Low (320×240), or MMS (176×44). Normally, you'll want to use Full HD unless you need to conserve space. The Video Quality options may vary depending on which device you have.
- **Image Adjustments.** Tap this button and then tap + or – to adjust the Exposure, Contrast, Saturation, and Sharpness settings.

TIP Of the four Image Adjustments, the one you'll need to change most often is Exposure. Increase the exposure if the automatic exposure setting makes the picture look too dark, such as when you have a subject positioned against a bright background. Decrease the exposure if the picture is too light and washed out.

- **Review Duration.** Tap this button and then tap the time period for reviewing the photo you just took. Choose the No Review option if you want to keep shooting and review the shots later. Otherwise, tap 5 Seconds, 10 Seconds, or No Limit.

- **ISO.** Tap this button and then tap the ISO sensitivity rating you want to use. Your choices are Auto (the best choice unless you need to set the ISO manually), 100, 200, 400, 800, or 1600.

> **NOTE** ISO controls how much light the camera's sensor captures while the shutter is open for a particular time. Setting a high ISO value (such as 800 or 1600) enables the camera to capture more light, but it also means you're likely to get more noise (wrongly colored dots) in the photo.

> **TIP** If your camera has a MAX ISO setting, use it to set the maximum ISO value you want the Camera app to be able to use. Some HTC cameras aggressively push the ISO setting higher than usual to get better photos in low light. The flipside of this is that shots with strong lighting may become overexposed. By setting MAX ISO to a sensible limit, such as 400, you can prevent the Camera app from running hog-wild with the ISO value and wrecking your photos.

- **Storage.** Tap this button and then tap the SD Card radio button or the Phone Storage radio button, as needed.

- **Continuous Shooting.** Tap this button and then check or uncheck the Continuous Shooting box, the Limit to 20 Frames box, and the Auto Review box, as needed.

- **Camera Options.** Tap this button to display the Auto Smile Capture check box and the Geo-Tag Photos check box. Check the Auto Smile Capture box if you want the Camera app to automatically capture a photo when you line up the onscreen aiming box on a smiling face. This feature seems odd, but it often works well. Check the Geo-Tag Photos box to have the Camera app automatically add GPS location data to each photo it takes.

TIP The GPS location data can be helpful if you want to be able to sort your photos by locations or see exactly where each photo was taken. But if you share your photos with others, the location data may be a threat to your privacy.

NOTE Auto Smile Capture works only for the rear camera. When you have switched to the front camera, the Camera Options section contains the Save Mirror Image check box instead of the Auto Smile Capture check box. Check this box to have the Camera app the mirror image of what it sees—so that in the photo you look the way you do in a normal mirror—instead of the real image.

- **Shutter Option.** Tap this button to display the Tap to Capture check box and the Shutter Sound check box. The Tap to Capture check box controls whether you can take a photo by tapping the screen rather than tapping the shutter button. The Shutter Sound check box controls whether the Camera app plays a shutter sound when you take a picture. Uncheck this box if you need to take photos discreetly.

- **Lock Focus in Video.** Check this box to turn on continuous auto-focus for those times when you are taking a video. Using this feature can reduce blurring at the cost of some battery power.

- **White Balance.** Tap this button and then tap the white balance setting to use: Auto (best for general use), Incandescent (old-style electric bulbs), Fluorescent, Daylight (for bright daylight, such as sunny conditions), or Cloudy.

TIP The Auto setting for White Balance usually works well, but you may need to override it when shooting in situations with mixed lighting. For example, if you're shooting indoors with both fluorescent and incandescent light, you may need to select the White Balance manually.

- **Grid.** Check this box to display the grid, which can help you compose your shots and videos.

- **Auto-Upload.** If you want to upload your photos automatically to the Internet, tap this button, and set the Auto-Upload switch to On. Tap the

Select a Service button and select the account to which you want to upload the photos (for example, your Flickr account). Tap the Frequency button to display the Upload Frequency dialog box and then tap the Immediately radio button, the Daily radio button, or the Wi-Fi Only radio button, as needed.

> **!CAUTION** Unless you take photos with extreme care and consideration, don't use the Auto-Upload feature. Normally, it is better to take photos freely, review them on your device, delete the duds, and then upload only the best of the rest.

■ **Reset to Default.** Tap this button to reset all the Camera settings to their defaults. Doing this can be useful if you have been experimenting with the settings and have messed up something, but can't identify what. Tap Yes in the Reset to Default dialog box that opens.

SHOOTING BOTH WAYS WITH DUAL CAPTURE MODE

When you want to add yourself to a screen, tap the Menu button and then tap the Dual Capture radio button in the Photo Capture Mode section of the pop-up panel. The feed from the front camera appears in a small window in front of the feed from the rear camera. You can drag the window to where you want it on the main picture; you can also pinch outward to expand it a little.

When you have lined up the shot you want, tap the Take Photo button or the Take Video button as usual.

BRINGING SCENES TO LIFE WITH HTC ZOE

The HTC Zoe feature gives you an easy way to capture a series of photos and save them as a video clip including the ambient sound. Tap the Zoe icon at the top of the Viewfinder screen to turn on Zoe mode; the icon goes blue to indicate that Zoe is on. You can then line up your shot and tap the Take Photo button to start the capture.

As your phone captures the Zoe clip, a red progress indicator gradually runs across the Take Photo button. When it finishes, you can tap the thumbnail to display the Zoe clip, which plays automatically.

Tap the blue Zoe icon at the top of the Viewfinder screen when you're ready to turn off the HTC Zoe feature again.

Index